THE COMPLETE
GUIDE
TO
ACTIVITY-BASED
COSTING

THE COMPLETE GUIDE TO ACTIVITY-BASED COSTING

Michael C. O'Guin

PRENTICE HALL
Englewood Cliffs, New Jersey 07632

PRENTICE HALL
Englewood Cliffs, New Jersey 07632
Prentice-Hall International, Inc., London
Prentice-Hall of Australia, Pty. Ltd., Sydney
Prentice-Hall Canada, Inc., Toronto
Prentice-Hall of India Private Ltd., New Delhi
Prentice-Hall of Japan, Inc., Tokyo
Prentice-Hall of Southeast Asia Pte. Ltd., Singapore
Whitehall Books, Ltd., Wellington, New Zealand
Editora Prentice-Hall do Brasil Ltda., Rio de Janeiro

10 9 8 7 6 5 4 3 2

This publication is designed to provide accurate and authoritative information in regard to the subject matter covered. It is sold with the understanding that the publisher is not engaged in rendering legal, accounting, or other professional service. If legal advice or other expert assistance is required, the services of a competent professional person should be sought.

. . . From the Declaration of Principles jointly adapted by a Committee of the American Bar Association and a Committee of Publishers and Associations.

Library of Congress Cataloging-in-Publication Data

O'Guin, Michael C.
   The complete guide to activity-based costing / by Michael C. O'Guin
     p   cm.
   Includes bibliographical references and index.
   ISBN 0–13–853318–0
   1. Cost accounting—Case studies. I. Title. II. Title: Activity
based costing.
HF5686.C8032   1991
657′.42—dc20   91–19963
ISBN 0-13-853318-0   CIP

Printed in the United States of America

PRENTICE HALL
Business Information & Publishing Division
Englewood Cliffs, NJ 07632
Simon & Schuster. A Paramount Communications Company

DEDICATION

Robin Cooper
Robert Kaplan
H. Thomas Johnson
Peter B. B. Turney
and the countless others who laid the foundations of *The Complete Guide to Activity-Based Costing*.

CONTENTS

Part II/DESIGNING AND IMPLEMENTING AN ABC SYSTEM

Part III/APPLYING STRATEGY ABC

PREFACE

Surprisingly, the genesis of this book can be traced to a war involving foreign powers fought halfway around the world. The battle for the Falklands lasted from April to June of 1982. Yet, during that time the Royal Navy depleted their entire war reserve of sonobuoys looking for a single Argentinian sub. A sonobuoy is a complex electromechanical device, which is dropped from an aircraft to search for submarines. The sonobuoy has a hydrophone for listening and a radio for transmitting the signal back to the aircraft. Sonobuoys are expendable ordinance, floating on the surface for about three hours before scuttling themselves.

Given the importance of anti-submarine warfare to the defense of our shipping lanes and sonobuoys in particular, the U.S. Navy was quite concerned. NATO sonobuoy supplies had diminished to dangerously low levels, while sonobuoy drops under these wartime conditions greatly exceeded expectations. The U.S. Navy needed more sonobuoys built, but the manufacturers were already running at full capacity. Concerned about limited sonobuoy production capacity, the U.S. Navy pressured Rockwell International to enter the sonobuoy manufacturing business.

During 1983, Rockwell began to gear up sonobuoy production at their El Paso, Texas plant. That summer, I received an exciting assignment. I became the project engineer for a robot to be installed in the plant. The robot dispensed epoxy onto circuit cards to protect them against shock and vibration. Tests had found sonobuoys were subjected to a force equal to one hundred times the force of gravity when ejected from an aircraft. Failure analysis had pinpointed electrical components breaking off under this stress causing multiple buoy failures. To cushion against the shock, an epoxy was used to glue some components to the board.

I spent most of the summer in El Paso, programming the robot, fabricating tooling, writing work instructions, training operators and developing the preventive maintenance schedule. After the robot was qualified, Rockwell brought in the public relations department to videotape the robot in action. As I watched the taping, I could not help thinking, "Where are all the savings the PR group claimed?" Here I was, an engineer making over $2000 a month plus travel expenses, spending over six months on this project. Rockwell had invested large amounts of tooling, maintenance and engineering support getting the robot operational. While the employees the robot replaced were paid only $8.20 an hour including fringe benefits. I was perplexed; by my calculations the robot would take until 1994 to pay for itself.

To satisfy my curiosity, I found the original robot justification and the sonobuoy project's budget. What I discovered disturbed me. Many of the costs my robot had created were buried in El Paso's overhead as well as my home division's. Our cost system did record all direct labor transactions charged against my robotic work cell, but the maintenance, tooling and other support costs were unaccounted for. These support costs went into the plant's overhead. My project was deemed a success because it reduced direct labor, but I knew it could not be saving Rockwell any money.

I then began to question why our division had established a plant in El Paso. I was told it was for low labor rates. Unfortunately, by offering only low wages we were unable to keep trained workers or attract skilled technicians. If we raised the wages, our justification for establishing the plant would disappear. So we just kept training new people and demanding technical support from the home division in California. Whenever I walked around the El Paso plant, I could not help but notice there were always several California engineers on site supporting the El Paso plant. I knew those engineer's costs were going into the home division's overhead and not El Paso's. I came to realize the way we recorded costs was the crux of the problem. By allocating all overhead costs on direct labor, the cost system led one to believe that direct labor was the only controllable cost. The cost system focused management's attention on direct labor and did nothing to control overhead. The system did not track overhead and provided no insight into what caused the overhead. The costs my robot caused were buried and only I knew my robot's true cost.

Over many years my feelings about labor-based cost systems became stronger. I saw companies large and small making very questionable decisions based on their questionable cost data. I have seen executives and managers lulled into poor decisions by fallacious cost information. In 1988 while conducting manufacturing strategy studies described in Chapter 6, I came across what I came to believe was the answer— activity-based costing (ABC). In fact, I found activity-based costing to be such a tremendously powerful tool, that I changed my career. I devoted myself to researching, designing, implementing and expounding ABC systems. This book is the cumulation of that work.

ACKNOWLEDGMENTS

I thank Bill Green for editing my manuscript as well as teaching me the finer points of shareholder value analysis. I would like to thank Dr. Charles Mecimore and Tom Deaver for their many constructive comments on the early editions of this manuscript. I want to thank John Derfus and Bruce Becker for their help in defining the relationship between ABC and MRP, as well as the editors of Prentice Hall for their support, especially Gerry Galbo and Ronald Cohen. I thank all those in industry and academia who allowed me to interview them and to learn some of their experiences: Don Begley, Garth Dour, David Galley, David Hildenbrand, Thomas E. Miller, James Reeve, Alicia Rodriguez, Peter Turney and Sheryl VanGorder.

Many thanks go to Al King of the National Association of Accountants for his help in getting this book published as well as his advice and counsel.

Lastly, I thank my wife Cindy for unending support through this long book writing process.

INTRODUCTION

This book describes the most significant advancement in management since the development of Frederick Taylor's Scientific Management eighty years ago. This new approach to management is activity management. Activity management broadens a manufacturer's perspective from producing products to serve markets to one of performing activities to satisfy customer needs. It seeks to portray a company as a series of activities designed to satisfy customer needs. Activity management breaks a company down according to all of the major activities performed and relates them to customer needs and their costs. This breakdown focuses on what triggers activities, how customers consume these activities and how much it costs to perform all a company's activities.

The mechanism for portraying the organization is a cost planning system called activity-based costing (ABC). This new cost system overcomes the shortcomings of today's labor-based accounting system. ABC provides a true picture of what products, processes and customers really cost. It explains how, as the number of vendors, part numbers, processes and customers increases, so does a company's complexity, resulting in overhead costs. Cost information is the basis for most management decision making, both tactical and strategic. ABC represents how activities consume resources and how products or customers trigger activities. These linkages allow management to assess the value creation of each activity to the customer.

This book shows how policies and systems drive costs and how management can use this information to match customer needs to their systems. ABC provides the basis for allowing executives to manage activities and not its symptoms—costs. In addition, activity management forces management to broaden their perspective from strictly products to satisfying customer activities. This new information allows executives to manage a company's activities for dramatically improved competitiveness. This book will help a company with the challenging task of designing, implementing and employing an activity-based costing system. Activity-based costing (ABC) differs substantially from traditional cost accounting systems and therefore requires breaking ingrained mind-sets. The system has new uses and provides new insight, which the book describes.

The Complete Guide to Activity-Based Costing is targeted for senior and midlevel managers who are working to improve their company's competitiveness. Part I introduces the reader to the shortcomings of today's cost systems, followed by an introduction in ABC and its benefits. Part II provides a very detailed description of how to design and implement ABC systems. Topics discussed range from choosing cost drivers to interviewing techniques, and from constructing the ABC system architecture to overcoming typical implementation problems.

This book will help the reader not only learn to design and implement ABC, but also how to use this new information effectively. It discusses in detail how to use ABC to achieve its full benefits. How can activity levels be lowered by permanently reducing costs? How can unprofitable products be returned to profitability while increasing customer desirability? To use ABC and improve a company's competitiveness, executives must leave their paradigm and view their business from a new perspective.

Part III describes how to use ABC. Using many examples from industry and case studies, the book gives the reader as much practical ABC experience as possible. The cases describe companies implementing ABC in a variety of industries and circumstances. The cases discuss why and how the companies use ABC to meet different objectives. In addition, why and how the companies were, or were not, successful in using this new information. Chapters 6 and 7 are detailed case studies describing how companies implemented ABC and how doing so changed their business strategy.

Other cases describe how companies used ABC information and what pitfalls befell them. In some of the case studies, to protect the company's identity, a pseudonym was substituted for the company name and industry. Given the strategic nature of most ABC work, revealing the company's identity would divulge confidential information to their competitors.

Chapter 8 discusses why traditional financial performance measures are obsolete and why shareholder value analysis should drive all decision making. The chapter discusses how shareholder value analysis depends on ABC, and how ABC depends on shareholder value analysis. The chapter demonstrates the power of shareholder value analysis in evaluation decisions as well as how to use it. Chapter 9 emphasizes the importance customers and a customer's activities must play in a company's success. Chapter 10 discusses how ABC fits into a company's competitive strategy, complete with five cases on company experiences. Chapter 11 specifically describes the effects of ABC on the organization of the factory. Chapter 12 describes how to use ABC for operational decision making. Chapter 13 discusses the effects ABC will have on American manufacturing in the 1990s—specifically, how ABC drives a company toward customer focus, speed and flexibility.

The final section, "Further Reading," discusses where more information on ABC can be found. This section lists many excellent articles and case studies.

This book is based on the author's personal experiences and extensive research. I have implemented ABC systems in both manufacturing and distribution environments. All available literature on ABC, published and unpublished, was read and analyzed. We also conducted a number of simulations on ABC data to validate recommendations on the number of cost drivers needed and costing error. I interviewed practitioners in the industry who have implemented ABC systems, along with leaders in academia.

CHAPTER 1

AMERICA'S ACHILLES' HEEL

There is something in the wind.

Comedy of Errors, Act III, Scene I
William Shakespeare

American manufacturing is in crisis, and there are plenty of signs.

- On September 13, 1990, Cincinnati Milacron—the last major American manufacturer of robots—quit the business by selling off its division to a Swiss company.
- In 1979, there were eight American television manufacturers; as of the early nineties, there was one.
- Imports now account for 40 percent of the domestic semiconductor and 50 percent of the machine tool market.
- The likes of Korea's Samsung have pushed Amana, Tappan, and Litton out of the microwave oven business and reduced General Electric to a sales and service outlet.
- Only 6 percent of West Germans surveyed believe "made in America" means quality products.

1

How has all this happened? The reason is that American executives have been forced to manage their Fortune 500 companies with misleading and distorted information for the past quarter century.

Until now, they have evaluated many of their business decisions—from replacing aging blast furnaces to establishing service policies, from fixing product defects to adding factory capacity, from training personnel to introducing new products—using our traditional labor-based cost accounting systems. Meanwhile, mechanization and automation frequently have driven this direct labor base to less than 5 percent of product cost, leaving material and overhead as a company's principal cost. This fact is for the most part ignored by today's cost systems.

Within the four walls of a business enterprise, labor, capital, and raw materials are converted into goods. The company knows what the customers pay for the goods leaving the building, and what the resources cost entering it. But does the company know how much in resources each product consumes during manufacturing? In most cases—no.

Executives in most companies intuitively don't believe their cost systems. They know that particular products are more expensive than the cost system reports, but they are not sure how much more. Most believe that the reported product costs are off by only a few percentage points. The fact is that many companies are manufacturing products without knowing what they truly cost. The products could cost twice as much or a third less than current cost systems report. In fact, as cases in this book show, it is not uncommon to find products undercosted by 100 or even 1,000 percent.

The cost accounting department, while appearing innocuous, is therefore the source of the most fundamental unit of decision making—cost. Management answers many of its strategic questions, such as capital investment, management incentives, pricing and marketing strategy, by employing cost information. Distorted information prevents a company from successfully competing.

Hence the crisis. However, just as the Chinese ideograph for "crisis" is made up of two characters, one meaning "catastrophe" and the other "opportunity," likewise, great opportunity lies within this predicament. If strategists can get accurate cost information and their competitors do not, the strategist can attack the most attractive market segments while competitors squander time and money on less appealing customers. Informed strategists can outmaneuver the competition with more effective product mixes, prices, sales policies, promotion efforts, and product designs.

This book describes a new system of management, activity-based management, of which activity-based costing (ABC) is its core. Activity-based management is a system that links resource consumption to the activities performed by a company and then links those activities to products or customers. This system dramatically improves executives' ability to manage their businesses. It provides executives with an entirely new view of the interrelationship between business processes and the customers. Activity-based management uses activity-based costing to measure and control these relationships.

As an added benefit, ABC focuses management's attention on activities. In turn, activity management concentrates not on squeezing budgets, but on controlling the source of costs such as the product mix, setup times, and backorder policies. ABC identifies how policies—such as offering numerous product options, 24-hour delivery, and minimum order quantities—create costs. Using ABC, decision makers can quantify the cost of policies and decisions in terms of the value that these activities provide for their customers. With ABC, one looks beyond costs and at the decisions that create activities and in turn generate cost.

This book

- Describes not only how to design and implement an ABC system, but how ABC changes one's perspective of the enterprise and therefore requires breaking ingrained mind-sets.

- Shows you how to overcome this hurdle as well as other pitfalls.

- Explains how to use activity-based information to better understand your business—how activities are linked to products, processes, and customers; how activities can be managed to ensure that customer needs are satisfied in the most effective manner; how to use ABC to control the company's activities.

But before implementing ABC, you must understand the state of our current cost systems and their corrosive effects on a business's ability to compete.

THE ROOT OF THE MANUFACTURING CRISIS

Performance Is Misdirected When Labor Is Overemphasized

Current cost systems place too much emphasis on direct labor, even to the exclusion of overhead. The systems typically assign overhead to products based on their direct labor content. This allocation makes labor look like the only controllable cost. This environment creates twisted performance measures, which encourage counterproductive behavior. To measure business performance, management uses measurements such as

- Machine utilization
- Individual operator performance
- Period-end absorption
- Direct labor efficiency

Whenever production methods are improved—reducing direct labor content— the production unit's labor standards are lowered. With lower labor content per unit, machine utilization and efficiency drop, direct to indirect ratios climb, and all the other measures indicative of performance seem to be falling. In reality, the company is reducing costs and thus is making itself more competitive.

Creating Inventory Buffers Hides Operating Ills

Measuring machine utilization and operator performance encourages factory supervision to keep the machines busy. Production managers are encouraged to run products with high labor content to earn standards, and in large batches to achieve learning curve efficiencies. This sacrifices flexibility and customer service. Large batches create large inventory buffers and queues throughout the factory, which bury many of the factory's shortcomings. Because enough inventory exists to cover up deficiencies, inventory lulls managers, supervisors, and suppliers into complacency. Operators and machines stay busy even if vendors deliver late or parts are defective.

Beside camouflaging deficiencies, inventory buffers create other problems.

1. They decouple the manufacturing process from demand, accentuating any demand fluctuations. If incoming orders drop, fewer products are shipped. With fewer shipments, a lower safety stock of finished goods is required, allowing safety stocks to be worked down. With fewer orders and safety stocks being worked down, the final assembly demand is cut by much more than the original drop. Each inventory buffer magnifies the drop in requirements. By the time the drop in orders of 10 percent reverberates down to raw material procurement, purchases could drop by 40 or 50 percent. When new orders come in, the orders trigger large batches, creating production bottlenecks throughout the shop. To compensate for the demand fluctuations and to improve delivery performance, companies invest in redundant equipment to increase capacity.

2. By definition, inventory queues create longer production lead times and backlogs. Parts spend the majority of their shop time waiting in front of a machine, instead of being processed. Since it is difficult to tell whether a parts order is holding up a customer shipment or going into inventory, customers' orders go wanting, as machines are busy building inventory for forecasted requirements. With long lead times to the customers, companies are vulnerable to more agile competitors.

3. Each inventory buffer increases cost. Every time a part is stored it takes up floor space. The floor space the inventory occupies increases the distance a part must travel and thus material handling costs. If a part is stored, it must be handled twice (into and out of stores), whereas if the part goes directly to the next workstation, it is handled only once. The inventory must be tracked and managed. Inventory must be counted and verified, and meanwhile it is vulnerable to being lost, damaged, or becoming obsolete. In addition, lots of inventory piling up in the aisles requires armies of people to schedule and track it, driving up overhead costs.

4. Quality problems are allowed to flourish. The factory can produce large batches of defective material before being detected at subsequent workstations. In addition, the inventory buffers create long queues, which delay problem recognition. The longer feedback takes, the less likely it will influence operator behavior.

5. Buffers tie up cash and create financial exposure by having large finished goods inventories, which must be insured and can become obsolete.

The Dysfunctional Factory

Allocating overhead on direct labor creates period-end absorption. At the end of a reporting period, either a company ships enough product (that is, earns enough direct labor standards to absorb the plant overhead) or it creates a negative overhead variance. This phenomenon creates a management mind-set that focuses on shipping targets and not on cost control. To make its targets, management believes it must ship a certain number of units. This creates the widespread and infamous "hockey stick" effect (see Exhibit 1-1). Companies ship most of the month's production in the last week of the month, disrupting any semblance of uniform flow. Manufacturing is pushed to "make its numbers" regardless of cost. The shop schedules overtime, expedites vendors, and "cherry picks" orders. The budgeting process then reinforces these cost overruns by basing budgets on historical performance.

I have known supervisors who spent hours analyzing direct labor variances, while overlooking overhead. This is remarkable, considering that direct labor is merely a fraction of overhead costs. By measuring the supervisor's performance on direct labor efficiency, supervision is encouraged to focus on improving direct labor productivity.

While "responsibility accounting" is supposed to give supervisors responsibility and accountability for budgets, supervisors find they have little control over their budgets. Overhead allocations, the largest portion of their budgets, are insensitive to

Exhibit 1-1 **THE "HOCKEY STICK" EFFECT**

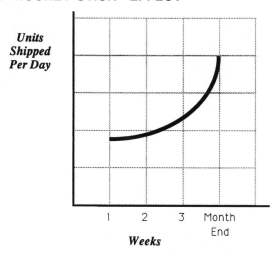

any of their actions. Because allocation schemes arbitrarily spread overhead (the approach is even referred to as "peanut buttering"), if supervisors manage to reduce overhead spending, they find their savings distributed across the whole organization. Instead, they spend their time trying to raise direct labor productivity. Shop supervisors feel victimized by the cost system and the high overhead rates their departments receive.

Furthermore, the overhead allocation does not relate the amount of support a department receives to the support's cost; consequently, supervisors compete for production engineering, tooling, and maintenance support. Supervisors have no incentive to refrain from demanding as much help as possible, because there is no cause-and-effect relationship between the support they receive and the overhead costs they are allocated. In effect, the supervisors are always trying to beat down labor costs while inadvertently driving up overhead spending. In fact, this competition

Exhibit 1-2   *WHERE TRADITIONAL COST SYSTEMS FOCUS THEIR ATTENTION*

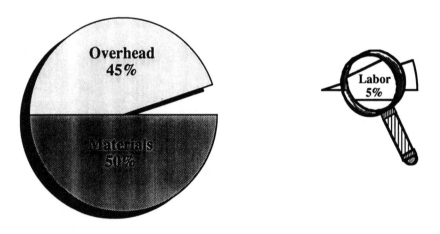

Today's cost systems pay too much attention to labor

for support frequently degenerates into a political battle for favoritism. Many productivity improvements are dependent on engineering or tooling support. Preferred supervisors (those getting the support) make their numbers—the others don't.

Chasing Low Labor Wages Around the World

By presenting all nonmaterial manufacturing costs as a multiple of direct labor, the cost system instills a mind-set that all costs are driven by and are proportional to direct labor. The cost system lulls management into believing that direct labor rates constitute the only controllable factor and the most crucial one in determining manufacturing costs—and hence competitiveness. This philosophy was reinforced by the success of low-cost imports from low-wage countries like Hong Kong, Taiwan, Singapore, and Japan during the 1960s and 1970s. This philosophy led many companies to conclude the only way to remain competitive was to move operations offshore to low labor rate countries. Between 1974 and 1986 the number of factories along the Mexican border under the in-bond or Maquiladora program grew from 450 to 1,100, and this number continues to escalate.

Subscribing to this philosophy, every major American television manufacturer, by 1973, established manufacturing facilities in countries such as Mexico, Taiwan, and Singapore. While American companies were moving production overseas, the Japanese were installing the latest design and production technology. The Japanese TV manufacturers switched to all solid-state chasses using automatic component insertion and extensive use of integrated circuits. These innovations slashed the average number of components in Japanese TVs from 1,200 in 1971 to only 480 in 1975, almost half the number of U.S. models. These advances not only removed labor content and manufacturing overhead, but vastly increased set reliability. It was estimated in 1977 that American color TV sets had a repair service call rate ten times that of Japanese brands.

By the end of the 1980s, only Zenith remained as an American-controlled manufacturer of television sets. Yet, all of the major Japanese companies now manufacture their television sets in the United States. Many of these Japanese-operated plants are the very same plants once used by American manufacturers, employing the same workers that the American manufacturers deemed uncompetitive. While more than 700 Japanese-owned factories have opened up in the U.S., American companies are chasing low labor rates around the world.

Allocating overhead on direct labor implies that by reducing direct labor, subsequent reductions in overhead mystically follow. Accordingly, engineers always target labor-intense processes like assembly operations for capital investment. The resulting capital justifications always portray automating direct labor as yielding large returns. In fact, this is rarely true. If a process is automated, then tooling, engineering, programming, and maintenance support invariably increase. Therefore, while direct labor is slashed, overhead (typically five to ten times as large as direct labor costs) increases.

Besides, human beings are versatile. People are very dexterous, possess a full range of sensory capability, can take verbal instructions, and can react to unanticipated stimuli such as product defects. Robots, on the other hand, are one-armed, blind, preprogrammed machines capable only of repetitive tasks. This makes replacing labor-intense processes one of the most difficult applications for automation. These factors explain why as many as 60 percent of executives are dissatisfied with their investments in automation.

However, some companies, recognizing that overhead reductions do not follow direct labor savings, prohibit overhead savings from being included in the capital justification unless the overhead reductions can be proven. While this certainly is a more rational approach, it leaves engineers little basis to justify capital investment. Because the traditional cost systems obscure the relationship between processes and overhead, it is difficult to identify the overhead affected by an automation project, much less quantify the savings. Therefore, capital justifications are forced to rely on direct labor savings, which are only a small part of a company's total cost. Most investment hurdle rates or paybacks are therefore extremely difficult to reach because they are arbitrarily set too high. This justification burden keeps capital investment down, concentrates investments on direct labor savings, and helps to explain why America has the lowest capital investment rate of any developing nation as a percentage of GNP. Yet engineers overcome this handicap by being very creative; they have learned to claim great direct labor savings on every project. No one knows how much capital has been misallocated over the years as a result of these fallacious justifications.

Even if the company has multiple cost centers, current systems make labor-intense processes appear more expensive than capital-intense ones. Labor-intense processes receive large overhead allocations, based on their labor content. Overhead—such as production control, industrial engineering, management and warehousing—are usually allocated on labor content. These large overhead allocations mislead industrial engineers into thinking labor-intense departments, like assembly, are expensive processes. Capital-intense processes such as die casting and machining, with their small direct labor content, receive only small allocations. This not only misdirects capital investment, but misguides make/buy decisions.

Obscuring the Sources of Overhead?

Because cost systems use arbitrary allocation schemes, there is no linkage between products or processes and the indirect costs they create. Management, with no reliable picture of what different processes really cost, is unable to see the connection between decisions and their effects on overhead costs.

- How much production control labor is created by adding another product line?
- How much does dedicating a production line save or cost?

- How much does special packaging and bar coding for one customer cost?

Without accurate measures, management has no clear understanding of what their decisions cost. Executives are forced to rely on intuition when negotiating with their customers, establishing order policies, or setting discount structures. This hinders cost reduction and process improvement. Without an understanding of cost, management is unable to control overhead spending, much less make effective trade-offs between costs and customer needs.

Lacking effective cost information, some managers attack its symptoms. Companies' response to profit pressure is either to cut budgets across the board or, in the words of a Casablanca police inspector, "round up the usual suspects." Management eliminates quality circles and preventive maintenance programs, while slashing capital and value engineering budgets. Usually, these moves only defer expenses. Yet, because the cost systems fail to identify the cause-and-effect relationships between costs and their sources, these "cost-cutting moves" can immediately drive up expenses elsewhere.

- An accounts receivable clerk was laid off, but her work did not go away. The very next week, a temporary could be seen entering payments into the computer. The temporary with agency fees cost about 10 percent more than the worker laid off.
- A company cut the customer service department by 15 percent to save money. As a result, customer time "on hold" and phone call abandonment rates skyrocketed, while customer service overtime increased and incoming orders plummeted. The long waiting times more than doubled the company's phone bill. At the same time, customers were livid. The customer service expenses actually climbed 10 percent.

These types of decisions sharply contrast with attacking the sources of costs. In the second case, other approaches, such as installing electronic data interchange (EDI) and increasing the discounts on multiple-unit orders, would have cut costs at its source. With customer service activity reduced, customer service could have been decreased without disturbing the customers. Lacking a solid grasp of what causes overhead, it is easy to botch a cost reduction.

The Distortion of Design Decisions

The traditional cost system encourages engineers to design standard labor and material out of their products, irrespective of their decisions' effects on overhead. To lower a part's direct labor, engineers route low-volume parts across automated high-volume machines. Since most cost systems fail to amortize the setup times across batches, the systems report cost savings. In fact, the automated machines' long setup times dwarf any direct labor savings.

To reduce standard material costs, engineers design unique parts with minimum material. For example, one manufacturer's designers created a short nonstandard screw. While the cost system reported saving three-tenths of a cent in material per screw, the cost system ignored the costs to plan, tool, inventory, and maintain this unique part. Current cost systems provide no incentive for engineers to follow the first rule of design-for-manufacturability—minimize the number of parts in a product.

The cost system of misallocating overhead costs to processes can result in engineers' designing products choosing the more expensive manufacturing process. In analyzing how to design a part, the engineer compares the part's cost using different processes with one another. If the process overhead is not correct, the designer has no way of knowing which process will cost more. A designer can, for example, be deceived into machining a part instead of sand casting it, or plating the part rather than powder coating it. When each process's true cost is assigned, the process chosen may change.

Confused Make/Buy Decisions

Management is often encouraged to outsource (buy from outside vendors) or relocate the labor-intense processes like assembly, thinking the move will eradicate assembly's large overhead. In fact, these processes require little overhead, while outsourcing or managing an offshore facility creates a great deal. When purchasing assemblies from a vendor, the vendor must be qualified, scheduled, and paid. Even though the parts require planning, inspection, and warehousing, they have no "direct labor" content, and therefore receive no overhead allocations. The vendor parts appear cheap but drive up overhead rates on all the plant's remaining processes. The outsourcing of assembly operations creates new inventory buffers. In addition, since assembly is typically the last operation before shipping the product to the customer, outsourcing wreaks havoc with schedules and lead times.

Yet these problems pale in comparison to those suffered by offshore facilities. Crossing the ocean and passing through customs add weeks to manufacturing lead times. Offshore manufacturing incurs new costs from tariffs, brokerage, and duties while exposing the company to currency fluctuations and foreign government regulation. Language barriers and culture differences aggravate communication problems between headquarters and the foreign plant. The ocean separating the design engineers from the manufacturing process may stifle a company's ability to innovate. It takes constant feedback from manufacturing to improve existing products and processes and to develop new ones. Consider, for example, what happened to the American television industry. After moving TV production overseas, the companies not only found themselves at an insurmountable disadvantage when new products like VCRs and camcorders came along, but fell behind in TV set technology as well.

Offshore operations typically require an enormous level of engineering, quality, tooling, facility, and material planning support. Unfortunately, this overhead typically ends up hidden in the U.S. operations. However, one should not say all offshore operations are losers. Rather, true costs and benefits are usually obscured.

Take the case of one medical products company that manufactures products ranging from catheters to blood pressure monitors. Each of its divisions is literally racing with each other to move manufacturing operations from California to Puerto Rico. While the illusion of low labor rates is the stated goal (despite the fact that labor constitutes only 6 percent of product cost), the real reason is more compelling. Each division is trying to get out from under the Irvine campus's crushing overhead. This huge overhead allotment consisting of engineering, quality assurance, customer service, and distribution functions, is assigned to each division based on its Irvine direct labor hours. However, the activities these functions perform are unrelated to where the division's manufacturing operations were located. As one vice president confided, each division is racing to Puerto Rico hoping the other divisions "will end up holding the bag"—or in this case—the overhead.

Since this company's cost allocation methods drove profitability reporting, these cost schemes in turn drove management performance measures and incentives. Despite the obvious deficiencies of the cost system, it was causing thousands of jobs to be lost in California and transferred to Puerto Rico without any true economic rationale.

Capital-intense processes—like machining, plating, and die casting, with very little direct labor—appear inexpensive, encouraging management to maintain these processes in-house and even to attract outside work with low hourly rates. The machining manager is encouraged to build parts for outside customers to keep the department's utilization high. The high utilization rates, in turn, attract more invest-ment—squandering the company's precious capital budget. Furthermore, capital-intense processes demand a high level of engineering, maintenance, and tooling support, so that the company subsidizes this outside work. The misallocation of overhead keeps the most expensive processes in-house and even grows them.

Concentration of Purchasing on Price Variances

Today's cost reporting focuses purchasing attention on price and price variances. Since no costs for rejected materials or late deliveries are tracked to purchased materials, the system forces buyers to judge vendors strictly on price and price variances. By concentrating on the lowest price, the system deemphasizes material quality and delivery. This creates downstream quality problems and forces the com-pany to maintain inventory buffers to compensate for poor delivery performance.

Measuring price variances also encourages buyers to increase order quantities for higher discounts, unfortunately creating the potential risk of excess inventory. Large orders also tie up cash, extend procurement lead times, increase inventory buffers, and create the need for more warehousing space. The large lots lumber through the factory like great lumps of work—choking receiving, inspection, and warehousing as they go.

The price fixation provides little incentive to consolidate vendors or to develop long-term partnership arrangements with them. By showing no loyalty to suppliers, the company fosters an adversarial relationship with suppliers. Knowing that a company buys strictly on price, vendors are unwilling to do anything extra for the company such as raise quality, improve schedule performance, or work to solve supply problems.

Undercosting of Complex Products

By allocating overhead on labor hours, complex products have their overhead greatly understated. Since direct labor content and complexity are poorly related at best, a simple product can have as much direct labor content as does a complex one. The simple product, with only a few part numbers, requires only minutes of planning, scheduling, and material movement. On the other hand, the complex product, with a large number of components, requires extensive planning and scheduling, tooling, and setups. Complex products usually have tighter manufacturing parameters because they require the successful interaction of many subcomponents. These tolerances not only create the need for more vigorous quality controls, but also result in quality fall out. Therefore, complex products require more inspection, test, and engineering support.

Complexity Triggers Activities

These activities consume time and resources; that is, they create cost. However, none of this cost of complexity is charged as direct labor. All of these costs are transparent to the cost reporting system and are haphazardly spread, via overhead allocations, across all the company's products. This undercosts the complex products and burdens the simple products with the cost of complexity.

While managers intuitively know the complex products are undercosted, they have no idea of the magnitude. Intuition is great for understanding the direction of the distortion, but extremely poor at quantifying it. Managers lack the cost data that would tell them how much different overhead activities cost and how many overhead activities the various products require. The complex products could be undercosted by 5 percent or 5,000 percent. Thus, management does not know if they are making or losing money in markets requiring complex products. On the other hand, management does not know how much more profitable the simple products are than what is reported.

Subsidizing Low-Volume Products

Today's cost systems subsidize low-volume, customized products at the expense of high-volume, standard products. Because overhead is allocated on direct labor hours or on the basis of some other measure of volume, high-volume products receive large overhead allocations. Conversely, low-volume products absorb small allocations. As more low-volume, complex products are introduced, the product costs of stable, high-volume products go up. The cost systems fail to recognize that many of the activities required to manufacture a product have economies of scale.

For instance, when in scheduling a job for 1 part or for 1,000, the planner takes the same amount of time. The same holds true for setting up a machine. Both a batch of 10,000 parts and a batch of 1,000 parts require only one setup. The cost of this setup is much less per unit for the 10,000 piece batch, but our cost systems do not account for it. Our cost systems do not amortize the cost of these or other activities like purchasing, receiving, and warehousing across a product's volume. Even though the cost is triggered by and, therefore, driven by the transaction, not part volume. Furthermore, in many cases a company's low-volume products are the most complex. These products not only require more engineering and test support, but also cause a disproportional number of the procurement, scheduling, and quality problems. The high volume repetitive products, on the other hand, are relatively problem free. How bad is the problem? In one recent study, we found low-volume products undercosted by more than 1,000 percent.

Because management intuitively knows these low volume products are undercosted (and because the market demands them), the company prices them at a premium, as it should. Ironically, this causes the cost accounting system to report the complex, low-volume products as having the highest (but fictitiously so) profit margins in the product line. Accordingly, marketing devotes inordinate resources to market segments which demand these products. Unfortunately, the company loses money on each unit sold because the "premium" price fails to cover the economic cost. The custom product only looks profitable because the cost system has unfairly overburdened the standard products.

Salespeople find it easier to sell unique products to niche customers. In fact, they frequently push to add new product options. While manufacturing people grapple with the problems of too many low-volume products, they lack any evidence to support their protests. Without supporting cost information, the company president frequently sides with the revenue-generating salespeople, who supposedly represent customer interests and are by their nature, convincing. The company is thereby suckered into manufacturing a huge variety of products. For example, with all of the options General Motors offers, a Chevy Cavalier comes in over 100 trillion configurations, even though GM ships only 200,000 units annually.

Companies constantly seek greater product differentiation through new products. Since the cost accounting systems do not penalize product proliferation with higher reported overhead, marketeers are unrestrained in deluging the American consumer with new products. In 1987 alone, manufacturers introduced 10,182 new supermarket products. Take toothpaste in particular, in 1979 there were seven major brands, today there are 31. Unfortunately, the introduction of these products unwittingly creates more and more overhead for not only the manufacturers but distributors and retailers as well.

Managing product permutations creates more overhead and higher inventory levels, but it also invariably leads to poor customer service. With broad product lines companies do not have enough working capital to stock every conceivable product with all of the options offered. Therefore, customer orders end up waiting for build-to-order products.

Burdening High-Volume Products

Consequently, by subsidizing low-volume products, management unwittingly overprices high-volume products. This leaves the company vulnerable to attacks by foreign competitors. In industries ranging from automobiles to color televisions and from semiconductors to door locks, America has seen Asian competitors attack the high-volume, standard market segments with aggressively priced products. These foreign competitors use focused factories to produce very narrow product lines.

As a result, Far East factories and products have minimal overhead. It is not uncommon to find Japanese plants with a half or a third of the indirect employees a comparable U.S. operation has. This low overhead allows foreign competitors to gain a foothold in the American market with low prices. American companies are unable to match these prices while simultaneously maintaining their diverse product lines. Because American systems overcost standard items, managers are convinced they would be selling these products at a loss. Their high prices on the high-volume products causes the American companies to lose the most profitable end of their market.

With little reported difference in margins across product lines, management is revenue focused. It responds to its falling sales and margins by increasing sales of the low-volume, specialty products. In these market segments, which management incorrectly believes are slightly more profitable, the company finds less competition. Chasing these customers creates even more overhead and further erodes profits. Because their cost systems do not reflect these products' true overhead, variances grow uncontrollably and management has no information explaining why.

Because their cost systems distort product costs, many American managers do not understand how foreign competitors can price so aggressively. These managers assume the lower costs stem from either low foreign wages or dumping (selling at prices in America below the foreigner's domestic prices). If American companies believe the low import prices result from low foreign wages, management usually starts moving operations overseas or to Mexico (a 1989 manufacturing survey of companies relocating facilities found over half the respondents still list seeking lower labor rates as the number one reason for relocating). While reducing direct labor costs, expatriating manufacturing operations incurs huge start-up costs and new overhead. The company must now deal with transportation, duties, brokerage, and coordination with a site hundreds if not thousands of miles away. In many cases, these "hidden" costs swamp the minuscule direct labor savings. Direct labor often constitutes less than 10 percent of manufacturing cost. Moving offshore also distances product designers from manufacturing operations thereby diluting design-for-manufacturability efforts. If American executives believe the Far East competitors are dumping, they lobby Congress for trade protection.

Japanese Companies Have Nearly Identical Cost Accounting Systems

Comparative studies of Japanese and American cost accounting systems have found that the only significant difference is the Japanese use of targets. The Japanese develop target costs; Niigata Engineering Ltd., a diesel engine manufacturer, is typical. Prior to designing a product, the company determines what the market price should be. Then the company calculates backward from the price what target cost the engineers must design to. All budgets are set based on this target cost. This "should cost" becomes the target cost the designers and production people shoot for. Each year the cost reduction target is 5 percent below the prior year's standard.

The Japanese allocate overhead, as do most American companies, on direct labor hours (this is not surprising since many of the systems were derived from American firms). The most remarkable aspect of the Japanese system is that Japanese executives pay little, if any, attention to their cost systems. Despite backgrounds in engineering or manufacturing, most Japanese executives are very intuitive and manage accordingly. The Japanese do not manage by the numbers. The executives' backgrounds and multifunctional job experience give them a feel for their business. They intuitively know what causes overhead and manage their business accordingly.

This distinction is critical. The Japanese managers place their faith in intuition while many American managers place theirs in numbers. This discovery is especially disturbing in light of the findings of social scientists. Extensive studies of decision making have concluded that "People tend to utilize whatever information is available—even though it might be erroneous or unrelated to the task at hand. Consequently, people may actually be hindered from penetrating to the core of a decision problem when they are overloaded with extraneous information. Without specific information, people tend to use whatever knowledge of logical analysis, statistical laws, and rational evaluation they can muster. When worthless information is given, they tend to use it and ignore the laws and rules!"[1]

This is exactly the situation American managers find themselves in. Most managers intuitively know their cost systems provide distorted information, although most have no idea of its magnitude. They continue to use these reported product costs for decision making because it is the only information available.

Yet, by examining their evolution, one can to see why cost systems are the way they are—so deficient. However, the state of accounting is not a failure of accounting or accountants. Managers have used financial information for a job it was never intended for—to manage operations. The intent of our cost systems as well as their evolution after 1920 has been to report financial performance after the fact—*not to manage and control operations*. The failure of our cost systems is not a

Exhibit 1-3   **THE EVOLUTION OF COST ACCOUNTING SYSTEMS**

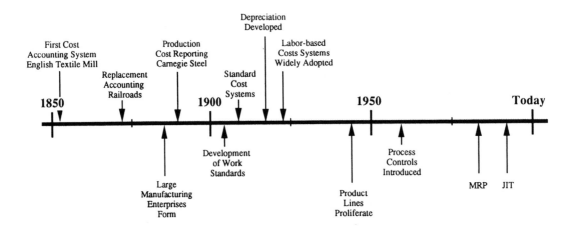

While manufacturing has changed – accounting has not

failure of cost accounting. Management, consciously or unconsciously, failed to develop appropriate performance measures. This shortsighted decision has imposed an ill-equipped system, which some managers religiously adhere to, upon American business. Therefore, the story of our cost systems is as much a story of American management as it is of cost accounting.

THE EVOLUTION OF AMERICAN COST MANAGEMENT

Double-entry bookkeeping systems in pre–Civil War textile mills were the first recorded American cost accounting systems. These records valued and controlled inventory. They measured the receipt and use of raw cotton and tracked the operation's efficiency at converting raw materials into finished goods.

In the 1860s, the world's largest enterprises—the railroads—adopted these primitive cost systems. Railroads such as the Union Pacific spanned half the continent and transacted annually the then unheard of sum of about $10,000,000. To manage these diverse operations, the railroads developed summary and sub-unit reporting. The owners also began to record operating statistics, such as cost per ton-mile, to improve their control and management over these growing operations.

With steam power came mechanization, and with mechanization came tremendous manufacturing economies of scale. By the late 1880s, large manufacturing enterprises in steel, oil, stockyards, wire, nails, sugar, and tobacco dominated the American economy. Because these enterprises were born of the newly discovered economies of scale and operated free of government interference, intense price competition ensued. Business leaders like Andrew Carnegie, John D. Rockefeller, Jim Fisk, and Henry Frick were obsessed with price competition. They sought to bankrupt their competition by undercutting prices with bigger and better foundries, railroads or coal mines. With extremely low sales expense and administrative costs, these early captains of industry priced their products strictly on variable costs. As a result, the *production reporting* which evolved only tracked direct labor and materials.

These captains of industry, watching every cent, kept meticulous accounting and sales records. Records for American Lubricating Oil Company include "daily stock reports." This report detailed the on-hand quantities of more than 50 different kinds of oils and greases. In one case, John D. Rockefeller wrote a refinery General Manager demanding to know why his factory listed his on hand inventory as only 6,000 barrel bungs, when, by Rockefeller's calculations, there should have been 6,750 on hand.

While these early systems made no allowance for capital costs, they eventually evolved into *replacement accounting,* which charged repair, maintenance and renewal costs as operating expenses. Thus, the cost systems of the 1880s and 1890s did not include any allocation of fixed costs to either products or periods.

The Birth of Scientific Management

Just after the turn of the century, Frederick Taylor pioneered scientific management, which pushed the idea of rational analysis and decision making. Taylor's overriding concern was improving productivity. He not only wanted to lower costs and raise profits, but also to make possible higher pay for workers. He worried about the labor movement's growing fascination with the radical and dangerous philosophy of one Karl Marx. Taylor hoped that by educating employees as to what constituted a "fair day's work" for a "fair day's pay," he would improve everyone's lot.

Standards Are Born

From this idea came work standards. Work standards defined how much work could be expected from one man per day, based on the optimum number and types of motions a man could perform. These work standards for direct labor quickly evolved into *standard costing*. Standard costing assumed each product absorbed an optimum and fixed amount of standard labor and material. By 1918, standard costing was widespread.

Another innovation of scientific management was a new organizational structure, one which separated the factory into specialized production departments. This separation greatly improved operating efficiency through specialization. It also created departmental measures and accountability, which had unintended results. As department managers became evaluated on direct labor efficiency, they grew inventory buffers between departments to avoid stock outs and subsequent work stoppages. To manage these new buffers, Ford Harris and R.H. Wilson developed the economical order quantity (EOQ) formula in 1915. This EOQ formula (see Exhibit 1-4) calculated the "optimum" order quantity or inventory buffer by weighing the cost of holding inventory versus the cost of processing an order. This formula became the cornerstone of inventory management for the next 70 years. EOQ encouraged the practice of running large batches and instilled the idea that setup times (part of ordering costs) are fixed.

The new organizational structure also separated staff from line functions. Taylor wanted staff organizations like engineering and accounting removed from production to enable standard setting and performance recording. Prior to this separation, non-production employees averaged less than 10 percent of a plant's work force. This reorganization expanded "factory burden," and led Taylor to advocate the allocation of overhead costs to products.

Exhibit 1-4 **ECONOMICAL ORDER QUANTITY FORMULA**

$$Q = \sqrt{\frac{2AS}{I}}$$

Where		
S	=	Setup or ordering cost
A	=	Annual usage expressed in dollars
I	=	Inventory carrying cost
Q	=	Quantity

At the time, Alexander Church, one of the standard costing pioneers, specifically warned against allocating overhead on direct labor hours. Church believed that, even though direct labor was 40 percent of the product value, allocating overhead cost would lead to serious errors in product costing. Unfortunately, this advice was not heeded and many companies use direct labor as a "simple," but "inaccurate" method of allocation.

The concept of the professional manager dates back to these days. In 1916, a French industrialist, Henry Fayol, wrote his observations on general management. He believed in the division of work by developing specialists, including management. Fayol regarded the elements of management to be planning, organizing, commanding, coordinating and controlling, which were equally applicable to business, political, religious and military enterprises.

Concurrently, Du Pont and General Motors (of which Du Pont owned a significant portion) decentralized into functional departments. With this change, Du Pont developed the return on investment (ROI) measure to rate business unit performance. In the early 1920s, as this measurement spread and with the institution of federal income tax, depreciation became included in our standard overhead.

An outgrowth of the ROI measure was the idea of "standard volume." Standard volume was the average volume each division could expect to sell over a period of years. This concept, developed and implemented at GM in 1925, was intended to compensate for the yearly fluctuations in ROI, by measuring it against an average output. Unfortunately this development had a very insidious long-term effect. The idea of "standard volume," which quickly spread to other companies and industries, inculcated a mind-set that volume and, therefore, market share were constants. The financial analysis, on which all operating and strategic plans were based, rested on the flawed assumption of standard volume. The analysis assumed if the firm did nothing, that is, no investments, no quality improvements, and so on—volume, that is, market share would remain constant. This contributed to the mind-set that market share did not have to be continuously earned.

Academics Come to the Forefront

By 1927, all of our present cost accounting practices and many of our current management concepts had been developed. Significantly, Frederick Taylor, Henry Gantt, Frank Gilbreth, Alexander Church and other pioneers were engineers by training and practitioners by vocation. These men concentrated exclusively on developing methods and tools for business. Accountants and scholars played little role in the development of our standard cost systems. However, since 1925, the accounting literature has been virtually devoid of practitioner developments. Until the late 1980s, accounting journals have relied almost exclusively on academic research.

After 1913, the government began to work toward standardizing financial reporting to ensure uniform and accurate calculation of income taxes. Regulations accelerated in response to the stock market crash of 1929. The Securities Acts of 1933 and 1934 founded the Security and Exchange Commission and gave it the power to ensure "full and fair disclosure" by corporations issuing securities on an interstate basis. Both the SEC and the New York Stock Exchange developed procedures for and instituted the auditing of corporate financial statements. These events caused the accounting profession to begin emphasizing the reporting of costs to meet external requirements, as opposed to internal needs. Accounting drifted toward cost accounting (i.e., cost reporting) and away from cost management (i.e., cost planning).

In addition, to meet the rapidly expanding tax preparation and auditing needs, the accounting profession and public accounting firms grew by leaps and bounds. The literature and teaching of accounting responded to this growth by emphasizing the preparation for public accounting and its examinations. With the greatest rewards, many of the accounting profession's best and the brightest were attracted toward public accounting. This "brain drain" helped stifle innovation.

The Gilded Age of American Manufacturing

In many ways World War II was won by American manufacturing. America was the arsenal of democracy. By 1943, the United States alone out produced the Axis powers in armaments by a factor of two to one. America outfitted not only its own forces but through lend-lease, Russian, English and French forces as well. In 1943 the United States produced one ship a day and one aircraft every hour.

America applied the techniques of mass production as never before seen to many items previously produced in only small quantities like aircraft, machine guns and ships. These techniques drove costs down dramatically. In 1943 it took over 40,000 labor hours to produce a B-24 bomber, by 1945 it was down to 8,000. When the call went out for a new long-range escort fighter, North American Aviation responded and had the P-51 Mustang designed and built from scratch in just 100 days. America buried the enemy in material.

After the war, American manufacturing turned its attention to consumers. An age of unheard of growth was ushered in. Product lines began to proliferate to meet the rising tide of "consumerism." Many factories shifted to a job shop organization to handle the increased number of small production batches.

Other trends emerged. General Electric lead a drive to develop complex, automated systems aimed at removing as much labor from the factory floor as possible. In the 1950s, believing economies of scale would build an insurmountable cost advantage, GE built its huge Appliance Park in Louisville, Kentucky. After this experiment GE would never try to build a facility on such scale again.

Artisan managers, men who had worked themselves up from the shop floor dominated the managerial ranks of American manufacturing. These men continually invested in the latest manufacturing technologies. They introduced process controls, like numerical control (N/C), accelerating the decline of skilled crafts and direct labor costs. Nothing better sums up the outlook of the American manufacturing executive of the 1940s and 1950s than the words of Newport News Shipyard's founder:

> *We shall build good ships here*
> *At a profit, if we can*
> *At a loss, if we must*
> *But, always good ships.*

With American manufacturing preeminent, John Kenneth Galbraith proclaimed in his 1958 book *The Affluent Society* that America had "solved the problem of production."

Accounting Shifts to the Esoteric

Meanwhile, in the accounting departments, few developments took place until the mid-1950s, when the time value of money concept came into vogue. Soon, dissertations on modeling discounted cash flows for investment analysis filled the accounting literature. Academic research focused on how to apply economic theory to accounting and not solving business problems. The research emphasis reflected the origins of the accounting in higher education. Accounting, as well as business education, grow out of the economics departments. Most of the professors of accounting, even today, originally majored in economics and not accounting or business.

During these postwar years, Fayol's philosophy of the professional manager was being discovered. It was not until 1949, that Fayol's book *General and Industrial Administration* was translated into English. Fayol's ideas that management skills and their application to be universal, was very attractive to management theorists. These theorists pushed the concept of general management and it became one of the foundations of management theory. These theories in turn became the basis for teaching of management in the business departments of the universities. However, this philosophy would not reach the corporate executive ranks for another 20 years when students schooled in this philosophy reached the corner office.

Later, during the 1960s, academia concentrated on applying operations research to cost accounting. The journals described how cost accountants could use linear programming, probability theory and regression analysis to improve forecasting and planning. In the 1970s, the literature's emphasis shifted again, this time to agency theory and information economics. Interestingly, information economics studies the value of information versus the costs of obtaining it. This idea can easily be applied to a new cost system.

America Gets a New Breed of Executive

During the 1960s, a new breed of executive ascended to the leadership of many manufacturing companies—these were men schooled in Fayol's philosophy of professional management. Men like Harold Geneen at ITT and Lynn Townsend at

Chrysler had been taught "managing by the numbers." Since dollars and cents were the only numbers available, this new managerial class was excessively cost focused. These men oriented their companies toward economies of scale and high utilization, striving to beat the competition on cost. These numbers men then began to push accounting numbers down into the organization. Suddenly, general managers found themselves measured on return on investment, and factory supervisors on the machine utilization and operator productivity. Gone were the days when operating managers were expected to think in terms of product quality, on-time delivery, and customer satisfaction.

Yet, the Go-Go years did well by these executives and their new philosophy. In fact, the biggest problem most manufacturers faced in the 1960s, was how to bring on capacity fast enough to meet demand. Room air conditioner and dishwasher unit sales almost quadrupled and clothes dryers more than tripled. U.S. machine tool, bicycle, and TV shipments doubled between 1960 and 1968. According to the Department of Commerce more than 90 percent of consumer markets were growing during the 1960s. Sales and profits soared. Companies went on buying binges, gobbling up small manufacturers and forming conglomerates.

As late as 1965, only 5,000 MBAs were being conferred. As management theory and teaching spread, so did Fayol's idea of the professional manager. Business schools, like Harvard and Wharton, developed curricula teaching basic management skills from case studies taken from not only all conceivable industries but also from government and nonprofit enterprises. In their effort to become more scientifically run and rational, many companies took up this new managerial class and earmarked them for the top.

Up until this time, American business was characterized by allowing anyone to work themselves up through the ranks. There was no limit to where a forklift operator could advance. However, by the mid-1970s a college degree became a prerequisite for advancement into the executive ranks and by the 1980s it was the MBA. No longer did companies need to ferret out and train potential executives from the shop floor ranks, companies got their managers from the business schools.

The belief a good manager can manage anything may seem justifiable in theory. After all, a manager must be able to plan, organize and control the organization to meet its schedule and budgets. This would seem to require the same skills in the production control department of a steel rolling mill as in the auditing department of a bank.

However, managers are required to make decisions and allocate resources. Under tense and trying circumstances, executives not understanding the details of the business, can be devastating. Assume the professional manager in question is the president of a manufacturing company and does not intuitively know the trade-offs involved in broadening product lines. Remember, the cost systems are untrustworthy, if not treacherous. The president is unsure to what extent 17 new part numbers will disrupt production, or to which degree the customers will appreciate the new products. This professional manager must depend on his flawed cost system and the advice and counsel of the controller, vice president of sales, and vice president of manufacturing; each of whom have their own partisan stake in the outcome. Under these circumstances managing by the numbers is impossible.

Ironically, just as these numbers people ascended to the helm of most companies, disenchantment with the numbers germinated. In the 1960s, leading companies found themselves dissatisfied with their cost information for make/buy decisions. Companies began to institute material burdening to understand the true cost of procuring material. Typically, these companies distributed purchasing, receiving, storing, and inspecting costs as a percentage of material cost. In the 1970s, as direct labor costs continued to shrink, capital intensive firms began switching from direct labor to machine hours as the allocation basis. This reduced some of the distortion between capital and labor-intense products.

The Coming of MRP

Concurrently, manufacturing was undergoing another very important change. In the late 1960s, Oliver Wight began to expound a new computerized system for ordering material and managing inventory. Its name is Material Requirements Planning or MRP. MRP was designed to be very robust and to handle the most complex of manufacturing environments—the job shop. MRP with fixed lead times and lot sizes best matches the needs of the popular job shop manufacturing environment— low to medium volume, with a wide variety of products and models. The job shop must be able to react to fluctuating mix and unpredictable demand. This environment is so complex, only a computer can handle it. As the system spread across the country in the 1970s, it brought a discrete lot production framework or perspective which *pushes* production through the factory.

The Japanese, on the other hand, developed just-in-time (JIT) as the cornerstone of their manufacturing approach (the story of how JIT was developed is discussed in Chapter 13). JIT which *pulls* materials through the factory, is specifically geared for the repetitive manufacture of high-volume, narrow product lines. With low inventory levels, the JIT factory reacts to fluctuating mix and demand by flexible production. Setup times are driven down, operators are cross-trained and systems streamlined.

A New Age Dawns

As early as 1971, George J. Staubus proposed management systems built on activities. In that year, he published *Activity Costing and Input-Output Accounting*. Unfortunately, at that time there was little interest in new forms of costing. Moreover, the computer systems needed to collect activity data did not yet exist.

However, by the early 1980s, industry and a few academics came to recognize the terrible flaws in our cost systems, and their ill effects. In spite of a stagnating domestic demand, with the dollar soaring to new heights, foreign competitors launched an invasion of the American market. These foreign competitors pummeled

American industry for the first time since the Depression. With growth stopped and earnings eroding, shareholders took action. Raiders began to force entrenched managers to divest underperforming divisions. Companies were taken private in leveraged buyouts (LBOs). Cash flow and shareholder value became the objective for many companies.

Automate, Emigrate, or Evaporate

Faced with sudden import competition from low wage countries, the battle cry for manufacturers became, "automate, emigrate, or evaporate." Robotics seemed to be America's only hope, and its newest growth industry. The number of American robot installations climbed from 5,000 to more than 20,000 in just four years. Conglomerates jumped on the bandwagon and not only installed robots, but began to build and sell robots as well. Westinghouse bought Unimation, America's largest manufacturer of robots, while Cincinnati Milacron and General Electric brought out their own lines of robots. Through the 1980s, General Motors not only spent $40 billion on automation and new facilities, but bought five machine-vision suppliers and formed a joint venture with Fanac to build robots. Meanwhile, other manufacturers raced to open manufacturing operations in low wage countries, such as Mexico, Malaysia, Taiwan and Korea.

Unfortunately, American investments in automation disappointed many executives and they came to realize their cost systems had betrayed them. Their systems told them automating direct labor was always a good idea. But, in reality, the costs of labor-intense operations were dwarfed by indirect costs.

Only after failing at automation did American companies begin to improve quality and emulate foreign practices like JIT. Yet, managers pushing for higher quality found no solace in their cost systems. The systems did a poor job of identifying quality problem areas and the associated high costs. Unfortunately, the cost systems provided no cost justification for quality improvements.

Companies also found their cost systems discouraging JIT practices, which were evidently crucial to Japan's success. Line stoppages would result in labor variances. High-quality vendors, which minimized or bypassed receiving and inspection activities, would apparently increase purchasing unit costs.

A New Cost System Is Born

In 1984 two respected accounting professors, Dr. Robert Kaplan, then at Carnegie-Mellon University and Dr. Tom Johnson of Portland State University, began to expound the shortcomings of today's cost accounting systems. Concurrently, Dr. Robin Cooper of the Harvard Business School developed a new type of cost system while consulting for Schrader Bellows. This new cost system allocated costs on overhead transactions or activity. This method was called activity-based costing (ABC). Shortly thereafter, Kaplan reported on a new cost estimating system which John Deere's Component Works had developed. It, too, assigned costs on measures of activity.

From these beginnings, ABC gained attention and spread. Northern Telecom, Hewlett-Packard, Honeywell, and Avery International are just a few of the companies who have instituted ABC or have undertaken ABC studies. At this time, the vast majority of the ABC systems are microcomputer-based and used strictly for product costing. Only a few companies such as Hewlett-Packard use ABC as their on-line cost system including inventory valuation. As practitioners, consultants and academics expound the benefits interest in ABC explodes.

WHAT YOUR COST SYSTEMS DON'T TELL YOU

What the traditional cost system does not tell management could fill volumes— thick ones. The traditional cost system gives management little idea of where to cut back spending if times get tough. The system only gives management reports showing where costs are spent and no indication of what is creating the costs. Management is forced to cut the organization back on intuition. Subsequently, management does not affect policies like minimum order sizes or backorders, which would lower activity levels. By increasing minimum order sizes, the company would receive larger orders and thereby cut order entry and billing work loads. These actions reduce work allowing staff reductions. While cutting staff without reducing activity levels, either leaves critical work undone, overburdens the remaining staff or drives up costs as temporary workers are hired to complete the work.

Lots of Dollars Are Left "Below the Line"

Traditional cost systems do look at a company's total cost. They ignore the so called "below-the-line" expenses, like sales, distribution, R&D and administration. At many companies, these costs are not assigned to different markets, customers, channels of distribution or even products. Many managers believe these costs are fixed. Therefore these "below-the-line" costs are treated as though they are equally distributed across all customers. Yet, some customers are much more expensive to serve than others and as this book will show these costs are some of the most variable costs a company incurs.

For example, one manufacturer sold to two types of customers—buying groups and distributors. A buying group is a collection of independent stores who negotiate with manufacturers as one group. This allows these small stores to leverage their buying power. Despite buying leverage these customers are expensive to serve. Each store in a buying group decides what products to buy for its store, and these stores are physically dispersed. Therefore, a buying group demands a great deal of sales force time, in addition to any marketing or training programs needed. Individual stores only order in small quantities. Small orders result in many customer orders, pick lists, bills of lading, freight charges and invoices—driving up order entry, shipping, freight and billing costs per unit.

A distributor is a product reseller. Distributors take possession of a manufacturer's products and sell and deliver it to their customers. Distributors have one or a small group of buying decision makers. Therefore, distributors require comparatively few sales calls. Distributors order products in large quantities and take delivery at only one shipping destination. Usually, they order only a select number of high-volume end items, once a month. The distributor requires only one bill of lading and one invoice per month. In addition, a distributor usually receives shipments as full truckloads. As one can see, buying groups create ten times the documents and transactions as does a distributor for the same sales volume. Thus, it is much less costly for the manufacturer to sell to distributors, but distributors can demand greater discounts.

Arbitrarily spreading distribution costs can fog decision making. One pet food company was considering building a new 400,000 square foot warehouse. Its other warehouses were at capacity. Increasingly, when a team visited the warehouses they found the warehouses filled to the brim with dog food. Why such overstocking was occurring was hard to understand until the team uncovered the method used to allocate warehousing costs. The company's warehousing costs were allocated on product value. Therefore, 4 cubic feet of dog food was allocated $3.89 in distribution costs per bag while a single case of gourmet cat food was hit with $12.00. This cheap storage cost allowed dog food product managers to order and ship products in very large batch sizes to the warehouse. By simply changing the allocation of distribution costs to cubic feet and number of units handled, behavior and operating policies changed. Product managers learned to manage inventory and no longer ordered in large batches. The dog food inventory shrank and the need for the new warehouse evaporated.

The cost of serving different markets varies tremendously. For example, one company sells wheelchairs in two markets—home care and rehabilitation. The home care market serves the aged with low-cost wheelchairs. The chairs are high-volume, simple products. The rehabilitation market serves injury invalids. Their chairs are customized or "prescribed" for particular individual needs. The chair is fit to each customer's body dimensions and has unique features such as removable left arms for persons with left-side paralysis. This market segment also includes very sophisticated sports and power chairs.

The home care products require little in the way of order entry, customer service or engineering. On the other hand, it takes days for the manufacturer to train dealers to prescribe a rehab chair. It takes 20 minutes or more to order just one rehab product. If the dealer or entry clerk make a mistake in ordering, the chair must be returned to the factory for rework. Between 1970 and 1977, one company introduced all of its current home care products, while none of the rehab products is more than four years old. Since innovation and new products are an important part of the rehab market, more than 80 percent of the company's R&D and engineering support it. The majority of the company's large product liability bill is traced to the rehab market. While the manual, home care products are sold to inactive, elderly patients, the rehab products go to injury patients who will live and work in the chair 10 or 20 years. The rehab market includes power chairs. The motor and batteries make the power chairs heavy and somewhat unstable. The drivers with their limited mobility can tip the chairs over. Consequently, the rehab products create much greater liability exposure and, hence, liability cost than home care chairs. By identifying the true costs of each market, the manufacturer can make more effective decisions about product pricing and resource allocation.

IN CONCLUSION

Our traditional cost systems do not accurately cost our products and misdirect our pricing and marketing strategies. Today's systems fail to help us improve our operations. We are forced to work with distorted information which discourages us from reducing inventory levels, improving customer service and building better products. These cost systems confound management decision making. We are beguiled into automating away direct labor or into chasing low wage rates around the globe.

These cost systems have not only given us wrong information on which to make decisions but have instilled management approaches which don't work. One may think I believe our labor-based cost systems are the cause of America's competitive decline. I do—or at least I think it has been a significant factor.

CHAPTER 2

STRATEGY ABC:
UNLOCKING AMERICA'S
COMPETITIVE EDGE

Invasions can be resisted, but not an idea whose time has come.

Victor Hugo

Accounting can shape the destiny of companies as well as that of nations. A superior accounting system can provide upgraded information for better decision making. This information allows management to allocate resources, as well as measure and control operations, more effectively. With a preeminent accounting system, as history shows, a nation can dominate world commerce and grow rich while doing so.

At the end of the twelfth century in what is now Algiers, an Arab master tutored a young man named Leonardo Fibonacci in calculation. Leonardo, a Pisan, was in Algiers while his father served as consul. When he returned to Italy, he brought back the Arab and Indian methods of decimal calculation he had learned. Fibonacci became quite famous for these findings, as well as for his own mathematical dissertations. Yet he received almost no acclaim for the obscure new Arab method of balancing income and expenditure that he brought back and that would have the most lasting influence.

At the time, European accounting was very primitive. It treated every transaction as a separate entity. With each transaction, merchants kept notes recording the details such as costs, interest, and sales. No one tried to bring all the transactions together into a comprehensive budget. It wasn't until 1340, over 100 years after Fibonacci's death, that his double-entry system made its first recorded appearance in practice.

The new system evolved as it spread from one Italian trading city to the next, first Genoa, then Venice and Florence. The new system significantly improved financial control and measurement. It was the Florentine Medici family who first made strategic use of the new system. In 1397 the Medici banking family started lending money on an international scale. Others had tried it before, but had gone bankrupt. The great economic recovery from the Black Death fueled the Medici's expansion.

The Medicis opened banks throughout Europe, providing bills of exchange and a credit system. Each branch provided flexible service based on an ability to make independent decisions. The new efficient double-entry bookkeeping methods allowed all of these services. Without the new accounting system, handling and controlling these complex and diversified transactions with varying exchange rates would have been impossible. The Medicis came to dominate Europe's money market because they could balance their books.

This new accounting system's importance cannot be overstated. It raised measurement and control to an entirely new plateau, allowing enterprises to conduct financial transactions of unprecedented scale at substantially lower risk. This new system created business enterprises of new scale and efficiency with autonomous decision making. This accounting system allowed banking, insurance, and trading to flourish in Italy. By dominating financial transactions, the Italians came to dominate commerce as well. The Italian peninsula became the trading hub between northern Europe's gold, grain, wine, and textiles and the East's spices, silks and cottons.

This accounting technique ushered in a new age. Their new wealth allowed Italians to found universities, libraries and museums. The world renowned Uffizi Gallery was built to house the Medici's family collection. Great churches such as the Cathedral of Santa Maria Del Fiore were built. In Florence, artists invented modern landscape painting and still life. The dark ages were over, Italian Renaissance had begun.

However, every competitive advantage is fleeting. It is hardly a coincidence that banking houses in France, Castile, Germany, and the Netherlands broke Italy's monopoly on international banking in the sixteenth century. In 1494, Luca Pacioli, a Venetian monk and mathematician, wrote a comprehensive instruction manual on the double-entry accounting system. The manual included an extended discussion of the critical issues of debit and credit. Once foreigners learned the new system, Italy's competitive advantage was lost forever.

THE GOAL OF ACTIVITY-BASED COSTING

Today, another cost accounting system, equally revolutionary and equally significant, is beginning its ascent. This system can restore America's competitiveness.

This new system, called activity-based costing (ABC), was developed to understand and control indirect costs. Yet it does much more than just cost products, it tells executives what triggers costs and how to manage them. Activity-based costing is the first true cost management system. Yet, never forget, cost management is an art, not a science.

ABC assigns costs to products or customers based on the resources they consume. The system identifies the costs of activities such as setting up a machine, receiving raw material, and scheduling a job. ABC then traces these activities to a particular product or customer that triggers the activity. Accordingly, the product's costs embody all the costs of these activities. Overhead costs are traced to a particular product rather than spread arbitrarily across all products. In turn, management can learn to control the occurrence of activities, and therefore, learn to control costs.

ABC:

- is a system for planning.
- does not try to establish a theoretical or actual (e.g., historical) cost.

Exhibit 2-1   **WHAT IS ACTIVITY-BASED COSTING?**

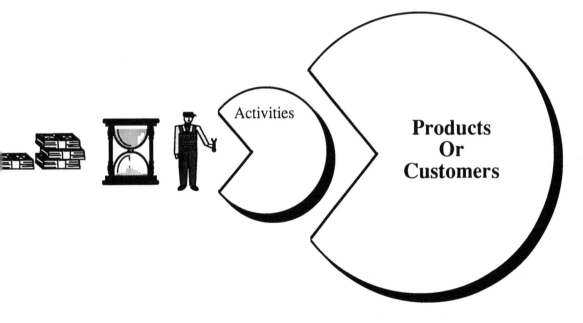

Activities consume resources and
products and customers consume activities

- reflects the company's best estimate of what it will cost to produce products in the future (i.e., later this year).

- is a managerial accounting system, not just an analytical study.

- is a system for costing products, developing budgets, measuring performance, and valuing inventory.

ABC debunks the myth of fixed costs. Using today's cost accounting systems, accountants assume many costs are fixed because they do not understand how to control these costs. However, costs are only fixed over a given time horizon. Over the long term all costs are variable—if one understands what creates the cost. This is the essence of business strategy—making all costs work to your advantage.

ABC allows one to identify the policies, systems, or processes that trigger activity, thereby creating cost. ABC, by ferreting out what really drives costs, allows us to attack and reduce the so-called fixed costs such as sales force expense, engineering, planning, and depreciation. In the long term, a company can sell its factory, move to another country, or even leave a business entirely. ABC, by identifying the activities that create cost and the triggers that create activities, allows a company to take control of its costs and destiny.

Tracking Costs to Products Activity

Activity-based costing assigns material costs to products in the same manner as present systems. Unlike traditional product costing systems, ABC does not start with the assumption that direct labor or direct material causes overhead. Instead, ABC presumes products incur indirect costs by requiring resource-consuming activities such as warehousing, scheduling, inspections, production setups, and so on. An activity, such as setting up a machine, causes overhead spending by triggering the consumption of an operator and machine time. Products create the need for indirect activities and, therefore, are assigned indirect costs based on the indirect activities they cause.

An activity-based cost system represents this resource consumption by tracking the relationship between indirect costs and their sources. It takes overhead costs and assigns them to products, based on measures of usage. The more activities a product requires, the more cost it creates. To track this relationship, an ABC system assigns costs to products based on the number of activities the product requires. To develop a cost per activity, divide the total overhead cost of the activity by the number of activities performed. This creates a cost per activity and a productivity measure for each overhead function (see Exhibit 2-2).

Trace Costs to Activities

Products then pick up these costs according to the number of activities or cost-driver units it consumes. For example, ABC tells a manager how much it costs to process a work order. ABC then assigns this cost per work order to each product based on the number of work orders it requires.

Exhibit 2-2

COST PER ACTIVITY = RESOURCES CONSUMED/OUTPUT MEASURE

COST PER WORK ORDER = WORK ORDER COSTS/# OF WORK ORDERS

$2.14 = \$47,255/22,123$

Companies use many different types of measures to represent the different types of resource consumption taking place. In some cases, resource consumption is proportional to the number of units produced. A cost such as direct labor fits this example. For each unit processed, some direct labor is consumed. Similarly, as more and more parts run across a punch press, the more worn the machine becomes. This wear creates the need for preventive maintenance or causes machine breakdowns. Therefore, ABC assigns the punch press's machine repair costs on the number of punches, insertions, or some other measure of production volume.

Triggering Activity

Even though most people and the traditional cost system tend to think of volume as creating all costs, often an activity is not related to the number of units produced. Some activities are not triggered by every unit processed but are triggered by a whole batch of units. These costs are driven by the number of batches processed. For example, doubling a product's volume does not double the number of machine setups. One must double the number of batches in order to double setup costs. Therefore, the ABC system assigns setup costs to batches of products.

These batch costs are then divvied up by each unit in the batch. Thus, a batch's setup costs are divided by the number of units in the batch to obtain the cost per unit. Consequently, the ABC system represents setup costs as proportional, very small in large batches, and very large in small batches.

Purchasing is another cost driven by batches. Traditional cost systems allocate purchasing costs to products on their material cost. This method does not reflect how a buyer works. A buyer creates, schedules, places, and coordinates purchase orders (POs). The work load is directly proportional to the number of POs processed—irrespective of the number of items bought or to the dollars spent. Therefore, ABC assigns purchasing costs to products based on the number of POs they require (see Exhibit 2-3).

While some purchase orders are going to take longer to process than others, differences average out. In the example shown, Product B, with ten times the number of purchasing transactions, creates ten times the purchasing work as Product A. If in fact this is not the case, purchase orders are not a good measure of activity.

Exhibit 2-3   **HOW ACTIVITY-BASED COSTING WORKS**

	PURCHASING COSTS		$200,000
	PURCHASE ORDERS		1000
	COST PER PURCHASE ORDER		$200

	PRODUCT A	**PRODUCT B**
PRODUCTION VOLUME	400	4000
PURCHASE ORDERS	4	40
PURCHASING COST	$800	$8,000
PURCHASING COST PER		
PRODUCT ITEM	$.20	$2.00

o Product A has only a few high volume components, while Product B has many. Product B, therefore, creates much more purchasing activity than Product A.

Activities Consume Resources

The warehousing department receives, stocks, picks, issues, and moves material to the production departments. In each of these functions, material is moved or transacted as a batch—individual bars or parts are not moved one at a time. Batches drive warehousing activities. The more batches issued, the more work for the warehousing department. Therefore, the warehouse's work load is proportional to the number of issues made.

Since a pallet of steel is just as time consuming to issue and move as one bar; the moving cost is not proportional to the number of bars moved. Typically, one single item like a bolt takes longer to move than a pallet of castings. Operators usually walk for a bolt instead of driving their forklifts. Therefore, ABC distributes warehousing costs on material issues. The costs of the material issue are then amortized across all of the parts issued in the batch.

The same argument holds for receiving. Time is spent and costs are driven by receipt transactions, not by the volume of items received. Thus, ABC assigns receiving costs to products on the number of receipts. Exhibit 2-4 shows the allocation bases for a traditional cost system versus activity-based costing. It should be noted that in an ABC system, you do not allocate costs, you assign costs. Allocating costs suggests arbitrarily spreading them to different cost centers. In an ABC system, you attempt to trace costs to their sources. Assigning costs implies a thoughtful application of costs.

Activity-based costing reflects a factory's economies of scale. When setup, planning, material handling, and warehousing costs are amortized across large production runs, these costs are very small per piece. Conversely, when amortized across small production runs, these per unit costs are very large.

Exhibit 2-4   **ALLOCATION BASES FOR TRADITIONAL AND ABC**

INDIRECT COST	TRADITIONAL	ABC
Production Control	Labor Hours	Parts Planned
Inspection	Labor Hours	Inspections
Warehousing	Labor Hours	Stores Receipts and Issues
Purchasing	Labor Hours	Purchase Orders
Receiving	Labor Hours	Dock Receipts
Order Entry	Labor Hours	Customer Orders
Production Setups	Labor Hours	Production Changeovers

ABC Overcomes Traditional Distortions

Exhibit 2-5 enumerates ABC's assignment of setup costs and compares it with the traditional cost accounting system. The exhibit demonstrates the cost distortion that the traditional system causes in high- and low-volume products. If the setup costs are assigned on labor hours, the high-volume products receive most of the setup costs. If, on the other hand, we assign setup costs based on the number of setups required, high-volume products receive proportionally small setup costs. The system accounts for the fact that low-volume products require a disproportion of setup costs. ABC system shows the low-volume products undercosted by 586 percent, while the high-volume products overcosted by 39 percent.

As you can imagine, this distortion is very dangerous. The traditional cost system, by allocating all overhead costs to products on volume measures, systematically undercosts low-volume products and overcosts high-volume ones. It is not uncommon to find products undercosted by 1,000 percent. This distortion can direct a company to drop profitable products in favor of products losing money!

The traditional cost system causes a similar distortion between complex and simple products. To manufacture a complex product with many part numbers and intricate functions requires more support activities—such as planning shop orders, processing engineering changes, placing purchase orders, conducting system tests, and moving materials—than a simple product. Complex products, therefore, place high demands on support functions. These demands trigger many more activities per unit than simple products, and are much more expensive. Yet the traditional system makes no such distinction. The traditional system allocates overhead costs on direct labor or machine hour content, which is a poor measure of product com-

Exhibit 2-5   **HOW ABC CHANGES A PRODUCT'S COST**

	PRODUCT X	PRODUCT Y	TOTAL
Volume	1,000	20,000	21,000
Direct labor per unit	4	3	
No. of Setups	30	40	70
Total Setup Costs **If Assigned on:**			
- On Labor Hours	$280	$4,200	$4,480
- On No. of Setups	$1,920	$2,560	$4,480
Traditional setup cost Per Unit (On Labor Hrs)	$0.28	$0.21	
ABC Setup Cost Per Unit (On No. of Setups)	$1.92	$0.13	
Change	+586%	-39%	

plexity. ABC, on the other hand, by tracking the triggering of support activities, identifies the real costs of these products. A complex product with many part numbers will require many purchase orders, more production planning, more inspection points, and so on. Each of these activities, by being traced to the product, are reflected in its product cost (see Exhibit 2-6).

It is important to remember that the misrepresentation of cost results in flawed decision making. Resources are not used effectively. Salesmen push the wrong products to the wrong customers at prices below costs. Engineers concentrate on designing out direct labor or material, unaware of the effects their decisions have on future overhead demands.

ACTIVITY-BASED COSTING IS TOTAL COST MANAGEMENT

Since all of a company's activities exist to support the design, manufacture, and delivery of products to its customers, activity-based costing seeks to assign all costs. ABC assigns the cost of activities either to the products or to the customers that trigger them.

Costs Vary by Customer

While the traditional cost accounting system ignores "below-the-line" expenses like sales, marketing, R&D, and administration, ABC assigns these costs to the

Exhibit 2-6   **HOW ABC REFLECTS PRODUCT COMPLEXITY**

	PRODUCT C		PRODUCT D	
VOLUME	1000		1000	
COST DRIVERS	DRIVER QUANTITY	COST PER UNIT	DRIVER QUANTITY	COST PER UNIT
LABOR HOURS	30	$.90	35	$1.05
PURCHASE ORDERS	30	.60	10	.20
SETUPS	20	.70	12	.42
TEST HOURS	4	.24	1	.06
PARTS PLANNED	14	1.40	7	.70
ENGINEERING CHANGES	22	.99	-	-
TOTAL COST PER UNIT LESS MATERIAL		$4.83		$2.43

o Product C is much more complex than D and requires more support costs like engineering, purchasing and test.

customers creating the need for them. Most executives are acutely aware that it is more expensive to serve some customers than others. Customer costs can vary widely depending on:

- Customer type
- Order size
- Service levels
- Product mix
- Channel of distribution
- Geography

Unfortunately, current cost systems do little to identify this difference in customer cost. ABC, on the other hand, enables management to compare exactly how much more it costs to serve a retailer's hundreds of stores than a national distributor's central distribution center.

Presale costs vary from customer to customer. Some customers require seemingly endless sales calls, while others place orders by phone after receiving a flyer in the mail. Large customers may require executive visits and long negotiation, backed up by sophisticated promotional or marketing campaigns, to conclude business. Some retailers may require a manufacturer to pay for coupon or advertising programs. Finally, some customers may require expensive services like custom engineering, nonstandard packaging, or training programs.

Distribution costs always vary by account. It costs more to ship cross-country than crosstown. Customers may require small deliveries or full truck load shipments. One customer may negotiate drop shipments (delivered directly to customer) while others receive all goods at their warehouses. It is important for executives to understand the magnitude and variance of these costs.

After-sales costs also differ. Based on the sophistication of the customers, some customers require more training and repair support. Other customers may need help lines or maintenance contracts. Some of these services might be lucrative for profit while others are just costly.

Identifying Customer Costs Produces Profit Improvement Opportunities

Given different costs, management can raise profits by offering different services and by developing different sales and distribution policies. By segregating these costs, you can identify the buying characteristics of different customers:

- Average number of units per customer order
- Number of locations shipped to
- Variety of sales promotions used
- Number of returns sent back

Exhibit 2-7   **ONE COMPANY SERVING TWO MARKETS**

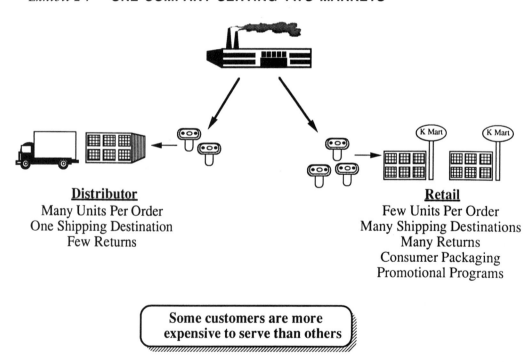

Distributor
Many Units Per Order
One Shipping Destination
Few Returns

Retail
Few Units Per Order
Many Shipping Destinations
Many Returns
Consumer Packaging
Promotional Programs

**Some customers are more
expensive to serve than others**

- Channels of distribution most frequently used
- Number of sales calls required
- Speed with which they pay their bills

From these buying characteristics, we can adjust our policies and systems to best service the customer's needs. In addition, a company can eliminate costly services to customers who don't require them, so that they can reduce costs and improve service to only selected niches. With detailed customer cost information, a company has a plethora of options.

For example, one electronic components distributor found it expensive and unnecessary to offer 1-day delivery to all customers. Many customers did not require it. Yet the distributor gave one customer a contract circuit board assembler, an order entry terminal, and a 24-hour delivery guarantee. The contract house enters its own orders at the end of the day, the distributor pulls and ships the orders on second shift. The contractor then has the orders first thing in the morning. This delivery system simultaneously keeps the high volume, high mix customer's costs and inventory down, as well as keeping the distributor's shipping and delivery costs at a minimum.

For another customer who makes pumps, the distributor consigns inventory at the pump manufacturer's facility. This customer demands a low mix of components in small quantities. Consigning inventory keeps the pump manufacturer's inventory and transaction costs low while ensuring supplies of components. For the distributor, the consigned inventory lowers the transaction and shipping costs while permitting a high margin to be charged. In this way, the distributor, by understanding the customer's buying habits, customizes its service, keeping its costs, as well as the customer's, down.

One ABC study showed how a manufacturer was losing money on 28 percent of its customers. Using activity measures, ABC assigned marketing, discounts, sales force, shipping, and customer service costs to its respective customers. After viewing this data, the manufacturer took the following actions to improve its profitability.

The firm expanded telemarketing, eliminated backorders, raised its minimum order quantities, and increased its use of wholesalers. Telemarketing cut sales expenses and allowed the sales force to concentrate on higher-volume accounts. At the same time, it allowed the company to reach new customers outside its traditional sales area—isolated, rural communities and cities without sales representatives. Raising order quantities and using wholesalers slashed distribution activities. Small orders were now handled by wholesalers who consolidated the orders, stocked the products and invoiced the customers. This cut the number of customer orders, bills of ladings, invoices, and freight charges, allowing the manufacturer to reduce its billing, order entry, and shipping staff. All together, these changes doubled the company's annual net profit within six months.

ABC Separates Product and Customer Costs

Therefore, activity-based costing splits costs into two different groups—one that is product driven and another that is customer-driven. Product-driven costs are the costs of designing and manufacturing products. These costs include procurement, warehousing, production planning, quality control, engineering, etc. (Chapter 9 discusses how to treat engineering costs, that is, excluding them from the cost of sales.) The second group is customer-driven costs: the costs of delivering, servicing, and supporting customers and markets. These costs include order entry, distribution, sales, R&D, advertising, marketing, etc.

Products obviously drive manufacturing costs. Yet engineering costs also trace directly to individual products. In some companies, engineers charge their time directly to the products they are designing. As with other aspects of the business, ABC can track engineering costs to products based on activities. In engineering, the cost drivers are activities such as number of drawings created and bills of materials developed.

Customers drive certain costs. Customers and their buying characteristics create order entry and sales costs. By having many employees involved in buying decisions, some customers require endless sales calls. A large number of orders are generated if the customer does not stock products and only orders them as needed, that is, "Just in Time."

Costs are separated for a few key reasons. To value inventory under generally accepted accounting principles (GAAP), customer-driven costs (and engineering costs) must be separated from manufacturing costs. Only the costs of supporting the production of a product can be inventoried. These costs include direct labor, direct material, and indirect manufacturing costs. Indirect manufacturing costs include indirect labor, utilities, supplies, rent depreciation, property taxes, and supervisor salaries. Inventoriable costs become expenses only when inventory is sold. When a company installs ABC as their integrated cost system, it is used to value inventory. Therefore, to report inventory costs, the cost system must be consistent with GAAP and segregate inventoriable from noninventoriable costs. An ABC system's product costs should include only inventoriable costs under GAAP. GAAP does not allow sales, distribution, engineering (except custom engineering), R&D, or other general and administrative costs to be inventoried. The company expenses these noninventoriable categories over its current accounting period.

Besides, costs are segregated to answer two very different questions:

1. How to manufacture our products most efficiently?
2. How to serve our customers most effectively?

Management needs a clear understanding of what it costs to design and manufacture a product. These costs must be derived irrespective of the product's customers. Among other things, this information allows management to decide whether it wants to manufacture, buy, or discontinue certain products. ABC avoids burdening the manufacturing process with costs such as freight or order entry, which have nothing to do with manufacturing. This puts responsibility for costs where they belong.

A company's poor choice of customers should not burden a product's cost. For example, a company had a product that was losing money when it was sold to retail stores. This was in spite of the fact the retail market was the product's original target. Management almost decided to discontinue the product. Instead, management experimented with selling the product in the original equipment manufacturer (OEM) market. The company found that in this market, with the lower customer-driven costs, the product made money. The experiment was expanded and the product is sold today to OEMs. If the cost system had portrayed all costs as product driven, management would never have seen the OEM opportunity. It would only have seen a product that was not profitable.

A cost system should avoid making certain products appear unprofitable, when, in fact, they are very economical to produce. Poor profitability may be tied only to the high cost of serving the wrong customers. Conversely, one market segment may be very inexpensive to serve, but the company may have few products for that market. This circumstance questions:

1. Should we introduce products for this market?
2. What will they cost?

The second purpose of cost segregation is to isolate the costs of serving different customers. Different customers have different buying characteristics triggering distinct activities and, therefore, varying service costs. Thus, some customers are more profitable to serve than others. Deciding which customers and markets to serve is the essence of a business strategy. To make an informed choice about which customers to serve requires accurate customer information.

Segregating product and customer costs does not mean the ABC system cannot analyze net margin of products. It simply means the ABC system reports customer-driven costs separate from product costs. The standard MRP database actually records all of this data in both product and customer files.

WHAT DOES AN ABC SYSTEM LOOK LIKE?

A Two-Stage Assignment

Activity-based costing assigns all resources such as direct labor, depreciation, supplies, and utilities to either products or customers to reflect the company's operation. Just as traditional systems assign costs in two stages, so does ABC. However, ABC uses more cost pools and assigns costs using a variety of more appropriate bases. The system also provides greater variety in choosing second stage drivers over traditional systems, allowing ABC to model substantially more complex cost behavior. Accordingly, ABC is more accurate than traditional cost systems.

Activity Centers

ABC first assigns all costs to the major manufacturing or business processes called activity centers. This first stage assignment does not differ greatly from traditional systems. The ABC system's first-stage drivers usually are more rigorous and depend more heavily on activity measures than traditional systems. From these activity centers, the system assigns these costs to products (see Exhibit 2-8). It is the second-stage drivers (the truly distinguishing feature of the ABC system) that separates it from the traditional cost system. The ABC system recognizes that many costs are not directly proportional to the number of units produced. Many costs are proportional to the number of batches processed. As such, the ABC system assigns costs to batches of parts. In addition, some costs, such as design engineering, are not related to units or even batches, but entire products. Therefore, some costs are assigned to products (although not included in inventory evaluation). These activity centers come in two groups—product-driven activity centers, where costs are assigned to products, and customer-driven activity centers, where costs are assigned to customers. In this way, ABC identifies the costs of serving different customers and groups of customers.

Exhibit 2-8 **ABC STRUCTURE**

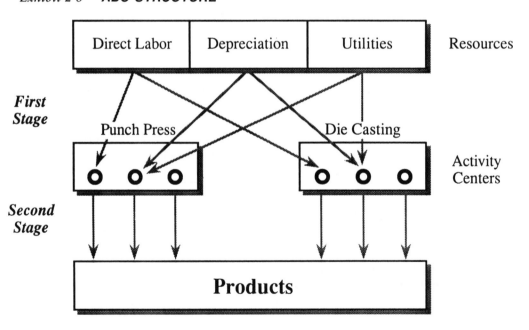

O Cost pools

The activity centers are either homogeneous processes like punch press, machining, or assembly, or a business process like procurement, distribution, or marketing. In either case, a product or customer directly consumes the activity center's costs. A punch press part consumes an operator and his machine time. Likewise, a pallet of steel bars (part of the product) consumes purchasing time and effort.

Second-Stage Drivers

Second-stage drivers are the measures of activity used to assign activity center costs to products or customers. In the traditional cost system, second-stage drivers are usually direct labor hours, material dollars, machine hours, or some other measure of volume. In the ABC system, second-stage drivers can be direct labor hours, machine hours, number of setups, setup time, inspections, warehouse moves, sales calls, or customer orders. Second-stage drivers reflect how an activity center's costs are consumed by products or customers.

For instance, a punch press department has two cost pools. One cost pool consists of production costs like direct labor and machine costs. These costs are consumed by products based on the production volume each product possesses. This activity center assigns these volume costs based on the number of machine hours a product requires. The other cost pool represents the cost of changing over from one product to the next. These costs include: creating work orders, moving material, setting up the machine, and inspecting the first article. These costs are irrespective of the number of production machine hours, but are triggered by each production changeover. These two punch press cost pools have their costs driven by different measures. In this case, the punch press activity center has two second-stage cost drivers: machine hours and number of setups.

An ABC system, by not assigning all costs on volume accounts for the differences in cost between products, caused by product and volume diversity. Some products, being more complex than others, will trigger more activities which ABC tracks. On the other hand, a low-volume product consumes more batch costs per unit than a high-volume product. This distinction is not lost in an ABC system.

Costs Occur at Different Levels

A very significant difference between traditional costing and ABC is the concept that costs are hierarchical. Costs are incurred at different levels. Some costs are triggered by units, some by batches, and others by products.

As in the example given, individual parts do not trigger all activity. ABC, by assigning costs to different levels, recognizes the great diversity in events triggering activities. Individual units trigger some activities. Batches or even market segments trigger activity. By allowing a company to attach costs to these different cost objects, ABC segregates costs for decision making. This is why an ABC system assigns costs to different levels of activity. The ABC system assigns some costs to individual parts while assigning others to batches and still others to products. Costs, like sustaining or design engineering, are not related to particular parts, but are attached to a higher level—directly to a product. Sustaining engineering costs should not be allocated to a particular part just because an engineering change modified it. A deficient product design or product enhancement triggers engineering changes. The product as a whole fails to perform, not simply one component. The cost of an engineering change should not burden an individual part's manufacturing cost, nor should it burden all of the product's parts manufacturing cost. Spreading the cost would distort reported manufacturing costs. Therefore, since the product is triggering the engineering change and the cost of the change is irrespective of the quantity of units or batches produced, the product should bear the cost of the change. Therefore, second-stage cost drivers assign costs to different levels to reflect activity being triggered by different levels.

Costs are assigned to different levels so that analysts can identify what costs are incremental for different types of management decisions. Some costs are short-term variable costs, directly related to production volume. Costs like direct labor, expendable tooling, or electricity fall into this category. Other costs are long-term variable costs that vary with the occurrence of activities. Costs like setups, inspections, scheduling, and creating work orders are long-term variables, and are not fixed, as assumed by traditional systems. These costs vary with the frequency of the part's production.

Costs are segregated to ensure only the appropriate costs are used for the appropriate analysis—to identify what costs are incremental for what types of decisions. For instance, changing the way a part is machined will only change its unit level costs. It will not affect the number or cost of setups, or the number of material movements that the batch triggers. On the other hand, discontinuing a product changes its unit, batch, and product-level costs.

Product-Driven Activities

Unit Level: Production costs assigned once for each unit produced (e.g., inserting a component and drilling a hole).

Batch Level: Manufacturing costs assigned once for each batch processed (e.g., setting up a machine and moving a batch to the next process).

Product Level: Costs to support the design or maintenance of a product line (e.g., engineering a product and processing engineering changes). Some of these costs are not used to value inventory.

Customer-Driven Activities

Order Level: Costs attributable directly to selling and delivery orders to individual customers (e.g., order entry, shipping, billing, and freight).

Customer Level: Nonorder-related costs that are attributable to individual customers (e.g., sales force, credit and collections, returns and catalogues).

Market Level: Costs required to enter or remain in a particular market (e.g., R&D, advertising, promotion and marketing).

Enterprise Level: Costs to remain in business, unassignable to any lower level (e.g., pension liability, licenses, and board of director fees).

There may be more or fewer levels for a business depending on the company's cost structure. For example, some companies have large costs associated with a channel of distribution, manufacturing process, or a facility. These costs could be established at their own level. A hierarchy of costs is shown in Exhibit 2-9. The total cost of manufacturing a product consists of unit, batch, and product-level assignments.

Many distribution costs can be traced to customer orders, however, some costs, like the sales force, are related to other transactions, like sales calls. The cost of these calls is traced to individual customers. Other costs like advertising and promotions, cannot be assigned to individual customers and are only attributable to a whole class of customers, like a market segment.

An ABC system distributes all of a company's costs. These costs may flow down to a part, a customer, or even a distribution channel. At first glance, an ABC system may appear very complex, but it is not. The ABC system mirrors the company's operation. ABC system assigns costs to products at every step (e.g., activity center) it goes through. The product absorbs activity center's costs just like a product consumes the activity center's resources. Likewise, the costs are assigned to the entity at which the costs are incremental, whether that be a unit, batch, or a product. The ABC system should mirror the company's operation—each step in the process and how the resources are consumed. An ABC system is not arbitrary.

Exhibit 2-9   **ABC ASSIGNING COSTS TO DIFFERENT LEVELS**

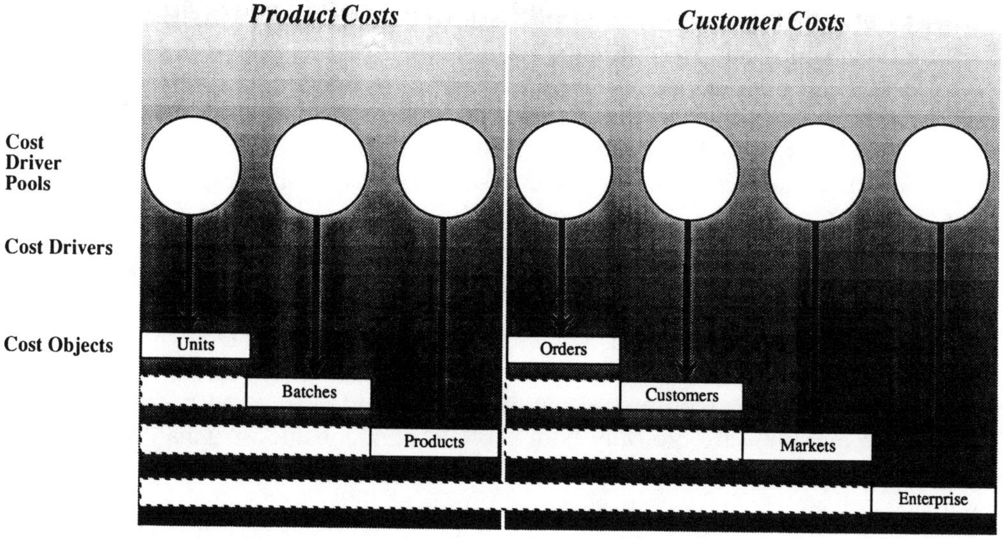

ABC in Different Businesses

This book concentrates on discrete manufacturing, but ABC principles and techniques apply equally well to process industries (in Chapter 10 there is a brief case study on a chemical company), job shops, and services. In each of these cases, ABC's application and implementation may have different requirements and problems.

Process Industries—The Forgotten Opportunity

ABC is very important to the batch processing industry. Process industries are usually capital intensive, having high process sustaining, marketing, and distribution costs. However, process industries like paper mills, oil refinery, and food processing are configured much differently than discrete part manufacturing; as such, these industries have very different ABC requirements.

High fixed costs. Process industries are capital intensive. Many process industries use period costing. Since time represents capacity utilization, it is a cost driver. The system charges direct labor not to a product, but to a process. Process time is assigned to products based on machine hours. The danger here is aggregating costs that are not time driven with period costs. Frequently, people designing ABC systems overlook batch costs and assign them on volume. Capital costs and, consequently, changeover costs (e.g., tank cleaning, lost machine capacity, and so on.) are very high in the process industry and should be allocated on production changeovers. These costs should not be assigned on a volume measure such as time. It is important to be very careful when assigning costs on volume. For example, in a paper mill, some grades of paper create much more scrap than others. The system should assign these scrap costs on some product attribute such as web thickness, not spread on product volume. While in some continuous process industries, such as petroleum refining and steel rolling, most costs are volume related, batch costs are still incured; while product changeovers occur, they are made in process, and no explicit changeover costs occur. However, implicit changeover costs frequently occur. Since process inputs are changing from one product to another, these intermediate products are not made to specification. Therefore, changing from one product grade to another, frequently results in yield fallout.

Since fixed costs in capital intense industries are so high, high-capacity utilization is critical to profitability. As such, you must look at variable pricing. In this environment, you usually calculate a cost of excess capacity so that fixed costs do not interfere with pricing decisions. Therefore, this must be part of the ABC system. In addition, the costs required to sustain the process, such as maintenance and process engineering, are large and fixed. Therefore, frequently ABC systems in process industries attach processing sustaining cost objects to production lines.

In industries like food processing, packaging, and labeling costs are high. The packaging machines are typically both capital and labor intense. Changeovers are frequent and time consuming. Major retailers, such as Ralphs and Albertsons, often demand private labeled products. These products, like sliced pineapples or apple juice, are identical to brand name products, with the exception of a different container.

The ABC system must account for these costs by assigning changeover costs to the customers creating them.

Some have dedicated processes. In some industries such as oil refining, the companies make it easy to assign costs to product lines. The refineries have dedicated production lines and storage vessels for particular product lines. The ABC system charges all these dedicated costs directly to those product lines.

In process manufacturing, changing over from one product to another may be expensive. Because today's cost systems usually allocate costs on volume, cost reporting in these industries are very inaccurate. Since these industries are capital intensive, management typically pays little attention to setup or changeover costs. Yet these costs can be very significant. In a process industry, product costs can vary widely.

For example, in jelly manufacturing, grape is much more expensive to produce than strawberry. To satisfy greater demand, the factory makes strawberry jelly in much larger batches than grape. With small runs, grape's setup costs are high. Since the business is capital intensive, changing over from one jelly to the next creates many costs. Production time is lost and each changeover requires setup and cleaning. Furthermore, since grape is very dark, it requires much more clean up when it is time to make strawberry jelly. In addition, jelly manufacturing has significant labeling costs. Many of these costs are incurred only when changing over from one batch to the next. When you amortize these costs across grape's small volume, its costs are quite high.

Most people would think that process industries with a large material content would not be good applications for ABC. They think ABC will report little change in product costs. Yet, one beverage processor had a ratio of 80 percent material to 20 percent labor and overhead, and still reported large swings in product costs.

High logistics costs. In many food processing industries, logistics costs tend to run at 25 percent of sales. The costs of serving different customers vary widely. The customer's sales volume, location, and product mix all affect logistics costs. This, combined with the need for high equipment utilization rates, allows traditional cost systems to steer management into some very unprofitable decisions. Without ABC, management is duped into chasing small customers with individual needs, and expensive delivery costs. The process industries' limited production flexibility compounds this problem. To compete successfully in this environment, management must understand its production costs. ABC aids them in increasing the sales and production of more profitable products, while leaving the less attractive niches to the competition.

Frequently lack sophisticated information systems. From an ABC implementation standpoint, process industries pose some difficult problems. Only 30 percent of process industry sites having more than $25 million in sales, have an MRP system of any kind. Because most process industries have simpler bills of materials, that is, fewer raw materials, many process industries do not require an MRP system. Those that do require an MRP system, tend to employ less sophisticated systems than discrete manufacturers. With less sophisticated information systems the companies may lack pertinent data.

Similarly, these companies are frequently saddled with primitive cost systems, as well. Many batch process manufacturers lack any cost accounting system. The company only knows how much it spent on labor, supplies, utilities, materials, and so on. When undertaking the ABC study, you must estimate the distribution of each of these costs. Some process industries do have not bills of material, but rather formula or recipe cards. Routings, as such, may not exist and must be developed.

Moreover, process industries typically have many alternative manufacturing methods. Process industries may have alternate sequences, different vessel sizes, substitute ingredients, and so on. If this is not enough, a process industry may produce products of different potency and yields. Process industries also create co-products and by-products that are problematic to cost, no matter what the system. Products may spoil. ABC provides no more answers to these costing problems than the traditional systems. All of these issues require management to make hard choices about costing assumptions.

Different requirements on ABC system. Process industries tend to have little routing diversity, as such, fewer cost drivers and simpler bills of activity are usually required. Product lines usually have dedicated process lines, allowing easy, accurate product costing. The challenge is to understand how products drive support costs, and how to increase throughput.

Because process throughput and yield are critical to process industry's profitability, the ABC system must concentrate on process variables. A process industry ABC system must correlate product attributes such as viscosity, density, and composition with process variables like energy usage, yields, and production throughout.

In addition, these industries are serial. If the factory is operating at capacity and one subprocess fails, the entire system stops production. As such, unscheduled work stoppages are tremendously expensive—sales are lost forever. Therefore, the ABC system must attach a cost to lost throughput. Lost throughput can be caused by inadequate preventive maintenance, capital investment, employee training, or even by the production of more difficult products. Luckily, process industries typically have fewer processes, standardized routings, and products. This keeps down the number of cost drivers, keeping system complexity low.

It is important to note that the ABC's representation of cost will be very different, depending on whether the facility is capacity constrained or not. If it is constrained, every production hour lost equals lost sales, in which case, lost time is extremely expensive. If the facility has excess capacity, lost time is much less expensive.

Getting a Better Price for a Job Shop

In a job shop environment, ABC is important for cost estimating and profit reporting. Many of the orders a job shop produces are one of a kind, therefore, profits depend on how well the shop estimates costs. Either the shop wants to make money on these unique jobs or it, at the very least, hopes to understand how much the job will lose. Since, by definition, the jobs are low volume, the transaction costs of order entry, planning, design, etc., are significant. An ABC system will estimate how much each type of transaction costs, and will determine the important parameters. Management can use this information to decide what work they wish to take on, as well as what price to charge.

Unfortunately, job shops, like process industries, are notorious for poor cost systems and lack of MRP systems. Forecasts are error prone. If the designers can overcome these hurdles, an ABC system adds substantial value by encouraging continuous improvement, and identifying transaction costs.

Services: The Next Opportunity

Service companies in insurance, banking, retail stores, tax preparation, and even hospitals offer one of the most important applications of ABC. Most services are transaction driven, accordingly, an ABC system can trace most of their costs with activities.

Lack Basic Cost Systems

Historically, many service industries have invested little effort in developing cost systems. Most accounting texts ignore service industries entirely, and services do not fit in with the traditional approach to manufacturing costing. Likewise, until recently, services like hospitals, banks, and airlines have been government regulated, which worked to restrain price competition and, therefore, cost containment. In the case of banks and insurance companies, operating costs mattered little. These costs were dwarfed by the cost of money for banks and claims for insurance companies. However, times have changed, and even hospitals are under extreme cost pressure.

Unfortunately, most service companies have little idea of their product cost. For example, most banks do not know how much it costs to process a teller's transaction versus an ATM's. Banks are uncertain how much it costs to open a checking account or process an out-of-state check. Without this knowledge, how can a bank intelligently price, or even effectively manage its business? A survey of 869 U.S. banks found that the transaction costs of check cashing and account maintenance increase with bank size (1). This survey seems to indicate that most banks are neither managing their costs effectively nor gaining economies of scale.

Services Are Transaction Intensive

At the same time, many consumers are leery of transactions fees, such as those charged by banks for automatic teller deposits. For most services, these charges create a precarious marketing and pricing environment. On the one hand, their business is transaction driven, but the market restrains them from pricing on a transaction basis. This makes "positioning" the key to business success for most services.

Therefore, ABC offers a substantial competitive advantage to most service industries. Their products are often transactions. Is it less costly for a bank to handle a check, or merchant card transaction? If the merchant card is cheaper, how should the company price it to encourage its use over checks? With ABC, a company can encourage the use of more profitable transactions, as well as target more profitable business.

By understanding the buying habits of different markets and their costs of service, companies can price and position themselves more effectively. For example, Shouldice Hospital, near Toronto, specializes in hernia operations. It has become an extremely low-cost provider by understanding and managing its transaction costs. Surgery patients stay at Shouldice for an average of 3 1/2 days, versus 5 to 8 days at most hospitals. Doctors, by specializing on hernias, can perform more operations per capita. By requiring patients to move themselves about, walking to and from their operations and the common dining room, the hospital requires fewer orderlies. In addition, Shouldice avoids the costs of wheelchairs, gurneys, and special elevators. These innovations lower Shouldice's fixed investment. All of this adds up to a very low cost, efficient organization, providing excellent patient care.

Yet, a lack of understanding can drive a service company into bankruptcy. Laker Air, for example, went out of business by failing to understand the cost of serving different customers as the airline expanded into new hubs.

In one bank, the marketing department was pushing to phase out passbook accounts and replace them with the new statement accounts. The passbook accounts are manually updated for each transaction. The statement accounts were seen as less expensive because a computer automatically generated the monthly statements. However, an ABC study showed the return on passbook accounts to be 2 1/2 times that of statement accounts. This discrepancy had nothing to do with the cost of handling transactions, but, instead, was related to the holders of passbook accounts. The passbook accounts, in general, were held by elderly, retired individuals who performed few transactions, typically only once a month to deposit Social Security checks. In addition, the passbook accounts received a lower interest rate. These factors made passbooks much more profitable than statement accounts with their higher ATM, deposit, withdrawal, and transfer activity. Lacking cost information, the bank almost discontinued one of its most profitable products (2).

If the service business positions itself correctly, it can have large economies of scale, while maximizing customer value. The key to positioning is identifying a group of customers whose needs can be satisfied at a reasonable price and acceptable cost. Therefore, a service industry profits principally from a customer profitability report. This identifies, for the enterprise, the cost of serving each group, and what factors drive its cost.

Lack Integrated Information Systems

Unfortunately, the big problem adapting ABC in many service businesses is the lack of a product oriented information system, such as an MRP system. MRP captures transactions systematically and relates them to particular products. These relationships are what you use to assign costs. Many service industries have no such database.

It is more difficult to define the product or output in the service business. Take a travel agency for example. Are the costs driven by every trip or by each element of the trip: the air fare, rental car, and hotel accommodations? Output is also less structured. A travel agency creating a trip itinerary may require many custom options, such as providing for special meals or unique tours.

Services do not necessarily have a structured list of all components available, or process steps required—the equivalent of a bill of material. This means this data must be structured and created prior to costing. Unfortunately, the activity may be very unpredictable and varied for the same service. For example, two patients in the same hospital for hernia operation may have very different costs. One patient may develop complications requiring a whole battery of diagnostic tests, while the other patient may have no such problems. Based on the length of the incision and the individual's recuperative powers, one may require a stay twice as long as the other.

In addition, many services require the use of common resources. Nurses, for example, perform an incredible number of tasks for different patients. Each of these tasks may be driven by a different affliction. In this environment, it can be difficult to segregate and record costs back to some driver.

Yet these problems and diversity make the ABC installation all that more valuable, because it provides such great insight. For more information on ABC in services, see the case studies listed, and the article by William Rotch, in the section "Further Reading."

ABC as Part of a Cost Management System

ABC is a cost planning system, it looks to the future. ABC is a cost system for continuous improvement. It portrays how much a product will cost to manufacture, given the company's current systems, policies, and operating conditions. An activity-based cost reflects the part's batch size, the screw machine department's scrap rate, and the cost of issuing material from the warehouse. In an ABC system, there is no ideal cost. The company can always drive an activity-based cost lower. The company can drive down the ABC cost by lowering its scrap rate, consolidating vendors, and reducing setup times. If you change your way of doing business, ABC costs will change.

Standard costing, on the other hand, assumes there is a theoretical or optimum cost: "Standard costing must be reflective of what cost should be." Unfortunately, whether it targets an "ideal" or what is "practical," standard costing presents a stagnant target. Standard costing does not promote continuous improvement. Striving for absolute performance, rather than for a simply acceptable or realistic showing, wards off complacency. As Stanley Davis said in his book, *Future Perfect*, "When managers manage the consequences of events that have already happened, their organizations are doomed always to be lagging behind the needs of their business."

Some mistakenly confuse ABC with *actual costing*. Actual costing is a cost reporting system, while ABC is a cost planning system. Actual costing portrays how much it *did* cost to manufacture a product. ABC portrays how much the company thinks it *will* cost to manufacture a product. ABC is a forecast, actual costing is a history. An actual system explains why costs happen, while an ABC tries to avoid costs. Actual costing is a report card, while ABC is a management tool.

In an actual cost system, you try to directly charge as many costs as possible. In an ABC system, you strive to understand cost behavior and what causes it. You want to identify what parameters or characteristics cause costs. In an actual cost system, you charge warranty costs directly to a product. In an ABC, you strive to understand what causes warranty costs. What parameters cause a product to break down and create warranty expenses? Once you understand which components cause field failure, you can assign warranty costs based on the number of these components. An ABC system proactively tries to identify and control costs. ABC focuses management attention not on the outcome, but on the process itself (e.g., activities).

However, an ABC system records average actual costs. The ABC system forecasts budgets and activity levels. After the fact, the system records actual dollars expended against different activity cost pools, and actual activity against different products. In this way, the system calculates average actual costs for products after the fact. ABC costs are then compared to average actuals. The ABC system is designed with an actual cost reporting system. Consequently, the system compares variances between the forecasted and actual budgets, and the forecasted and actual activity. Therefore, the actual costs reflect the product's actual cost using the ABC methodology. This allows us to continuously improve the ABC model. In addition, this average actual product cost is used for cost reporting, such as inventory evaluation.

Much More than a New Cost Accounting System

ABC is much more than a new cost system. ABC brings order and clarity out of chaos. In today's company, despite all of their incredibly detailed computer systems, management receives little or no information on what causes overhead. Costs grow from year to year with little or no explanation. However, ABC provides a clear picture of what creates overhead costs. ABC does for business what Copernicus did for the solar system.

By the beginning of the sixteenth century, the world was in crisis. The Julian calendar was wrong by about 11 days. An observation that could be seen by even the most ignorant observer. The problem was a theological one. No one could make sense out of how the heavens corresponded to the passage of time. At the time, everyone believed the earth was the center of the universe. The sun, moon, and stars revolved around the earth. Unfortunately, a lunar month is 28 days long, making for a lunar year of 336 days, which is 29 1/4 days shorter than a solar year. This meant that the lunar and solar years were only in sync once every 19 years. This discrepancy caused the church great problems. The beginning of many holidays, such as Easter, depended on both a date and a phase of the moon. When the phases of the moon did not follow the calendar, no one knew when to start celebrating the Easter festival.

To resolve the crisis, the secretary to the Pope asked a relatively unknown mathematician, Copernicus, to look into the problem. Copernicus replied that nothing could be done about calendar reform until the relationship between the sun and moon had been resolved. Through his study of astronomy, Copernicus developed conclusions, which he published in 1514. He suggested that the earth revolved around the sun, and that the moon revolved around the earth. This elegant, yet simple, conclusion brought order to the heavens. Suddenly, the confusing movements of the sun, moon, and stars were clear. Copernicus was truly a genius. In the words of C.W. Ceran: "Genius is the ability to reduce the complicated to the simple."

In the same way, ABC is genius. ABC brings simplicity to the operation of a business. ABC takes the confusion out of cost creation and shows how activities create it. ABC traces the relationship between what triggers activity, and costs that the activities create. This perspective results in a whole new approach to business. ABC changes the way everyone views his or her business. People see the enterprise process, and not just its outcome.

Managers come to see how product or customer characteristics drive activities. Products with many unique parts require much purchasing, production control, and warehousing support. Customers who do not stock products, order frequently, driving up order entry and shipping costs. Management understands how activities create cost. It begins to concentrate its attention on the process (activities), not the outcome (cost). Rather than worry about treating symptoms, executives seek to revise policies that are creating costs. The company learns to manage activities, not costs. People clearly understand the sources of cost, and become sensitive to them.

Forecasting and ABC

In an ABC system, all costs are volume dependent. Therefore, a company cannot use historical production volumes to calculate product costs. If a company just recently introduced a product, using historical volumes to calculate the product's cost will overstate it. By the same token, if the company is allowing a mature product to be cannibalized—sales are falling, historical volumes will understate costs. Worse still, if a customer can order a unique product with a set of options that has never been made before, the product will have zero cost if historical activity is used.

Since all costs are volume dependent, you must use the most accurate volumes available. The most accurate forecast volumes should be the production forecast. *This is the forecast the factory is planning to build.* Whether this forecast is annual, quarterly, or weekly, it is used to forecast costs. The ABC system will use different forecasts for different purposes and analysis. The company will use multiyear forecasts for strategic "what-if" analysis, and annual or quarterly production forecasts for establishing budgets and ABC costs.

ABC Requires Simulation

A simulation module is more than a desirable feature in an ABC system, it is a necessity. Since all costs are volume dependent, and most strategic decisions involve one volume trade-off or another, all future cost analysis is volume dependent. Simulation determines whether the operation actually can eliminate any people along with discontinued products. After all, a company cannot eliminate half of a person. It is too difficult and complex to analyze these changes with anything but a simulation module. Simulation allows you to analyze the volume affects on cost. The simulation module calculates activity level forecasts for varying sales forecasts over different time horizons. Overall, costs are calculated using these forecasted activity levels.

Since all costs are volume dependent, you cannot assume that, by eliminating a product, all of its associated costs are eliminated. If a product's sales volume or the factory's product mix changes, not only does the one product's cost change, but so will

Exhibit 2-10 **MRP AND SIMULATION**

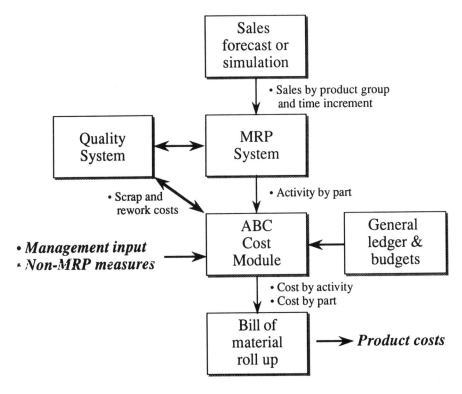

the costs of other products. To illustrate this, suppose products A and B have a common part XYZ. Discontinuing product B will reduce the volume of part XYZ and, therefore, increase part XYZ's unit cost. This, in turn, raises the cost of product A.

As volume drops, less activity occurs, but with some costs being fixed, the cost-driver rates change. If the company has more than a few parts, calculating the changes becomes onerous. Therefore, an ABC system must have simulation capability to identify precise cost changes with different production levels and product mixes.

Fortunately, most MRP II systems possess just this type of capability. The MRP packages allow you to run different sales forecasts and calculate different activity levels. This information can then be used to simulate cost changes and identify true savings.

In addition, analysts input different cost-driver rates for evaluating different decisions into the simulator. You can run rates that exclude depreciation and other fixed costs to estimate product line or customer cash flows. Using different rates, engineers can estimate changes in profitability if a process is outsourced, or they can perform sensitivity analyses making various assumptions about which costs are fixed and which are variable. Since some costs are variable in the short term (i.e., overtime pay), while other costs are only variable in the long term (i.e., building leases), the simulation must allow different cost rates to be used over different time horizons. Some costs would be fixed in the first year but variable thereafter. Other costs would be fixed in the first two years but then variable, etc.

As can be seen in Exhibit 2-10, the ABC system must be integrated with the company's manufacturing system, in most cases an MRP II package. The MRP II system not only contains almost all the measures of activity the ABC system requires, but also bills of material, routings, links to the general ledger, and simulation capability. Just as the factory's operations are dynamic, so is cost reporting—activities are always being undertaken and costs accumulated. The only way to maintain data integrity between what is happening and cost collection is to have the costs updated on-line. Given the similar logical operations and capabilities of MRP and ABC, it seems dubious that even flat-file transfers between the two systems would be effective. An integrated MRP II system with an ABC module is the only design that makes sense.

You will perform almost all cost analysis using simulation. Long-term simulations will be used to forecast a new product's cost over it's life. Forecasted activity levels will help budget departments for next year. Even new marketing strategies will be forecasted to see their affects.

ABC Must be the Official Cost System

Many ABC studies have been successful from the standpoint of improving a company's competitive position. These studies have changed a company's strategic direction, or targeted improvement opportunities. The studies have determined which products and customers are truly profitable to produce and serve. It shows the cost of each process, allowing more effective pricing, make versus buy, investment, and relocation decisions. However, the ABC's studies influence is typically short-lived. Failing to install ABC as its cost system, a business greatly hinders its acceptance, and forfeits the benefits of continuous improvement.

At the present time, the vast majority of ABC installations are PC-based systems. Companies use ABC information for pricing, investment decisions, make/buy analysis, and many analytical cost studies. However, these systems are not being used for performance measurement or financial reporting, such as valuing inventory or reporting divisional profits and losses. While building a PC-based ABC model is a logical progression from the traditional cost system, it is only an interim step. ABC systems must become a company's on-line integrated cost system to be effective.

You will even find that senior management is reluctant to use the ABC system if it is not the "offical" system. People are suspicious of a cost system that the controller is not using to report with. The vast majority of people are risk adverse, and given, or left with the choice, employees always choose the least risky alternative—in this case, using the traditional cost system. Employees know their superiors will not criticize them for performing analysis with the standard cost system, unless specifically told not to. Therefore, people continue to use the standard system until it is replaced.

Companies do not want to have two cost systems. Two cost systems create user confusion about which system should be used. It also induces skepticism about both systems, and cost accounting in general. In companies running two systems, you will find analysts coming up with "crazy" numbers based on some information from both systems. In addition, maintaining two systems creates large amounts of system and data maintenance, and invites complex reconciliation between the two systems.

An on-line integrated ABC system has many operating advantages over the PC-based system. If the ABC system is PC based, access to the system is severely limited. Because the data integrity of a cost system must be controlled, you cannot clone the PC-based system throughout the plant. As such, the system ends up being used by a limited number of people for only a number of limited applications.

PC-based systems also lack features required on an ABC system. PC systems are not dynamically updated for closed-loop feedback. In addition, because all ABC costs are volume dependent, you must simulate activity levels for cost prediction and "what-if" analysis. An ABC system integrated with an MRP II system will have this capability, a PC-based system will not. In addition, the on-line system uses MRP data files. The on-line system is automatically updated by the MRP system, thereby eliminating errors and inconsistencies. The PC-based systems require bills of material, routings, and general ledger information to be down-loaded. This duplication of data invites data inaccuracies. In addition, the sheer quantity of data for most companies overwhelms PC-based systems. On the other hand, the on-line system is more timely and accessible to users. Faster feedback to employees increases the system's influence on behavior.

Operating managers, like everyone else, only do what the company rewards. The rewards, in turn, are based on the financial reporting system. Unless the ABC system is on-line, management will not be measured against it. They will not use a system against which they are not measured. At Tektronix, engineering refused to use ABC for design decision making, unless the controller made the system the company's cost system. Engineers would not want to use one system, while being held accountable to another. If ABC is merely a microcomputer-based system, purchasing agents will still buy for favorable price variances. Designers will still concoct products with many unique part numbers, and production will still build inventory buffers.

Hewlett-Packard uses only one cost system at many of its divisions. Management reasons that two systems would be costly to maintain. It would also require continuous reconciliation. With two systems, people would use selected data from each and, thus, perform some "crazy" analysis. How much faith will employees put in a system that management is afraid to install?

ABC Is a Catalyst for Change

These changes are dramatic, yet evolutionary. When first exposed to ABC, you see many opportunities. More improvement opportunities appear months later. ABC revolutionizes the business. The sooner a company implements ABC and educates its employees, the faster the business reaps ABC's tremendous benefits, as described in Chapter 3.

CHAPTER 3

WHY ABC IS THE SECRET WEAPON OF THE 1990s

We have improved the effectiveness of our financial management system and sharp-
ened the measurement tools to direct management's actions. We are introducing
activity-based costing throughout the company, which will provide managers with
a much more accurate approach to cost accounting in order to measure all of the
costs of delivering a product to market.

Avery International, Annual Report 1989, Pasadena, California

On the misty morning of October 14, 1066, William of Normandy led his invasion force of 7,000 men up a ridge to attack English defensive positions. William hoped to fulfill his dream of becoming king of England. After being repulsed, William rallied his men and led cavalry charges, alternated with flights of arrows, against the defenders. Feigning two retreats, he drew a substantial number of the English from their positions and used his cavalry to annihilate them.

While the English rode to the battlefield on horseback, they fought on foot. Horses were considered too unsteady a platform from which to fight. However, the Normans had a secret weapon, the stirrup. This device allowed the Norman cavalry to stand secure in their saddles and ride down the English, letting the weight of their charging horses drive the lances home.

The stirrup carried the day. The Anglo-Saxon forces were routed. Near nightfall, King Harold, the English leader, was killed. With his two brothers already dead, no English leader of sufficient stature remained to raise a new army and contest William's claim to the throne. This secret weapon led to one of the most decisive victories in history, and the last successful invasion of England. Without the stirrup, this book might very well have been written in Latin (Anglo-Saxon would be considered too crude for intellectual thought).

Just as the stirrup was the decisive advantage in the Norman conquest, ABC will be the decisive advantage for American business in the 1990s. It promises to revolutionize business, just as the stirrup revolutionized warfare.

That is why innovative companies like Hewlett-Packard, General Electric, Texas Instruments, Merck, and Perkin-Elmer are installing activity-based costing systems. These leading firms realize ABC provides them with a substantial competitive advantage. ABC helps them reduce overhead spending, improve product design, raise quality levels, and focus on profitable products and customers. ABC places a business in an environment of continuous improvement. ABC will drive American companies to reshape world manufacturing.

ABC PROVIDES SUPERIOR INFORMATION FOR SUPERIOR DECISION MAKING

The traditional cost system causes tremendous distortions in the information with which everyone, from cost accountants to vice presidents, makes decisions. Every company has a finite quantity of resources. Cost distortions misallocate these resources. Salespeople push the wrong products to the wrong customers, marketing introduces products that lose money, and engineering automates processes they should discontinue. Only an activity-based cost system provides the right information for making the right decisions. ABC provides substantial insights into costs and cost behavior. It shows what causes costs and which costs are fixed versus variable. This information is of paramount importance to effective decision making.

Separates the Winners from the Losers

Indirect costs dwarf profit margins. Typically, indirect costs amount to 40 percent of sales, while pretax margins average less than 10 percent. When overhead costs are reassigned on an activity cost basis, many products are suddenly found to be losing money. This dramatically changes the way executives look at their products and markets. Suddenly, executives discover entire product lines and markets losing money. A company can be forced into changing its business strategy.

Prior to an ABC study, one valve manufacturer believed it was unable to make its corporate profit targets because it was stuck in a low-margin business. However, an ABC study showed the manufacturer that their market was not the problem. The company was losing money on 80 percent of its products.

There is probably no greater strategic information for an executive than knowledge about which products are making money and which ones are not. Product profitability drives most strategic decisions, such as which markets to pursue, and where to invest R&D and capital.

Indicates Which Customers to Chase

Likewise, it is not uncommon to find that it is unprofitable to serve the majority of a company's customers. At Kanthal, a Swedish manufacturer of electrical resistance heating elements, ABC found the company only sold profitably to 40 percent of its Swedish customers. These accounts generated 250 percent (two and one-half times their annual profits) of realized profits (1). This means the rest of its customers dissipated the other 150 percent of profits. This ABC information allows a company to change its targeted customers to correct this problem.

This information provides a company with substantial first mover advantages. Imagine being able to "cherry pick" the market's juiciest customers—the most profitable—and leaving the dregs for your competitors. This is exactly what ABC allows. The competition, deprived of ABC information, does not understand the market's true economics. Competitors can only blindly react to the ABC-inspired moves and will vigorously pursue the rejected customers. The informed company concentrates its resources on, and improves services to, the target customers. This is every chief executive's dream.

By understanding which accounts are really the most profitable, the sales and marketing departments are able to better focus their efforts. Prior to ABC, reported product and account margins usually varied little from product to product. Consequently, sales and marketing focused exclusively on increasing revenue (the "top line"). With ABC, margins vary significantly from product to product and increased profits (the "bottom line") become the focal point of decision making—not revenue. After Kanthal installed an ABC system, profit margins on individual customer orders ranged from -179 to +65 percent. Previously, almost all of these orders were thought to be profitable (1).

With ABC, management has better information to measure marketing and sales performance. Are advertising dollars being spent on the right market? ABC helps answer this question by identifying advertising and marketing costs by segment and channel. Since telemarketing costs $45 per call and a salesforce call costs $175, are salespeople four times as effective as telemarketers?

ABC information helps set discount and service policies. The company now knows how much a consolidated order, to one shipping destination, saves. At one company, ABC showed that telemarketing and special pricing would allow the firm to reach a much smaller customer than was previously thought accessible.

Some channels of distribution are much less expensive than others. Knowledge of these costs can help a company reorient its distribution strategy. The company may find that selling through wholesalers is too expensive, or that direct customers are not worthwhile because they order too many low-profit units.

Managers with detailed ABC information are able to negotiate contracts with distributors and other customers more effectively. One company, before installing ABC, spent a large amount of time and effort trading discount points for the elimination of drop shipments. ABC showed the company that the discount points they traded were worth four times as much as the cost of drop shipments.

One certain result of an ABC customer profitability analysis is the discovery that just-in-time (JIT) delivery is very expensive. If a customer demands JIT, the firm probably has a dedicated finished goods inventory for the JIT customer, many bills of lading, high shipping costs, and high freight costs. The company either charges the JIT customer for these extraordinary costs and services or, hopefully, works with him to eliminate the high JIT costs. The firm can install electronic data interchange (EDI), commence automated billing, and institute piggyback deliveries to reduce costs. Otherwise, the JIT customer simply transfers his costs of doing business to the manufacturer.

Redirects Capital Investment

ABC eliminates distortions that are caused by today's labor-based cost systems and hinder investment decisions. Labor-based cost systems undercost capital intense processes, while overcosting labor intense processes. ABC provides more accurate process cost information which lays the foundation for better capital justification. Using ABC, companies can now see how much indirect cost is really associated with each manufacturing process. Exhibit 3-1 shows the huge changes in punch press overhead before and after ABC. The punch press department's parts were 30 percent more expensive with the ABC system. You can imagine the affect the labor-based cost distortion had on a capital investment decisions.

ABC highlights setup time as a major cost driver, encouraging its elimination. Setups typically amount to half of activity center's batch cost. Management recognizes this cost as nonvalue-added as well as an impediment to flexibility. Quantifying the costs of setups provides the organization with a ripe cost reduction opportunity.

ABC allows setup costs to become central to evaluating each capital investment. Using activity-based costing, one company reanalyzed an automated punch press line that was already on order. The analysis showed the previous labor-based capital justification was in gross error. Not only were nonexistent overhead (allocated on direct labor) savings assumed, the financial justification also ignored the automated line's long setup times and high support requirements. When the estimated 12-hour changeover times were included in the analysis, the anticipated savings disappeared. Management canceled the project.

Exhibit 3-1   CHANGES IN DEPARTMENTAL OVERHEAD

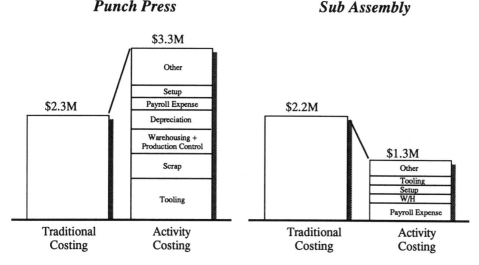

Overhead shifted from labor-intense departments to capital-intense ones

Using ABC, management not only knows what each process's real overhead amounts to, but what it consists of. The system tells management how much tooling, maintenance, and utilities each process consumes. These costs can be used in capital justifications or as targets in cost reduction programs.

Justifying Flexibility

ABC allows companies to justify flexibility. With the number of changeovers, and their costs quantified, engineers can calculate the costs of machines with varying degrees of changeover flexibility. In Exhibit 3-2, a proposed machine with quick changeover times is compared to the current machine. The current setup time is three hours, with an hourly cost of $45 for operator wages and fringe benefits. The new machine allows much faster setups, which means a saving on every setup forecasted. The proposed machine's faster setups will save $14,175 a year.

ABC improves the whole justification process. Engineers can now justify projects on overhead (50 percent of product cost) savings. Previously, engineers could only justify projects on direct labor (only 5 to 10 percent of product cost) savings. With ABC, engineers are able to identify how overhead is caused and how it can be

Exhibit 3-2   **PUTTING FLEXIBILITY INTO THE FINANCIAL JUSTIFICATION**

```
CURRENT MACHINE

    AVERAGE SETUP TIME  X  COST/HR  X SETUPS/YEAR =    TOTAL

         3   HOURS      X  $45/HR X     140     = $18,900

PROPOSED MACHINE

         45 MINUTES     X  $45/HR X     140     =  $4,725

                        SAVINGS FROM FLEXIBILITY =  $14,175
```

reduced. For example, by installing bar code readers, warehousing, data entry, and inspection time can be saved.

In addition, ABC practically forces the company to streamline operations, thus eliminating nonvalue-added activities. This makes every investment in automation that much more productive. Robots will no longer insert studs—the studs will already be designed out of the product. Automation projects are no longer crutches for design deficiencies.

Ensures Accurate Relocations

In Exhibit 3-1, you can see the countervailing affect that ABC has on the subassembly department's overhead. While punch press overhead increased by $1 million, the subassembly department's overhead dropped by a similar amount. This had a marked affect on one company's manufacturing strategy. Due to the subassembly department's large reported overhead, the company was considering relocating the operation to Mexico. Much of the forecast savings were illusory. Expected savings were based on $2 million in direct labor-allocated overhead. Not only did ABC report the subassembly department's true overhead for a more realistic savings estimate, but the measures of activity also provided management with insights into what kinds of and how much support the Mexican operation would require. The company still decided to go to Mexico, but had more realistic expectations and planned for more support.

Another benefit of ABC is the identification of special project costs. During one ABC study, the project team identified the costs of starting up an overseas facility. Once again, the budgeted and reported costs were very different from actual costs. The budgeted start-up dollars for the overseas plant were $1.2 million, but the team found most middle managers spending 25 percent of their time working on start-up problems. The actual cost of supporting the overseas plant was $2.3 million. The unreported difference was buried in the domestic plant's overhead.

If this company had implemented ABC prior to making the plant relocation decision, executives now would not be chasing illusory labor savings in Taiwan. Imagine the value of ABC information.

ABC DRIVES A COMPANY TO UNDERTAKE STRATEGIC IMPROVEMENTS

In the past, our cost systems have discouraged a number of important actions that enhance competitiveness. Namely, the traditional cost systems do little to encourage a company to implement JIT, improve product design or raise quality. The traditional cost systems fail to identify the true savings that come from these initiatives. In fact, our cost systems misdirect operating improvements toward direct labor efficiency and away from these truly strategic improvements. However, this is not the case with ABC. ABC not only encourages these actions, it drives a company toward them. Simply by implementing ABC, a company starts on the road to each of these initiatives:

- Implementing JIT
- Improving product design
- Closing the quality gap

Implementing JIT

Initially, many manufacturing executives were concerned that ABC, by measuring transaction costs, would discourage just-in-time (JIT). The goal of JIT, after all, is a lot size of one, or millions of transactions per year. In fact, and counterintuitively, activity-based costing drives a company toward JIT. JIT substantially reduces inventory, throwing off cash, as well as improving operating efficiencies. Therefore, implementing JIT is one of the best methods of increasing shareholder value. However, with ABC, management does not blindly try to reduce batch sizes to implement JIT. To achieve JIT production, a company must become extremely flexible. Employees must push activity rates—the costs of receiving, warehousing, and setup—to zero.

Management understands it must first reduce batch costs before cutting batch sizes; otherwise, indirect costs escalate rapidly. Batch costs are transaction costs and include setting up jobs, moving material, processing POs, creating shop orders, etc. With ABC, management sees the high cost of transactions, and views them as nonvalue-adding activities. Therefore, reducing batch costs is one of the best opportunities for cost reduction in the company. An ABC system drives management to measure, control, and reduce all batch costs.

To achieve JIT, a company increases the number of transactions, reducing batch sizes and lowering inventory levels. These moves can be economical only if the company simultaneously changes its business methods, either by eliminating activities such as receiving and receiving inspection, or by streamlining them. Armed with ABC information, executives force the company to streamline systems and procedures. This drives down the cost per transaction. ABC encourages vendor agreements, the elimination of nonvalue-added activities, part number reduction, and standardization, all of which contribute to JIT.

The transaction costs for a low-volume part are so prominent that they make part number reduction and part standardization high priorities with design engineering. Engineering redirects itself toward part number reduction and away from squeezing pennies out of material costs. One Tektronix division found it had more than 200 different kinds of nuts, bolts, and screws. ABC encouraged the division to standardize the number to 12. With a traditional cost system, this part reduction would increase the product's direct material costs (the standardized screws fit more functions and were more expensive) and associated overhead. With an ABC system, overhead savings cause product costs to fall.

With smaller lot sizes, the number of transactions climb. Simultaneously, management drives down setup, receiving, purchasing, and warehousing costs. Transaction costs fall to zero, allowing lot sizes of one or perfect flexibility. As management slashes its batch costs, it finds itself able to run smaller and smaller batch sizes. Smaller batches cut production lead times and inventory levels. Cutting inventory smooths production flow, cutting costs. It also increases flexibility, allowing the company to improve its customer responsiveness dramatically, for improved profitability. In addition, lower transaction costs make the production of low-volume products more economical.

You find that inventory buffers are no longer required. Moving to smaller batch sizes also leads to better quality and lower scrap. If a worker only makes one of a part and passes it on, the next worker discovers it does not fit in the assembly. Thus operators discover defects quickly and their causes are corrected almost immediately, avoiding the production of large lots of defective parts. Likewise, as B.F. Skinner tells us, quickly learning the effect of his or her workmanship naturally motivates a worker to improve. As the time lag between performance and effect shortens, the influence on behavior becomes greater.

ABC exposes and quantifies transaction costs. Suppliers are seen in a new light, particularly with respect to the costs of interfaces between the company and its vendors. Using ABC, management can see the costs of receiving, receiving inspection, purchasing, accounts payable, and defective material. Management sees the savings from qualifying vendors to eliminate receiving, receiving inspection, purchasing, and accounting costs, as well as quality defects. Buying decisions are based on quality and capability instead of purchase price. Purchasing stops shopping for the lowest price and chooses suppliers for their capability. Therefore, ABC improves supplier selection. The company develops long-term supplier relationships that eliminate receiving, receiving inspection, and vendor qualification. The accounting system works to push companies toward JIT, instead of just being pulled along, dragging its heels.

Reducing transaction costs becomes critical to offering low-volume products. With transaction rates being batch costs, the system amortizes these costs across a part's volume. Unless a company drives down its transaction rates, producing low-volume products with unique part numbers is prohibitively expensive. If a company wishes to broaden its product line, it knows it must drive its transaction rates down.

Improving Product Design

Between 1954 and 1974, the number of parts in a car door lock mechanism fell from 17 to 4. This reduced manufacturing costs by 75 percent. Why? In addition to being more reliable, products with fewer parts are less costly to build and operate.

The more complex the design—more parts—the greater the demand on overhead functions. More part numbers mean more inspection, warehousing, purchasing, and planning costs. ABC highlights and quantifies for engineers how much overhead each of their decisions is creating—from introducing new part numbers and vendors, to routing products through the automatic testing station. This dramatically improves the information available for designers. No longer are designers only pushed to rid the products of direct labor and direct material, but complexity. Consequently, many of the initial ABC systems, such as those at Tektronix and Hewlett-Packard, were developed specifically to improve engineering design.

A product's design locks in as much as 70 percent of a product's cost. Hence design represents the single greatest opportunity for cost and productivity improvement. ABC encourages a company to reduce the number of nonstandard and low-volume components a product contains. However, ABC, in most cases, makes only a limited allowance for the ease of manufacture. Many products are poorly toleranced, and have trouble fitting together or performing properly after assembly. While an ABC system tracks this type of quality fallout and attempts to predict cost, it is far from comprehensive. ABC's real contribution to design for manufacturing is to encourage reductions in part numbers. A company can slash part numbers, incorporate standard components, or modularize its design. Each of these steps dramatically cuts the overhead activity in a firm.

For years, John Deere's Waterloo, Iowa factory manufactured components including hydraulic cylinders for Deere's construction equipment. These cylinders provided the thrust to move a scrapping blade or lift an excavator shovel. However, these cylinders had become so expensive, that the construction division threatened to outsource the cylinders overseas. Waterloo decided to take action: The best way to get the cost down was to redesign, cutting the number of parts in the cylinder. Waterloo redesigned the product, slashing the number of parts from 405 to 75, which lowered the cylinder's cost by 35 percent. Not only did Waterloo save the construction division's business, but they began to sell hydraulic cylinders to other companies.

Modularizing the design allows you to customize products without creating a high number of unique part numbers. You can design a product family with a restricted list of components or modules that the designer must draw from. For example, pump engineers can modularize the different stages, diffusers, and intakes. When the engineer designs his pump, he selects various combinations of stages, a diffuser module, etc.

One of the key steps Lee Iacocca took to save Chrysler was a product-line reduction and part standardization. In 1979, the product line was slashed from seven basic car designs, or platforms, to two. The number of parts manufactured was cut from 75,000 to 40,000. This simplified operations allowing overhead reductions, doubled labor productivity, and dropped inventory $1 billion. It is interesting to note that as soon as financial health was restored, Chrysler went back to proliferating its models and parts.

General Electric took the modular design approach when designing its very successful commercial jet engines, CF6 and CFM56. These engines helped GE capture the leadership of the jet engine business from archrival Pratt-Whitney. GE's modular design allowed them to cut manufacturing costs while being able to quickly and economically adapt the engine to different aircraft. The design has also had the additional benefit of slashing the cost to repair and overhaul the engines. The GE engine design allows repair facilities to swap out the affected module and return the rest of the engine to service. This cuts repair time and gets the very expensive unit back into the field. This is in contrast with Pratt-Whitney's design that requires a more thorough disassembly, tying up the entire engine for the duration of the repair.

Big savings come from eliminating unique, low-volume part numbers from a design. When redesigning a product using design-for-manufacturability principles, the first step is removing as many fasteners from the design as possible. You can value-engineer the product, reducing needless features of costly components. Value analysis was developed in General Electric's purchasing department in 1947. *Value analysis* is a system of analyzing a product's design to meet the customer's needs, at the lowest cost. Where product design engineers use it, it is known as value engineering. *Value engineering* is the system of examining each component's cost versus the functions it is performing in the product. Is a part's price worth the function it is performing? Is there a less costly way of performing the same function?

In addition, ABC affects even the selection of components. At Wang, they implemented an ABC system in an incremental approach. They started by developing an ABC procurement costing. They then moved on to the other business functions. At Wang, procurement costs are very important, and effective material acquisition is paramount to competitiveness. Wang developed activity procurement centers for major classifications of parts: boards, integrated circuits (ICs), and OEM products— mechanical and electromechanical. Since the cost of buying, inspecting, and storing each of these components varied widely, each had its own procurement rates. A receiving lot of electromechanical components, with its complicated functions, is much more expensive to test than a lot of ICs. However, prior to the ABC system, procurement overhead was assigned on acquisition cost. The changeover to ABC significantly redirected the costs of procurement overhead, which amounted to 7 percent of total manufacturing costs.

Part Family Percentage Change in Rate

Raw PCB boards	+32 percent
ICs	-38 percent
OEM	No change
Mechanical	+21 percent
Electromechanical	+50 percent

As you can imagine, this cost shift can redirect design decisions. These new rates encourage designers to use more ICs to replace electromechanical systems.

After installing an ABC system at Hewlett-Packard's Roseville Network Division, the designers had some very important guidelines for reducing cost. Manual insertion was three times as costly as automatic insertion. Component reliability was critical. Each field breakdown cost more than $1,000. The designers developed procedures to favor using preferred vendors with parts whose failure rates and safety margins were known. Connectors that could not pass through a wave solder and that had to be inserted and soldered manually added more than $2.00 per component.

The designers used ABC-provided insights to design better products at lower cost, and with superior quality. Designers began to see their designs in terms of cost attributes, rather than pure functionality.

Closing the Quality Gap

For a country that has produced the majority of the world's quality experts, America's quality performance is abysmal. Men like Walter Shewhart, Harold Dodge, Joseph Juran, Edward Demings, and Armand Feigenbaum founded the quality profession and most of the quality improvement techniques. Nevertheless, foreign competitors continue to outstrip American products with superior quality. Only one American car—the Buick LeSabre—made J.D. Powers' 1990 list of the top ten most trouble-free cars. According to a Roper survey, the percentage of Germans who say "Made in America" is a mark of quality is—six! Why?

Total quality management rests on five pillars:

1. Customer focus
2. Total involvement
3. Measurement
4. Systematic support
5. Continuous improvement

The third pillar, measurement, has been America's weak link. Quality departments collect reams of defect and process variation information; yet, companies lack the most crucial measurement—cost. Scrap and rework expenses are buried in overhead variances; they are not tracked back to the vendors, departments, or designs that created them. This hides their sources. Inspection, quality engineering, and testing are lumped into overhead and are treated as another cost of doing business. Lacking cost information, management has adopted a fallacious economic view of quality—that high quality and low cost are mutually exclusive.

During World War II, in order to manage the procurement of large quantities of arms and munitions from multiple sources, the War Department developed the concept of acceptable quality levels (AQL). Every production lot purchased was inspected to determine whether the lot had sufficient working units to pass. If too many defects were found, the lot was rejected and sent back to the supplier. Implicit in this approach was the belief that higher quality is more expensive than lower quality. Economists have developed and propagated this idea with economic models like the "indifference curve." Without cost information to the contrary, American companies bet their competitiveness on this view until the 1980s.

When Joseph Juran recognized this problem in 1951, he coined the phrase "cost of quality." Rather than attempt to develop an entirely new cost system, he aggregated all the costs of quality—inspection, test, rework, and scrap—into a single number to draw management's attention. Juran believed that by identifying the huge cost of quality, management would react by continually striving for improved quality. Over the years, this led to cost-of-quality reporting, whose sole purpose is to convince management of the great opportunity in quality improvement. Most of the cost-of-quality measurement systems in use are not (there are some exceptions) intended to trace costs to their source.

In 1979, Phil Crosby published his landmark—and controversial—book, *Quality Is Free.* Within a year, NBC aired its white paper, "If Japan Can...Why Can't We?" highlighting Japan's successful quality push.

On March 25, 1980, Hewlett-Packard shocked American business by revealing the results of tests on 300,000 16K DRAMs from six different suppliers. The three American suppliers had an incoming inspection failure 20 times greater than the three Japanese firms. The study showed that the highest-quality American suppliers were inferior to its worst Japanese suppliers. The quality discrepancy can be traced to the American approach of compensating with low yields by adding more component testing, while the Japanese concentrated on raising yields with process improvements.

Incidentally, production delays resulting from yield problems plagued the next generation DRAMS, 64K, such that Americans permanently lost their dominance of the memory chip market.

These events helped convince American companies to rethink their view of quality, ushering in a quality resurgence in the 1980s. Contrast three headlines about Ford Motor Co. from the beginning of the decade and ones from nine years later:

- *The Wall Street Journal,* October 1979—"Car Trouble, Ford Has Its Problems as Big Autos Falter...Investigations, Pinto Blazes and Recall Record Hurt."
- *Forbes* magazine, October 15, 1979—"Can Ford Keep Up? They Have Started Whispering About Ford. The Chrysler of 1983?"

- *Monthly Detroit*, April 1980—"Can Ford Put It Back Together? Portrait of a Company in Trouble."

Years later, after Ford rediscovered quality.

- "Ford Still the Most Profitable Carmaker"—*Newsday*, February 1988.
- "As Ford Shows, Quality is Key to Long Business Life"—*The Louisville Courier Journal*, June 1988.
- "Ford's New Styling Scores Again with Probe, Lincoln"—*Reuter's*, July 1988.

Unfortunately, while America made progress, Japan has redoubled its efforts. Even though American carmakers have decreased the number of defects in their cars by more than half, they still lag behind Japanese cars. America still has tremendous quality potential that ABC can unleash.

Today's cost systems stifle quality improvement at every opportunity. Not only do they fail to report the true costs of quality, they camouflage them in variances. In only a few rare companies is the cost system linked to the quality system, so that managers know how much a casting defect or an out-of-spec washer costs them. Demonstrating the low priority that quality had in the 1970s, when MRP was developed, the classic MRP system does not have a quality module. If it did, quality reporting would be integrated with cost reporting.

ABC reports quality costs for a number of different purposes:

- Identifies the size of the quality improvement opportunity
- Identifies where the opportunities exist
- Enables management to set improvement targets and establishes plans to meet them
- Measures progress toward these goals

Identifies the size of the quality improvement opportunity. In an ABC system, the total cost of quality is not hidden. The size of the improvement opportunity is identified. Management can see how much poor quality is really costing throughout the organization. It is not unusual to find scrap and rework costs alone amounting to 15 percent of sales. This 15 percent is lost profit. It absorbs productive capacity and creates the need for inventory buffers throughout the organization.

ABC helps the company reduce costs in the short term by identifying these costs of poor quality—scrap, rework, warranty claims, and returned goods. With ABC identifying the total cost of quality, the potential savings drive management to improve quality. One company, discovering over $800,000 in punch press scrap, traced the problem to worn dies. Management immediately began a die rehabilitation program to upgrade the dies.

The sources and costs of quality defects are the missing link in most total quality management programs. Management cannot pinpoint its quality problems, nor does it know which ones are the most expensive. The greatest hindrance to further quality improvement in this country is the executive who does not know what poor quality really costs. In the 1987 ASQC/Gallup survey, more than 63 percent of executives believe their cost of quality is less than 10 percent of gross sales (44 percent think it is less than 5 percent). Quality experts estimate the American average to be more than 20 percent of sales. Executives are underestimating the cost of quality by more than half. They will never fully address quality problems until cost systems reveal its true cost.

Identifies where the opportunities exist. ABC does more than just measure quality, it tracks it to its sources. ABC identifies the sources of poor quality. The costs of defects are identified and then tracked to their sources, whether the source is a vendor, process, or a design. By tracing scrap and rework costs to the responsible party, ABC identifies where the greatest improvement opportunities lie. By tracing quality losses to product attributes, parts, processes, engineering, and vendors, management can take corrective action.

By integrating ABC with the quality reporting system, the cost of poor quality is assigned to its sources. The system records and costs the expense of buying defective material. The system tracks and costs vendor returns by vendor and part; purchasing understands the true costs of buying from particular vendors. The company's system no longer forces purchasing agents to buy strictly on price. Scrap costs in most cases are assigned back to its product. A product that is not producible shows a high scrap and rework cost. In other cases, such as an operator error, the scrap cost is assigned to the process's overhead. This provides management with clear pictures of who is causing defects and of how much they cost.

Frequently, the quality department is overwhelmed by data collection. It spends most of its time inspecting parts and recording data. It spends little time analyzing the data or trying to prevent problems. ABC arms the quality department with defect and rework cost information. It tells the department where to concentrate its quality improvement efforts. All defects are not equal. Some defects are more costly than others and some mean much more to the customers than others. We must use cost information and customer input to prioritize quality improvements. A company cannot fix all of its quality problems simultaneously—although it should shoot for that goal. ABC helps identify the problems of highest priority. Which processes are costing us the most? Do we have casting, operator, or drawing problems? Which should we fix first?

With ABC, the quality department has the answers to these questions. The department can collect more quality information where it counts, and cut back elsewhere. The quality department simultaneously cuts scrap while reducing quality department costs. Quality personnel even have time to develop defect prevention programs.

ABC puts dollar figures to the cost of poor quality, driving companies to concentrate their effort where the money is. At a door-lock manufacturer, the screw packing department reported a very large number of defects. The screw packing department sorted and packaged installation screws into plastic bags. The quality engineers were spending hours trying to develop systems ensuring that the right screws, of the right length, were in the right bags. After completing an ABC study, the quality assurance department reached two important conclusions. First, the quality engineers should quit working on screw packs and start fixing the plating rework. The study identified the high number of defective batches in the barrel-plating department. The investigation discovered a huge, hidden, expensive rework cycle.

Second, screw packs were not a costly problem, unless you considered the cost of processing the defect reports. The company president, after reviewing the ABC results, immediately realized carrying 120 different screw packs was ridiculous—creating many transactions. The company had this many screw packs because its standard cost was lowest if each bag contained no extra screws. The costs of planning, scheduling, inspecting, and setting up of these different screw packs were transparent to the company's traditional cost system. Hence, the system reported no savings for standardizing screw packs. The president ordered engineering to standardize the screw packs and give away extra screws. Engineering cut the number of screw packs down to 14, eliminating $74,000 in transaction costs. This standardization also eliminated the mispacking problem.

ABC quality information provides management with quick justification for changing vendors, training machinists, or upgrading drawings. Purchasing can evaluate whether Acme Screw Machine House, with its history of poor quality, will be a truly cheaper supplier than Metric Machining. Using an ABC system, an analyst can justify replacing an old mill or implementing a statistical process control (SPC) program on the scrap the mill is creating.

Warranty and return costs are also tracked back to their products. This gives management a much more realistic picture of product life-cycle costs and true product-line profitability. This eliminates the tendency for a product manager to rush a product through testing, or ship defective goods to make his sales targets. It also helps design engineers justify fixing defective products, rather than designing new ones. Since engineers have much better information on past quality problems, they can avoid designing them into new products.

The Japanese have been working to design quality into their products since the 1960s. America has continued its attempts to weed out defects using painstaking inspection. Americans have finally realized that 60 to 80 percent of a product's cost is designed in, as is most of its quality. ABC provides the designer with the critical quality cost information he does not have today. How much does a high-quality vendor save? Which processes create scrap? Where have warranty costs been high?

Enables management to set improvement targets and establishes plans to meet them. With this cost information, management can establish challenging improvement targets for every organization. Management can require purchasing to reduce vendor quality costs by 20 or 50 percent in a year. The number of engineering changes can be targeted to be cut by 30 percent. Each organization, even those outside of manufacturing, can establish cost reduction targets. Warranty and customer return costs can be tracked back to engineering or order entry. Since ABC product costs are forecasted based on budgets, the budgets are constructed incorporating improvement targets. This puts the improvements into the product costs.

Measures progress to these goals. Management can then track the company's performance to these targets. If improvement targets are not met, the failure shows up as a variance in the ABC cost reporting system. Quality improvement never just happens, it is planned and managed.

Management establishes quality improvement targets for all the organizations. Management budgets these targets into the ABC product cost. Any "unanticipated defects" immediately show up as variances. The variances force management to develop a better understanding of what is causing the variances—improving quality understanding, while simultaneously encouraging management to eliminate the source of the problem. This feedback allows management to continually plan and track all quality improvement programs.

Justifies Quality Improvement Projects

Management also has the financial justification for quality improvement projects. By tracking scrap and rework back to processes, management can quantify quality savings as part of a capital investment justification, as well as customer value improvements, as described in Chapter 9. This encourages quality engineering to track down the problem. Are the dies worn or the machine out of calibration? By identifying the cause of the problems, the company can fix the problems.

With ABC quantifying the cost of inspection and quality defects, management sees implementing statistical process control from a new perspective. Management realizes that even though direct labor productivity appears to suffer, inspection savings dwarf this cost. They also know that by giving the operator responsibility for inspecting his own work he takes ownership of their process. The operator begins to control his process, making the feedback loop instantaneous. Operators can correct their own process before it starts to create bad parts. In addition, with SPC, operators begin to adjust and calibrate their own machines. This improves quality as well as trimming maintenance costs. Operators enjoy greater challenge and job fulfillment.

Supports Quality Planning

ABC, by forecasting quality costs, creates quality planning. In a short amount of time, this approach shifts the quality effort from quality reporting to quality planning. The company changes its emphasis from where costs occurred, to where they will occur. ABC provides the justification for quality planning. By planning quality, the quality emphasis shifts from inspection and defect identification to process control and defect prevention. As defect prevention reduces process variation, the company becomes more sophisticated and pushes quality improvement farther upstream into the design process to control design tolerances. Quality assurance establishes controls on vendors and processes, eliminating the need for inspectors. The factory controls process variations, or engineering designs products with wider tolerances.

BRINGS ACCOUNTING AND MANUFACTURING TOGETHER

With improved cost-management information, the operating departments see the benefits of working with accounting to improve operations. In addition, the ABC information is complex, requiring accounting to work very closely with the operating departments to collect accurate data. The accountants spend more time in the production, engineering, and sales departments, observing and developing an understanding of how these departments work and interrelate. This improves the working relationship between the operating departments and accounting.

WHAT IS GOOD COST INFORMATION WORTH?

Many executives resist ABC because they believe slightly better cost information is not worth the trouble, or they believe they have more pressing problems. Others believe the time and trouble of implementing a new cost system may be worthwhile, but they would rather wait until more companies have proven its benefits.

This book, it is hoped, will demonstrate the dramatic changes in profit that ABC provides. The value of ABC can be summed up by considering actual ABC installations and the benefits the companies reaped. Had these companies not installed ABC, they never would have made the decisions that they did. The savings generated by most ABC studies are measured in millions.

Today, most executives admit certain products cost more than their current cost systems report. However, executives believe they compensate for this error. They know which products are undercosted, but are unsure of the magnitude. Executives guess that the product is undercosted by 5 to 10 percent, when, in fact, it is undercosted by 500 percent. Intuition suggests the direction of a distortion, but not the magnitude. Executives attempt to compensate for the bad information, but fall far short of the true costs.

One way to look at the cost of distorted information is to examine all the daily decisions being made with it. You can assume that most decisions are wrong, because the information with which they are made is so distorted. Buyers choose the high-cost vendors, engineers add needless costs to products, and salespeople make the least profitable sales. These decisions all add up to millions of lost dollars in most companies.

WHO BENEFITS THE MOST?

Companies that reap the greatest benefit from an ABC system are those that suffer from high manufacturing overhead costs. These costs could result from a diverse product line, capital intensity, or vertically integrated manufacturing. Because

ABC is designed to understand and control overhead costs, companies with large overhead reap more value from ABC.

Firms with large distribution, sales, and marketing costs reap substantial benefits from ABC. ABC identifies which customers are the most and least profitable. The system gives management insight on how to improve its operations. What discounts are appropriate for large orders? What size accounts should salespeople no longer call on? How effective is advertising to different markets? And much more.

A firm suffering from sluggish or declining profitability on rising sales is the first sign of uncontrolled growth. The company is most likely selling some products at a loss to some customers. ABC determines which products and customers are generating profits and which are not.

Even with a diverse product line or customer base and very high profitability, a company lacking an ABC system is surprisingly vulnerable. Product profitability probably varies widely across the company. Highly profitable products present an irresistible target to new market entrants. Management should know which products are reaping enormous margins, so they can erect barriers to entry.

ABC provides strategic, as well as tactical, benefits. The strategic benefits are usually a one-time occurrence—companies probably will not change their business, pricing, manufacturing, or distribution strategies from year to year. On the other hand, ABC provides ongoing tactical benefits—JIT support, design decisions, quality improvement, overhead reduction, and capital investment. ABC not only provides one time savings, but also works to improve profitability over the long haul.

Companies seeking to improve competitiveness throughout the 1990s need an ABC system. Just-in-time and total quality management are merely symptoms of a wider, more significant trend—flexibility—the critical success factor of the 1990s. As life cycles shorten and customer focus becomes increasingly important, economies of scale will disappear. The successful factories of the 1990s will be focused, but flexible, able to introduce new products quickly and to produce very small batches economically.

ABC changes the employees' perspective of the company. They understand the costs and activities required to process invoices and bills of lading. Wherever they see paperwork, they see cost. They do not simply look at symptoms. They look at causes. Why do we have so many invoices? Why are our purchase orders so involved?

ABC encourages a company to push its cost-driver rates down. This reduces setup times, streamlines purchasing, and cuts product development times. By attaching costs to each of these activities, management can finally measure and plan improvement.

PROFITING FOR ABC

However, ABC by itself provides no benefits; ABC is only a tool—a tool for strategic and operating changes. The information ABC provides is a great catalyst for change. The benefits of ABC are in the actions taken from the information ABC supplies. While these potential benefits are tremendous, most companies have achieved, and future implementors will continue to achieve, only scant benefits at best. Some significant obstacles stand between companies and ABC benefits. The first obstacle is that until the ABC system becomes the company's integrated cost system, few people will use its information. Unless ABC is the integrated cost system, executives, managers, engineers, and purchasing agents will continue to rely on their traditional cost system for decision making. People will always perform to their measurements, and, in the end, they are measured against the traditional cost system.

People do not like working in ambiguous environments, such as having two cost systems. People just do not have confidence in a cost system that the controller has no confidence in. The perception will be: if the controller had confidence in ABC, it would be the cost reporting system.

Another hindrance to ABC is the counterintuitive nature of some of its conclusions. Most managers in the real world make their decisions based on past experience and not intellectual arguments. The argument that cutting product lines will increase profits is not obvious. Only if the managers can understand activity-based management, from the standpoint that some products create much more work than others, will the managers truly understand the results of ABC. This understanding can only be reached through education.

Furthermore, unless a company is in crisis, many executives lack the desire to radically change the company's direction. Cutting product lines, reorienting the business toward different customers, outsourcing departments, and implementing JIT are uncomfortable. All of these actions are risky and challenging. Many managers also have their egos on the line. They have, in the past, argued for exactly the measures that put the company in its current condition. Most managers have insufficient incentive to take on innovative actions, despite the benefits each of these actions promises. If the board rewards executives for taking such risks, then executives will take them. If the shareholders make it clear that they will fire management if the company in crisis is not turned around, then, too, executives will take bold action.

To improve a company's competitiveness dramatically with ABC, a company must implement ABC as its integrated cost system. The president and his or her staff must commit to an ABC philosophy, and follow its conclusions. Lastly, the shareholders must reward management for outstanding performance. Outstanding performance is the benefit of following ABC.

SUMMARY

Activity costing has arrived. It provides a significant competitive advantage. Because its effects are so widespread and so dramatic, ABC promises to revolutionize manufacturing. ABC encourages behaviors such as JIT and design-for-manufacturability, which positively impact profitability. ABC provides superior information for making superior decisions. Consistently making the right choices separates those businesses that dominate their markets from those that seek Chapter 11 protection.

There is no substitute for accurate cost information. Mistakes are too expensive—buying the wrong machine, chasing the wrong customers, and building the wrong products. Typically, activity-based costing leads to changes in a company's marketing strategy, product pricing, service polices, factory configuration, and product design. Budgets are planned, managers are rewarded, and overhead is reduced.

Activity costing must be the company's on-line cost system, and not just a file in the controller's personnel computer. All the company's employees must have access to activity-based costing information. Every week, hundreds of decisions are made using cost information. Salespeople decide which products to push, buyers choose vendors, and engineers design new products.

Activity costing is not a substitute for business judgment, but ABC does provide substantially better cost information for superior decision making. Activity costing represents the interrelationships between products, processes, and customers. ABC transforms executive thinking. Yet, you must heed the words of Dr. Denis E. Waitley, author of *Winning the Innovation Game:* " . . . innovators are people who realize that change brings both threats and opportunities."

ABC is a two-edged sword—ABC brings both threats and opportunities. ABC can destroy a company if your competitor implements it first, because the information it provides is so powerful.

CHAPTER 4

DESIGNING AN ACTIVITY-BASED COSTING SYSTEM

Think of the end before beginning.

Leonardo da Vinci

An ABC system design mirrors the company's operation. Designing the ABC system may seem overwhelming, but it is easy, as long as you remember how the organization incurs costs. The assignment schemes should all be simple and straightforward. The system should only become complex when all of its pieces are brought together and the designer faces a large cost model.

This chapter provides guidance for designing and structuring an ABC system. The discussion defines the ABC system's elements and features—activity centers, bills of activity, and so on. Also described are the nuances of choosing cost drivers, including what type and how many cost drivers the system should have.

The greatest challenge—in fact, the art of designing an ABC system—is choosing the cost drivers. To choose cost drivers, you must correctly identify what triggers activity; these activity triggers are cost drivers. ABC cost assignments reflect the manner in which the organization works and incurs costs. This chapter puts together some rules for making the ABC implementation process less overwhelming, while

Chapter 5 outlines the process of getting started: undertaking the design of an ABC system, establishing the cost database, and interviewing the people who will make ABC work.

DESIGN GUIDELINES

Guideline 1: Keep the system simple. Concentrate on the significant costs. Focus on relevance rather than precision. Keep the system understandable. The system should reflect how the company incurs its costs, but not to extreme detail. Ask yourself: What are the most important costs within the company? Substantial time and effort can be lost tracing every cent. Meticulously pursuing immaterial costs distracts management from more important costs. The number of different tasks taking place in most businesses extends into the thousands. Consequently, attempting to assign costs on all these tasks becomes economically prohibitive. Instead, tasks should be combined into significant activities allowing costs to be assigned on fewer cost drivers.

Simplicity is key. It is better to be approximately right than precisely wrong. In the words of John Tukey of Princeton University: "Far better an approximate answer to the right question, which is often vague, than the exact answer to the wrong question, which can always be made precise."

Many costs have no ideal or perfect measures of activity, but you must attempt to assign these costs in the most equitable manner possible. For example, a production engineering department estimates it spends 50 percent of its time supporting the N/C machining department. The actual figure of 48 percent is not salient. The cost system should reflect the more important point that the N/C department is a major consumer of production engineering resources. Additionally, the cost system hints that a dramatic change in the N/C department's work load will have a corresponding effect on production engineering's activity.

Do not become overly enamored with tracking costs and create an extremely complex ABC system that measures a large number of activities. Many of the activities should probably not even be performed and, by tracking these activities, you only help to institutionalize them. For example, at one company, the designers considered establishing an activity center for the process of editing (checking and correcting) customer orders. But the team realized that editing was a nonvalue-adding activity. Editing provided no value to the customers. Being nonvalue-adding, editing shouldn't be tracked, it should be eliminated.

Adding unnecessary detail creates the need for more cost drivers, which makes the ABC system more expensive to design and maintain. Complexity is usually added by including an excessive number of second-stage drivers. The ABC system does not need to represent every cost behavior and nuance—just the important ones.

Keeping the system simple makes it more understandable. If the ABC system becomes so complex that employees cannot understand it, the workers will ignore it and make decisions based on intuition.

If the designer faces a tough decision about making the system more or less complex, he should err on the side of less complexity. If, as a result, cost behavior is distorted, the designer can improve the system incrementally.

Guideline 2: Every company is different. The nature of costs varies widely from company to company. As such, cost drivers should be different.

What is important in one company may be trivial in another. When you talk about cost reduction in aluminum smelting, you talk about energy conservation. When you are in semiconductor manufacturing, you talk about yield.

The same type of costs may be assigned using different cost drivers in different companies. For example, at one computer manufacturer, purchased materials amount to more than 70 percent of the cost of manufacturing. Effective purchasing is considered critical to remaining competitive. Since buying and inspecting a circuit card costs substantially more than an integrated circuit (IC), this company developed different procurement costs for different part types. Most other companies assign procurement costs to materials based on the number of purchase orders and receipts.

This computer manufacturer established four procurement centers for different part families to account for the large difference in costs by type of component. They divided all incoming materials into printed circuit boards, integrated circuits, and mechanical and electromechanical parts. Each group, in effect, had its own material acquisition activity center. The costs of planning, purchasing, receiving, incoming inspection, warehousing, and accounts payable were then assigned to each activity center. These cost pools were then assigned to part numbers based on planned parts, POs, receipts, lots tested, stores receipts, and invoices. As with this example, ABC system is customized to each company's needs.

At one company, there was a substantial difference between order entry of a stock product and of a custom product. A stock product required only a few seconds to specify the stock number. On the other hand, a custom product required a lengthy interchange, taking as much as an hour of the customer service representative's time. In the former case, stock order entry costs were assigned on the number of customer orders, since most of the ordering time involved taking down customer information (name, shipping address, etc.). Custom ordering costs, however, were directly proportional to the number of units ordered. Therefore, the custom product's order entry costs were assigned to customers based on the number of custom units ordered.

Guideline 3: Understanding what objectives management wants the cost system to support. A company's management has a great number of decisions to make regarding the ABC system's design. These decisions affect the choice of cost drivers, the system's complexity, and whether it is configured as an on-line system or not.

The design team needs a clear understanding of what decisions management intends to use the system for, so that the system can be designed to meet those needs.

STEPS IN ABC SYSTEM DESIGN

The following summarizes the steps required in designing an ABC system:

1. Develop fully "burdened" department cost from the general ledger.
2. Segregate costs into product driven or customer driven.
3. Split support departments into major functions. Functions must
   a. Have a significant cost
   b. Be driven by different activities

4. Split department costs into function cost pools.
5. Identify activity centers (homogeneous processes).
6. Identify first-stage drivers.
7. Identify second-stage drivers, based on:
   a. Data available
   b. Correlation with resource consumption
   c. Effect on behavior

8. Identify activity levels.
9. Choose number of cost drivers based on:
   a. System use
   b. Company complexity
   c. Resources available

ORGANIZING AN ABC SYSTEM

Activity-based costing attempts to assign all resources to either products or customers to reflect the company's operation. Where resources are labor, utilities, materials, supervision, and all of the other classifications found in the general ledger, ABC assigns costs in two steps. First, costs are assigned from indirect departments to activity centers, and from activity centers to parts/products (see Exhibit 4-1). The starting point for any ABC system is the general ledger, which records all costs.

Develop a Fully Burdened Cost of Each Department

The first step in the design is to develop the fully "burdened" cost of each department. All of the company's costs such as salaries, wages, occupancy, depreciation, and fringe benefits are assigned to their departments. By assigning all costs to particular departments, the design team is able to quickly organize the data into a manageable form. This approach also allows the team to identify the company's

Exhibit 4-1 **ABC STRUCTURE**

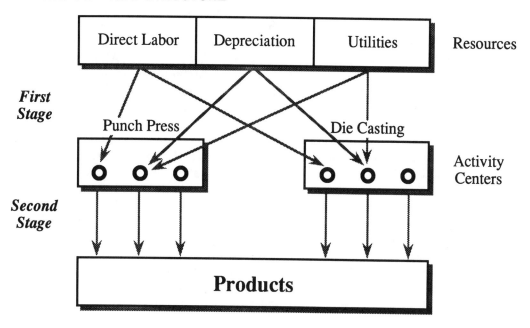

O Cost pools

major costs and most influential departments. I will assume your cost system has sufficient detail for this analysis.

Split Departments into Functions

After obtaining the fully "burdened" cost of each of the departments, you can begin the process of assigning support department costs to the activity centers. The support departments are all of the functions that have their resources indirectly consumed by products. The support departments include tooling, maintenance, warehousing, data processing, and industrial engineering. You divide the support department's total cost into major functions. The support department's total cost is then split into these major functions. In this way, each function has its own cost pool.

For example, the tooling department typically breaks down into three functions. The first function is tool construction—designing and fabricating tooling. The second is tool repair, and the third is tool cleaning. Each of these functions meets two criteria:

1. The first criterion is that the function's cost pool be of sufficient magnitude to warrant separate treatment.
2. The second criterion is that each of these pools must be driven by different activities.

Tool design and fabrication costs are caused by the creation of new parts that require dies or fixtures. Tool repair is the rehabilitation of tooling as it wears, as a result of use. Tool cleaning, on the other hand, is the removal, following a production run, of flash and chips from dies. Every time a die is run, the tool must be cleaned. In this case these three activities are driven by different occurrences. After identifying tooling's burdened departmental cost, the tooling's $1.2 million cost is divided into the three pools (see Exhibit 4-2). The department cost is split, based on the number of people who performed each function. Eight of the 16 tooling people repair tooling, four construct new tooling, while four clean tooling.

In another company the stores department breaks down into three functions. The first function is raw material warehousing. The second is work-in-progress (WIP) inventory, and the third is finished goods. The raw material warehouse receives and stocks raw material from outside vendors. Their activity is caused by the receipts of raw material shipments. WIP inventory receives and stores WIP inventory from the fabrication departments, and issues the parts to the assembly departments. This function's work is driven by the number of receipts and issues the function must process. The last function, finished goods, receives and stores all completed products. Their work is proportional to the number of batches of parts completed in assembly. While dividing department costs by headcount is usually fairly accurate, you must examine all of the departments costs and treat any large costs that are unique to one function separately.

In most cases, if you split a support department into more than two or three functions, the ABC system begins to take on too much detail. In most cases, a cost pool should not be less than two equivalent people. Typically, you also do not want

Exhibit 4-2   **SPLITTING TOOLING DEPARTMENT COSTS INTO FUNCTIONS**

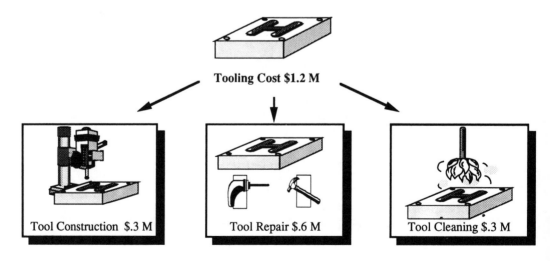

Tooling Cost $1.2 M

Tool Construction $.3 M   Tool Repair $.6 M   Tool Cleaning $.3 M

to divide cost pools into less than 1 percent of total manufacturing cost, otherwise the system becomes too detailed. During or after implementing an ABC system, the accounting department will probably restructure the general ledger so that its sub-categories match the ABC cost pools.

Assign Cost Pools Using First-Stage Cost Drivers

The function's cost pools are then assigned to each of the activity centers, using first-stage cost drivers. Through these activity centers, all of the company's support costs are assigned to products or customers (see Exhibit 4-3). This exhibit shows how tool cleaning costs flow down from the tooling department, through the injection molding department, to piece parts. First, each of the tooling department's function's cost is distributed by first-stage drivers to activity centers. In this case, the activity center—the injection molding department, receives an assignment of tool cleaning costs. The cost then passes through the activity center by way of the second-stage drivers. In this case the activity center assigns tool cleaning costs on the number of batches run for each piece part. Using this methodology, an analyst can determine exactly how much injection molding tool cleaning cost is assigned to each part.

Developing the total activity center cost allows summarized reporting and identifies the process overhead for make/buy, design, and investment decisions. Assigning the cost of support functions to activity centers is familiar to cost account-ants. They have used similar techniques with the traditional cost system for years. The assignments are usually straightforward. As an example, consider the inspection function. Typically, inspectors are assigned to particular production departments. If a company has 12 inspectors and 3 are assigned to final assembly, then final assembly is assigned 25 percent of the inspection pool. Departments like maintenance and tooling usually use time cards to charge specific departments. If utility costs are significant, meters can be installed to track energy consumption by department.

Going through this process of assigning support costs will reveal support de-partment costs that must be assigned to other support departments. Costs like data processing, nonproduction purchasing (i.e., toilet paper and pencils), payroll, and personnel will be assigned to other support departments, which, in turn, are passed through to the activity centers.

Identifying Activity Centers

The next step is identifying activity centers within the company. Activity centers are functional or economic groupings of homogeneous processes. You must segregate activity centers into one of two major groups—product-driven and customer-driven activity centers. Product-driven activity centers assign the costs of designing and manufacturing to products. These costs include procurement, warehousing, produc-tion planning, quality control, engineering, and so on. (Chapter 9 discusses how to treat engineering costs, i.e., they are not included in the cost of sales.)

Exhibit 4-3   **ABC STRUCTURE**

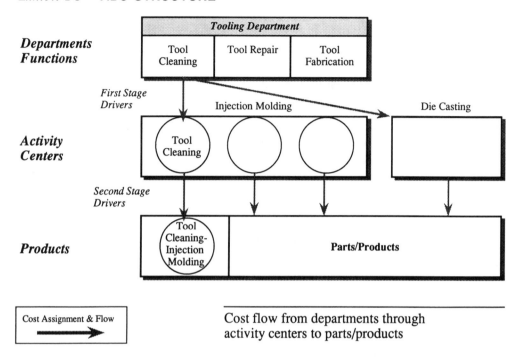

| Cost Assignment & Flow | Cost flow from departments through activity centers to parts/products |

Certain costs are driven by customers. Order entry and sales costs are created by the customer, and by his purchasing characteristics. If the customer has many employees involved in buying decisions, many sales calls are required. A large number of orders are generated if the customer does not stock products, and only orders them as needed, that is, "just in time."

Activity centers are not support departments. Support departments perform functions that cost objects indirectly consume. The support departments include tooling, maintenance, warehousing, data processing, and industrial engineering. Activity centers are processes that have their resources directly consumed by products or customers.

Activity centers must be defined with care. An activity center must be a homogeneous process. Aggregating activity centers with different economics should be avoided. For example, a machine shop with both N/C (numerically-controlled) and manual machines should be split up into two different activity centers. Operating N/C and manual machines have very different cost characteristics. N/C operators are paid more than operators of manual machines. N/C machines require programming and incur four to five times as much setup, maintenance, and depreciation expense. Manual machines run at lower operating efficiencies and generate more scrap and rework. A machine hour on a manual machine may cost $45 per hour, while an N/C hour costs $125. Given one shop rate, the manual machining rates are prohibitively expensive, while the inexpensive N/C rates would attract work. Over time, this cross-subsidization influences design decisions. Designers begin to design more complex jobs, requiring N/C machining, because the reported cost is so "reasonable." In this type of environment, you see simple brackets being machined on million dollar Flexible Manufacturing Systems (FMS), as occurred at one prominent defense contractor's facility. These processes have very different costs per unit of output and behaviors; therefore, these processes should be separated.

Yet, you do not want to establish activity centers for every machine either. Such systems are too cumbersome and expensive to use or maintain. Activity centers should be relatively consistent with the company's departmental organization structure. Otherwise, the implementation team will have to have routings changed and departmental budgets split up, which creates a great deal of work. However, you can easily consolidate different departments into one activity center, if the processes are similar and not sufficiently large enough to warrant being an activity center, for example, the activity center's costs amount to less than 2 percent of the cost of goods sold.

If a department has a large number of machines, varying widely in size, and the department consumes more than 20 percent of the company's manufacturing cost, the designers may wish to split the department up into large and small machines. It is not uncommon to find an injection mold shop with presses ranging from 20 to 5000 tons. The costs of operating these machines as well as their capabilities are drastically different. In departments of this size, it is not uncommon to find a few of the largest machines consuming a huge proportion of the department's cost. In this way, products designed for smaller-tonnage machines are not subsidizing parts that must go across the large machines.

In companies that have advanced into cellular manufacturing, the autonomous work cells are the activity centers. The cells are treated as a homogeneous process by manufacturing. Manufacturing cells produce a particular kind of part—a dedicated processing of a particular type of part. From this perspective, the cell is a homogeneous process. The ABC system treats the cell the same as any other activity center with a unit cost driver and a batch cost driver. Costs are assigned to cell parts based on their volume and batch. In this way, the cost system mirrors how the factory views the cell. Tracking costs below the cell level would create an excessively detailed ABC system, requiring extravagant data collection—creating nonvalue-added work.

A second grouping of activity centers is for customer-driven costs: the costs of delivering, servicing, and supporting customers and markets. These costs include order entry, distribution, sales, R&D, advertising, marketing, etc.

On the customer-driven side, activity centers can include:

- Customer service
- Finished goods warehousing

- Shipping
- Distribution centers
- Transportation
- Marketing
- Sales
- Administration (general catch-all—billing, credits, legal, etc.)

All of the support department costs assigned to the activity center, plus the activity center costs such as direct labor, supplies, indirect labor, and fringe benefits then pass through the activity center to piece parts or customers using second-stage drivers.

After the study, but prior to the integrated system's implementation, the team may recommend new departmental organizations (i.e., activity centers and resource categories). Activity centers should be defined so that they represent a homogeneous process. If the company has nonhomogeneous processes with different cost behaviors in the same activity center, one process will subsidize another.

The activity centers must also be defined with accountability in mind. At what level in the organization is process ownership desirable? Each activity center has its own rates and budgets, giving its supervisor or manager process responsibility.

What Are First-Stage Cost Drivers?

First-stage cost drivers assign indirect support costs to activity centers. These support costs include utilities, maintenance, tooling, quality assurance, and industrial engineering. The first-stage cost drivers represent the resource consumption of support by the activity centers. Examples of first-stage drivers include:

Number of work orders scheduled

Number of inspectors

Kilowatts of power used

For instance, tool and die makers record on their time cards which department's tools they are working on. The consumption of tooling department resources by the production departments can be tracked by the tool and die makers' time-card records. Quality control and material handling costs can be distributed to the departments that the inspectors and material handlers are assigned to. The industrial engineers (IEs) can assign their time to production departments based on the number of routing changes and IE work orders completed for each activity center. Utility costs can be assigned by installing and surveying gas and electricity meters in key departments.

Being higher-order costs (further removed from actual production, that is, resource consumption by products), first-stage drivers require less accuracy than second-stage drivers. A 10 percent error in a first-stage driver has much less effect on a product's cost than the same error in a second-stage driver. First-stage drivers are principally used to budget activity centers. In addition, the first-stage drivers only indirectly affect product cost; their assignment scheme can be much less rigorous. Less rigor allows designers much more latitude in choosing these cost drivers. You can use surveys or organization charts to quickly assign many support costs to activity centers.

Of course, it is preferable to use measures of activity as first-stage drivers. Measures such as store issues and receipts in the warehousing activity center act as productivity measures for continuous improvement. They are also continually updated and have closed-looped feedback. Any changes in activity levels alert management. Most important, measures are usually much more accurate than surveys. Unfortunately, for some departments (i.e., legal department or president's staff) no good measures exist.

What Are Second-Stage Cost Drivers?

The crux of an ABC design is selecting second-stage cost drivers. The use of second-stage drivers is the greatest difference between the traditional cost system and ABC. Second-stage drivers determine the system accuracy and complexity.

The total cost of each activity center is divided into cost-driver pools. Each of these cost-driver pools has its costs assigned to products using a second-stage cost driver. Each cost pool is unique to one cost driver. The second-stage cost drivers are activity measures that occur whenever resource consumption is triggered from the activity center. A cost-driver pool is distributed to products based on the number of cost-driver units it consumes.

The most common second-stage driver in the traditional cost system is direct labor, whether it is direct labor hours or direct labor dollars. Some other companies use machine hours if the manufacturing process is capital intensive with little direct labor content. Each of these drivers assumes that resource consumption is directly proportional to the number of units being processed. Therefore, in the traditional system, each activity center usually has only one cost pool.

However, in the ABC system, an activity center usually has more than one cost pool, because usually all of the activity center's costs are not consumed in proportion to the number of units produced. In fact, many different cost objects trigger resource consumption. Some costs are consumed by the number of batches of each type of product. Costs like setups, material movements, and planning are incurred every time a batch is processed, irrespective of the number of units produced. Therefore, most activity centers need a batch driver, as well as a unit driver.

Activities have a hierarchy. Some activities are triggered by parts, some by batches, some by product lines, and still others are triggered by the existence of the business enterprise. Likewise, costs are related to these different levels of activity. Accordingly, second-stage cost drivers assign costs to different levels. Some manufacturing costs are assigned to units, while others are assigned to batches of parts, and still others are assigned to products.

Assigning Costs to Different Levels

Costs such as sustaining or design engineering are not related to particular components, but are attached to a higher level—directly to a product. While sustaining engineering costs, the cost of engineering changes and product enhancement, can be traced to a particular component, the component's cost should not bear the cost of engineering change, just because an engineering change modified it. The engineering change was driven by a required change in the product's performance, not the component's. These costs are not driven by, nor should they be allocated to, parts. These costs should only be assigned to the product.

Costs should be assigned to the level at which they are incremental, meaning that if the part, product, or customer is eliminated, the cost will disappear. These costs are also segregated so that only relevant costs are considered in an analysis. For example, product-level costs are not affected by buying components instead of making them. Product-level costs, like that of engineering changes, are incurred regardless of where the components are manufactured (although the manufacturing location may affect the magnitude of the cost). If, on the other hand, the product is discontinued, all the product-level costs, such as the cost of engineering changes, would be eliminated. A decision like exiting a market involves the most costs—unit, batch, product, order, and customer.

The hierarchy of costs is shown in Exhibit 4-4. The number of levels varies from one company to the next. On the product-driven side, the level from lowest to highest, are unit drivers, batch drivers, product drivers, and, if the company has multiple facilities, facility-level drivers. On the customer-driven side, the levels from lowest to highest, are order drivers, customer drivers, market drivers, and enterprise drivers. The order costs are those costs directly traceable to individual customer orders. These costs include discounts, invoicing, shipping, order entry, and freight. A customer's cost is all of the costs associated with maintaining a customer. These costs include those of making sales calls, sending samples, catalogues and other mailings, handling information requests, managing collections, and all other nonorder-related costs. A market's costs are the costs relating to developing and maintaining a presence in a marketplace. These costs typically include advertising, promotion, product liability, trade shows, marketing staff and general R&D (not engineering, but research and development). The enterprise-level costs are the costs of being a business entity such as licenses, fees, or outstanding liabilities.

Cost drivers take many forms and distribute costs in many different ways to model various types of cost behavior. Second-stage cost drivers can be unit measures such as labor hours worked, machine hours processed, square footage plated, or units shipped. Batch cost drivers can be transactions such as work orders, setups, or receipts. Cost drivers might even be product attributes, such as the number of layers in a circuit board or whether a part is painted.

Unit drivers. Cost drivers in the traditional cost system are unit drivers. These drivers are assigned in proportion to the number of items processed. These drivers

Exhibit 4-4 **HIERARCHY OF COSTS**

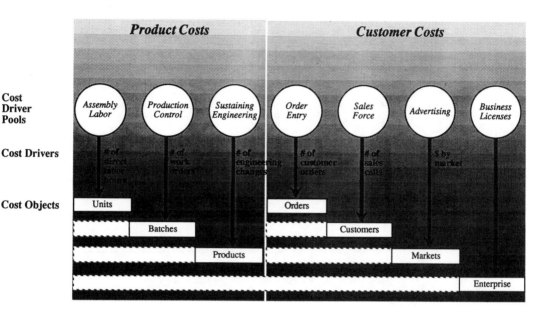

represent all the tasks that are performed every time a unit is produced. Therefore, as more and more production volume passes through an activity center, more and more costs are incurred. The costs driven by production volume are aggregated for each activity center. Unit drivers model cost behavior as if resource consumption has no setup costs and its costs are directly proportional to production volume (see Exhibit 4-5).

A unit measure can be standard labor hours in an assembly department, machine hours in a die-cast department, or the number of insertions in a printed circuit board (PCB) assembly department. There may very well be more than one volume driver per activity center. For instance, in a PCB factory's insertion activity center, manual insertions are twice as expensive as dip insertions, which are three times as expensive as axial insertions. Therefore, a PCB assembly department has three volume-driven cost drivers—manual, dip, and axial insertions.

At another installation, in one very significant activity center, the circuit board hole-drilling costs were found to vary significantly by hole size. Each hole size required different feed rates, drill life, and drilling depth. Therefore, with this one activity center, six different volume cost drivers were used—one volume driver for each of the hole sizes drilled. The different rates compensated for the different costs of each of the hole sizes.

In most installations, some surrogates are used in lieu of true measures of activity. Surrogates are used to represent cost behavior, if the cost behavior is complex.

Exhibit 4-5 **VOLUME COST-DRIVER BEHAVIOR**

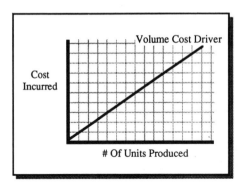
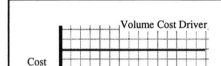

A volume driver's cost rises in direct
proportion to number of units processed

A surrogate is a measure like direct labor, machine, or test hours. The surrogate does not represent how the product consumes activity, but provides a measure of per unit consumption. Standard direct labor hours is a good example. Standard labor is a surrogate representing the number, speed, and difficulty of a variety of human motions. The human motions are the actual activity being performed. However, the huge variety of different motions performed would overwhelm any cost system. Therefore, using standard labor hours simplifies the cost system. In the same way, machine hours represents the number of passes a face mill makes, and the number of holes drilled. The number of tools and passes required is a function of the amount of material to be removed, the parts configuration, the material type, and finish required in concert with the capability of the machine tool. Obviously, this is a very complex relationship. It would be valuable to understand this relationship, but prohibitively expensive.

Therefore, the designer has the option of using surrogates, as well as true measures of activity. Surrogates can greatly simplify the system. But the surrogates must be understandable to the system's users.

Batch cost drivers. Batch drivers are activities triggered by groups of parts—not by individual units. Many of a company's activities consist of processing batches of units, not individual units. Resource consumption is proportional to the number of batches processed. For instance, when ordering parts from a vendor, rarely is a solitary part ordered; usually, hundreds are ordered. The cost of making the order is irrelevant to the number of items ordered. The cost to order is the same for 1 or

1,000 units. Therefore, when these batch costs occur, they are amortized across all of the units in the batch.

The number of setups is a batch driver. Doubling the number of items in a batch does not create any higher setup cost. Hence, it is the occurrence of a setup that causes a fixed cost to be assigned to the production batch (see Exhibit 4-6). A batch driver assigns the cost to the batch, or group of items, for which the transaction was created. This batch cost is then amortized across all the items in that batch to get a cost per unit. A shipper's bill of lading is another batch driver. The bill of lading's cost is the same, regardless of the number of units it contains. If a bill of lading costs $50 to process and it includes ten line items, each line item is assigned $5.

Batch Costs Are Typically Understated

A common mistake committed by inexperienced ABC designers is overstating volume costs and understating batch costs. For many years, accounting has viewed all costs as volume driven. It is difficult to break that mindset, but a break is necessary for accurate costing. Many ABC installations will assign all of an activity center's cost on one cost driver.

For example, one printed wiring board (PWB) fabricator assigned all the manufacturing process costs on some production measure. The cost of the circuit-drilling activity center was assigned on the number of holes drilled, lamination was assigned on number of panels processed, and plating was assigned on the number of square

Exhibit 4-6 **BATCH DRIVER COST BEHAVIOR**

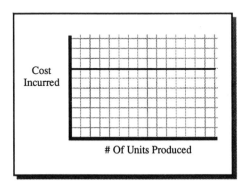
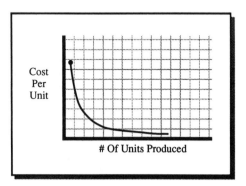

Batch costs are incurred irrespective of production volume.
However, batch costs per unit fall as batch size increases

feet plated. While these cost drivers correlate with some of the costs of processing, they ignore setup and changeover costs. These costs are extremely significant and should not be overlooked. Each of these activity centers should have at least two cost drivers: a volume driver and a batch driver. The batch driver assigns costs to a batch of products every time the line is changed to produce a different product. The hole-drilling machine, the laminator, and the plating line all require setup. Changing over from one product to the next triggers material movements, shop order transactions, and inspections.

Most discrete manufacturers will find that 30 to 40 percent of a production department's total cost can be traced to changeovers. Frequently, even when a transaction driver is established, its costs are greatly understated. Usually, if an activity center's costs are divided between volume and batch, fringe benefits are assigned to the volume pool. But this is wrong. Fringe benefits are driven by an operator's time. When the operator is setting up a machine the transaction time is consuming fringe benefits. Therefore, the fringe benefits must be split up between the volume pool and the batch pool. As indirect labor is assigned to a setup pool, so should a corresponding amount of fringe benefits.

The same argument holds true for equipment depreciation. Depreciation should not be assigned entirely on volume. Depreciation is best equated with the value of available capacity. Production absorbs capacity, but so do setups and changeovers. Therefore, changeovers should include some equipment depreciation to represent the capacity they are consuming.

Hewlett-Packard's Loveland Division avoided having more than one driver for each activity center. Loveland calculates the number of insertions each batch of products requires and then adds a fixed number of insertions to represent the setup time. This equivalent number of insertions is multiplied by the cost per insertion to calculate the total batch cost. This batch cost is then amortized across the units produced. This approach is not recommended. Since setup costs are calculated and not dynamically measured, a manager cannot see or track savings from setup reductions. This obscures the transaction costs and hinders continuous improvement.

Hewlett-Packard's Roseville Division's volume and batch drivers were one and the same. Roseville's batch size was one unit. Therefore, all batch costs were unit costs also. A lot size of one is not only the goal of JIT, but also a way of simplifying ABC!

Drivers Can Take Many Forms

Batch drivers are not necessarily a production measure. Cost drivers can be product attributes, where the product attribute induces activities. At Johnson & Johnson, a dyed Tylenol capsule costs more to produce than a clear capsule. Whenever a production run of dyed capsules is produced the dye room must be set up, the colors mixed, the dye machine filled, and so on. If a capsule is dyed, its batch incurs a dye charge. These costs are insensitive to production volume and are driven by the number of batches with the particular attribute. While an attribute is not an activity, it is a surrogate for one or several activities. The dyed attribute encompasses all the activities involved in the dyeing process.

Another example of an attribute driver is floor loading of ship containers. A floor-loaded ship container is one with its boxes loaded on the container floor without pallets, which can take as much as eight person-hours to unload. The same container with pallet-loaded boxes takes one person with a forklift about 20 minutes to unload. Therefore, a container of stereos from Korea costs $300 (8 hours times $37.50 per hour) more if it has the floor-loaded attribute.

Another approach I have seen is that of developing equivalent cost-driver units for batches. In these cases, the cost driver is assigned on some factor based on the product type. For instance, suppose customers are able to order two types of products—A and B. A, on average, takes twice as long to order as B. For cost assignment, an A order counts as two and a B order as one. The two problems with this approach are that it is somewhat confusing and the relationship between A and B must be continually validated.

Another interesting cost driver that has been used is *variety capacity*. On some machines, like a four axis N/C machining center, there are only a limited number of tool holder locations on the tool chain. If only a limited number of tools are used on a given machine, the tools are only changed when they become dull. If, on the other hand, each job requires many different tools, substantial time can be lost changing tools in and out. If this is a significant cost, you can assign the costs of the tool changing and lost capacity to the number of tools a job requires, or, more likely, to the number of nonstandard tools a job requires (typically, well run shops have standard tool libraries to avoid this problem).

In the cardboard packaging business, presses are limited to one, two, or only a few different color inks. If a package needs more colors than the machine's capacity, the package must be run through a press multiple times, which doubles the processing time and cost. In addition, as the number of inks available increases, the cost of the press also increases. Therefore, in this business, the number of colors a package requires is very important to the product's cost, which the ABC should account for.

At Hewlett-Packard's Roseville plant, setup costs are assigned on the "slot" spaces. For a component to be inserted into a printed circuit card, the component must occupy a pickup position, that is, slot, on the insertion machine. Each insertion machine has 200 slots for the insertion head to pick up components. Roseville's managers believe the number of slots limits the capacity of the insertion equipment. The number of different components required per board determines the number of machines the board must cross. A circuit board with 200 different components is only run across one insertion machine, while a board with 600 components is run across three machines. Management believes this is an important cost and wants to encourage the designers to use as few unique part numbers as possible. Each part number receives a "slot" charge, this "slot" charge is then amortized across that part's volume.

Product cost drivers. Some costs are consumed to develop or maintain product lines. These costs are not related to the number of units or batches produced, but the number of products. These are the costs of drawing new components, creating bills of material, prototyping products, as well as managing the product's marketing. The vast majority of these costs are the costs to develop and introduce new products—the cost to prototype, design, test, tool, and promote. These up-front costs are extremely important in evaluating whether to invest in new products, and selecting markets. Some products, like software packages, have almost all their costs up front. In addition, some markets are more sophisticated or capital intense than others, which means they require proportionally more up-front investment. Management needs to understand these costs to manage its product portfolio properly.

The development costs are segregated and traced to products, but are not a "cost of sales" product cost under Generally Accepted Accounting Principles (GAAP). Yet, these costs are tracked against products so the company can analyze the net present value of different product lines and markets. These product costs reach the financial statements by being deducted as period expenses.

After committing the costs of developing a product, these costs are sunk. As such, this up-front investment has no effect on the recurring manufacturing costs. Therefore, sunk development costs have no place in deciding whether to discontinue a product or not. Once a company has sunk this up-front investment, no operating decisions will ever bring this investment back, although you can sell the rights to the product.

However, it is crucial for a company to understand how much it costs to develop particular products. This information is critical to accurately estimating the up-front investment required for other new products. The size of this investment in many cases determines the resulting attractiveness of any product line decisions.

In fact, when development costs are excluded, product-level costs usually become insignificant. This is becoming more true as product life cycles shorten. The costs of correcting design errors are usually very small compared to costs of fabricating tooling, conducting experiments, making prototypes, and creating drawings and software programs. The sustaining engineering costs are usually assigned to product lines on engineering changes. An engineering change usually results from a change in an engineering drawing, or as a revision to the bill of material.

Part Number Costs

A common ABC design mistake is associating large costs with maintaining part numbers. This is a mistake. With the exception of development costs, having part numbers per se creates no activities. The only resources consumed by maintaining an active part number are the costs of storing inventory, dies, tooling, and engineering drawings. However, the cost of introducing a new part number is great, but that cost is sunk. A large number of part numbers flowing through a factory triggers large amounts of planning, scheduling, warehousing, purchasing, inventory control costs, and so on. Part numbers are a poor surrogate for assigning these costs. These costs are accurately captured by the number of planning tickets, work orders, stores receipts, and so on. Except for the engineering change costs and storage costs for dies, drawings and such, maintaining a part number costs virtually nothing. Since older products tend to have more part numbers than newer ones, allocating indirect costs on part numbers overburdens old, stable products, despite the fact these products have been in production a number of years and no longer create production problems. Likewise, such an allocation scheme would underburden poorly designed new products that are actually consuming all the sustaining engineering costs.

Theoretically, these development costs are assigned to products with activity measures that are usually product attributes, such as the number of part numbers, number of bills of material, and number of routings. In practice, however, the design process is so complex and so poorly understood—but so very important—that companies usually track hours and costs directly to products using time cards. In this way management can record exactly how much time and money was spent against a particular product. The basic problem with activity measures, in terms of design, is that the cost per activity is very high, and the variance between one performance of the activity and the next is very great. Take the design of a pump casing. In some cases the designer can use a previously designed casing with little or no modifications; however, a subtle design specification change, like requiring the pump to operate in a nuclear power plant where it will be exposed to low-level radiation, would require changing the casting's material. This material, with different tensile and shear strengths, requires an entirely new casting design. Thus, in one case, the pump casing requires a few thousand dollars in design and test costs, and in the latter case, it costs tens of thousands of dollars.

Other installations will have product group costs. These are costs inseparable between products, but associated with a whole class of products. These costs could include facility costs of a common production line, like those found in chemical plants. A system of reactors and distillation columns that only produces a limited product offering should have all its costs assigned to that product offering. These costs are especially important in calculating the costs of excess capacity.

Order cost drivers. These are activities that are directly triggered by customer orders. A large number of activities are triggered by every customer order. These activities include order entry, order picking, packing, shipping, delivering, invoicing, and collecting. For example, customers consume order entry time by placing the orders. The resources consumed by the calls are proportional to the number of orders received. Therefore, the order entry costs are assigned to customers based on the number of orders placed.

Customer drivers. Customer costs are the nonorder-related costs of obtaining or maintaining an individual customer. Customer costs include the cost of the sales force. The purpose of the sales force is to make sales calls. These calls create market awareness and distribute product knowledge and literature, while developing a personal relationship with the customers. These actions, in turn, lead to sales. In most companies, it is not the job of the sales force to take orders; customer service takes orders. Therefore, sales force costs are assigned to customers based on the number of sales calls the customer receives. The more sales calls a customer receives, the more company resources the customer uses.

Customers also create other nonorder-related activities, such as negotiating sales contracts. Some customers require promotional programs or special discounts, both of which should be recorded against that customer. Some customers, such as retailers, generate more returns than a distributor, for which returns should be tracked to that customer. These returns may be caused by end users' buying habits, habitual ordering errors, or even consigned inventory becoming obsolete.

Some customers need more after-sales service than others and therefore create more cost [i.e., the sale of an information system (I/S) such as an MRP system]. Surprisingly, large companies with expensive installations require comparatively little after-market support. This is due to their extensive and experienced internal information systems staff. A mid-sized company, on the other hand, may have very limited I/S capability, and has to depend on the software supplier extensively.

A special category of customer costs is the costs to add a new customer. In banks, for example, opening an account triggers a whole set of transactions—taking down customer information, entering the data, ordering and supplying checkbooks, etc. These transaction costs actually create a net loss for the initial year in accounts averaging less than $2,000 in deposits. Therefore, these costs are important for decision makers evaluating marketing programs, such as promotions.

Channel drivers. Channel-level activities are particular to maintaining a channel of distribution, and are not driven by customer orders or individual customers. These activities include the costs of operating and stocking warehouses, maintaining delivery truck fleets, or advertising the outlets. Distribution channels are the method through which customers buy and have products delivered. Not only can one market use multiple channels of distribution, but customers can, and frequently do, order the same product through different channels. One week, the company may buy the product through a distributor, and the next week, directly from the factory on a rush order. When distribution channels compete with each other it is called channel conflict; channel conflict is a frequent occurrence. This channel conflict, along with the innumerable ways a product can typically reach the customer, makes segregating costs between channels and markets a challenging task.

Market drivers. Market level activities are those activities required to maintain a place in a particular market segment. These costs include marketing administration, trade shows, service centers, advertising, product liability, and research and development. These costs, like advertising, should not be assigned to a particular customer, but should be assigned to the target market. Advertising rarely reaches all the market segments a company serves. A medical equipment manufacturer that places ads in *Homecare* magazine is trying to reach home care dealers, not medical distributors or rehab dealers. Therefore, distributors and rehab dealers should not be allocated any part of this advertising expense. By the same token, who is the booth at a trade show targeting? Trade shows and other marketing programs can usually be traced to a limited segment of the market. Once the costs are assigned to the target market, the market's true profitability can be determined.

The total cost of serving a channel are its order, customer, and channel's cost as well. A market's total cost includes all product- and customer-driven costs.

Enterprise drivers. Some costs are related to the business itself, and not any of its operating components. Executive and board pay, debt payments, pension obligations, some legal expenses, and taxes fall into this category. These costs are only variable at the business unit level. Unless the business unit is sold or enters bankruptcy, there is very little or nothing the company can do about these costs. Yet, a company like Manville Corporation finds that these costs (its asbestos liability) are one of its most significant costs.

Further comments on cost drivers. All the relationships between the number of activities and costs incurred have been assumed to be linear, meaning the costs rise in direct proportion to the number of cost-driver units consumed. However, more complex cost behavior can be modeled.

A company can rethink its cost drivers too. At Hewlett-Packard's Roseville plant, test costs were significant. Initially, the designers assigned costs on the "number of tests." Later, when updating the ABC system, they switched to a new cost driver, "test hours." The designers felt uncomfortable with the "number of tests," because some boards took much longer to test than others. The complex boards were being subsidized by the simpler, easier to test boards.

Cost-driver pools. An activity center's cost pool may include first-level distributions from several different departments and functions. For instance, when the punch press department is changing over from one product to another, a batch of parts is issued from the warehouse to the punch press department. Likewise, a production setup takes place. Because the warehouse moves, and setup costs always occur together, costs assigned from two different support departments are combined into one cost pool. This pool's cost driver could be either the number of warehousing issues or the number of setups, which are the same.

Choosing Cost Drivers

The three most important considerations when choosing cost drivers are:

Current availability of data

Correlation of data with resource consumption

Effect the cost driver will have on behavior

Current availability of data. You should attempt to only use data that are currently collected as second-stage cost drivers. If data are currently collected, the figures tend to be more reliable, and the company avoids the additional expense of gathering new information. When using data collected strictly for cost reporting, you frequently find discipline problems in keeping the data accurate. Measures of activity currently recorded and found in historical records are preferred. These records help test how well the cost drivers predict resource consumption.

Fortunately, current materials requirements planning (MRP II) and distribution requirements planning (DRP) systems record an incredible number of activity measures. In these systems, you can find a large number of good, accurate activity measures already in place. Exhibit 4-7 lists 11 examples of MRP fields. A typical MRP system has thousands of such fields.

ABC literature has virtually ignored MRP in its discussions. Yet, MRP should be integrated with any ABC installation. To be successful, an ABC system must mirror the MRP system operations. MRP, by its nature, reflects how the company operates. At the same time, it records almost all the information the ABC system needs. A good ABC designer needs to understand the ABC system's organization and capability. In addition, a successful ABC system depends on accurate information, which is only available if the MRP database is accurate.

The preferred measures are those that are already part of the computer's database (this is why having an MIS rep on the team is so valuable: they know what data are being collected). These measures are free. You will want to avoid time-card distributions, if possible. While highly accurate, they are expensive to fill out, collect, input, and reconcile. Time cards only tell you how long something took to accomplish. They are only a record of resource consumption. Time cards give little insight into why costs were incurred. What initiated the resource consumption? You would rather measure what is causing the resource consumption.

A frequently overlooked alternative to data collection is rules. Rules may substitute for measures of activity. For instance, if a factory is organized into manufacturing cells, there is no reporting within the cell. But, based on the product's attributes, you know which machines will process the product, and, therefore, a rule can be devised to calculate the number of setups taking place. The same applies to flat bills of material and back flushing—transactions are implicit. A company does not need bar code readers capturing each transaction; to make the product, transactions must have taken place. A product, as it back flushes a rule, can register that a setup took place on a given machine, because the setup must have taken place for the transaction to take place.

Where data are lacking, rules can suffice. Rules can approximate the number of sales calls a customer receives. For example, at one company, major accounts with over $10 million in sales are visited once a month. Therefore, it was assumed that each major account was called 12 times a year.

The big concern with rules is that they are open loop. If behavior changes, the rules must be updated, even though no feedback loop exists to indicate a change has occurred. You must ensure rules stay current. Since this system is not automatically updated, vigilance is required to keep it accurate.

Exhibit 4-7   **TYPICAL MRP II DATA**

MRP FILE	FIELD DESCRIPTION
Product Master	Year To Date Issues
Product Master	YTD Times Customer Ordered
Product Master	Weight Per Unit
Product Master	Batch Size
Product Master	Order Quantity
Product Master	YTD Quantity Scrapped
Shop Floor History	Quanity Moved
Shop Floor History	Quantity Scrapped
Shop Floor History	Scrap Reason Code
Sales Invoice History	Commission Paid
Sales Invoice History	Discount Paid
Sales Invoice History	Freight Charged
Sales Invoice History	Ship-To Number

Correlation with resource consumption. The second factor in choosing cost drivers is how well the drivers correlate with resource consumption. The number of cost-driver units accumulated by a product must be proportional to the amount of resources consumed. In statistical terms, the coefficient of correlation should be close to 1. Exhibit 4-8 shows two volume cost drivers with varying degrees of correlation. In

Exhibit 4-8   **VOLUME DRIVER WITH VARYING DEGREES OF CORRELATION**

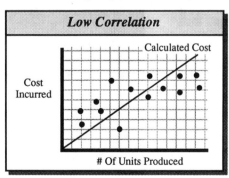 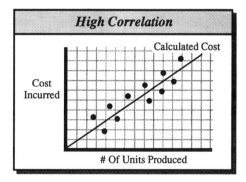

• Actual observations

the first example, the cost driver predicts resource consumption poorly, while the second is much more accurate.

For instance, is the customer service representative's time proportional to the number of orders taken? To find out, the department can time the rep's work by order. If the time spent per order is approximately the same for different orders, assigning cost on the "number of customer orders" is a good measure. If, on the other hand, it takes the representative five minutes to enter one type of order and an hour to enter another order, the "number of orders" measure has a low correlation with resource consumption and is a poor measure. You can compensate for this distortion by allocating some of the cost on the number of options called out on the order, or on some other parameter. Alternatively, an entirely new measure may be chosen.

You can judge correlation of a cost driver with resource consumption by tracking the actual observations of processing time of the activity for various kinds of products. This is the most accurate and preferred method of evaluation. The industrial engineers can perform this type of study. You can also track variation in the activity measure over time. If you observe large variations in activity, but do not see backlog or overtime grow, then the department has excess capacity, or the measure is poorly correlated. In general, the less frequent the observation (i.e., activity measure), the less accurate it will be. If the shipping dock's costs are assigned on the number of trucks loaded, you will probably find greater error than if you used number of pallets loaded. Measuring in smaller units usually yields more accurate results. Typically, during the fact-finding interview, the department manager will point out a poorly correlated measure.

The best critics will be the department's workers. They are acutely aware of what they do, and to what their work is proportional. They also will be more than willing to help. The problems usually encountered when dealing with line personnel, are that they have trouble articulating and quantifying their work, and they tend to push for too much detail.

Obviously, the cost correlation of a cost driver is much more important for the significant costs than for small costs. If a cost driver is very important, you must make every effort to verify the accuracy of the cost driver and develop accurate cost drivers for that pool.

In some cases, a cost pool will be large and a simple linear measure will not reflect the product diversity of the process. In these cases the design team must design the system to account for product complexity. Take the system test of one medical instrument. The test cost is very large and varies substantially from product to product. The time to test the product ranges from a few minutes to eight hours. Assigning test costs strictly on number of tests would fail to properly account for the product diversity. Complex products with long test times would be subsidized at the expense of simple, easy to test products. In this case, the designers decided to use the test time, instead of number of tests, to assign test costs.

Effect the cost driver will have on behavior. The last consideration when choosing cost drivers is: What will be their influence on behavior? Cost drivers will affect behavior as long as management considers them in evaluating performance. By allocating costs on setups, managers may be encouraged to schedule larger batch sizes, or work toward shortening their setup times. By allocating sales force costs on sales calls, management may inadvertently discourage salespersons from calling on small customers, or just stop reporting those calls. The effects on behavior of cost allocation schemes, as well as their use, deserve careful scrutiny. People do exactly what they are rewarded for doing.

At John Deere Component Works, one of the very first ABC studies, ABC changed employee behavior. By assigning procurement, setups, planning, and other transaction costs to jobs, the cost of small batch sizes climbed. Management responded to this in precisely the wrong way. They increased their batch sizes and manufactured low-volume products less frequently, despite the fact that doing so results in longer customer lead times, poorer quality, and larger inventories. Instead, management should have worked to reduce procurement, setup, and other transaction costs.

Some proponents of ABC argue that the ABC system should be designed to encourage certain types of behavior. They advocate the allocation of costs on part numbers to encourage designers to reduce the part count in new products, or cycle time to encourage fast throughput. While these approaches have the best of intentions—to encourage design and manufacturing excellence—they do not reflect how the factory incurs costs.

The philosophy that a cost system should encourage a particular type of behavior is wrong, and this is not the purpose of a cost system. The "behavior modification" philosophy runs counter to a cost system's purpose. A cost system's objective is to report costs as accurately as possible. To encourage or discourage behavior is not the prerogative of the cost system, but that of the management incentive system. If a system allocates costs to encourage behavior and not to report true costs, it blurs the information with which managers make trade-off decisions.

Cycle Time Costing

For example, some theorists advocate allocating overhead on in-plant cycle time. They argue that overhead is driven by the time from order receipt till it is filled. They believe the longer a part stays in house the more activity is created. While there certainly is some correlation between cycle time and overhead, simply having a part on the factory floor does not mean it is creating more work orders, setups, moves, or inspections. While you can certainly argue that the work in process consumes floor space and working capital, these costs are relatively insignificant in most factories. While reducing lead time is an admirable goal, and allocating costs on lead time would encourage its reduction, it is still an arbitrary measure. Allocating costs on cycle time provides no more guidance into what triggers overhead activity than allocating costs on direct labor. Such a system does not provide information for effective trade-offs or highlight true cost drivers. If the cost system fails to predict costs, employees can only guess what actions will reduce costs the most. A product with a short lead may trigger more activities than a product with a long lead time. In addition, under a cycle time cost system, cutting ten minutes out of a product's queue time would save twice as much as cutting five minutes out of its processing time—despite the fact that a part in production consumes more resources than the part in queue.

One of the most confusing and difficult to understand ABC systems is at Tektronix. Tektronix assigns indirect costs on part numbers. But it is not obvious how a high-volume product in production for a number of years with a large number of part numbers creates a lot of overhead cost. This system is simple, but it does not represent how costs are actually incurred. To the user, such a system seems arbitrary. An ABC system must reflect how the company incurs costs.

A cost system should predict cost. If a cost system is designed solely to influence behavior and not actually report costs, after taking the encouraged actions, a designer should not find the resulting product cost a surprise. Just as designers found that overhead did not decline by cutting direct labor in half, designers will find that by cutting cycle time in half, indirect costs will not fall by half. The cost system confuses management about what really happened. A cost system should be close looped, with the result of actions fed back to the decision maker.

Zytec, a manufacturer of power supplies, designed a new cost system allocating indirect costs on cycle time and supplier lead time, where cycle time was the time from receipt of raw materials to shipment. Supplier lead time was the time lag between ordering a component and its arrival. The system's objective was to make the cost system consistent with the company's continuous improvement program. The company's cycle-time reduction was intended to reduce cost and improve quality.

The system failed. Both drivers measured elapsed time, which does not correlate with resource consumption by products. For example, a product with a short manufacturing cycle may still have a high failure rate, or demand large amounts of engineering support. Conversely, a resistor and a custom integrated circuit may have the same lead time, but the IC requires substantially more receiving, testing, and engineering support than does the resistor. Management found that the lead-time-based system did not report accurate product costs. Managers were confused. No one was able to explain differences in cost from one product to the next. The system lacked credibility and failed. (1)

It is important to remember that, at one time, manufacturing's chief variable cost was direct labor. By allocating overhead on direct labor, cost systems were successful at driving it out of products. Unfortunately, the direct labor measure is still influencing behavior, and not reflecting true costs. The labor-based systems continue to drive direct labor out of products, in many cases inadvertently creating more overhead costs than savings.

Assessing Costing Error

To help you manage the ABC system design's trade-off between accuracy and complexity, you must assess cost-driver error. However, a product's cost can only be estimated. Even in an actual costing system, some assumptions will be made. Companies are just too complex to assign all costs accurately. Therefore, you can only estimate what products really cost. Since actual costs are never known, you can only measure reported costs against other reported costs.

You compare the less accurate estimate with what we know is a more accurate estimate. Therefore, to estimate costing error, we compare product costs, determined by fewer cost drivers, with costs calculated by using more cost drivers. The resulting deviation is called *induced error*, because it is error that you choose to induce to simplify analysis. It is important to keep in mind that error means products are either being over- or undercosted.

The next section discusses costing error, the induced deviation between a more detailed (i.e., more cost drivers) costing and a less detailed costing (i.e., fewer cost drivers).

How Many Cost Drivers Do We Need?

As you identify the cost pools and cost drivers, you must consider how much detail to portray in the cost system. How many cost pools and drivers are really needed? The answers depends on:

- The intended use of the system
- The company's complexity
- The company's resource availability

You can have as many first-stage cost drivers as you want, at little additional cost, since these first-stage drivers are used principally in budgeting and variance reporting.

The number of first-stage drivers is not as crucial as the number of second-stage cost drivers. First-stage drivers do not assign costs directly to the products, and they add little complexity to the system, as they are used much less frequently than second-stage drivers. Application of first-stage drivers to activity centers is straightforward and creates little user confusion. However, the number of second-stage drivers is critical. Second-stage drivers create system complexity and cause user confusion. These drivers are the ones to manage.

Second-stage drivers hold the key to system complexity. The more second-stage cost drivers, the greater the cost of designing and maintaining the system. Second-stage drivers must be used each time a part cost is calculated or a part is designed. Calculating part costs is a process performed every day. Everyone, from buyers to designers, from cost accountants to industrial engineers, uses part cost information.

Each must understand and have access to this information. The number of second-stage drivers also drives the amount of cost required to program the ABC system.

The intended use. The objectives of the ABC system are very important in determining the optimal number of cost drivers. If the company intends to use the ABC system strictly for product costing, the number of cost drivers can be quite small. By effectively modeling the top 85 percent of costs, a system will have very little error in reporting product cost. This allows many cost-driver pools to be consolidated, slashing the number of cost drivers. Consolidating two or more cost drivers induces little product-cost error if the cost pools in question amount to less than, say, 5 percent of a product's cost.

However, beyond product costing, management may wish to use the cost system to answer certain specific questions, or to better manage certain costs. Such demands increase the detail and accuracy demands on the system. If the company intends to use ABC for continuous improvement, a much greater level of detail is required. To support continuous improvement, each manufacturing process and indirect department needs at least one cost driver. In this way, every manager or supervisor has ownership of a cost driver and can put his or her people to work toward continuous improvement. Each activity center most likely needs at least two drivers. Two cost drivers are usually necessary so that one driver assigns costs on volume, while the other assigns costs on batches. The batch cost reflects any setup or changeover costs—nonvalue-added costs. The costing of changeovers is critical to improving the company's flexibility. These costs must be measured to be managed. To support increased flexibility, batch costs must be driven to zero, permitting a lot size of one. If there are no changeover costs, a company has already achieved a flexible process.

The more detailed the cost information, the more potential it has to help managers improve their operations. Detailed cost information allows detailed trade-offs. Are blanket POs more or less costly than regular POs? Is one buyer more efficient than the others? But, pursuing answers to such questions is not worth the effort and can distract management from eliminating the activity all together. If the purchasing cycle is very complex, it will require many drivers. But it should first be streamlined to eliminate the complexity.

Supporting design decisions requires a large number of cost drivers because the system must mirror the complex process of cost estimation and all its trade-offs. You cannot eliminate any cost drivers that create part cost distortions (as opposed to reporting costs accurately on the product level). To report part costs accurately, to 95 percent, requires exponentially more cost drivers than to report product costs accurately. If any part's costs are distorted, it leads to a design trade-off error. Therefore, each part's cost must be accurately reflected. For instance, at one printed circuit board (PCB) manufacturer, the cost to insert a DIP component was estimated at $.25, while a radial was $.17, and an axial was $.08. Because each PCB can contain hundreds of these parts, the product cost would be greatly distorted if an aggregated cost per insertion were employed. This aggregation could result in design engineers losing this valuable design trade-off information.

Even the company's competitive environment influences the number of cost drivers. At one electronics manufacturer, two divisions with the same manufacturing process had different numbers of cost drivers. Since the division that made computer peripherals had a very cost-competitive marketplace, they required much more detailed and accurate costs than the other division that manufactured medical electronics. Therefore, the peripheral division had more cost drivers for more accurate product costing.

The company's complexity. The number of cost drivers depends on the company's complexity—the complexity of its manufacturing process for the product-driven side and the complexity of its distribution system for its customer-driven side.

Factors Creating More Cost Drivers

PRODUCT DRIVEN

- Number of production processes
- Total indirect costs
- Product diversity

CUSTOMER DRIVEN

- Number of distribution channels
- Steps in distribution system
- Variety of items sold
- Customer diversity

The number of cost drivers principally depends on the process diversity of the company. If the factory produces only a few products, in approximately the same volume and following similar routings, few cost drivers are required. Clorox's Huntington Park plant, producing bleach and cleaning solutions, is a good example. The plant produces only four products, all of which are processed, packaged, and distributed in the same way. This plant requires only a few cost drivers to cost its products accurately.

A factory producing only one product does not even need a product costing system, or any cost drivers. If, on the other hand, the company has a large variety of products, processes, routings, and customers, many cost drivers are required. As an example, Snap-On Tools produces pliers, wrenches, chisels, screwdrivers and many other tools, whose unit sales range from millions a year to less than a hundred. Some products are die cast, some are molded, some are stamped, while others are purchased externally in completed form. In this complex environment, Snap-On requires a large number of cost drivers to cost its products accurately.

If the company has large indirect costs, it needs more cost drivers, simply because more costs are significant. If the products are very different in configuration, more cost drivers will be needed to reflect their differences. At H-P's printed circuit board assembly plants, they were able to eliminate all but one batch cost driver. This is because all the products follow the same routing and, therefore, all the setup and transaction costs are accumulated into one cost-driver pool.

The more complex the distribution system, the more cost drivers are required. The more diverse the products handled, the more cost drivers are needed. McKesson, for instance, handles bottles of aspirin and hospital beds. Obviously the ordering, handling, and shipping costs for these two products are very different. To model this cost behavior would require more than a few cost drivers.

The company's resources availability. Other factors also affect the optimal number of drivers. If the company has an unsophisticated data processing system, the number of drivers may be limited by the data currently being collected. An unsophisticated system may only collect a few measures, or may not be flexible enough to process the ABC information. The company's culture and sophistication are also factors. By their nature, some companies are not comfortable with detail—if this is the case the ABC should reflect their approach to business.

In one case, the scarce resource was time. A circuit board manufacturer designed a very simple ABC system because the company was losing money and needed an operational system as soon as possible. The simple system saved design and training time. In addition, management wished to know immediately where to concentrate its attention.

Even in the simplest systems, each manufacturing activity center usually requires at least one volume driver and one batch driver. However, if there is little difference in cost by product type in a particular activity center, and the system is only used for product costing, one cost driver may be sufficient.

The procurement functions usually require between three and ten drivers. The exact number depends on the complexity and diversity of the purchased components, and the significance of procurement costs.

On the customer-driven side, the number of cost drivers depends on the number of different distribution channels used, and the number of steps in each channel. For instance, a company distributing through master warehouses, distribution centers, and retail outlets may require 2 dozen drivers. A direct mail company may only have 7 or 8. Typically, a customer-driven side will have between 15 and 30 cost drivers.

Given the conflicting desires of low cost and simplicity with accuracy, a company should simulate the affects on product costing of various combinations of drivers. The changes in part and product cost should then be compared to the system's objectives.

BILLS OF ACTIVITY

Product costs are usually summarized as bills of activity in an ABC system. The bill of activity in Exhibit 4-9 summarizes the costs a product incurs in each activity center. The design team should write a program to convert manufacturing

Exhibit 4-9 **BILL OF ACTIVITY**

BILL OF ACTIVITY
PRODUCT LATCH CLIP
QUANTITY: 10,000

ACTIVITY CENTER	COST	COST PER UNIT
UNIT/BATCH COSTS		
RAW MATERIAL	$20,000	$2.00
PLANNING	2,500	.25
PROCUREMENT	10,500	1.05
PUNCH PRESS	32,000	3.25
POLISHING	12,000	1.20
SUB-ASSEMBLY	7,000	.70
ASSEMBLY	15,500	1.55
MANUFACTURING COST PER UNIT	**$100,000**	**$10.00**
PRODUCT COSTS		
ENGINEERING	5,000	.50
PRODUCT COST PER UNIT	**$105,000**	**$10.50**

---

routings into bills of activity. Typically, this conversion will add numerous cost attachment points to the routing. This approach substantially reduces system maintenance by avoiding the creation of a totally new and different set of bills. Within each activity center, a part has a detailed bill of activity that defines the cost drivers charged against it (see Exhibit 4-10). In this example, the punch press department has only two cost drivers, machine hours and production changeovers. The latch clip requires .03125 hours of machine time, for which each product receives $1.00 in machine-time cost. The exhibit shows the cost-driver buildup. The buildup shows all the first-stage cost assignments that go into making the machine-hour rate pool. In this case the pool is made up of direct labor, utilities, machine repair, equipment depreciation, and supplies. The 1,244 units take 38.875 hours total.

The changeover rate buildup includes costs from indirect labor, warehousing, shop floor control, and the depreciation cost consumed by setups. From the calculations, you can see that the punch press department had 600 changeovers last year,

Exhibit 4-10 **DETAILED BILL OF ACTIVITY**

DETAILED BILL OF ACTIVITY

PRODUCT: LATCH CLIP
ACTIVITY CENTER: PUNCH PRESS

COST DRIVERS	QUANTITY OF C/D	C/D RATE	TOTAL COST	COST PER UNIT
# OF MACHINE HOURS	38.875	$32	$1244	$1.00
# OF PRODUCTION CHANGEOVERS	4	$700	$2800	$2.25
ACTIVITY CENTER COST			**$4044**	**$3.25**

CALCULATIONS:
   MACHINE HOUR UNIT COST

   03125 HOURS X $32/HOUR = $1.00/UNIT
COST DRIVER BUILD-UP

   COST DRIVER: MACHINE HOURS

COST POOL	PUNCH PRESS ASSIGNMENT ($000)
STANDARD LABOR (PLUS FRINGE BENEFITS)	$300
UTILITIES	85
MACHINE REPAIR	35
PRODUCTION DEPRECIATION	220
TOOL REPAIR	290
SUPPLIES	30
TOTAL MACHINE HOUR POOL	**$960**

   $960,000/30,000 MACHINE HOURS = $32/HOUR

   PRODUCTION CHANGEOVER UNIT COST

   4 PRODUCTION CHANGEOVERS X $700 = $2800
   $2800/1244 UNITS = $2.25/UNIT
COST DRIVER BUILD-UP

   COST DRIVER: PRODUCTION CHANGEOVERS

COST POOL	PUNCH PRESS ASSIGNMENT ($000)
INDIRECT LABOR (PLUS PAYROLL EXPENSES)	$240
WAREHOUSING	65
SHOP FLOOR CONTROL	15
DEPRECIATION COST IN SETUPS	100
TOTAL PRODUCTION CHANGEOVER POOL	**$420**

$420,000/600 PRODUCTION CHANGEOVERS = $700/PRODUCTION CHANGEOVER

---

of which the latch clip created four. Dividing the total changeover cost pool by the number of changeovers results in a cost of $700 per changeover.

From the cost-driver buildup, you can see that the total cost of the punch press is $1,380,000 ($960,000 + 420,000). This cost is split into two groups—cost driven by machine hours and cost driven by changeovers. The cost driven by machine hours is

Exhibit 4-11 **USING ABC TO CALCULATE VARIABLE AND FIXED COSTS**

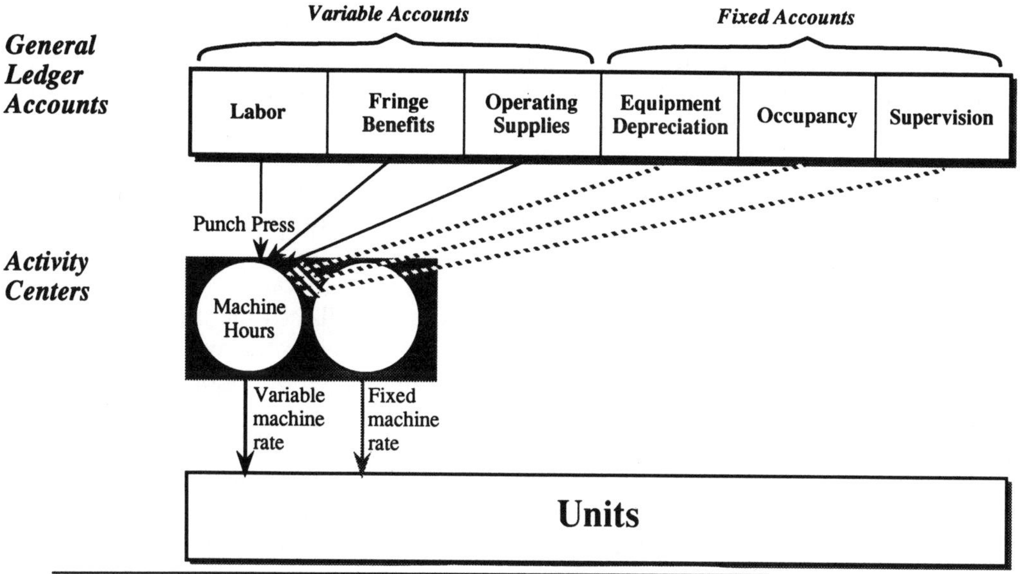

By segregating the general ledger accounts flowing to parts one can create variable and fixed cost drive rates

---

$960,000; this cost supported 30,000 machine hours of production; thus the machines cost $32 an hour. The changeover costs of $420,000 supported 600 changeovers or $700 a changeover.

If the ABC system is in database format, you can go into the detail behind an activity center's rate and flag all the general ledger categories as being fixed or variable. Once flagged, an analyst can have the fixed and variable components of each cost driver rolled up. In this case, the analyst would have fixed and variable machine-hour rates and production changeover rates. For example, within the tool repair component of the machine-hour rate of $32 per hour is $9.67 per hour. By examining the tooling department's general ledger accounts, the analyst finds that 73 percent of the dollars that are in these accounts are wages, fringe benefits, operating supplies, and so on, that are variable. Therefore, of the $9.67-per-hour punch press tool rate, $7.35 is variable. Rolling up the general ledger detail of all accounts allows the analyst to calculate fixed and variable rates for all cost drivers. These rates allow the analyst to calculate the incremental cash flow implications of any potential decision.

QUALITY REPORTING AND PLANNING

While few issues are as critical for success as quality improvement, today's cost systems virtually ignore quality improvement as one of the objectives. Current systems provide little, if any, help to quality professionals in pinpointing or quantifying the costs of poor quality—scrap and rework. ABC, on the other hand, seeks to assign all costs to their sources, including scrap and rework.

Tracking the costs of poor quality back to their sources is not difficult in a disciplined, actual-costing environment. In this environment, all costs are traced to products, scrap and rework are no exception. With actual costing, you simply report which raw material, parts, or products were scrapped or reworked, and these costs are charged to the end product. In addition, the system can allow the costs of processing defect reports, taking corrective actions and all the other preventive and corrective quality costs to be charged directly to products. In this way, the average actual cost system reports not only the total cost of quality, but, more importantly, where the costs are coming from. This type of cost system puts a cost on each defect and pinpoints the products, creating the bulk of the poor-quality costs.

However, the shortcoming with actual costing is that it is a reporting system and not a planning system. The system only keeps score and provides little guidance on where costs will occur in the future. In addition, actual costing does not push the company to identify what is causing the products to incur scrap or rework costs.

However, ABC is a cost-planning system. ABC forecasts all costs so that management can take preemptive actions and avoid costs. In an ABC system, all costs are forecasted, including poor-quality costs. Accordingly, an ABC system needs to be integrated with a quality system to capture, report, and plan quality costs. While a quality system, as described, is of paramount importance, in most cases, it does not exist and must be developed.

Nonintegrated Cost Systems

While most companies have a quality system of one kind or another, usually these systems are not integrated with the company's MRP system, much less the cost system. As discussed in Chapter 3, the original MRP design need not include a quality module and, as such, usually has been inserted into the MRP system design as an afterthought, or as a stand-alone system in most companies. Thus, in most cases, a company will need to develop a quality module, as well as an ABC system, to support a total quality management (TQM) program.

The quality system requirements, from the standpoint of the ABC system, are as follows:

- The quality system must provide the ABC system with activity data, such as the number of defects, inspections, and test hours, to be used as cost drivers.

- The quality system must report to the ABC system quality losses by part number, responsible party, items scrapped, corrective actions, etc.
- The two systems must be integrated so that each automatically exchanges data and updates the other's files.

Capturing Actual Costs Is the First Step

The ABC system reports average actual costs for all products and customers, after the fact, for comparison to the ABC forecasted costs. The quality system must report all defects and the resources loss to the ABC system, so that it can calculate actual costs. The actual product cost includes any scrap or rework costs incurred against it. The quality system must pass the following information to the cost system:

- Defect report number
- Date
- Part number
- Quantity of items scrapped
- Hours reworked
- Rework code
- Any other charges
- Responsibility code
- Last process step completed
- Vendor
- Corrective action number

This information allows the cost system to calculate a cost for every defect reported. The ABC system must know the time and material already added to the product, which is why the part number, number of items scrapped, rework hours, other charges, and last process step completed are reported. The rework code informs the system that performed the rework so the proper rate can be applied. The ABC system can calculate the cost of the items on this defect report and record these costs against the proper end product. In addition, the ABC system passes the cost of this defect report back to the quality database for quality analysis.

ABC Predicts Costs

However, the ABC system must predict costs as well as report them, including the costs of poor quality. Ideally, a company would use statistical process control (SPC), coupled with design experiments, to be able to analytically calculate the percentage of quality losses. The SPC program would define and control process variance. The design experiments would determine the quality losses resulting from process variation on a given product's design specifications. However, few companies have a quality system anywhere near this level of sophistication. Therefore, the ABC system must attempt to pinpoint the activities or attributes that trigger quality losses. The system can assume that unless specific corrective actions are put in place, per a corrective action report, the costs will recur. The ABC system forecasts product costs assuming the same quality problems will repeat themselves. If a corrective action report is filed against this defect report, the source of poor quality is assumed corrected. If no corrective action is filed, a proportional quality loss is forecasted for every occurrence of the activity or attribute.

Tracing Quality Losses to Their Sources

The quality system reports quality problems by responsibility code, which defines whose fault caused the problem. This responsibility code directs the forecasted scrap costs to a particular product attribute, or to a product, process, vendor, or customer-cost pool. Distinct quality-loss cost pools are established for a particular product attribute when these costs are significant. Typically, a company will only have limited number of cost pools strictly for quality losses. For example, take a steel mill that is designed to run strips 48 inches wide. When strips of 60 inches or more are run, it increases the likelihood of uneven gauge and shape problems, reducing yield. It also overworks the rolls, resulting in more frequent replacement. Since these yield losses are very significant, all width quality losses are aggregated into a cost pool, and plant metallurgists developed a model that calculates expected yield factors. Using last year's quality losses due to width, the company estimates the quality losses over the next quarter. The ABC system then uses this factor, times a product's tonnage, to forecast quality losses. This forecasted quality loss is assigned to products for inclusion in their product cost.

Take the case of a manufacturer of injection-molded components for aircraft interiors, such as tray tables and galley doors. While the manufacturing process consists of molding, painting, finishing, and stamping, the cost of molding dwarfs the other processes. Over 70 percent of supervision, quality control, and tool maintenance support this area. In addition, molding also generates large quality losses. Unfortunately, these quality losses and indirect support of molding vary greatly by product complexity, which is difficult to measure.

The molds for some parts have moving parts like rollers, lifts, and sliding cores to ensure that the injected plastic fills all cavities. These moving parts must align and function with accuracy and precision, to avoid producing scrap material. The more moving parts a mold has, the more tool wear it experiences, as well as requiring more inspection points. These molds also tend to create more rejected material, and require close supervision. By the same token, the size and length of the part also affect the support requirements. Larger parts, because molten plastic must flow over and cool them uniformly, require greater process control and injection tonnage. The machine pressure and heating and cooling cycles must be monitored closely. This increases capital investment, supervision, machine maintenance, and quality control needs, as well as generating more yield loss.

Exhibit 4-12 **COST DRIVERS FOR A MANUFACTURER'S INJECTION MOLDING ACTIVITY CENTER**

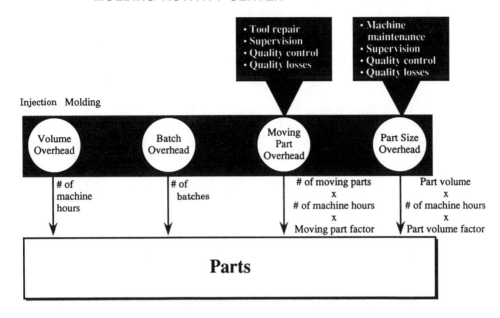

This ABC System reflects part diversity and more accurately assigns quality costs

In this factory, costs are assigned to parts based on the number of moving parts and part size, plus machine hours and batches (see Exhibit 4-12). As the exhibit shows, the injection molding activity center has four cost drivers. The moving-part pool consists of all the costs that grow in proportion to the number of moving parts in a part's die. The pool consists of costs from tool repair, supervision, quality control, and quality losses. The quality losses consist of the costs of the parts scrapped and the cost to process the scrap (filling out defect reports, creating new work orders, etc.). Since resource consumption is not directly proportional to the number of moving parts or to machine hours, an engineering study was undertaken to better understand the relationship. The study correlated support consumption with the number of moving parts. It found that the tool repair, supervision, quality control, and scrap losses were proportional to the number of moving parts in the die, and the number of machine hours the parts were run. However, the study also found that this relationship was not linear. For example, a mold with two moving parts may consume 50 percent more tool maintenance per machine hour than a part with no moving parts. Therefore, factors were developed to compensate for this nonlinear relationship.

The moving-part pool was assigned on machine hours, times the number of moving parts, times the factor. The same nonlinear relationship held true for the part-size pool as well. This information can then be used to guide design decisions and to target quality improvement programs.

The remaining quality losses that are not assigned to product attributes are added to aggregate-cost pools that are already in existence. In this way, significant quality losses are highlighted for cost reduction, yet the system is not overly complex.

All quality losses are proportioned to the expected change in activity of the cost pool. A scrap or rework cost is assigned to the end product if the responsibility code links the product design or product specification problem. Defect costs are assigned to vendors if the vendor fails to meet the procured materials specifications. The costs are assigned to customers if the product is returned, but the product has no defects or the product was misordered. All other costs are assumed to be caused by the process and put into process overhead.

Poor Designs Cause Costs

Costs are assigned to the end product to reflect nonprocess-related defects. Warranty costs are a product-level cost. The costs of filling warranty claims are usually reserved, and are forecasted for the ABC product costs. These costs will also accrue against the product's actual cost. These product-level defect costs increase as the sales of the products increase, unless corrective actions are taken. Therefore, forecasted product warranty costs should be proportional to the sales of that product.

Vendors Cause Quality Problems

Some vendors provide higher-quality components than others. Purchasing needs data to trade off effectively quality costs versus purchased price. Therefore, the costs of poor vendor quality are traced back to each individual vendor. The system forecasts a certain markup quality cost for each vendor based on the vendor's historical performance. This cost is represented in the cost system as a vendor quality surcharge on all material purchased from this vendor. Of course, you must be very careful with these numbers and customize them to each company. A vendor should be held responsible for defective material only if the materials supplied do not meet the purchasing specifications. If the specifications are in error, the responsible party is engineering, that is, the product, not the vendor. Likewise, you must adjust the system if one vendor supplies many components, some of which have much higher reject rates than others. For example, 256K DRAMs have higher failure rates, as well as higher costs, than 64K DRAMS, regardless of vendor. Therefore, purchasing should not discriminate against a vendor when evaluating 64K DRAMS quotes just because the vendor also supplies 256K DRAMS with higher failure costs. Costs are distorted if the vendor defect cost is applied equally to both.

Customers create defect costs by returning nondefect goods. Some customers cause more return costs than others. For example, Black & Decker can expect many more returns of perfectly good power drills from retailers than from builders. Some customers are also more likely to misorder products than others. These costs should be traced back to the actual cost of serving that customer, and be included in the customer-driven costs.

Processes Cause the Majority of Quality Losses

Processes are responsible for creating the majority of defect costs. These defects are caused by an operator inputting the wrong feed rate into a mill, or the machine being worn and no longer holding tolerances. These costs are the result of a poorly managed process and should be included in the process's overhead. Some defect types may be related to the volume processed, such as hole run-out, while other process scrap costs, such as an operator running the wrong program, are related to the number of batches run. The ABC system should split poor quality costs into the most appropriate overhead process pool possible. Even though many defects put into the process's overhead are not the process's fault, per se, such as damaged while being handled, or the operator being given the wrong drawing revision, the organization created the possibility of the defect by having the process. If a vendor was manufacturing the part, the vendor would not be able to pass these costs on to the company. Therefore, having the process creates the potential to have the scrap. In addition, this approach is used for the sake of simplicity.

Unless specific corrective actions are taken to eliminate the cause of the defect, you should assume a repeat of the problem. Defect costs are forecasted as proportional to the increase or decrease in its activity center's volume. For example, last year the die-cast department had $50,000 in scrap costs traced back to the process, and no corrective actions have been taken. Next year, the die-cast department's volume is forecasted to increase by 10 percent; so the forecasted scrap costs for die casting are $55,000. This cost is then included in the die-cast departments cost-driver rates.

From this information, the cost system passes back the total cost of the items on the defect report. The quality system will record much more information on the defect, such as cause code, inspector, disposition, corrective action, etc., but this information is not required by the cost system. The quality system will be a quality planning system. It should be in a database format so that defect analysis can be examined from numerous points of view.

While the ABC system shows the magnitude of poor-quality costs and focuses management on specific attributes and activity centers that are receiving more defect costs than others, the quality system drives the TQM program. Engineers are forced to identify the areas causing the most significant quality problems and explain what characteristics drive quality losses. The system reinforces corrective action and monitors its effectiveness. With the link to the ABC system, the quality system will be able to track down and analyze all poor-quality costs. The ABC system, through its actual cost reporting, provides a feedback loop. If forecasted quality costs have large variances to actual costs, it means the company's engineers cannot model the causes of quality losses. The variances then force the company to better understand quality problems, to reduce these variances. This quality reporting will put the fifth pillar back into TQM.

COSTS OF EXCESS CAPACITY

An issue management must wrestle with when designing the ABC system is whether to report the costs of excess capacity separately. Calculating excess capacity costs can identify the costs of underused facilities. This issue has long been debated by accountants, as well as microeconomists. From a theoretical standpoint, it appears reasonable that you should not burden products with the fixed costs of idle capacity. Burdening products with excess capacity costs can have catastrophic effects on pricing. On the other hand, understanding capacity costs can help a company better understand how to manage these costs, as well as help it obtain more work. In practice, the application of this theory is somewhat difficult.

Some accountants insist that the cost of excess capacity should be treated as a separate line item—a cost of the period written off in the income statement. When designing the ABC system, this is certainly a management decision. Activity-center cost pools could be identified as capacity costs; these costs would only be allocated as production capacity was absorbed. From an execution standpoint, this would increase the system complexity somewhat, but the real problem would be defining the elements. What is capacity and what are capacity costs?

In a process industry, such as oil refining, capacity is relatively straightforward—defined as so many barrels per day. Unfortunately, in discrete manufacturing, capacity is usually a guess. Production capacity in a discrete factory depends on the bottlenecks within the plant, which, in turn, depend on the product mix. A capacity analysis quickly becomes incredibly complex. Rarely, if ever, is a discrete manufacturer able to model a factory accurately to determine what the capacity would be under different product mixes. The imprecise nature of capacity "guessing" introduces error into any excess capacity calculations.

The next problem with the cost of excess capacity is defining which costs are really fixed, and which are variable. Depreciation, rent insurance, and taxes are conventionally considered fixed costs, but what about energy? Is preventive maintenance fixed or variable? Managers have an inherent incentive to argue their costs are fixed. Such a claim relieves budgetary pressures, and helps avoid painful cost control. But which costs are really fixed, and what is the best way to manage them? Does defining a certain production volume as capacity, and certain costs as fixed, support continuous manufacturing improvement?

The typical definition of capacity costs is those that are independent of production throughput, and are required to sustain the process. Under this definition, preventive maintenance, supervision, occupancy, space heating, and process engineering would all be considered excess capacity costs. If you established an excess capacity cost, you would create a process-level cost with all these elements. In addition, none of these costs would be included in a cashflow calculation.

When working with an ABC system to calculate a cost of excess capacity, rather than dividing the cost pool by the forecast activity level to develop a cost-driver rate, you develop a consumption rate for each of the excess capacity pools. This consumption rate is the fixed cost, divided by the theoretical production capacity of the activity center. For example, a test lab costs $300,000 a year to support a refinery's cracking plant. The cracking plant has a capacity of 3,000,000 barrels of oil. Therefore, the test lab consumption rate is $.10 per barrel. This consumption rate is then assigned to every barrel forecasted to pass through the cracking plant. Any unabsorbed costs are designated excess capacity.

When ABC simulates product costs at various production levels without isolating the cost of excess capacity, the product costs reflect these fixed costs. ABC shows product cost reductions as production volume increases; therefore, the costs of excess capacity are implicit in ABC. Nevertheless, there is much value in showing management a defined cost of excess capacity. The cost of excess capacity can be very important if the cost information is used for pricing. You do not want to price products higher to cover excess capacity, or you could exacerbate low-capacity utilization by driving away business. For participants in the semiconductor or steel business, where capacity utilization is extremely important, estimating the cost of excess capacity is probably worth the effort.

Chapter 5 describes how to go about implementing the ABC system.

SUMMARY

When designing an ABC system, you must account for the diversity of not only the products being sold, but the customers being sold to. However, the designer must concentrate on relevance rather than precision. The ABC system must not be too complex, or else the system will be too difficult to understand and expensive to maintain. The system design must consider not only the company's environment, but its capabilities as well. Can the company accept a complex costing system? What data are available? And finally, for what decisions will the system be used?

CHAPTER 5

IMPLEMENTING AN ABC SYSTEM

Well done is better than well said.

Ben Franklin

One must learn by doing the thing, for though you think you know it—you have no certainty, until you try.

Sophocles

In the early 1970s, a number of companies began to report the same story over and over again: lower inventories, faster customer service, and better ability to respond to changes in the business. These companies all had similar systems, but with different names. Today we know these systems as materials requirements planning (MRP). These systems changed the way companies operated. MRP raised materials planning out of obscurity and into the limelight. Production and inventory management, which used to be looked on as clerical work, had come of age.

A parallel exists between MRP and ABC; both are planning systems that forever change a company. Both systems require an education of the entire business. Neither system is possible without computers and accurate data reporting. However, their implementations are quite different: while MRP forces change, ABC encourages change. In many cases, implementing an MRP system requires the company to change its way of doing business to coincide with the MRP system. Most MRP systems are based on simplifying assumptions and standard methods of operation.

Unfortunately, it seems that in every company there are exceptions to these rules. Because the MRP system plans, schedules, and controls the factory, these exceptions must either change or work outside the system. This creates conflicts and problems in any MRP implementation. There is no such requirement imposed by ABC. ABC forecasts, monitors, and reports the operation of the factory. These functions do not create any such conflicts. Yet it is hoped that by implementing ABC, a company will discover many ways to improve its competitiveness.

While each ABC implementation is different, they all are exciting. It is invigorating to develop a system that helps a company see its business from a new perspective. However, you will face challenging problems when implementing the new system—mostly behavioral problems, but some technical. Most people are resistant to change and new ideas. For proposing new ideas, Galileo was put under house arrest; Socrates was put to death. It is doubtful any retribution for implementing ABC will be as harsh!

This chapter describes an approach that practitioners have successfully used to implement ABC systems. In addition, the chapter discusses the pitfalls that some practitioners have encountered. Typically, implementers begin by undertaking an ABC study prior to implementing the ABC system. The chapter concentrates its discussions on undertaking the ABC study and not on the implementation of the integrated system. In practice, this two-step approach is preferable to jumping in with both feet and immediately attempting to redesign the cost system. In the latter case, the system would fail because the designers lack ABC experience and full understanding of the company's cost behavior.

The following discussion identifies who should be on the design team and who the team members should interview. The chapter recommends questions that the design team should ask and describes how to configure the cost database.

CRITERIA FOR A SUCCESSFUL IMPLEMENTATION

For an ABC system to be successful, the company must embrace this system and use it as the basis for all management decision making. The successful system depends on four key factors:

1. The system has top management support.
2. The ABC methods are understandable and explainable.
3. The system is accessible.
4. Internal people take ownership of the system.

1. Top management support is critical. An ABC system changes a company's perspective of its business. As such, the organization has winners and losers. The losers are likely to fight the system unless senior management voices confidence in it. At one company, senior executives led ABC briefings, as well as training classes.

In addition, most people are resistant to change, and unless change is forced, a new idea can wither away.

You can compare companies and see the difference that top management support made. At one company, the ABC system was advocated and developed by corporate staff. Even though the team built substantial consensus among the plant personnel, the plant's executives remained skeptical, and in the end, the system's results were ignored. At a second company, on the other hand, the system was initiated and developed on the cost manager's recommendation and approved by the divisional president. This installation resulted in significant changes in the company's strategy. At Superior Faucet (Chapter 6) and Excel Medical (Chapter 7), the company presidents were the system's most ardent supporters. Another important distinction was that Superior, Excel, and the second company mentioned in the foregoing were all in serious financial difficulty at the time of the study. The executives' futures depended on making changes.

2. For the ABC system to be successful, the company's employees must understand the system and its results. Simplifying assumptions is not only allowable, but necessary; the system cannot become too complex. A successful system will not require a Ph.D. to calculate a product's cost. If a system is not understandable, it is not credible.

At the same time, the system must accurately report product costs. The results must appear intuitively correct. The ABC system must represent how the company's activities consume resources and how its products or customers trigger those activities. Assignment schemes should not be arbitrary. If one part is more expensive than another, and the difference cannot be explained, as with Zytec, the system will not have credibility. Without credibility, the system will fail.

3. All potential users of an ABC system must have timely, convenient access to the cost system. This is one important reason that an integrated cost system is superior to a stand-alone system. Integrated cost systems are accessible from any information system terminal in the company. Only an integrated system can match this availability.

Lack of accessibility is one of the key reasons that many PC-based systems fail. Most personal computer systems lack the networking capability to support multiple and diverse users. Typically, the system overseers rebuff suggestions to clone and disperse the system, for fear of losing control over its configuration. Therefore, access to the PC-based ABC system is limited. This creates an enormous burden on those operating the system. At Union Pacific, after implementing an ABC system, the accounting group was deluged with 500 cost analysis requests per week.

Restricting access to the system also breeds distrust. Users are naturally skeptical of new systems. Many users only feel comfortable with the system after prolonged experimentation.

If access is limited, it will only be used for specific decision making processes. After developing an ABC system, one company found that it was missing out on most of ABC's benefits—such as encouraging better designs, improved performance measures, and better pricing—because access to the system was so limited.

4. The implementation site's personnel must gain ownership of the system. This holds true for all new systems. Unless someone internally is committed to the new idea and champions it, overcoming all obstacles to its implementation, the idea bogs down and withers away. A cost system is no exception. In addition, only with in-house expertise will the system become an evolving entity, growing and responding to new company needs.

An ABC study does not need to meet all these requirements to be successful in the short term. For an ABC study to be successful—that is, to enable a company to improve its competitiveness—only takes top management support, although top management support typically depends on the understanding and buy-in of the organization. A study usually results in only strategic decisions, which top management, alone, makes. Management's belief in ABC and its willingness to act on the study results is all that is really required for success.

GETTING STARTED—CONDUCTING AN ABC STUDY

The first step in implementing an ABC system is to undertake an ABC study. The ABC study provides a historical baseline of the company's product, process, and customer costs. The study allows management to immediately begin reaping strategic benefits such as:

- Changing prices
- Refocusing marketing efforts
- Modifying distribution policies
- Restructuring product lines

Yet, more importantly, the study convinces management of the importance of ABC. The ABC team paves the way for system implementation by educating the organization and prototyping the system's architecture. The study allows the team to model the organization with different cost drivers, and identify and test the most appropriate mix of cost pools and cost drivers.

An important point to remember is that the ABC architecture is far from perfect on the first design attempt. After the study is undertaken, design decisions will be made early in the process, and some of these will require correction. This is inevitable, even if the team includes people with ABC experience. Today's ABC technology and collective experience are simply too limited to expect an optimal model on the first pass.

The ABC study analyzes the whole organization, not just manufacturing or marketing. ABC provides maximal benefits when it is a comprehensive, company-wide system. An ABC study that is performed only on one particular product line will overlook the cost shifts to other product lines and organizations. Strategic benefits come from looking at cost shifts across the company. To demonstrate these cost shifts adequately, the pilot area must produce products with volume or configuration diversity. If the products are homogeneous, the ABC study will reveal little, if any, product cost differential. These cost shifts alert management to its past misallocation of resources. Only by seeing the effects on the whole organization, can management effectively address pricing, marketing strategy, and factory focus. If a company has limited manpower or time, management should opt to sacrifice the thoroughness of the study, rather than the scope (if diversity exists across the company).

UNDERTAKING THE ABC STUDY

Top Management Support

It is crucial that the team receives top management direction and exposure. A company or division's top executives must decide if and how to use the information. A company's executives are the ones who benefit the most from an ABC system. The study provides a truer picture of the costs to manufacture each product and to service each customer.

Only with top management involvement and understanding can ABC be successful. A steering committee oversees the design team. Typically, the steering committee consists of the vice presidents of each of the divisions or the company's major organizations—marketing, manufacturing, and finance—as well as the president. The steering committee determines the study's scope, informs the organization of the study's intent, and solicits everyone's cooperation. Over the study's duration, the steering committee will meet for one to two hours, every three weeks, to be briefed by the team on its progress and any outstanding issues. The steering committee ensures that consensus is built and the schedule adhered to. The team reports its findings to the committee, and, in turn, the committee gives the team direction and guidance on policy issues. For example, the steering committee would decide whether the ABC system would report the cost of excess capacity separately, or include it in product cost.

Typically, most managers who understand ABC support it. Additionally, middle managers do not hesitate to support an ABC system if they know the president backs it.

More often than not, the ABC team finds and presents information of such strategic value, that top management begins improving the company's competitiveness even before the design's completion. As an example, the president of one company, anticipating the results of the ABC study, ordered a concurrent marketing survey. The president realized the ABC study's findings would prompt the company to reduce its product offering. Marketing research was conducted that assessed customer needs, allowing the company to begin altering its product line immediately.

The study is typically conducted on an off-line personal computer, using historical data for product line and customer profitability analysis. The steps in the study are as follows:

- Forming the team
- Creating the cost database
- Conducting the interviews
- Costing the products
- Testing the system
- Analyzing the data

Forming the Team

To reflect correctly the workings of the company, a multidisciplinary team must be assembled to design the ABC system. This team should be selected and assigned to the project full-time. It should be composed of three to five people, depending on the organization's size and complexity, and should include representatives from manufacturing, marketing, management information systems (MIS), and accounting. All team members must be open-minded, knowledgeable about the company's operations, and well respected. A knowledge about cost accounting is not required. The caliber of the resulting cost system will reflect the quality of the team members chosen.

The benefits of the team approach include smoother implementation and greater design effectiveness. Members from across the organization also ensure a broader acceptance due to better communication, transfer of knowledge, and awareness of the benefits.

The manufacturing representative must understand how products are processed through the factory and how they are planned. He must know who the knowledgeable, key individuals are within each department, how the factory actually works, and how that differs from the way it is supposed to work. The cost system must reflect how costs are actually incurred. Questions that the manufacturing representative will answer, or will know where to obtain an answer for, are:

- Which processes have quality problems?
- How good is the tooling?
- Are the manufacturing routings accurate?

The marketer must understand how the company's products are sold and distributed—who the customers are, how their buying characteristics differ, and which customers the sales force calls on. The ABC system has such significant marketing implications that marketing's involvement is critical to maximizing the strategic benefits. The ABC system identifies which customers and products are really profitable.

One of the most affected and critical organizations in an ABC implementation is also the most frequently overlooked—the information systems (I/S) group. To be a success, an ABC system must mirror the MRP system operations. MRP, by its nature, reflects how the company operates. At the same time, it records almost all the transaction information that the ABC system requires. The involvement of an I/S representative is not only recommended, it is mandatory.

A good I/S analyst is worth his/her weight in gold. The I/S analyst must know what type of data is collected, where the data is located in the system, how much history the records contain, and how the data is collected. Most of the required cost-driver information, it is hoped, is already collected. As the team interviews management, a good analyst will volunteer data fields currently collected, and probe whether these fields would make good measures of activity. The analyst, by knowing where and how the information is collected, can help determine the data's accuracy. Inaccurate data is one of the largest stumbling blocks of an ABC implementation.

An ABC study is very data intensive. The team requires dozens of reports detailing the number of POs created by product line, the number of bills of lading by each customer, etc. An I/S analyst is a big help in describing the team's data needs to the I/S department's programmers. In addition, this person will probably manage the on-line ABC system's design.

A cost accountant's detailed knowledge of the costs included in each general ledger account is critical. The cost accountant should know what costs are included in which accounts. For example, is hazardous waste disposal buried in plant overhead? The ABC system must reassign these costs to the waste generating plating department.

The cost accountant will probably be aware of any past cost studies. For example, at one company, the cost manager knew of a study, recently completed by the facility engineers, to identify energy usage by department. The design team used this study to assign energy costs to the appropriate production departments. The technical necessity of having a cost accountant on the team is relatively obvious. The accountant ensures the data integrity of the system. Usually, other team members, such as people from marketing or engineering, are less concerned with precision than accountants. Additionally, they help to obtain buy-in to the process and pave the way for accounting's "ownership" of the system, after its design.

Design engineering and industrial engineering are heavily involved with the team's efforts. Design engineering helps define the critical parameters of product cost and how new product development costs are incurred. As one of the ABC system's principal users, engineering's involvement helps educate the team about the company's cost drivers. It also promotes buy-in to the system. Industrial engineering is usually asked to conduct work sampling of various departments to develop activity measures for improving the team's understanding of the process, or to assess a proposed cost driver's accuracy.

Creating the Costing Database

Collecting the cost data. The team begins its study with the company's general ledger. The team aggregates all costs into departments. Putting the data into departmental budgets quickly collects the company's costs into manageable units. You reverse out any allocations to or from other departments. You must validate these allocations for yourself. In addition, any corporate allocations should be assigned as an enterprise-level cost. Prior to interviewing, the team calculates the fully-loaded cost of each department. The team should assign the costs of occupancy and fringe benefits to its sources. This gives a much clearer picture of what each department really costs. Once the cost database is established, the team begins to assign costs.

The ABC study, unlike the eventual on-line system, is historical. The team analyzes last year's costs and production. In this way, the study provides a baseline, allowing comparison of ABC costs with those recorded by the traditional system. Historical data are used to increase the study's credibility. You face the criticism of wishful thinking if forecasted data are used. At most companies, people do not believe their budgets, and never believe their sales forecasts. Using historical data makes data checking and reconciliation easier, because the data can be checked against other historical records.

Configuring the off-line system. Prior to undertaking an ABC study, the most frequently asked question is whether a piece of ABC software exists that, essentially, can perform the study. The answer is no, but there are software packages that can help configure and analyze a company's ABC data.

The approach that most companies have taken for building the off-line costing system is either to use a customized model to develop cost-driver rates on a personal computer system, or to use a packaged piece of software to configure the data and perform the analysis.

One simple approach to the ABC study is to construct spreadsheets on a PC. The output of this system is cost-driver rates, which are then uploaded into the company's mainframe or minicomputer system for calculating product costs.

The team inputs the general ledger costs into the spreadsheets. (A database program is preferred, due to the enormous amount of data the ABC study generates. In addition, a database format allows much more analysis flexibility than a simple spreadsheet does.) All data inquiries and cost-driver analyses are queried from the MIS system and manually input into the PC. The spreadsheet is used to assign the indirect costs to the activity centers via the first-stage distribution. The spreadsheet lists all the production departments in the left-hand column and all the support departments across the top row. The spreadsheet was essentially a matrix. Each column spreads the support department's costs to the production department's. Then the team segregates the support cost assignments into cost pools for each activity center (see Exhibit 5-1). The cost-driver rates are calculated by dividing these cost pools by the number of cost-driver units.

This spreadsheet approach is relatively straightforward for calculating cost-driver rates. However, this approach puts the difficult part of the analysis on the information systems group. They must program the system and configure data to calculate each product's ABC cost on the main computer system. Therefore, this

Exhibit 5-1   *CONCEPTUAL LAYOUT OF COSTING SPREADSHEET*

CONCEPTUAL LAYOUT OF COSTING SPREADSHEET

| Activity Centers | Support Departments | | | | | | | | Total |
| | Maintenance | | Tooling | | Production Control | | Warehousing | | |
	$	%	$	%	$	%	$	%	
Punch Press	$40K	10%	$500K	50%	$30K	20%	$120K	20%	$690K
Die Casting	$20K	5%	$200K	20%	$9K	6%	$36K	6%	$265K
.	.	.	.	.	.	.	.	.	.
.	.	.	.	.	.	.	.	.	.
.	.	.	.	.	.	.	.	.	.
Final Assembly	$20K	5%	$10K	1%	$15K	10%	$60K	10%	$105K
	$400K	100%	$1,000K	100%	$150K	100%	$600K	100%	

approach depends on good MIS support and capability It is most effective when the company has a large number of products to be costed, although this model becomes complicated if the company has numerous activity centers and cost drivers. The latter situation evolves into a series of linked spreadsheets because the cost database becomes so large. The major shortcoming of the PC-based spreadsheet approach is that the spreadsheet only develops cost-driver rates. The team is forced to depend on the mainframe or minicomputer (requiring MIS support), which is cumbersome and expensive. In addition, the analysis capability of the main system is very limited.

Today, the other option is to purchase a packaged PC-based software package to analyze the data. This system typically requires downloading activity records, routings, bills of material, and general ledger information into the PC. Therefore, the data processing group must create download programs. Unfortunately, the amount of data you can download and analyze is limited. With the large files of bills of material and routings, the number of product lines analyzed is usually restricted to a sampling. The package provides a structure and analysis tool. The team must still configure the system and define resource categories, cost pools, measures of activity, and cost targets. Some of the systems even have diagnostic subroutines to identify data integrity problems. After the package is configured, it generates a variety of product-line and customer profitability reports.

This packaged system provides the user with much more flexibility, after bringing up the system. Endless analyses can be performed, whereas, with the spreadsheet system, each analysis is cumbersome. The packaged system requires an upfront expenditure and user training. Most of the sellers are actually trying to sell consulting services rather than software. Therefore, some packages are not designed for ease of use.

The PC software package approach is best if the factory is complex, and the analysis involves many activity centers and cost drivers, but only a few important products.

No PC-based solution is a viable long-term approach to product costing. Because a PC-based system is not integrated, it must be maintained separately, inviting data integrity and maintenance problems. Additionally, PC-based systems are not accessible to a large number of users and, therefore, have limited influence on the organization.

Conducting the Interviews

The next step in the ABC system design is extensive interviewing to develop a detailed understanding of the company's operations. The team identifies the individuals, within each department, who are most knowledgeable about how each department works. Typically, these key people are the department's managers or supervisors, but can also be engineers and quality inspectors. The team starts interviewing in the indirect departments, and then moves on to the activity centers. The goals are to discover what each department does and, ultimately, which are the most appropriate cost drivers.

It is important for the interviewer to make the interviewee understand and feel comfortable with the ABC study. This is an important part of the consensus building within the organization. The interviewer must work to get a balanced picture of the organization, yet not impose his or her opinion or preconceptions on the interviewee. Most interviewees feel uncomfortable giving the percentage of time that was spent working on different activities. They think that the interviewer wants exact answers, which they are incapable of giving. The interviewer must explain that only approximate answers are necessary.

The first step is to identify the major functions being performed by a department. Typically, the way a department is organized splits it up into different functions. For example, the materials department is usually split into inventory planning, production scheduling, and shop floor control. Each of these groups represents a different activity.

The first interview question the team asks is "How is your department organized?" Typically, departments are organized around major functions that signify cost pools. For example, one company's quality assurance department was organized into quality engineering, inspection, and the test lab. Each of these groups performed different functions and had different drivers.

The team should use the time devoted to each activity by department employees to determine the portion of the department's total cost spent by each activity. However, if any significant nonpersonnel related expenses are associated with only one of the functions, it should be accounted for separately. For example, one production engineering department was separated into three functions—floor support, N/C programming, and tool design. While the headcount was equal for all three groups, the $200,000 in software, equipment depreciation, mylar, and maintenance only supported N/C programming. Therefore, these computer costs were treated separately from the rest of the department's costs.

Once a department is split into activities, the team identifies how many equivalent people are consumed by these activities. The ratio of workers will be used to divide the department's costs. If 4 of the department's 16 people work in production scheduling, scheduling receives 25 percent of the department's cost. Unless the supervisors or managers are actively involved in performing work, the team should not count them as departmental personnel.

A typical interview between Bill Green (BG) and tooling manager Scott Feldmann (SF) goes much like this:

BG: How many people work in the tooling department?

 SF: About half.

BG: No, what I mean is how many people are in the tooling department?

 SF: Eight, nine including myself.

BG: Do they all perform the same jobs?

 SF: No, two just clean dies and six repair tooling.

BG: The two men who clean dies, do they clean dies for all of the departments?

 SF: No, they only clean die-casting dies—Department 314.

BG: What creates their work?

 SF: A die needs to be cleaned after every run, so I suppose whenever a part is run.

BG: So, after every batch a die is cleaned.

 SF: Yup.

BG: Does it matter how many parts were die cast?

 SF: No, it doesn't matter how many parts were manufactured.

BG: The six men who repair tooling, which departments do they support? Do you keep any records?

 SF: No, I don't keep any records. Sandy works in 314 (die casting) full-time; Eric, Steve, Jim, and Dale spend most of their time in 312 (punch press), and Sam spends some of his time in 312 and 411 (screw machines).

BG: How much time does Sam spend in 312 versus 411?

SF: I'd say about 60–40. Sixty percent in 312 and only 40 percent in 411. But to tell you the truth he doesn't do much work at all. . .

BG: What causes their work—tool repair?

SF: Tool wear. The more parts punched or machined the more tool repair needed.

BG: How do you know when to repair the tools? Are some parts more likely to need more repair than others?

SF: Yeah. Some parts are terrible. The departments send us a tool repair request like this (hands Bill a form). The operators spot tool wear and send it over. Except in punch press, of course. In punch press we clock how many punches a die stamps and as soon as it reaches 30,000, back it comes.

BG: Do you have records of tool repair requests?

SF: See that file cabinet behind you, plus we send a copy to accounting and I've no idea what those guys do with it.

BG: If a die reaches 30,000 punches is a tool repair form created?

SF: Yes.

BG: Would it be accurate to assign costs to parts based on the number of tool repair requests created?

SF: No. A die-cast die takes much longer to repair than a punch press die.

BG: I understand, but with punch press dies?

SF: Yeah. Most of our dies are pretty similar and take about the same amount of time.

BG: Do you actually work on tooling?

SF: No, I've got my hands full just watching these guys, I only get involved when we've got a real tricky job like fixing that 12HX-14 behind you. I'll tell you that die is such a mess, the idiot who designed that one should be . . .

BG: Thank you for your time. I'm going back to my office and write this up. Tomorrow I'll be back to show you what distribution I came up with and you can critique it.

Exhibit 5-2 shows how you would break out and use cost drivers based on this interview. First, the tooling department is broken into two functions: tool repair and die cleaning. Two out of eight people support die cleaning or 25 percent of the department's cost, while the remaining 75 percent of the cost goes to tool repair. The rest of the costs are broken down similarly.

The real interviews take much longer than the script shown and are much less to the point. You should figure at least one hour per interview, and usually more than one interview per person.

Another example is a purchasing department that has six buyers, each of whom is assigned to buy parts by commodity code. One buyer handles brass raw material,

**Exhibit 5-2   *TOOL DEPARTMENT COST ASSIGNMENTS
BASED ON INTERVIEW***

Tool Department Cost Assignments Based on Interview

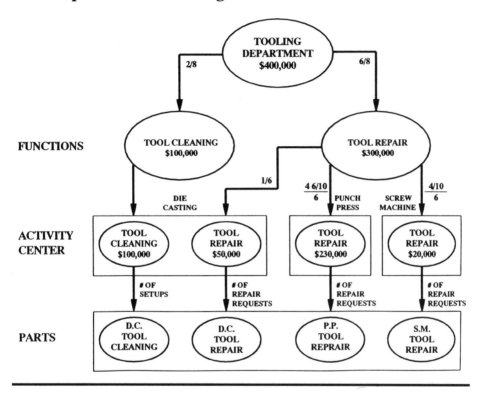

one handles steel products, one handles castings, one handles supplies and all non-production items, and the last handles forgings. In this case, one buyer purchases only 12 different forgings, all of which come from a vendor in Spain. Because this buyer travels back and forth to Madrid, his job incurs much more cost than the typical buyer's. Since other buyers purchase hundreds of line items, the other parts have substantially less procurement cost per line item than do the forgings. Therefore, to cost purchased components accurately, this team splits purchasing costs into cost pools by commodity code.

Another approach is for a department, like design engineering, to use time cards to charge its work to products. The team can then correlate this data with some activity measures. If not, filling out time cards may be required, which is expensive. However, accurately reporting the cost of new products is more than worth the effort at many companies. Hopefully, the team will find some measure that can be used to estimate the department's resource consumption.

If no measures exist, and a group of costs are significant, industrial engineers can conduct a study to identify how much time or other resources various activities consume. At one company, utility costs are very significant. The plant installed meters at selected locations to measure usage by department. In this case, over half—$150,000—of natural gas was going into die-casting, a single department.

Where no measures of activity exist, you may be forced to use the assignment method of last resort—surveys. Executives rarely punch time clocks, for example, but their costs are significant. Their costs can be assigned with the help of surveys. The interviewer asks the executive to identify the processes, product lines, new products, plants, or customers that usually demand his attention over the course of the year. This can have some interesting results.

At one company, 40 percent of the average manager's time was spent resolving problems associated with a new plant in Taiwan. Meanwhile, the relatively neglected domestic plant was filled with broken-down machinery, annually scrapping $2 million in parts, and routinely missing customer delivery dates. These management costs were not reflected in the Taiwanese plant's books, and were completely absorbed in the domestic plant's overhead. This distortion resulted in a large understatement of the new facility's start-up costs. The ABC study reversed this misconception and made the president acutely aware of management's neglect of the domestic plant's operating problems.

When no activity measures exist, you still hope to avoid directly charging any product (a single-stage assignment) or lumping costs in overhead categories. Not only is direct charging difficult to forecast, but it implies a failure to identify or measure the activities causing resource consumption. For example, product costing requires a forecast of future product warranty expense. If you understand which components wear out, their mean time between failure, and the cost to make field repairs, you can predict warranty costs. More importantly, by analyzing these costs, management can begin to control them at their source—product design. The choice of components and ease of repair would become design variables with target costs.

After interviewing members of indirect departments and delineating departmental costs, the team reviews the cost distributions with the interviewees. The interviewee then has had a chance to mull over the cost assignment. By feeding back the results, the team identifies any misinterpretations and verifies the accuracy of the chosen activity measures. Consensus is rarely a problem because most interviewees want management to understand their work. In addition, this feedback helps consensus building and ensures that, if queried, the interviewee will verify the accuracy of the work distribution.

Next, the team interviews representatives of the activity centers. Activity center representatives are interviewed after the indirect departments, so that the team can probe more deeply into the consumption of support costs by the activity centers, as well as how individual parts trigger indirect support requirements. The questions are much the same, except the emphasis is on how costs are driven by products. The team needs to develop an understanding of how products are processed through each of the production departments. For instance:

- Why do different products take more time than others?
- What are their characteristics?
- Do certain products require more engineering, maintenance, or tooling support than others, and why?
- Are build-to-stock parts processed differently than build-to-order parts?

You need to identify whether or not the proposed activity center includes multiple processes with different cost behaviors. The interviewer should develop an understanding of all of the processes within the department and identify whether any significant nonhomogeneous processes coexist. If such a nonhomogeneous process does exist within the activity center, is it significant? If it is expensive enough, the team should first try to create a separate activity center for this process. On the first ABC study, the team usually tries to avoid developing new activity centers, as it creates substantial work, especially calculating product costs using the standard manufacturing routings.

It is very important to identify any cost behavior that varies by product line. The characteristics that cause products to require more resources than others must be identified. It is precisely these types of characteristics or parameters that should either be cost drivers or help identify them.

Identifying activity centers. Identifying activity centers is relatively straightforward. They are production departments. During this study phase, the team should avoid attempting to "reorganize" the company into new departments. The team should organize the activity centers around existing budgetary units. The team can compensate for different processes within one activity center by using multiple drivers for one activity center. For example, the costs of machining five-axis (part configurations that require simultaneous movement in five directions) work is much more expensive than three-axis work. Consequently, the ABC team could develop five-axis and three-axis machine hour rates.

If there are no formal budgetary units, or if no established "burden centers" exist, the team will have to devote a few days to dividing up costs into activity center budgets. This will require segregating labor costs, indirect labor, depreciation, utilities, and all other charges.

Developing customer activity centers. To simplify reporting of customer-driven costs, the team must define customer activity centers. Customer activity centers are major groups of functions or steps in the distribution process. These groupings can include distribution, warehousing, sales, marketing, and administration.

Just as with product-driven activity centers, you must be careful not to aggregate nonhomogeneous processes. You should be sure to separate warehouse storage if some warehouses, or parts of warehouses, are refrigerated, chilled, dry, high security, or bulk stacked versus rack. In these instances, not only is the space cost different, but handling costs will vary substantially under these different conditions.

If transportation costs are large, a transportation activity center is appropriate. The activity center may include pools for your own truck fleet, as well as hired trucks and rail transportation.

Identifying customer groups. The customer side of ABC is somewhat different than the product side. The customer-driven side is usually simple enough to model on a PC spreadsheet. There are fewer steps and fewer support functions in distribution than in manufacturing, and no bills of material. On the customer side, the team will not analyze each customer, but will consolidate customers into manageable groups. However, the customer groups must be established with great care.

The ABC team must classify customers according to buying characteristics. Some characteristics of interest include order size, total dollar volume, number of buying decision makers, product mix, and number of shipping locations. These are some of the parameters that determine the costs of serving various customers. The team consolidates the customers into a dozen or so groups to make the cost reporting information digestible. If you are not careful, you may consolidate too many customers and lose sight of distinct classes of customer niches. Typically, the marketing department will already have some classifications, but in many cases these classes need to be updated or validated.

As the team designs the system, the members should document who they interviewed and what functions the department performs. The documentation need not be extensive, but must describe the activity measures and their data sources. From year to year the cost system will evolve; it is very useful to be able to trace the system's development. You may find that the company's cost behavior is changing, or that you just understand the cost behavior better.

Costing the Products

As interviews are completed, the team requires many data processing reports. These reports are used to understand departmental activity and their sources. The team may require reports summarizing:

- Number of warehousing issues by department
- Number of purchase orders by product
- Number of invoices by customer

This information is used to create the cost database, as discussed earlier. Treat these reports with skepticism; they frequently contain errors (see "Implementation Problems" on page 158). In all cases validate your data!

The team needs to create a database for all of last year's production. The part database lists all of the parts and their quantity produced last year. The team applies last year's costs against this database. To create the part database, you calculate all of the end units produced last year. Next, the database is multiplied by all of the end units' bills of material. This listing is then adjusted by adding all of the parts scrapped out last year, and any changes in part inventory. From the spreadsheet, cost-driver rates are calculated. These rates are then entered into the company's computer to calculate part costs. Then these costs are rolled up into end-unit costs.

This analysis can be made simpler by aggregating and analyzing product families and not individual products. This can reduce the number of items analyzed from 10,000 to 50 or even 10. It saves a great deal of time and effort. However, you may miss data errors by calculating the costs of all parts in one total.

Testing the System

Prior to disseminating the results of the ABC study, the team should test its ABC model. First, to verify the cost database's accuracy, the team reconciles the sum of all of ABC-costed parts and customer costs with the company's profit and loss statement. This step verifies that all costs are being absorbed.

The costs of various products with different characteristics and volumes are calculated to see if the results make intuitive sense. If the costs make sense, the system probably works as intended. If not, it either has a bug, the assignment scheme is incorrect, or the team has discovered an unforeseen cost behavior. If the problem is the former, the team must correct it immediately to maintain the system's credibility. If it is the latter case, revealing unanticipated cost behavior, the ABC team is well on its way toward demonstrating the system's worth.

The team must be very sensitive to any system output that does not make intuitive sense. The team must rigorously test the validity of any counterintuitive results, or perform what is known as a "sanity check." Are these answers reasonable? If not, why?

Analyzing the Data

At a minimum, the team should conduct the following analysis on the ABC data:

- Changes in activity center total overhead cost
- Profitability by:
  Product
  Product group
  Division
  Customer
  Channel
  Market segment

- Cash flow by:
  Product
  Product group
  Division
  Customer
  Channel
  Market segment

See Chapter 8 for the importance of cash flow and its calculation. Chapters 10, 11, and 12 discuss how to use this information.

IMPLEMENTATION PROBLEMS

Data Integrity Problems

The greatest challenge facing the ABC implementer can be summed up in two words—accurate data. New packaged MRP II systems collect and record just about all of the data needed by the ABC system and even have simulation capability. Unfortunately, many companies have no MRP system. About half the MRP installations are homegrown, and have limited data collection and recordkeeping capabilities.

A more insidious problem that you face is data integrity, or the lack of it. The accuracy of most companies' MRP systems is low.

The team is likely to find many data problems as it undertakes the study and implements the system. There are very few companies with at least 95 percent MRP system data accuracy. The errors are spread throughout the database in routings, bills, planning rules, and vendor listings. For example, some parts will lack MRP planning codes. Moreover, some companies manufacture products that are lacking bills of material. Since the team assigns costs based on this data, costing errors will occur. As the team goes through the process, team members must correct all data that will skew the results. On the other hand, the ABC system uses so many cost bases that it is much less susceptible to data errors than a traditional cost system.

But an MRP system is not required to have an ABC system, although it is desirable. Chapter 9 contains a case study, called California Sunroof, in which the company developed an ABC system with no MRP system.

Scrap Reporting

The team may run into problems assigning scrap and rework costs. One of the major hindrances to quality improvement is the absence of a quality module in the standard MRP system. Quality reporting is not integrated with manufacturing planning and, worse still, the cost systems. Typically, scrap reporting is haphazard at best. At one company, more than $3 million in scrap costs were identified, yet this number was significantly understated. The rest of the scrap was being reported as a process inefficiency. Nevertheless, scrap costs can be very significant and must be accurately assigned.

The goal is not only to capture the scrap cost, but also to assign it to its sources, whether the source is a poor design, out-of-control processing, or worn tooling. In this study, you should be happy if you can reasonably assign scrap costs to an activity center. However, assigning scrap costs down to parts, vendors, and products is better. Typically, quality reporting requires the assignment of responsibility for all defects. Whether or not the reporting is accurate is another question. You should use reports from the quality system to assign scrap and rework costs.

It is important to note that the quality system reports quality costs at values generated by the traditional costing system. This data must be converted into ABC costs.

Engineering and New Product Costs

One problem the design team will face when designing the ABC system is what to do with engineering and other product introduction costs. It is obvious that engineering is directly traceable to products, but engineering costs are expensed as period costs, not amortized or included in product cost. When a new product is being developed and designed, these costs are expensed. Theoretically, these costs should be treated as any other investment and amortized, but our tax laws (and GAAP) permit us to expense them, thus reducing current taxable income. Therefore, while engineering costs are tracked against products, they are not included in product costs. How to evaluate product lines including engineering costs is discussed in Chapter 9.

The two pieces of engineering costs that are inventoried as part of product cost are custom and sustaining engineering. The costs of customizing products should be traced directly to the product. Costs such as revising bills of materials and processing engineering changes are frequently incurred by complex or poorly designed products. These costs should be assigned to products based on the number of engineering changes or program notes. By tracking these costs, engineering is encouraged to avoid them.

TRAINING

After completing the ABC study, the team disseminates the new knowledge it has gained. Concurrently, the team begins educating the company about ABC and how it works. The strategic and operating benefits of ABC will be lost unless it is accompanied by an effective training program, nor will people trust the system or its results without training. The elements of such a training program include:

- What is ABC?
- How does it work?

- How was the system designed?
- What were the results?
- How should the results be interpreted?

The attendees should understand ABC, so they can help you design the on-line integrated system. It is very important that the attendees understand how to use the preliminary ABC data because misuse of this data can lead to poor decisions. I highly recommend using some Harvard Business School cases in the training class. The cases give the students excellent examples of ABC design and implementation. Typically, I use the John Deere, Schrader Bellows, and Kanthal cases listed in the bibliography. The company should train everyone who uses cost information.

Yet, the only way to really learn ABC is to try it. You must calculate product costs and perform analyses. If the company trains people to use ABC, the company creates the expectation that everyone will have access to the ABC system. Lack of access is one of the problems associated with an off-line system. If the company copies and distributes the ABC database, control over the data's integrity is lost. If the company tries to localize the database and allows only authorized people to use it, many of the system's benefits are lost, which is why you must implement ABC as the integrated cost system after completing the ABC study.

The following case briefly describes the steps gone through by one company, that was implementing ABC.

CASE STUDY
Goliath Aerospace Company—Providing a New Look

Recognizing problems with its current cost allocation system, Goliath decided to pilot a new cost system. The company made electronic systems such as signal processing and communications systems for the Department of Defense (DOD).

The company was concerned that its declining labor base distorted product costs. It also felt that its rising overhead rates created the customer perception of inefficiency, and focused excessive attention on overhead rates, and not total product cost. Over the years, Goliath had tried a multiple overhead rate structure and central service allocations, but was still dissatisfied. Goliath watched its competitors use creative accounting such as creating satellite plants, or entire new divisions to reduce overhead rates.

The company felt the present system promoted suboptimal decision making. The company retained excess direct labor employees. The system directed the company to invest in only labor-saving automation, ignoring overhead. Most significantly, Goliath was concerned that its cost system encouraged it to bid and win contracts for less profitable business.

An internal champion pushed management to study the problem. Between May and December, personnel from Goliath contacted and visited ABC sites at General Motors, Tektronix, and Hewlett-Packard. In addition, they interviewed consultants from the Big Six accounting firms and CAM-I (Computer-Aided Manufacturing-International, Austin, Texas). Given the nature of their business—defense contracting, Goliath decided to develop a prototype site first. In this way, Goliath could understand and test the system, gain an early success, and explore the disclosure implications with their DOD customers.

The pilot site chosen was its printed wiring board (PWB) fabrication plant. The PWB factory was an autonomous unit with its costs easily segregated from the rest of the company. The factory had a total cost of $16 million and 220 employees. The pilot manufactured over 1,000 different part numbers.

To undertake the pilot, Goliath formed a cross-functional team. The team included representatives from finance, industrial engineering, production, and management information systems (MIS). Starting with the company's general ledger, the team identified all the costs associated with the pilot site. The team interviewed the various factory employees to identify activity centers, first- and second-stage drivers. The team identified 30 activity centers on their first pass. The activity centers included each major manufacturing process such as oxide treatment, lamination and CNC drilling, plus activity centers for scheduling, buying, material handling, production control, administration, and quality/defect analysis.

The team assigned the general ledger dollars to the activity centers based on accounting records, industrial engineering analysis, or activity measures. For instance, indirect labor and depreciation were assigned on accounting records while floor space costs and utilities were assigned on square footage.

They analyzed each activity center in detail. The team identified each of the major tasks performed and labeled them value or nonvalue added. The team identified 15 second-stage cost drivers (see Exhibit 5-3). These second-stage drivers are divided into two columns. The first column includes product characteristics that assign manufacturing process costs. For instance, square foot area is the total area of each circuit board. This area determines the amount of material deposited on the board during the plating, cleaning, and electroless copper deposit. The second column represents manufacturing characteristics that correspond to the quantity

Exhibit 5-3   **GOLIATH'S SECOND-STAGE COST DRIVERS**

Product Characteristics	Manufacturing Characteristics
Roll requirements	Work orders
Panel volume	Moves
Man-hours	Purchase orders
Holes	Plan packages
Tests	Defects
Inspection hours	Production volume
Check hours	Value-added
Sq. ft. area	

of support activity consumed. The workload of production control is proportional to the number of work orders each product requires. The number of defects triggers defect analysis.

The team used a PC-based model to analyze the data. To simplify the data analysis, the team did not cost every product but developed 54 families of products. After entering the data, the team spent a substantial amount of time debugging and analyzing. The team also made multiple iterations, simplifying the system.

After completing their study, Goliath discovered that results found over 70 percent of PWB costs changed by more than 10 percent. The team spent considerable time educating the organization on the results and creating "buy-in." Goliath discovered that one of its high-density two-sided PWBs was overcosted by 100 percent. Meanwhile, the study found multilayer PWBs to be undercosted by as much as 80 percent.

This study took approximately six months, with three equivalent people, to complete. The implementation program included verifying the pilot, developing a training program, and extending the pilot into other manufacturing areas. The company is also working with the DOD to develop a coordinated implementation plan and resolve contract issues.

Lessons Learned

As this case demonstrates, with an ABC implementation even a pilot can take a great deal of time and effort. Yet, the knowledge of pursuing less profitable products and pricing them below cost dwarfs this expense. Goliath recognized that it had a problem, and convinced management to undertake a study. The company formed a multidisciplinary team to undertake the study. The team researched and visited people with ABC experience. Goliath selected a pilot area easily segregated, manufacturing a wide range of products, using a number of processes. The team conducted extensive interviews and analysis, and used a packaged PC-based system to analyze the data. The team spent substantial time debugging and analyzing the data.

Despite spending substantial time and resources investigating and developing the ABC pilot, Goliath fell into the common trap of assigning each production process overhead to a single second-stage driver. Goliath missed the significant batch costs of each process. However, Goliath's ABC study still reported huge swings in product costs.

Goliath also developed a pilot in the most challenging of cost accounting environments—Department of Defense contracting. The DOD has a number of stringent rules, called cost accounting standards (CAS), regarding how products are bid and priced. If the DOD finds a company reporting inaccurate costs, it can sue the company for defective pricing and stop all of the company's DOD work.

All cost accounting changes in the defense environment must comply with

- CAS 401—Consistency in Estimating, Accumulating, and Reporting Costs
- CAS 414—Cost of Money as an Element of the Cost of Facilities Capital
- CAS 418—Allocation of Direct and Indirect Costs

Many defense contractors are concerned with whether ABC meets these CAS requirements. In fact, CAS 418 requires that the accumulation of costs be made in homogeneous pools, and allocated in causal or beneficial relationships. From the wording of 418, not only does it appear that ABC systems meet the government's requirements, but the traditional systems, by allocating overhead on direct labor, are in violation. In other words, the DOD has no problems with ABC, and the Defense Contracting Audit Agency (DCAA) has publicly said so. However, any defense contractor making a change to the cost system must carefully follow government procedures when implementing the change. You must file a disclosure statement and provide a notification to an administrative contracting officer (ACO), along with a cost impact study.

CHAPTER 6

SUPERIOR FAUCET—
AN ABC TURNAROUND

*Most ailing organizations have developed a functional blindness
to their own defects. They are not suffering because they cannot
solve their problems, but because they cannot see their problems.*

John W. Gardner

Every executive should know that, according to a survey of turnaround executives, declining margins is the best early warning signal of a company headed for trouble. Yet, in spite of years of warning, many executives are unwilling to anticipate change. They would rather not alter their course in order to avoid the storm of shifting circumstances, but wait until they are in the midst of a hurricane to escape.

Everyone finds change difficult, but without it there is no progress. The greatest hindrance to achieving the benefits of ABC is not technical issues, but the admission that you must change—to act on the information ABC provides. The one advantage of a turnaround situation, as we shall see, is that the organization admits to itself that it must change. In a turnaround company, a deteriorating financial position forces the company to admit that a crisis is at hand. The company realizes that its past abilities no longer guarantee success. Turnaround companies are the companies most susceptible to change—because they are willing to act on new ideas.

This is the story of how one troubled company turned its factory around. The case study describes how activity-based costing directed an attack against the company's sources of overhead cost. The company focused its factory by outsourcing processing (buying parts from outside vendors as opposed to making them in-house) and pruning product lines. These actions streamlined the company, cutting costs and, simultaneously, improving customer responsiveness. ABC led the company to alter its strategic direction and, subsequently, return to profitability. The case study describes:

- How Superior Faucet got into its predicament
- Why the study was undertaken
- How the cost database was constructed
- What information was used to assign costs
- How piece parts were costed
- What the study results told Superior
- What actions Superior took and what their effects were

SUFFERING FROM AN ALL-TOO-COMMON MALAISE

The company, which we will call Superior Faucet, suffered from an all-too-common malaise. Throughout the 1960s and 1970s, Superior's sales grew by leaps and bounds. In fact, demand frequently outstripped capacity. Faced with industry-wide capacity constraints, Superior developed the philosophy of making and finishing every knob, screw, and plug itself. Superior believed that self-reliance was critical to maintaining quality standards and meeting schedule commitments. In the late 1960s, Superior was bought by a conglomerate, yet Superior retained its original owner-managers. In the late 1970s, Superior's executives laid out a plan for the future—relocating operations under one roof. As the relocation was completed, the previous owner retired.

Until a replacement could be found, the conglomerate's group president assumed the divisional president's responsibilities—the divisional president position would remain open for the next eight years. In 1978, the building business was deluged with orders. Superior's backlog grew to nine months. Believing that most of the backlog was inflated by double and triple ordering of products as lead times extended, the group president's first major decision as acting president was historic. He canceled half of the customer's orders unilaterally. He believed that his move was imperative to setting realistic schedules and production plans. However, it created animosity that Superior's customers have never forgotten.

In 1980, the recession, induced by the collapse of new construction, hammered Superior and the building industry. However, Superior was doubly hit. The parent company was taken private in a leveraged buyout (LBO). With the prime rate at 21

Exhibit 6-1   **SUPERIOR FAUCET SALES AND NET PROFIT**

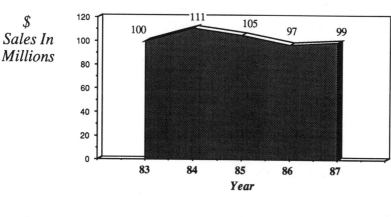

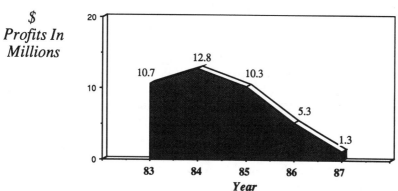

percent, Superior was buried under a debilitating need for cash to meet its staggering debt payments. Desperate, Superior's capital budgets evaporated, maintenance budgets were cut, and new product investment was furloughed. For the next five years, Superior's operations were virtually ignored as management was distracted by debt financing and restructuring. By 1984, sales and profits had recovered; however, budgets were never restored to their previous levels.

Since 1984, sales had stagnated and profits had evaporated (see Exhibit 6-1). Over the next few years, Superior's response was typical of many companies. Initially, Superior brought back memories of the LBO by tightening its budgets. Management slashed expenditures on quality circles, preventive maintenance, research and development, tool repair, and capital investment. Superior brought back in-house parts being purchased from outside vendors. Management believed that this "backward integration" would improve factory utilization and increase overhead absorption.

In 1987, after more years of stagnating sales, the company launched a bolder, more aggressive strategy. To increase sales, Superior introduced variations of existing products. Management instructed the industrial engineers to develop new time standards and improve factory methods. Superior invested capital in labor-saving automation, and opened a maquiladora (a Mexican border plant) to take advantage of low Mexican labor rates for polishing and assembling the faucets. The result: Sales remained flat while overhead exploded, driving the company into the red. Meanwhile, imports from the likes of Taiwan had now risen to 30 percent of the U.S. market, up from 7 percent in 1978. Superior and its American competitors filed an antidumping suit with the Justice Department. In 1988, the parent company finally filled Superior's president position. Meanwhile, Superior's group president, who had become a multimillionaire as part of the leveraged buyout group, retired.

A New President Arrives

The new president, wanting a fresh look at the operations, brought in a consulting team to make an evaluation. The consultants pulled no punches, writing, "Superior is an unfocused company with a confused product line and a hodgepodge of processes." Its product lines were so broad that one product could be ordered in 3,126,786 variations of style, function, finish, and length. The processes under Superior's roof included die casting, plating, polishing, machining, cold heading, and assembly, most operating below 40 percent of capacity. To remain competitive, these processes required large investments in capital and talent, resources that were in short supply. The lack of focus resulted in a manufacturing overhead of more than 55 percent of the cost of goods sold. To turn the company around, overhead had to be reduced through streamlining.

Neither Superior nor the consultants knew where to begin. Superior's traditional cost accounting system did not provide this type of guidance. Therefore, the team decided to develop a cost system to identify where the company's real cost reduction opportunities existed. The new system was to portray what was creating manufacturing's huge overhead. Originally, this new cost system was intended only to relate manufacturing overhead to the different manufacturing processes based on measures of usage. However, when completed, this new system was an activity-based costing system that went well beyond our expectations.

DEVELOPING A NEW COST SYSTEM

A team consisting of one consultant, the MIS manager, and the cost accounting manager were given six weeks to develop the cost system. The team designed the system to assign costs in two stages. The first stage assigned all manufacturing costs to the production processes (each process was a separate department). The second stage was to assign these process costs to each of the parts produced last year.

The team operated under the assumption that the study was strategic and, therefore, of long-term outlook with all costs being variable. The team intuitively believed that Superior could reap significant savings from outsourcing (buying all of the parts for a particular process from an outside vendor). Therefore, the team wanted to identify the cost of each department that would be eliminated if the department was outsourced. If outsourced, floor space would be freed up, equipment sold off, supervisor positions eliminated, and overhead support cut. The team expected to outsource enough floor space so that the "fixed" cost of occupancy could be leased out.

Starting with the prior year's departmental budgets, the team determined the total cost that was created by every department. While the departmental budgets included wages, salaries, operating supplies, and some direct charges from other departments such as tooling, the team added occupancy, depreciation, workers compensation, and other miscellaneous costs.

Creating the Database

Next, the team built a computer spreadsheet to distribute the overhead costs to the production departments. The spreadsheet listed all the production departments in the left hand column and all the support departments across the top row (see Exhibit 6-2). The spreadsheet was essentially a matrix that showed how each of the indirect departments' costs were assigned to the production departments.

Assigning Support Overhead to Processes

To understand how the production departments created the need for overhead support, the team interviewed each support department supervisor. Through the interview, the team tried to comprehend what each overhead department did, and

Exhibit 6-2   **CONCEPTUAL LAYOUT OF COSTING SPREADSHEET**

CONCEPTUAL LAYOUT OF COSTING SPREADSHEET

Activity Centers	Support Departments								
	Maintenance		Tooling		Production Control		Warehousing		Total
	$	%	$	%	$	%	$	%	
Punch Press	$40K	10%	$500K	50%	$30K	20%	$120K	20%	$690K
Die Casting	$20K	5%	$200K	20%	$9K	6%	$36K	6%	$265K
• • •	•	•	•	•	•	•	•	•	•
Final Assembly	$20K	5%	$10K	1%	$15K	10%	$60K	10%	$105K
	$400K	100%	$1,000K	100%	$150K	100%	$600K	100%	

how the production departments triggered the consumption of the overhead department's resources—which event triggered the overhead department's action. The team always looked for some measurement of these trigger events. In addition, if overhead activity was triggered, would it define an equivalent amount of support work for each production department? For example, would the average machine repair request take as long to complete in the punch press department as in the screw machine department?

Warehousing

The team asked the warehousing supervisor what his people did. He replied that they moved material. They pick it up from the receiving or production departments, move the material to the warehouse, verify the item count, input the transaction into the computer, and move the material to its storage location. The warehouse person also performs the reverse, issuing material from the warehouse to the production department.

The warehouse occupied over 200,000 square feet, yet occupancy costs were proportionally very small. Therefore, warehousing costs were not assigned on square feet. The vast majority of the warehousing department's cost was tied to personnel. The personnel's work appeared to be driven by the number of moves into, and out of, the warehouse. The supervisor told the interviewer that the distance traveled by the batch was not a good measure because other tasks took up a lot of time and driving a forklift was pretty fast. He also suggested that the number of parts handled mattered little, unless the batch was extremely large, thereby requiring more than one trip—a rare occurrence.

Fortunately, the computer recorded the number of warehousing transactions, corresponding on a one-to-one basis with the number of material movements. The team had the data processing department provide a report with the number of issues sent to, and from, each department last year. The team used this report to assign Superior's warehousing costs of $1,104,000. The team distributed warehousing costs on the prior year's 86,890 warehousing issues. Thus, the average cost of an issue was $12.70. Since the punch press department transacted 5,022 issues last year, the team assigned the punch press department $63,808 in warehousing costs.

Tooling

A similar interview with the tooling supervisor revealed that the tooling department built and repaired tooling. The traditional cost system allocated tooling costs to processes on depreciation dollars, which seemed like a reasonable method. However, the screw machine department, with its new equipment, had the largest depreciation expense, and used no tooling support. Therefore, under the traditional system, the screw machine department received $300,000 in tooling cost allocation, but should have received less than $20,000. When asked which departments he supported, the supervisor said that his people filled out time cards recording the departments they were working on. The records told the team how many hours each department was charged last year. Over 50 percent of the tooling department cost was charged to the punch press department. However, a significant portion of the tooling charges were not charged to a production department. Time spent cleaning the tooling area, fixing the department's equipment, etc., were charged to the tooling department's overhead. The team wanted to assign tooling cost fully, so it assigned all tooling costs on the percentage of time charged to each department.

Maintenance

Maintenance department personnel also used time cards to charge their hours to particular production departments. The team used time card records to distribute tooling and maintenance costs.

Inspection

Since quality control inspectors worked in particular production departments, their $800,000 budget was assigned based on the number of inspectors working in each department. Two of the sixteen inspectors worked in the assembly, so assembly got 2/16 of the department's $800,000 cost.

Material

Scheduling and planning costs amounted to $450,000. These costs were driven by, and assigned, on the number of shop order releases required by each department.

Utilities

The cost accounting manager dug up a two-year-old facilities study that analyzed utilities usage by department. Two years ago, gas and electric meters had been temporarily installed to record energy consumption by department. Since little had changed over the last few years, this study was used to assign utilities costs.

Scrap and Rework

Because the scrap cost of defective parts was in the millions, the team wanted to assign these costs to the processes generating it. Unfortunately, the quality system did not attach any cost information to its defect reports. Using the number of defects to assign scrap costs would distort any analysis. Although mispunching a washer and drilling an oversized hole in a brass handle are counted as only one defect each, the latter costs 500 times more. A washer costs two cents, while a brass handle costs more than four dollars a piece. The quality reporting system made no allowance for the defect's cost.

However, Superior did record each part scrapped and which department discovered the defect. Unfortunately, many of the defects were discovered late in the production process, and the department responsible for the defect was unidentified.

To distribute scrap costs, the team decided to assign scrap to each production department's overhead, based on the value added to the scrapped part. It was believed that the majority of the processes that added value also produced more scrap. If, for instance, the screw machine department added $.50 of labor and overhead cost to a part that was subsequently scrapped, the screw machine department received $.50 of scrap in its overhead. The results of this, admittedly post hoc, method seemed reasonable. The processes that were known to create scrap coincidentally received large scrap assignments.

Procurement

Initially, the team assigned receiving, receiving inspection, and purchasing costs to the first department requiring the purchased materials (cost assignments were based on the number of receipts and purchase orders). This approach was mistaken. To conduct make/buy analyses, the team needed to quantify the costs of procuring material. Therefore, the team removed procurement costs from each process's overhead, and assigned the costs directly to incoming materials based on the number of batches ordered and received. Assigning procurement costs in this manner allowed the team to calculate how much each procurement transaction cost. These transaction costs, when added to the purchase price, give a clear picture of the total landed cost of buying material.

Some indirect costs were difficult to assign. Departments such as industrial engineering, manufacturing engineering, and facilities engineering had no clear records or measures of where they spent their time. In addition, much of their work was spent on one-time projects. You would like to think that the support departments spent the majority of their time in the departments where the majority of costs are incurred, but this was not the case. Projects seemed to be randomly spread throughout the factory. The industrial engineering (IE) department used to complete IE work orders that the supervisor felt would have been a good measure, but these forms had been discontinued as needlessly bureaucratic. The team was forced to rely on each engineering department's supervisor's best estimate of how much support each production department received.

Management costs were another problem. Managers had difficulty relating their work to particular activities, with the exception of being able to estimate time spent on new products. However, lacking any alternative, the team still used surveys to allocate these problem costs.

Dealing with Nonmanufacturing Costs

The study identified some elements of the factory's overhead as not being manufacturing related at all. These costs represented introducing new products and supporting the foreign plants. These costs were included in the local plant's manufacturing overhead, despite the fact that they were not their costs. So the team created separate categories for new product introductions, and the support each of its new plants required. (Superior was establishing one plant overseas and one in Mexico.) These three categories consumed more than $1.5 million in expenses per site each year. The inclusion of these costs in the plant's overhead distorted product costs.

Identifying the hidden costs of the overseas operations created quite a row. Only dedicated personnel, supporting the overseas operations, were being charged into these budgets. But during our interview stage, we found many of the managers estimating 40 to 60 percent of their time dealing with overseas problems. The controller admitted that these support costs were ignored to avoid upsetting the president. Reporting these new cost findings had many ramifications. The foreign operations were much more expensive to establish than previously reported, and were not going to deliver anywhere near the forecasted savings. In addition, with all of the time being spent on the foreign operations, the local facility, with its delivery and quality problems, was shown to be neglected.

Data Analysis

After completing the interviews and some additional analysis, the team reviewed with departmental supervisors the cost distributions they had gleaned from the interviews. The supervisors were asked whether the cost distribution reflected how their people spent their time. These reviews improved the accuracy of the activity-based costing and gained departmental concurrence. In most cases, the supervisors recommended some minor changes.

After seeing the distribution of which departments the janitors were charging, the maintenance supervisor adjusted it. He commented that it was difficult enough to get the non-English-speaking janitors to punch in, much less charge the correct department. He said that janitors habitually charged departments that were centrally located. The initial cost distribution did not represent how the janitors worked.

The traditional allocation schemes are compared with the ABC assignments in Exhibit 6-3. In general, the recosting shifted overhead from the labor-intensive to capital-intensive departments. There were dramatic swings in some departments' overhead expense. Punch press's and autopolishing's overhead increased by $1 million each. Knob and inner assembly's overhead decreased by $900,000 and $300,000, respectively.

COSTING PIECE PARTS

At this point, the team originally intended to end its analysis. The team had developed total manufacturing overhead for each department, believing that this was sufficient for a make/buy analysis. They intended to compare the total cost of each department with the total bid from outside vendors for all of the department's parts. If this approach was followed, it would have not been necessary to assign the department's overhead to each piece part. However, Superior's president insisted that the team cost each and every piece part.

Exhibit 6-3   **FIRST STAGE OVERHEAD ASSIGNMENT METHODS**

Type	Rationale	
	Before	After
Maintenance	Depreciation	Time Card Changes
Tooling	Depreciation	Time Card Changes
Scrap	Excluded	Scrapped Parts Explosion
Utilities	Depreciation	Facilities Engineering Study
Support Engineering (i.e., M.E., T.E.)	Earned Hours	Management Survey/ Activity Review
Quality Control	Earned Hours	Inspector's Department Assignment
Warehousing	Earned Hours	Stores Issues
Shop & Production Control	Earned Hours	Material Issues
Purchasing & Receiving	Earned Hours	Purchase Orders

How Do Parts Absorb Cost?

Therefore, the team needed an effective method to allocate costs to each part. Likewise, the team knew something had to be done about Superior's product line. The breadth of the product line would bog down any outsourcing or streamlining efforts. The 1,200 parts in the punch press department, many with annual requirements of fewer than 1,000 parts per year, would scare off many potential vendors, as well as take years to make the transition to a vendor. Despite knowing intuitively that Superior's product line would have to be trimmed, the team knew they would have to prove it to Superior's "by the numbers" president with dollars and cents. Therefore, costing the piece parts would have to show the high cost of low-volume parts, which would provide the justification to eliminate them.

Accordingly, the team examined how the parts were processed, and determined what drove their costs. While many costs were driven by production volume, many were not. It occurred to the team that many production costs such as setup, planning, inspection, and material handling were caused by production changeovers or batches (i.e., moving a batch of parts into or out of a work center).

Splitting the Costs into Volume and Batches

On a personnel computer spreadsheet, the team created a matrix with all costs split by production department. Each row represented a production department, and each column represented a support department's budget. The team segregated the support cost assignments into either volume or batch costs for each production department.

The team had spirited discussions deciding whether a given support cost was volume or batch driven. Some costs such as direct labor, maintenance, utilities, tool repair, and operating supplies were driven by volume; other costs such as setup, planning, scheduling, warehousing, shop floor control, and tool cleaning were driven by batches. Some costs such as fringe benefits and equipment depreciation had to be split. Fringe benefits were driven by whatever the touch labor operators were working on. The fringe benefits were split between volume and batches according to the percentage of time operators spent setting up machines, versus direct labor operations. In the same way, equipment depreciation was split by the percentage of time the machines were down for changeovers, versus making production.

One large cost pool that was debated was lost labor efficiency. Where lost labor efficiency is the difference between the earned standard labor hours and actual direct labor hours extended. Some team members took the traditional view that this lost time should be spread over products on production volume, as if to represent a department realization. However, others argued that the principal reason operators did not make standard was that their work stopped before they reached the bottom of the learning curve. These people argued that lost labor efficiency was driven by production changeovers. With each production changeover, learning curve efficiency was lost, and a new product had to be learned. A worker had to change over to new materials or dies, a factor that was not reflected in the setup times. In addition, with a disruption in the process, workers were more likely to take a break. The assumption here is that the principal reason operators did not meet standards was because their work was disrupted by production changeovers. This is also the basic assumption on which Fredrick Taylor developed labor standards. Every worker should meet standards if not interrupted. Therefore, the cost of this lost efficiency was assigned on batches.

Most frequently, the other reasons a production run is interrupted were that the operators ran out of material, or ran into a production problem. These problems were more prevalent in infrequently run parts than in high production units, where lost labor was not related to volume. Likewise, these costs were driven by batches.

Calculating the Rates

Then the team consolidated each activity center's costs into two pools—a volume pool and a batch pool. The volume pools totaled 56 percent of manufacturing overhead, while batch costs were 44 percent. The volume pools in the fabrication and finishing departments were assigned to products based on each product's machine hours. In the assembly departments, these volume pools were distributed on direct labor hours.

The batch pool included all the costs driven by production changeovers (i.e., batches). Every time a machine was changed to produce a different part, the change-over had to be planned, a setup was triggered, material was moved, etc. These costs were assigned on production changeovers.

The team's MIS analyst created a part database on the company's mainframe computer. The team would apply last year's costs against this database. The database was calculated by multiplying last year's end unit sales history, adjusted for changes in inventory, times all of the end unit's bills of material. This created a listing of each piece part manufactured, as well as its quantity. By multiplying the quantity times each part's machine hours or labor hours, the computer calculated each part's volume. Then, using each part's routing, the MIS department calculated the number of standard labor hours worked by each assembly department, and the number of standard machine hours experienced in the fabrication and finishing departments during the prior year. These hours represented each department's production output. The team divided each department's volume cost pool by these hours to calculate a volume rate for each production department. Calculating the number of changeovers was less straightforward.

A part number creates a changeover every time a batch is run, in each department the part passes through. Using Superior's inventory planning rules, the number of production runs for each part received could be calculated. According to the inventory planning rules, high volume parts were run every four weeks or 13 times a year. The medium volume parts were run once a quarter, or four times a year, while the low-volume parts were run twice a year. In fact, the team discovered some parts that were run once a year. Therefore, the team created a fourth category for parts receiving one transaction per year.

To calculate the number of transactions performed last year, a program was written for the mainframe. Using Superior's production volume for each part, the inventory planning rules, and their routings, the mainframe calculated each part's trans-actions, as well as each department's transaction count—the number of changeovers that each experienced last year. This transaction count was assigned to each department that the part passed through. For example, part 12-12534-001 is a high-volume part with 13 transactions a year. Since this part goes through the punch press and secondary operations departments, each of these departments receives 13 transactions.

By dividing each department's batch pool by the total number of transactions, a batch rate for each department was calculated. For instance, the die-cast department ran 1,140 batches and had a batch pool of $800,000, for a batch rate of $702 per batch. Hence, $702 was incurred every time a batch of parts was cast in the die-cast department. This cost consisted of setup, inspection, production planning, scheduling, warehousing, and all the other costs driven by batches of parts moving into, and out of, the departments. Therefore, each batch was assigned $702, which was am-ortized across the number of units in that batch.

Assembly Is Different

Superior could not use inventory planning rules to calculate the number of transactions in the assembly departments. The assembly departments built to order, not to stock. The assembly departments only built a particular batch of parts when a customer order was received for them—assuming that every time a customer order contained a particular part number it triggered an assembly transaction. The team calculated the number of customer orders containing each assembly part number. This count was used for assembly transactions.

In retrospect, this method was wrong. It overstated the number of assembly transactions. In fact, an assembly transaction was not triggered every time a part was ordered. The assembly departments had in-process stocking of subassemblies. Only when a subassembly stocking location ran out of parts was an assembly transaction triggered. A customer order was almost always assembled, not from individual parts as the team assumed, but stocked subassemblies. The transactions for the assembly departments should have been calculated from the number of customer orders containing each assembly part number, divided by the batch size in each stocking location.

Superior's ABC system architecture is shown in Exhibit 6-4. The system had 42 activity centers. Each had a volume and a batch overhead assignment to parts.

Exhibit 6-4   **THE ABC STRUCTURE USED AT SUPERIOR**

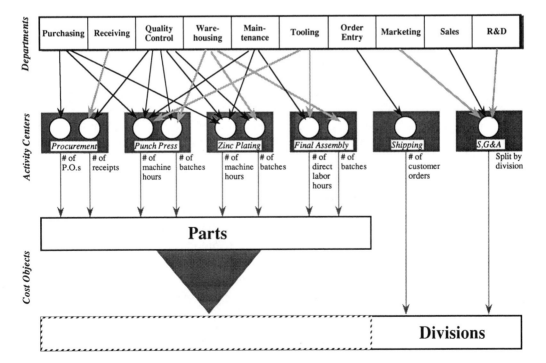

However, three activity centers—production planning, purchasing, and receiving—assigned costs on work orders, POs and receipts. In addition, all sales, engineering, and general and administrative costs were assigned directly to the different divisions for divisional profitability analysis.

These batch and volume rates were then entered into Superior's mainframe and used to create a cost database for all last year's parts. An ABC cost was calculated for each part. The part's per unit volume was multiplied by the volume rate, and the transaction count was multiplied by the batch rate. This batch cost was then amortized across the number of parts produced. These calculations were performed for each department through which the part passed. In Exhibit 6-5, the total part cost is shown to be the sum of the material cost, plus the labor cost and the two overhead assignments (volume and batch).

The high-volume or "A part," 12-03121-003 is run in 13 batches a year. Therefore, the part has a total of $9,389.90 (13 × $722.30) in batch costs assigned to it. This batch overhead is then spread across the part's 1,292,929 annual production to calculate the part's batch cost per unit. The part's volume overhead is simply the part's machine hours times the die-cast machine hour rate.

Part 12-03123-003 is a low-volume part that is only run in two batches during the year. Therefore, this part's batch cost is $1,444.60 (2 × $722.30). This cost is then amortized across the part's 21,191 parts for a per piece cost of $.07. As you can see, even though the low-volume part only incurred two transactions, its per unit batch cost is significantly higher per unit.

The ABC System Developed

The ABC system at Superior only included manufacturing costs in part costs. Yet, the system developed had 42 activity centers—which seems like a lot, but the company has over 70 different departments. The system has 22 first-stage cost drivers and 62 second-stage cost drivers. Each production department had two cost drivers: a volume and a batch driver. Plus, the system assigned production planning costs on work orders, procurement costs on purchase orders, and receiving costs on receipts (see Exhibit 6-6 for a listing of all second-stage drivers).

Two-Driver Activity Center

I believe that this approach, using two cost drivers for each activity center (one for volume-related costs and one for batch-related costs) is superior to all the other ABC architectures I have seen. Every activity center needs a batch driver to compensate for setup costs and other nonvalue-added changeover costs. By assigning costs on batches, the system encourages a reduction in these nonvalue-added costs. With only two drivers, the system is kept simple and consistent across the whole company. In addition, the two-driver approach allows you to create bills of activity with ease. You merely add a new overhead assignment to every activity center in

Exhibit 6-5   **CALCULATING A PART'S ABC COST**

**CALCULATING A PIECE PART COST
IN SUPERIOR'S ACTIVITY-BASED COST SYSTEM**

DIE CAST PART: 12-03121-012

BATCH OVERHEAD CALCULATION:
MRP CODE: C = 13 BATCHES PER YEAR
DIE CAST BATCH COST = $722.3/BATCH

TOTAL BATCH COST:
$722.3 X 13 = $9,389.9

ANNUAL QUANTITY: 1,292,929

BATCH COST (PER UNIT):	($9,389.9/1,292,929)
	$0.00726
LABOR COST:	
(.0008977 X $13.1)	$0.01176
MACHINE HOUR OVERHEAD COST:	
(.00066 X $37.38)	$0.02467
MATERIAL COST:	$0.04376
ABC COST PER ACTIVITY	$0.08745

DIE CAST PART: 12-03120-003

BATCH OVERHEAD CALCULATION:
MRP CODE: C = 2 BATCHES PER YEAR
DIE CAST BATCH COST = $722.3/BATCH

TOTAL BATCH COST:
$722.3 X 2 = $1,444.6

ANNUAL QUANTITY: 21,191

BATCH COST (PER UNIT):	($1,444.6/21,191)
	$0.06817
LABOR COST:	
(.001253 X $13.1)	$0.01641
MACHINE HOUR OVERHEAD COST:	
(.000853 X $37.38)	$0.03189
MATERIAL COST:	$0.03788
ABC COST PER UNIT	$0.15435

Exhibit 6-6 **SECOND-STAGE COST DRIVER LISTING**

ACTIVITY CENTER - COST DRIVER	C/D POOL (in $000)	C/D RATE (in $/CD unit)
SWISS AUTO. - MACHINE HRS	$144	$38.1
SWISS AUTO. - BATCHES	$74	$185.1
COLD HEADERS - MACHINE HRS	$921	$127.7
COLD HEADERS - BATCHES	$218	$504.2
DIE CAST - MACHINE HRS	$791	$73.2
DIE CAST - BATCHES	$238	$714.8
DELRIN MOLDING - MACHINE HRS	$472	$69.2
DELRIN MOLDING - BATCHES	$181	$427.5
SCREW MACHINES - BATCHES	$755	$246.3
SCREW MACHINES - MACHINE HRS	$1,926	$55.6
PUNCH PRESS - MACHINE HRS	$3,620	$97.0
PUNCH PRESS - BATCHES	$702	$112.2
POWER WASH - BATCHES	$194	$19.2
POWER WASH - MACHINE HRS	$419	$51.2
THREADING - MACHINE HRS	$1,029	$52.3
THREADING - BATCHES	$275	$168.4
2ND OPERATIONS - MACHINE HRS	$1,014	$31.0
2ND OPERATIONS - BATCHES	$299	$121.7
ANODIZING - MACHINE HRS	$506	$148.6
ANODIZING - BATCHES	$95	$280.9
BURNISHING - BATCHES	$317	$54.0
BURNISHING - MACHINE HRS	$528	$59.5
CHROME PLATING - MACHINE HRS	$875	$62.4
CHROME PLATING - BATCHES	$396	$109.8
ENAMELING - BATCHES	$785	$73.8
ENAMELING - MACHINE HRS	$1,444	$41.4
DC PLATING - MACHINE HRS	$738	$257.1
DC PLATING - BATCHES	$206	$210.7
ZINC PLATING - MACHINE HRS	$857	$102.9
ZINC PLATING - BATCHES	$182	$43.0
HAND POLISH - BATCHES	$955	$122.2
HAND POLISH - LABOR HRS	$1,073	$24.5
AUTO POLISHING - MACHINE HRS	$2,226	$101.7
AUTO POLISHING - BATCHES	$690	$324.7
HAND PLATING - BATCHES	$96	$120.5
HAND PLATING - MACHINE HRS	$551	$321.4
BARREL PLATING - MACHINE HRS	$573	$231.0
BARREL PLATING - BATCHES	$120	$77.9
VALVE ASSY - BATCHES	$992	$1.6
VALVE ASSY - LABOR HRS	$2,351	$19.6
INDUCT VALVE ASSY - LABOR HRS	$2,017	$19.2
INDUCT VALVE ASSY - BATCHES	$545	$0.7
L SERIES ASSY - BATCHES	$415	$2.9
HI VOL ASSY - LABOR HRS	$892	$21.0
HI VOL ASSY - BATCHES	$426	$4.5
K SERIES ASSY - LABOR HRS	$504	$19.6
K SERIES ASSY - BATCHES	$354	$2.3
E SERIES ASSY - BATCHES	$241	$3.3
E SERIES ASSY - LABOR HRS	$511	$22.0
INNER ASSY - LABOR HRS	$1,288	$19.5
INNER ASSY - BATCHES	$759	$4.6
M SERIES ASSY - LABOR HRS	$284	$21.3
M SERIES ASSY - BATCHES	$210	$1.7
S SERIES ASSY - BATCHES	$268	$5.0
S SERIES ASSY - LABOR HRS	$321	$16.7
X SERIES ASSY - BATCHES	$136	$2.6
X SERIES ASSY - LABOR HRS	$213	$22.4
KNOB ASSY - LABOR HRS	$538	$34.5
KNOB ASSY - BATCHES	$250	$2.3
# OF WORK ORDERS	$927	$8.2
# OF RECEIPTS	$486	$18.7
# OF P.O.S	$247	$10.7

the manufacturing routing. This approach allows one to create bills of activity automatically from the manufacturing routings. This is a critically important feature
to keeping the initial development and ongoing maintenance burden low and data
integrity high. However, setups and other batch costs such as material handling are
not perfectly correlated. Warehousing moves do not correspond with production
setups when batches are very large. If a batch is very large, it is moved through the
shop in multiple loads, so there are more moves than setups. Therefore, assigning
warehousing moves on setups understates warehousing costs. Yet, with large batch
sizes this undercosting is insignificant—the cost distortion disappears when amortized across a large batch. For example, say a large batch, 100,000 units, requires
three moves instead of one. At a move cost of $26 per batch, the ABC system
undercosts the batch by $52 or $.000052 per part—an insignificant change.

The same argument holds true for other batch costs such as inspection or
receiving; a very large batch may take up more time, yet this distortion is buried when
amortized across the batch. In fact, all of an activity center's batch costs become insignificant when amortized across a large batch. Therefore, consolidating all batch costs
into one pool induces an insignificant change, while substantially reducing system
complexity.

The ABC Results

When the company's part costs were recalculated to include batch costs, the
costs of low-volume parts skyrocketed. Exhibit 6-7 shows the per-piece cost of parts
with similar configurations but different volumes, under the traditional cost system
and ABC. As you can see, under the traditional system, as volume drops the per-
piece costs rise slightly. However, this rise is nowhere close to the cost escalation
the ABC system reports. Under ABC some parts were undercosted by more than
10,000 percent.

When these part costs were accumulated and rolled up by the mainframe into
products, the results were staggering. Product lines thought to be cash cows were
actually losing money. Product lines perceived as mediocre were stars. One high-
volume product's manufacturing cost fell by over 17 percent, while some low-volume
products' costs rose by over 5,000 percent.

To assess the profitability of Superior's different divisions, the general, administration, and sales expenses were also assigned. The R&D costs were split by surveying
the engineering manager as to the number of people working on each division. Sales
and marketing costs were already segregated into divisions. The MIS and accounting
managers estimated the labor power and budget support to each of the divisions.

The new Far East start-up factory was assigned to the commodity division,
since it's products were dedicated for that division.

Exhibit 6-8 displays the changes in each division's manufacturing overhead.
The custom division produced low-volume, customized products which required
large amounts of overhead support. The fabrication division produced both low-

Exhibit 6-7 **A COMPARISON OF TRADITIONAL PART COSTS AND ABC COSTS**

COMPARING THE UNIT COST OF SIMILAR PART NUMBERS
USING A TRADITIONAL LABOR-BASED VERSUS ACTIVITY-
BASED COST SYSTEM

SCREW MACHINE PARTS

ANNUAL QUANTITY	TRADITIONAL COST (PER PIECE)	ABC COST (PER PIECE)	% CHANGE
2,013,351	$0.13776	$0.11553	-16.1%
1,115,148	$0.17008	$0.13959	-17.9%
234,548	$0.17727	$0.15895	-10.3%
169,798	$0.13424	$0.13432	0.1%
118,385	$0.16501	$0.16962	2.8%
92,758	$0.19130	$0.20372	6.5%
49,119	$0.14032	$0.14182	1.1%
37,014	$0.17971	$0.16538	-8.0%
33,848	$0.12253	$0.13750	12.2%
11,318	$0.14660	$0.17574	19.9%
7,859	$0.11739	$0.17038	45.1%
4,869	$0.13335	$0.22962	72.2%
395	$0.15033	$0.85316	467.5%
119	$0.25410	$5.10924	1910.7%
26	$0.26044	$22.65385	8598.3%

INJECTION MOLDING

ANNUAL QUANTITY	TRADITIONAL COST (PER PIECE)	ABC COST (PER PIECE)	% CHANGE
9,587,987	$0.00919	$0.00939	2.2%
6,062,170	$0.01243	$0.01303	4.8%
5,248,411	$0.01274	$0.01303	2.3%
1,540,566	$0.04929	$0.05185	5.2%
974,739	$0.02961	$0.03260	10.1%
613,444	$0.01576	$0.02437	54.6%
107,459	$0.03542	$0.05028	42.0%
49,575	$0.05805	$0.09004	55.1%
20,738	$0.03464	$0.05264	52.0%
8,660	$0.09437	$0.19111	102.5%
888	$0.47055	$2.42005	414.3%
6	$0.01693	$73.00000	431087.2%

and high-volume fabricated parts for the company's Canadian subsidiary. The electronic division was a new venture and, at this point, dedicated production and test production principally consisted of prototypes. This division also required many new skills, such as electrical engineers, component buyers, and electronics inspectors, and equipment that had nothing in common with the rest of Superior's operations. However,

Exhibit 6-8   **SUPERIOR FAUCET'S CHANGES IN MANUFACTURING OVERHEAD BY DIVISION**

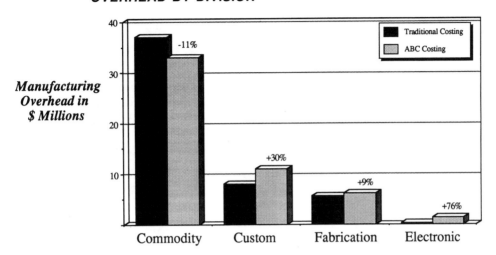

under the traditional cost system, the electronic division received its overhead allocation based on its miniscule direct labor content. Therefore, the division's cost was greatly understated.

Exhibit 6-9 shows the changes in divisional profitability. Results revealed that the custom division was losing 30 percent of sales. The "Commodity" division was making more money than expected. While not shown, changes in individual product lines and end items costs were as high as 10,000%.

The team identified the custom division and certain low-volume product lines as unintended loss leaders. The ABC analysis also shifted manufacturing overhead to the capital intense fabrication departments. With this new overhead information, many manufacturing processes appeared ripe for outsourcing. Using the cost database, the team presented the various manufacturing options to Superior's senior management. By identifying the overhead associated with each product, the team was able to simulate the effects of pruning the product offering on the company's cost structure. The team ran the company's annual requirements, less items to be discontinued. The inventory planning rules then calculated new activity levels for this product offering. The team assumed that only the sales of the product lines that were discontinued would be lost. Multiplying these new activity levels by the cost driver rates would calculate new costs. Since the manufacturing strategy would be implemented over a number of years, all costs were assumed to be variable. If the punch press department were outsourced, its equipment would be sold and its floor space redeployed. The total of these costs would be the company's total cost.

Competitive bids from outside vendors were used to calculate savings from outsourcing. Actual JIT and maquiladora case studies were used to estimate the

Exhibit 6-9 **SUPERIOR FAUCET'S CHANGES IN RETURN ON SALES BY DIVISION**

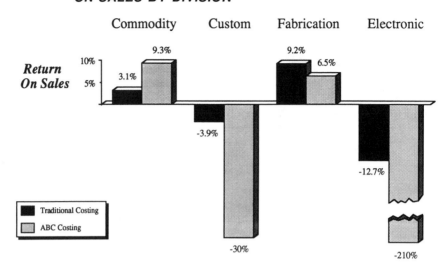

overhead savings that each of these options would bring. Considering different product combinations, the team generated different activity levels from which new costs were calculated. These new activity levels, savings estimates, and sales numbers allowed the team to create a series of product and facility options, showing superior's cost, sales, and profitability. After developing these simulated costs, the team validated these cost estimates by calculating the number of people the new plant configuration would require. This allowed Superior's executives to validate intuitively the recommendations and savings estimates.

SUPERIOR CONDUCTS A MARKET SURVEY

Early during the study, the consultants came to the conclusion that Superior must prune its product line. Superior had too many low-volume products. Many vendors would simply refuse to bid all of Superior's work, or bid them at outrageous prices. The consultants also knew that their cost study would show these low-volume products as loss leaders. Therefore, the consultants were convinced that Superior must reduce its product offering.

Yet the consultants were acutely aware that a poorly implemented product line reduction could have a devastating impact on a company's market position. Therefore, the consultants pushed for Superior to undertake a product line survey of its customers. The president refused. He believed that the product line needed to be looked at, but it was not a pressing issue. The consultants disagreed; they believed a successful implementation of the manufacturing strategy depended on rationalizing the product line.

The consultants badgered the president into authorizing a market survey of its customers. The study was conducted without revealing Superior's name. Superior did not want to taint the results, or indicate to the market any of the actions that Superior was considering. The interviews, as well as mailed questionnaires, were used to ask a variety of questions. The study asked the customers what product lines a faucet manufacturer must offer to satisfy their needs. The customers were asked to rank the attributes that were most important in their buying decision. The market study surveyed the customers for their opinion of Superior and its competitors.

This study was of immense value. The study put the voice of the customer into the strategy decision making process. This study determined the importance of product line breadth (see Exhibit 6-10) and which products the market required. The survey found that rapid delivery was much more important to customers than product line breadth. The team knew that delivery performance and customer service would improve with a narrower product offering. Low-volume products are always the ones that hold up shipments. Not only do low-volume products get the lowest priority when scheduling the factory, but they have the greatest demand variability and, therefore, most frequently have part shortages. By eliminating these low-volume products, fewer shipments would be held up and product lead times would fall because machines would be tied up with fewer setups.

Surprisingly, the study found that Superior was perceived by customers as having the narrowest product offering in the industry, when, in fact, from the manufacturing standpoint, Superior had the broadest. From the manufacturing viewpoint, Superior's products could be assembled in more ways than any competitor's products.

Exhibit 6-10 **CUSTOMER VALUE SURVEY RESULTS**

Average Rating By Survey Participant

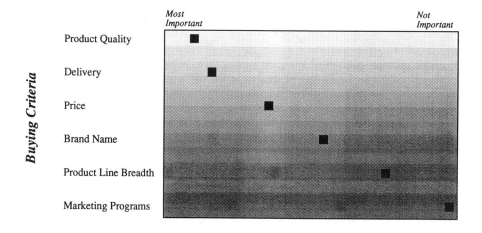

However, this distinction was lost on the customers. It appeared that customers viewed product line breadth not as manufacturing permutations, but as the number of styles offered. Thus, Superior could cut its manufacturing permutations, lower overhead costs, and, at the same time, improve its customers' perception of its product line by reducing the number of options, finishes, and functions offered, but adding more styles.

Superior's Turnaround

Superior decided to turn the company around by undertaking four major programs: divesting a division, reducing the product offering, focusing the factory, and outsourcing some of the fabrication departments. The analysis estimated that these actions would raise Superior's return on sales from a lethargic 4 percent to an incredible 20 percent!

Selling the Custom Division

The Custom Division manufactured an extremely wide variety of products. Unfortunately, these low-volume products caused an inordinate amount of overhead. Because the Custom Division and the Commodity Division were both in the same factory, the large overhead pool was spread across all of the company's products. The commodity division was subsidizing the custom division. To make matters worse, the Custom Division produced low-volume products in a high-volume plant. Consequently, the factory always gave the custom products second priority, upsetting the Custom Division's customer with inconsistent delivery and service. These factors encumbered the custom division so much that it was denied the chance to ever become a successful business.

Therefore, the Custom Division was sold for $10 million, a price based on the traditional cost system's reported profit and loss. Within two weeks of the Custom Division's divestiture, the factory's production throughput rose 20 percent, to an all-time high. Moreover, the Custom Division's new owners were able to focus the factory and configure it for rapid customer response. New machines were bought with quick changeover times, and the product offering was cut. These actions dramatically improved its delivery performance. The smaller focused factory permitted big cuts in overhead, too. To everyone's amazement, within four months, the custom business was made profitable.

Shrinking the Product Offering

The ABC system reported losses from a number of the Commodity divisions low-volume product options. Therefore, Superior discontinued a number of low-volume, money-losing product lines and options. Removing these offerings reduced net sales by 3 percent, but slashed Superior's active part numbers by 87 percent. The punch press department saw the number of stamped parts fall from 1,250 to 341, while part numbers requiring polishing decreased from 1,930 to 300.

Shrinking the product line is usually the surest route to higher profits and improved cash flow in a turnaround company. Turnaround experts contend that the earliest signal of a company headed for trouble is a proliferation of products. Proliferating products consume overhead and load up the balance sheet with slow-moving inventory. As sales grow, the company's ability to compete declines. Yet, many businessmen see sales growth as synonymous with success. However, growth is not synonymous with success.

Focusing the Factory

The next major element of Superior's strategy was focusing the factory. The commodity division produced both build-to-stock and assemble-to-order products. Although these two product types are incompatible from a manufacturing process perspective, they were being manufactured side by side. By segregating these two product types into their own "factories-within-a-factory," manufacturing systems for both product types could be streamlined. The build-to-stock factory would concentrate on reducing costs by using high throughput machines. The assemble-to-order factory would concentrate on quickly assembling products from stocked components. Each factory would have different systems to support different needs. This would cut costs and improve customer service.

Vertical Disintegration

Seven processes were outsourced saving $2 million a year. Superior, with so many diverse processes, was unable to remain competitive in all these technologies. Therefore, Superior found small, focused vendors with minimal overhead to make the parts currently manufactured in-house.

For example, Superior's die-cast operation consisted of only four die-casters. The industry rule of thumb is that six machines are required for minimum economical operation. The team found that half of Superior's die casting was already being bought from vendors because the internal operation lacked the capacity or skill to perform the work. The die-cast vendor selected, had many advantages over Superior's operation. The vendor was also another division of the parent company. The vendor not only had newer equipment with process controls, but had preventive maintenance and die rehabilitation programs. The vendor controlled critical quality variables like the ratio of remelt to raw material and had a testing lab to sample all incoming materials. These advantages allowed Superior to cut die-casting costs by 7 percent in the first year, while receiving higher quality components. In addition, this outsourcing raised shareholder value, freed up fixed assets, and cut in-process inventory, and provided a surge of cash for Superior. Superior divested underperforming assets, lowered inventory levels, and avoided future capital investments.

Overall, ABC allowed Superior to save $8 million a year, while improving customer service and making the company more competitive. In addition, all the changes were consistent with and supported the company's business strategy. Superior was focusing its business away from the builder market and toward the retail market. Builders required greater product variety and allowed longer lead times. Retailers, on the other hand, made their money by quickly turning their inventory. Therefore, the retailer desired quick delivery of only a limited number of fast-turning items. By slimming down the product line, volume would increase on the items left, and service would improve on all items.

To achieve these savings, management cut not only the activity levels, but then had to slash employment. As the work went away, management had to follow up the drop in activity by cutting out the costs—the people. Management had to redo the lay out of the factory to consolidate floor space. This allowed a portion of the factory to be leased out. Some of the costs like material, utilities, and supplies would simply disappear as their requirements—activities—disappeared.

After concluding the study and embarking in a new strategic direction, Superior's management was dismayed to discover its engineers still designing products based on the discredited standard cost system. In spite of an extensive training program on the new ABC system, the engineers were neither standardizing parts nor developing quick changeover machines. They were still squeezing out seconds of direct labor. On further investigation, the president discovered the ABC study's findings were having little or no impact on operational decision making. Superior had used ABC to set its strategic direction, but wasn't using it to streamline processes or standardize designs. The president realized the only way to ingrain ABC for operational decision making was to retire the traditional system and convert the company to an integrated ABC system. Therefore, the president instructed the controller to replace their traditional cost system with an ABC system.

CHAPTER 7

EXCEL MEDICAL—THE CASE OF THE MISSING DISTRIBUTION STRATEGY

Businessmen go down with their businesses because they like the old way so well they cannot bring themselves to change . . . Seldom does the cobbler take up with a newfangled way of soling shoes and seldom does the artisan willingly take up with new methods in his trade.

Henry Ford, My Life and Work, 1922

Up to this time, most companies implementing ABC have concentrated their attention on manufacturing costs. In manufacturing, most companies already have existing cost systems and feel greater comfort. They have ignored customer-driven costs. In the few ABC installations that have included sales and general and administrative costs, the systems treated these costs as extensions of product costs. However, this case shows how one company developed an ABC system for customer-driven costs and its powerful effects.

The genesis of distribution cost systems dates back to the 1950s and early 1960s. Yet, few companies have bothered to implement these systems, even though, over the years, consulting firms have charged millions of dollars for conducting just these types of studies.

Interestingly, distribution cost systems resemble ABC systems much more than the traditional manufacturing cost system. This was for two reasons. First, the distribution process lacks a universal measure of volume, such as labor standards, which permeates the organization. Lacking standards, distribution cost systems rely on measures of activity. The second reason is that the distribution process tends to be much more transaction oriented as products pass from one step to the next. Products go from shipping, to trucks, to warehouses, to trucks, to distributors. The cost of each step is much more a batch cost than a volume cost.

This case study will show the powerful effects of tracking customer-driven costs. The case study will describe how a customer-driven ABC system was designed, how the ABC system identified key distribution policies that created cost, and how the new system helped Excel develop a new distribution strategy.

EXCEL MEDICAL—THE BED COMPANY

Excel Medical annually sells $100 million of durable medical equipment (DMC) beds. The company sells no products to end users. The company sells most of its beds directly to its customers (i.e., dealers), while Excel sold the remaining 20 percent through distributors who resell the product. The company served two market segments—home care and rehab products. The method of reimbursement characterizes each of these segments.

Two Markets

The reimbursement method determines how price sensitive the buyer is, and what options the end user can afford. Most home-care beds are bought through Medicare. Medicare has a low ceiling on reimbursement dollars and strict guidelines on options and accessories covered. The private insurers, on the other hand, generally buy rehab beds. Private insurers have a much higher reimbursement cap and permit latitude on the choice of reimbursable options and accessories. The elderly typically use home-care products, while people with debilitating diseases or injury victims use rehab products. Consequently, the rehab patient may spend years in a rehab bed, while the average home-care patient spends less than six months.

Outflanked by the Competition

Excel's chief competitor, GAC, was growing rapidly. Five years earlier GAC had seen the advantage of "bundling" products. At that time, all the durable medical equipment manufacturers sold directly to dealers. GAC noticed the increasing market share of drug distributors. Hospital supply manufacturers, such as Baxter or Johnson & Johnson, no longer served pharmacies directly. These manufacturers were saving money by selling through distributors such as McKesson and Bergen-Brunsick. These distributors by selling, order taking, handling, and delivering hundreds of manufacturer's products, have economies of scale in logistics, unmatched by a single manufacturer. Therefore, the distributors saved the manufacturer money while making a profit. In addition, a national distributor will have 16 to 25 distribution centers across the United States, compared to 4 to 10 for a manufacturer. These geographically dispersed stocking locations provide much faster delivery and more frequent sales calls. GAC correctly foresaw that the same forces would eventually reshape the medical equipment market as well.

GAC saw that it could reduce costs and improve service by providing a full product line to its customers. It began acquiring other durable medical equipment (DME) companies in wheelchairs, disposables, and oxygen. These products filled out GAC's DME product offering. GAC also set up a separate division to become its own distributor. This full product line provided its customers with "one-stop shopping." With its full line, GAC decided to compete across-the-board on price.

For four years, Excel watched GAC's strategy unfold before entering sales agreements with Independent Distributors. Excel had a large, well-paid sales force, and four distribution centers around the United States. In spite of spending a disproportional amount of money on sales and distribution, its customers complained that Excel was "difficult to do business with." At the time, the company was only breaking even, despite being the market share leader.

Excel—Its Own Worst Enemy

Its new agreements resulted in Excel's having competing channels of distribution. Its distributors were trying to sell to the same customers that its own sales force was calling on. When a salesman talked to one of the dealers, the dealer commented that he was the third Excel representative that he had talked to today. The direct Excel salesman, as well as salesmen from two different distributors, had called on the customer that day. Salespeople and competing distributors were fighting over the same customers. Since distributors were new to the durable medical equipment market, many geographic regions did not have any distributors. Consequently, every distributor was trying to develop clients in areas like Atlanta. Atlanta has a high population density and no established distributors (a dense population keeps a distributor's costs low and sales high). Therefore, of Excel's seven distributors, four were fighting for this market. Unfortunately for the manufacturers, it is illegal to restrict distributors to a particular region. Therefore, Excel's distributors were fighting for the same business. Since all the distributors sold the same product, they typically competed on price, creating extreme pressure on Excel's prices.

In addition, unless distributor and dealer pricing is established very carefully, distributors, with their higher discount, can undercut a manufacturer's direct sales to the independent dealers. This phenomenon is called *vacuuming* the sales base. Since distributors have lower margins, their vacuuming of Excel's direct customers transforms dealers from high-margin sales to low-margin sales. This creates market confusion, needless price pressure, and erodes profits. Unwittingly, Excel had not set its discount strategy with this phenomenon in mind. Consequently, its distributors were vacuuming many of Excel's customers.

What's Excel to Do?

Given GAC's "one-stop" shopping and Excel's competitive position, how should Excel distribute its products? To develop a new distribution strategy, Excel chartered a multidisciplinary team. The team needed to understand Excel's distribution costs, as well as the customers' needs to develop this new strategy. To understand Excel's costs, the team undertook an ABC study of Excel's customer-driven costs. The study would identify the real cost of serving its customers through each channel. The team conducting the ABC study had two people assigned full time. The consultant and the financial analyst had four weeks to develop the cost model and another three weeks to conduct all the necessary analysis. Concurrently, other members of the team developed and conducted surveys of Excel's customers.

UNDERTAKING AN ABC DISTRIBUTION STUDY

The ABC study consisted of

- Classifying customers into groups
- Collecting cost data
- Interviewing management
- Selecting cost drivers
- Applying and analyzing costs
- Making a new strategy recommendation

Classifying Customers into Groups

To make sense out of Excel's 2,000 individual customers and simplify the analysis, the team first defined customer groupings. Typically, a company's marketing group has some customer classifications already, but I recommend validating them. Frequently, these classifications are out of date or inconsistent.

The customers are segregated into major groups that represent different buying characteristics, end users, service requirements, packaging needs, sales volumes, product mixes, etc. In this case, we will say that there were five customer classifications:

- Distributors: These are product resellers who stock products, make sales calls, take orders, deliver products, and collect payments.
- National accounts: The national accounts are large multilocation health care institutions like the Veterans Administration, Kaiser Permanente, or other HMOs. These customers buy large fleets of home-care products for internal use, as well as sell some rehab products to patients.
- Independent dealers: The independent dealers are small, unsophisticated, "Mom and Pop" stores that sell durable medical equipment directly to end users.
- Buying groups: These are groups of dealers who form a cooperative to leverage their buying power to obtain large discounts when negotiating

sales contracts. With the exception of averaging slightly larger sales per store, these dealers are identical to independent dealers.

- Rehabilitation centers: These are independent medical clinics that specialize in helping seriously disabled people adapt to a new life. The centers are paid for by either the end user or private insurers.

One problem that plagued the study team throughout the study was Excel's marketing department. Marketing, on more than one occasion, changed the classification of individual accounts from one customer group to the next. This indecision caused the team a substantial amount of rework on the analysis. (Excel's marketing department's reclassifications were a cost driver for the ABC team.)

Collecting the Cost Data

The ABC structure for this study is a two-stage model, similar to the structure of a product-driven study. The structure defined each step in the distribution channel, or major function, as an activity center. In this case, the team defined the activity centers as

Distribution	$4.1 million
Customer service	2.1
Sales	1.8
Discounts	3.2
Marketing	3.9
R&D	2.3
General and Administrative	1.5
Total	$18.9 million

The team developed a spreadsheet to assign costs to each of the customer groups. From Excel's cost records the team already had most of the costs assigned to departments:

- Salaries and wages
- Utilities
- Rent
- Supplies
- Equipment depreciation
- Information systems charges
- Freight

To get the full cost of each department, the team added occupancy costs on square footage. Fringe benefits were added as a percentage of payroll dollars and medical insurance costs were calculated based on the number of people in each department. The team also added financing charges for finished goods and accounts receivable at a cost of 12 percent (per the controller). The team found many customers with their own private label products (unique products for only one customer that carried the customer's label and not Excel's), which created a large finished goods inventory. Accounts receivable were also large and varied substantially by channel. Some accounts were more than 180 days outstanding. Therefore, the team accounted for both costs in the analysis.

Interviewing Management

The team interviewed representatives from each of the activity centers to determine the functions that each department performed, how the department was organized, and what measures could be used to assign its costs. The team asked each manager:

- How is your department organized?
- Can the team have an organization chart with head count listed?
- What increases or decreases each group's work?
- How is the department's work measured?

So much computer work was needed that the team was assigned a management information systems (MIS) analyst full time. After the interviews, the team would discuss with the MIS analyst what measures the MIS system recorded. The team identified cost drivers and fed back the cost distribution to the managers for concurrence. If the managers agreed, the team would use the results; if not, the team discussed the results and where they had gone astray.

Selecting Cost Drivers

Distribution Activity Centers

Excel shipped from the factory and four distribution centers around the company. The team split the distribution function into eight cost pools. The shipping office created the bills of lading, coordinated pickup with the shipper, scheduled the dock, and reconciled freight charges. The first cost driver was the number of bills of lading. This cost driver assigned all the shipping office costs. While a bill of lading with ten items took longer to process than a bill with two, the team believed this difference was insignificant. Clerks in the shipping office spent most of their time confirming customer information and arranging shipment. Therefore, the analyst used the distribution requirements planning (DRP) system to calculate the number of bills of lading each customer group had created for Excel last year. Then she calculated an average cost per bill and assigned these costs to customers.

The next pool was the shipping dock. The shipping dock collected all the items required by the bill of lading. The team observed the forklift operators. They spent most of their time traveling back and forth from pick locations to the consolidation point. Their work appeared correlated with the number of pick locations. One line item equaled a pick location that the forklifts must visit. The team saw little difference if the operator picked up a single unit or a pallet using the forklift. Therefore, the number of line items, and not the number of items, drove the handling costs.

The team used two different ways to assign the costs of holding finished goods. Since private labels were held for individual customers, the team assigned this inventory directly to the name on the side of the bed. Multiplying the value of the private label inventory by the cost of money created the inventory charge. The team assigned the rest of the finished goods to the market segment that the product was from. Based on the number of units of that market type bought, the team assigned costs to each customer group. Spare parts shipping consisted of pulling, packing, and processing each order. The team assigned its costs on number of customer orders shipped.

The only difference between assigning the shipping department's costs and that of the distribution centers (DCs) was that the system assigned DC costs only to units that pass through them. Excel shipped beds directly to customers in the Eastern United States from the factory; therefore, these products did not incur any DC costs. Since units had to get to the DCs, units shipped through the DCs also had the freight costs of shipping beds from the factory to the DCs assigned on the weight of each unit.

Freight records were a shambles: There were supply charges in the general ledger's freight accounts, and freight in the wrong accounts. The team reconstructed last year's total freight bill from shipper-provided billing records. The team then sampled Excel's way bills to assign costs to customers. An analyst went through two months of way bills and classified the freight charges into customer groups depending on which group the customer belonged to.

Customer Service Activity Centers

The customer service (CS) department consisted of four groups: customer service reps, order editing, parts reps, and returns. The customer service reps spent most of their time taking customer orders. When interviewing the CS manager, the team found that the time to take an order varied widely, according to order type. The home-care orders took only a minute to write down customer information the catalog number desired. However, rehab orders, with all of their confusing options and features, frequently took a half hour (it was amazing how many different ways a bed could be ordered). From order entry, both order types went to the order editing group to check for errors.

There was actually another group of customer service reps—the national account reps. These reps strictly serviced Excel's large accounts. Therefore, their costs (based on the number of national account reps) were subtracted from the home-care and rehab groups, and assigned directly to this group.

Through customer interviews, the team found that the customers were very unhappy with Excel's customer service. The customers complained that Excel's reps didn't seem to know what they were doing. The team believed that the department had two major problems. First, the reps were not taking the orders right initially, resulting in all orders going through the nonvalue-added order editing process. The most experienced people, the editors, were not on the phone with Excel's customers. The least experienced people were on the phone with the customers and as soon as they gained experience, management promoted them off the phone.

The second major problem was customer service's lack of accountability. Excel had organized the CS department as a pool. When a customer called in, the first available rep took the call. After taking an order, if the order came back with corrections from order editing and required customer approval, the first available rep would call back the customer. There was no feedback or accountability on order mistakes to the rep who made them. The customers had a random point of contact—the reps and the customers never developed any personal relationships. Also, the reps were not responsible for resolving any customer's problems. In fact, since the reps were measured on call volume, there was a disincentive to solve a time-consuming problem. If a tough problem came in, the rep would simply try to get the customer off the phone, knowing that if the customer called back it was likely that another rep would get the call.

To solve these problems, the team persuaded management to split the customer service group into two groups, rehab reps and home-care reps, while eliminating the order editing altogether. The team recommended splitting the group because, even with enhanced training, the rehab products required much more product knowledge than many of the reps had. The more experienced reps would handle only the complex rehab products, while the less experienced reps would take orders for the simple home-care products. While having to make some changes in the computer system, these changes cut Excel's staff by five people. This change simultaneously improved service by putting knowledgeable people on the phone and cutting the order-entry cycle time.

After splitting up customer service, Excel split up its costs based on the number of people assigned to each group. Since ordering of home-care products took only a few seconds, the number of units ordered did not drive costs. The number of customer orders drove home-care product's ordering costs. The rehab orders, on the other hand, were still very time consuming. The time it took to order a rehab product depended on the number of units ordered. Therefore, the team assigned rehab order-entry costs on the number of rehab units ordered.

By assigning reps to territories, Excel solved the accountability problem. Reps now were responsible and accountable for all rehab or home-care orders from a particular group of customers. If a customer had a problem, a rep got feedback and knew he or she had to fix it, and that it was his or her responsibility. This new organization drastically changed the whole department's attitude; reps had responsibility, as well as new authority, and could develop personal relationships with the customers. In fact, reps began to refer to customers as "my customers."

While the team did not discover it during the study, the customer service reps spent a considerable amount of time answering customer questions regarding order status. Later, the team learned that it could have had a report created that would have listed the number of customer inquiries by customer. About 15 percent of the customer service reps' cost should have been assigned on this measure. Some customer groups were more prone to call in than others.

The parts ordering group strictly took orders and telemarketed for spare parts. As with home-care products, order entry was quick and simple. The order-entry costs were associated with processing the order. The team used the number of customer orders taken to assign the parts order costs.

The returns group processed customer returns. The cost of returns area included the cost of fixing returned goods minus restocking fees. The costs of processing a return were insignificant when compared to the cost of returned goods. Therefore, the team assigned the cost of returns to customers, based on the dollar value of returned goods from each customer.

Sales Activity Centers

The sales costs were broken down into two groups—sales force and commissions. Management believed that the purpose of the sales force was to make sales calls. These calls created market awareness, distributed product literature, while developing a personal relationship with the customers. These actions, in turn, led to sales. Excel's management did not see the sales force's job as taking orders— customer service did that. The team believed that the best way to assign sales force costs was on the number of sales calls made to each customer. The more sales calls a customer consumed, the more of Excel's resources the customer was consuming. To develop a distribution of whom the salespeople were calling on, the team had an analyst sample two months' worth of sales call reports.

The team found the buying groups and rehab centers to be the most frequent salespeople stops. Buying groups (collectives of many independent dealers) were not exclusive Excel customers. Therefore, despite a national sales contract, Excel still had to convince individual dealers (and there were a lot of them) to buy from Excel. On the other hand, the sophisticated users that were staffing the rehab centers demanded substantial sales and technical support.

Excel commission records were in terrible shape (Excel was concurrently undertaking an internal audit to get the records straight). Excel did not give the sales force a commission simply based on a percentage of a product's gross sales. Excel's commission structure had different percentages for different products, and these percentages changed, based on the number of units sold this year versus last year. This complicated commission structure forced the team to apply Excel's complicated commission formula to each customer group to estimate commissions.

The controller argued that the distribution of sales commissions should be the same as the sales force distribution. She argued that salespeople are smart and they do exactly what they are rewarded to do. Therefore, she argued, the salespeople spent their time exactly where their commissions came from. The team disproved this argument. The team found Excel's salespeople getting commissions on products sold through distributors, even though they did not call on these customers. Excel had a policy to encourage the sales force to work with distributors, instead of against them. Excel's sales force received commissions from distributor sales without any work. The second case, where the sales force received commissions, but did no work, was orders from small dealers. These orders came from either pull marketing or word-of-mouth sales. Excel would have received these sales even if they had no sales force.

Discounts

Every customer received a discount off the standard trade discount. The customers' sales contracts, of which Excel had over 2,000, defined these discounts. The MIS department gave us a report that calculated the average discount by customer group. However, the team needed to include in this discount the effects of net pricing.

Net pricing is the practice of agreeing, in the sales contract, to a fixed price for a particular product. Net pricing was an effective discount. It had exactly the same effect as a discount, except it was calculated differently. Items that were net priced amounted to a significant portion of Excel's sales, although no one knew how much. There were no reports that detailed net-priced sales. However, you could not ignore net pricing, or it would have made certain customers appear to have much lower discounts and gross sales than they effectively had. So, after compensating for net pricing (much easier said than done), the team calculated the average discount by customer group, which included the effective discount of net-priced items.

It was interesting to note that because only a few products per customer were net priced, and net pricing was not reported as a discount, net pricing had very little visibility to management. Consequently, management paid little attention to it. As such, management always negotiated with customers on discounts, and gave them whatever they wanted on net pricing as an afterthought. The analysis showed that the single most important cost factor, in two out of the five customer groups, was net pricing. While the number of products net priced was small, the net-priced items were all the customers' high-volume items. Net pricing was where all the money was in contract negotiations. Even though Excel's largest customer only had seven items net priced, these units amounted to 56 percent of his sales revenues.

Marketing Activity Centers

The team traced all the marketing costs (advertising, trade shows, promotions, market administration, and literature) to markets or channels. The team spread these costs as a percentage of market sales to each channel. For example, 20 percent of the rehab sales went to buying groups therefore, this customer group received 20 percent of the rehab advertising assignment.

The team found that most advertising costs could be tracked to either the home-care, rehab, or parts market. The team assigned ads in *Homecare* magazine to only the home-care market. The team assigned to the rehab market the cost to put on a rehab trade show.

Research and Development Activity Centers

The team traced R&D costs to one of the markets. These costs were not the costs of engineering the products. Engineering costs are product-driven costs. Most of the research had some user need in mind. By identifying which customer category this user fell into, you could assign the costs. If the research was for the aged, its costs went into the home care pool; if it went toward injury recovery, it went into the rehab pool.

Administration Activity Centers

The administration category was a collection of other assignable costs, such as billing, accounts receivable (AR), product liability, and credits. The billing department billed customers monthly, so the invoices were not directly related to customer orders. Therefore, the team assigned billing department costs on number of invoices.

The accounts receivable cost was the AR times a 12 percent cost of money. The team noticed wide variations in payments while undertaking the study. The company was also beginning a new marketing program of giving 90-day terms on some products. The costs of AR was directly traceable to every customer.

The team discovered that one large customer checked each bill Excel sent him for errors. He would dispute any bill that was off by even a cent. He did this to draw out his payments until all the mistakes could be checked. This customer had more than 120 days outstanding in AR, and almost 18 percent of the company's credit authorizations. This customer was using Excel as his bank!

The team assigned the credit department costs on the number of credit authorizations and credit holds each customer required. Most of the product liability and legal fees could be traced to rehab business, so the team interviewed Excel's insurance advisor to split these costs between the different markets.

Applying Costs to the Customers

The team assigned all the distribution costs to our customer groups on our spreadsheet. Exhibit 7-1 shows customer-driven costs as a percentage of revenue for each of the customer groups. One notices distributors are the least expensive to serve. Naturally, the first question to be asked is: Why do some customers receive more costs than others? Of course, the question should really be: Why do some customers cause more activity than others?

Why are sales costs so large for buying groups? While buying groups negotiate national contracts and receive large discounts, each store makes its own buying decisions. Therefore, buying groups require the sales force to call on each store. In addition, the sales force always considered the buying groups Excel's most profitable customer group, and so spent much time catering to them.

Discounts were always one of the principal negotiating points of each customer's contract. Discounts (including net pricing) were the largest expense to distributors, national accounts, and buying groups. Each of these groups bargained with sub-

Exhibit 7-1   **EXCEL MEDICAL'S CUSTOMER-DRIVEN COSTS BY CONSUMER TYPE**

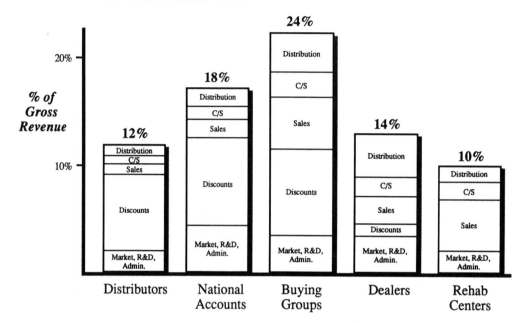

stantial buying volume and received large discounts. The discounts came in two forms: either secondary discounts off the standard discount that everyone, even small dealers, got; or through net priced items. What this chart does not show is that net priced items made up more than half of the effective discount distributors received. Prior to the ABC study, Excel's management had only sales information with which to negotiate discounts. Thus, Excel gave discounts to customers principally on sales volume, although management gave greater discounts if the distributors bought in large truck-load volumes. Unfortunately, as the ABC study showed, Excel gave away discounts worth thousands of dollars, in return for shipping large orders that only saved hundreds of dollars.

By examining the cost drivers, one can see how different customers drive different costs. Exhibit 7-2 shows how the number of home-care units per customer order vary by customer group. You can see that distributors are by far the least expensive customer group to serve. Distributors stock products and, typically, order only once a month. This bundling of orders allows Excel to only enter and track one order. Excel creates only one invoice and bill of lading. Excel coordinates the shipment with only one trucking company. On the other hand, dealers often carry little inventory except displays, and place orders whenever they accumulate enough sales to exceed the minimum order limit.

Surprisingly, the study uncovered little difference between the order size of a buying group member and a dealer. Looking at the other distribution characteristics,

Exhibit 7-2 **HOW THE AVERAGE NUMBER OF HOME CARE UNITS PER CUSTOMER ORDER VARIED BY CUSTOMER TYPE FOR EXCEL MEDICAL**

	Distributors	*National Accounts*	*Buying Groups*	*Dealers*	*Rehab Centers*
Average number of units per order	34	7	1.8	1.7	2.1
Number of orders per 1000 units	29	143	556	588	476

Some customers cause more activity than others

---

the team found buying groups had somewhat higher sales per store. Otherwise they behave just like dealers. However, from a profit perspective, there was a major difference: dealers got slim discounts and buying groups got fat ones.

In fact, the study found that Excel lost money on over 80 percent of the sales they made through buying groups. Buying groups had not only negotiated good discount terms over the years, but also grew to monopolize the time of Excel's sales force. These buying groups, being small shops spread around the country, had no economies of service, causing Excel to incur huge service costs. These costs eroded all of Excel's profits.

Only a few of the study's uncovered customer characteristics were a surprise to Excel's management. However, by attaching costs to these characteristics, management was astounded. Management could not believe that buying groups were as expensive as the study showed. Therefore, the study team went through the analysis and results in detail, to convince management of the study's validity.

Now management knew how much each group cost to serve, as well as why. Management could now make more effective sales contracts to encourage customers to order in larger quantities without Excel paying too much in discounts.

Distributors' service costs were very low, in spite of paying for free freight on truckload quantities. The distributors only handled the simple home-care products and consolidated orders before faxing them. This kept order-entry costs low. Salespeople did not call on distributors. Nor did they call on distributor's customers, the distributors had their own salespeople. Nonetheless, Excel salespeople did receive commissions on products that were sold through distributors. Discounts and net pricing were most of this channel's cost. These discounts were the markup distributors receive to sell and distribute Excel's products. Administration costs were high, even though distributors did not buy many of the rehab products with their high R&D and insurance costs. Excel devoted a great deal of time to developing specialized promotional campaigns just for their distributors. The team assigned these costs directly to this channel.

National accounts were also relatively cheap to serve, but their volume allowed them to negotiate some very favorable discount terms. They also received some special promotional programs and required significant management time, which was reflected in their administration costs.

Dealers were expensive to service; however their small discounts offset these costs. Located around the country and with a high failure rate, dealers require substantial advertising just to learn to carry Excel's products. Each year a hundred or so dealers go out of business. This created the need for credit checks on all new customers, and a high incidence of credit holds and bad debt. The customer costs factor all of these costs into the administration category.

Rehab centers, with their small sales volumes, received virtually no discounts, but being sophisticated customers, required substantial sales-force time. The rehab units, being much more expensive, made their distribution and customer service costs appear low as a percentage of sales. These costs were just amortized across higher sales dollars.

HOW ORDER AND SHIPPING POLICIES DROVE COSTS

From this ABC study, Excel was able to see the relationship between many of its policies and their costs.

With over 2,000 unique sales contracts, Excel now understood why it had so many people in billing, in spite of having an automated invoicing system. There were so many contracts that the MIS group could not accurately maintain the records. Excel's billing department was forced to correct many bills manually. Still, many incorrect invoices slipped through, creating a high number of credit authorizations and large accounts receivable, as customers disputed their bills.

By allowing Excel's distributors to have private label products, they created a high finished goods inventory. Since private label products were specially configured with different colors, options, and labels from any of Excel's standard products, these products forced Excel to carry more finished goods. The private labels also increased the risk of switching distributors. Since distributors had their name on the product, end users were developing distributor brand awareness and not Excel's. Should Excel drop a distributor, Excel could find that the end users have more brand loyalty to the distributor than Excel.

By offering free freight on orders with three units or more, Excel inadvertently created many backorders and doubled its freight charges. This policy stemmed from the finding that freight costs per unit were much lower when shipping three units or more. Therefore, they offered free freight on all orders with three or more units. So Excel's customers ordered two stock units every time they ordered a custom unit. Since custom products had to be built to order, with stock units inventoried, the plant shipped the stock units immediately with free freight. The factory, meanwhile, put the custom unit on back order. When the custom unit was complete, the factory shipped it with free freight. Excel's policy had inadvertently doubled freight costs, in addition to creating backorders and more invoicing. Excel's policy had backfired, but, until this study, no one recognized it.

When the team listened in on dealer calls in customer service, they discovered some important customer dissatisfiers. First, the frequency at which dealers intended to buy long-discontinued products, or product configurations that were no longer offered, surprised the team members. One of the customer service representatives explained to the team that Excel had not updated the product catalogue in a number of years, despite changes in the product line. Most of Excel's product literature was obsolete. The customers using the old catalogue would only discover updates if they happened to order one of the obsolete products or they maintained files on all product announcements (most dealers maintained haphazard records, if any). In fact, Excel had not updated the catalogue in six years. This, in turn, created high order entry costs, because the customer service rep would have to educate customers on the current product line while on the phone to them. The team began recording the time spent discussing obsolete products. They estimated that Excel lost seven percent of the customer service representative's time because the product catalogue was not being updated. This also caused lost sales and dissatisfied customers.

The team found that the marketing department considered the budget for the product catalogue a discretionary item. In recent years, the company's poor financial performance had necessitated budget cutbacks, and new product catalogues were usually one of the first items waylaid. The team also thought that the marketing department deemphasized the catalogues because they would rather spend their time on the more exciting advertising campaigns and new products.

The team quantified the customer service time wasted due to obsolete literature, and identified from the marketing survey the number of customers dissatisfied with the catalogue. This information ensured Excel would introduce new catalogues next year.

Another problem that was identified by listening in on customer calls was the confusion about how to order products. More specifically, the customers frequently did not understand what product options went with which products. Customer service reps were spending valuable time explaining options and pricing on the phone.

The service reps explained to the team how poorly organized and confusing the catalogues were. One of Excel's customers told the team that Excel's catalogue was "like a phone book without names!" One of Excel's sales reps told the team that she believed it took an average dealer a half hour to prepare an Excel order before even reaching for the phone. She said the catalogue was just too complicated.

She also commented that a similar product from one of Excel's competitors, Beds R' Us, could be ordered in about five minutes. When asked why, she explained that Beds R' Us supplied dealers with order forms patterned after Medicare reimbursement forms. The DME market is very reimbursement driven. Just about every time a dealer orders a DME product the dealer will send in a reimbursement form, either to Medicare or to an insurance company. The insurance companies patterned their reimbursement forms after the Medicare forms. Beds R' Us, by patterning its order forms after reimbursement forms, allowed dealers to copy most of the information off the reimbursement form onto the order form. The forms even had notations describing what options were reimbursable and which were not, and the forms could be faxed instead of phoned. These order forms must have saved Beds R' Us a bundle by slashing ordering time. The order forms also cut the dealer's cost of doing business with Beds R' Us by slashing the time to order its products. The study highlighted the costs of poor product literature for Excel. Excel began to develop order forms just like Beds R' Us.

MAKING A STRATEGY RECOMMENDATION

Assessing Customer Needs

Customer surveys are critical for effectively configuring the distribution process. From the survey, the team identified what was important to the customers (see Exhibit 7-3). In both markets, order accuracy was critically important, due to the high cost of correcting a mistake.

In both markets, delivery times were very important, but the delivery time requirements were different. In the rehab market, superior delivery was eight days, while in the home-care market it was three days. This difference recognizes the difference in the products. Rehab units are customized with many options and have to be assembled to order, while dealers stock home-care units.

These delivery requirements configured the distribution system. To deliver a home-care bed anywhere in the country, within three days, required Excel to stock the home-care products in six locations across the country. Assuming Excel could take the order and pull the unit in one day, that left two days to deliver the product. From six locations, United Parcel Service guarantees two-day delivery to 95 percent of the continental U.S. population. The customers required eight-day delivery for rehab products. Excel could organize its factory to take an order and assemble a rehab product, from components, in three days. This left five days for delivery of the rehab products. UPS can deliver from Excel's factory to anywhere in the continental United States in five days. Therefore, Excel only needed one assembly location for the rehab products to meet the eight-day cycle. In this way the customer's delivery requirements drove the distribution configuration.

Exhibit 7-3   ***DISTRIBUTION ATTRIBUTE IMPORTANCE***
                 FROM CUSTOMER VALUE SURVEYS

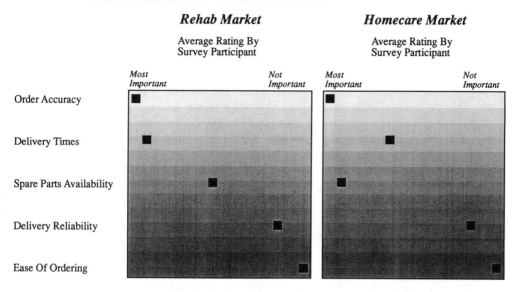

Weighing the Strategic Options

Excel basically had two options. Either it could sell all products directly, which would require Excel to reconfigure its distribution centers and factory, or it could sell its home-care products through distributors. This option would allow Excel to sell off its distribution centers, while still reconfiguring its factory. A distributor performs most of the sales and service functions for its suppliers. Distributors sell the products, inventory the product, take customer orders, handle customer questions, and deliver products to the customers.

When contracting with a distributor, a manufacturer must create incentives for the distributor to perform all these functions satisfactorily. If a distributor does not inventory the product, the manufacturer is forced to drop-ship products either directly to the customer or to the distributor. Either way, the customer gets slow service.

A manufacturer also wants the distributor to provide incremental sales—sales to new customers that the manufacturer has not sold to before. Whenever a new distributor adds a company's product, the company benefits from incremental sales to the distributor's customer base. However, over time, the distributor will usually pick up most the manufacturer's local customers, a process called "vacuuming." If a dealer changes from going direct to a distributor, the company loses margins because distributors have better discounts than dealers. Therefore, only when the dealer transaction costs exceed the change in discounts does the company make more money.

In addition, Excel had to weigh whether a distributor's less well trained and less focused sales force could sell Excel's product as effectively as its own sales force. If not, how much sales would be lost? In addition, would sales rise because a distributor offers a full product DME line?

To assess the costs of these two options the study team constructed cost models of each of the alternatives. To meet the customer's home-care delivery requirements demanded that Excel add two more stocking warehouses to its distribution system. To meet a three-day delivery, Excel had one day to enter and pull the order, leaving two days for delivery. (The team even debated what was meant by three-day delivery. Did the day the product was ordered count as one day?) It took six warehouses for UPS to cover the 95 percent of the U.S. population with two-day delivery (see Exhibit 7-4).

To understand the importance of bundling—selling a full DME product line—the team called distributor customers and asked them if one-stop shopping was important to them. The team found bundling was important to 40 percent of the dealers interviewed. This 40 percent was mainly medium-sized accounts. These accounts believed that bundling cut their transaction costs and provided them with more sales volume, and, therefore, greater buying leverage. Large customers felt

Exhibit 7-4   **EXCEL'S CURRENT AND REQUIRED DISTRIBUTION SITES**

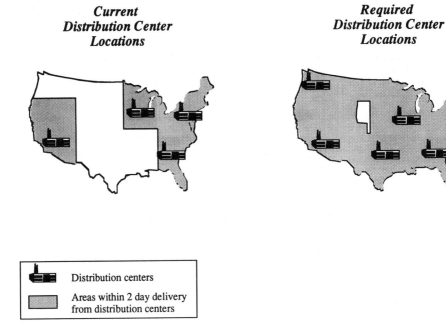

Current Distribution Center Locations

Required Distribution Center Locations

Distribution centers

Areas within 2 day delivery from distribution centers

that bundling was not important, since they already enjoyed good discounts. Small accounts, because they did such little volume, felt that bundling was not important.

The team also identified whether these distributor customers represented incremental sales or were vacuumed from Excel. (Incremental sales are sales to customers that Excel has never sold to before.) The team found that the percentage of incremental customers varied widely by distributor. In addition, the team found that incremental sales decreased rapidly over time.

After reviewing the cost information and the customer interviews, the team recommended that Excel reverse its business from 80 percent direct and 20 percent distributors, to 80 percent distributors and 20 percent direct. The team estimated that this strategy would save Excel approximately $1.5 million a year, and free up cash from sale of the warehouses and inventory reductions. The distributor strategy would also improve customer service through quicker delivery and increased sales by providing the customers with a bundled product line.

The distributors with more than six warehouses could offer much more rapid delivery then Excel could hope for. The distributors with their own sales force would allow Excel to slash its sales force. Excel would ship products in full truckload quantities as distributors would stock Excel's products—allowing Excel to close its DCs, freeing up cash and reducing distribution costs. In addition, distributors would reduce Excel's transactions in billing, order entry, and the shipping office.

By shifting to distributors, Excel solved another problem. Excel's use of distributors confused its customers. Dealers found Excel's sales force and distributors competing with one another. Since the strategy removed Excel's sales force from these accounts, that part of the problem ended. To eliminate, or at least reduce, conflicts between distributors, Excel would only ship products to specified cities for each distributor (it is illegal for a manufacturer to impose territories on distributors). This did not stop a distributor from selling in Atlanta, if his home territory was New York. Yet, it did increase his costs, because the distributor would have to pay the freight to get the bed to Atlanta. These changes would hopefully reduce the distributor competition.

The strategy also recommended that Excel renegotiate its distributor contracts, trading a distributor's increased sales volume for discount reductions and customer service incentives. Using the ABC data and knowledge of distributors' operations, the team was able to construct a cost model for each of Excel's distributors. Armed with this information, the team estimated the increased volume's effects on each distributor's costs. Therefore, Excel's negotiators had a very good idea how much of a discount reduction Excel could squeeze out of each distributor. The team also wanted to ensure improved customer service; so the team included delivery times, sales penetration, and other criteria into the distributor contracts.

The team also used the ABC data to persuade Excel's management to invest in Electronic Data Interchange (EDI) terminals for its distributors. This electronic link would cut both parties' order-entry costs, and help to reduce both parties' inventories. Excel could monitor the distributors' orders and deliveries, while the distributors could see Excel's finished goods inventory and build schedules.

Probably most important, the team proved to Excel that the company could not compete on price with GAC. GAC had too many cost advantages. Our surveys showed that the customers perceived Excel as the high-quality manufacturer and not as the low-cost leader. The team convinced Excel to switch its business strategy from low cost to differentiation. This strategy, it was hoped, would end the markets destructive price war.

The team did not use this information for evaluating market segments. In fact, the team made little use of the market cost information at all. The reason was that any market segment decisions required manufacturing cost and product profitability information. The team did not have time to develop it. The team had the company's traditional costing reports, but they knew that these reports were worse than useless. Worse—because with them, you think they know product line profitability. Unfortunately, experience shows that the traditional reporting is wrong. Therefore, the team would rather have nothing, so they never forget that they lack true cost information. For this study, the team believed that it was not critical to have product line profitability, because the team was not going to make any product line additions or subtractions, only distribute them through different channels. The team operated under the assumption that sales would not change significantly if business switched to another channel.

Lessons Learned

This case shows the powerful effects ABC can have beyond manufacturing. It shows how cost control can be extended to all areas of a company's operations. The case shows how costs can be applied to customers, and how ABC can be used to track down what systems and policies are creating costs.

However, Excel's decision to undertake a distribution study was not based on finding a new application of ABC. Excel desperately needed to unravel its distribution system. Its costs were too high and its poor distribution system was driving away customers. The decision to undertake a distribution study was a decision based on marketing imperatives.

While ABC played a crucial role in developing the new strategy, as well as identifying a significant number of cost reduction opportunities, it had only a supporting role. ABC was merely a support tool that provided valuable cost insight on which to base the strategy. This is ABC's true role in business: providing superior information for superior decision making. The lesson here is that ABC should be applied wherever the company's most important decisions must be made.

TARGETING MARKET SEGMENTS

Beyond a distribution strategy, a company needs to consider what customers the company should be pursuing. Which customer segments Excel Medical should pursue, and with how much resources, are complex decisions. They depend on each segment's growth and Excel's competitive advantage, as well as the strengths of its competitors, access to distribution channels, investment required, and much, much more. ABC supplies some very important pieces of information: how much it costs to serve a particular market segment, and what margin the company really makes on these products. ABC tells management the gross profit margin and how much customer-driven costs each segment is absorbing.

This information is critical for management to make resource allocation between segments. In addition, ABC records how much investment in working capital, fixed capital, and new product development each market segment requires. This information allows management to make more informed decisions about each segment's cash flow.

One implication of portraying customer-driven costs is the desire to charge different customers different prices. It would improve the functioning of the market if all customer-driven costs could be directed back to each customer through pricing. However, federal regulation, such as the Robinson-Patman Act, specifically prohibits the practice of pricing discrimination. The Robinson-Patman Act, supposedly, allows price differentials if there are cost differences. ABC definitely improves the ability of a company to substantiate these claims. Unfortunately, even with ABC, costing is not an exact science and objections can be raised, and the Federal Trade Commission usually sides with small businesses. Small businesses are the very ones with high transaction costs and are the ones most likely to be hurt by activity-based pricing. Therefore, a company must be careful in its application of this ABC information for customer pricing.

CHAPTER 8

BUILDING SHAREHOLDER VALUE WITH ABC

For one who has no objective, nothing is relevant.

Confucius

Chapter co-authored by William F. Green II of Lockheed Corporation

When queried about their corporate objectives, chief executives proffer a variety of responses: profits, market share, sales growth, industry leadership, etc. However, these responses are not what a company's owners desire. A company's owners want value creation—shareholder value creation. Shareholder value creation is an increase in the present value of a company's stock. This value can come in the form of stock price appreciation or stock dividends.

Shareholder value analysis (SVA) is the process of predicting how business decisions will impact a corporation's market value of equity. SVA provides a single unifying concept with which to evaluate business decisions. Calculations of the net present value of expected cash flows are the fundamental core of the shareholder value approach.

However, without ABC, any shareholder value analysis may be so distorted that it is rendered meaningless. The benefits of shareholder value analysis can be fully realized only in an ABC environment. Conversely, the benefits of ABC can only be fully achieved by performing shareholder value analysis and managing the business accordingly. To accurately evaluate shareholder value, you need ABC, and to use ABC effectively, you must work to maximize shareholder value.

Since the 1940s, when business strategy was called long-range planning, the basis of strategic analysis has been financial projections. Over the years, business has given the revenue side of the financial projections a great deal of attention. Companies have developed sophisticated sales forecasting and market research tools to help them accurately project future revenues. However, business has done little with cost forecasting. Companies have merely forecast costs based on historical records, and those records inaccurately portray overhead relationships.

However, before discussing how to use ABC, there must be agreement on the criteria for to judging business decisions.

BY WHICH CRITERIA TO MEASURE PERFORMANCE?

One reason some companies have let themselves become undervalued is that their managers have been measuring corporate performance against the wrong standards. Executives have relied on earnings per share (EPS) growth, return on assets (ROA), and return on equity (ROE) to judge business performance. While these measures have been around since the 1920s, they mislead decision makers. These measures do not predict or correlate with the creation of value for owners. All of these measures focus on past history, not the future. These tools, like the rest of the financial tools that management has been forced to use, are reporting tools, not planning tools. These accounting measures are not up to the task of measuring economic value that manifests itself in the price of a stock.

EPS growth does not account for the amount of capital that is required to achieve a particular growth in earnings. This growth only adds to shareholder value if the rate of return exceeds the cost of capital. If not, growth in sales and earnings actually destroys shareholder value. For instance, Wheeling-Pittsburgh's EPS advanced 28 percent between 1978 and 1988, but shareholder value actually dropped. On the other hand, Berkshire Hathaway delivered a shareholder return of 40 percent, despite an EPS growth rate of only 12 percent, while Sun Oil gave its shareholders a 14 percent return, despite a 33 percent EPS decline.

The essential problem with both ROA and ROE is that they do not take into account a company's cost of capital. Both measures are accrual accounting returns, relying on accounting conventions. Ford Motor Company has had an anemic return on assets; in 1988 its ROA was 4 percent. Nevertheless, its average annual shareholder return for the ten previous years was 24 percent.

ROA does not compensate for higher risk, and, therefore, ignores the higher cost of capital that risky business units incur. A real estate business with a solid capital base can obtain less costly capital than an emerging biotechnology division. The real estate enterprise has substantial collateral such as large property holdings, while the biotechnology division has only intangible assets such as the expertise of staff Ph.Ds.

Comparing divisions using ROA can be very misleading—for example, assume two divisions are identical, except that one division owns its property while the other leases. An ROA comparison would show the division owning its property to be underperforming the leasing division. The balance sheet reports the property as an asset, against which executives judge the division's return.

As a performance measure, ROA distorts decision making by including in the analysis undepreciated investments which the company has already made (i.e., sunk costs). ROA considers capital investments, but ignores investments in R&D and software because accountants expense these items. In fact, as with capital, these investments are discretionary commitments that management must weigh against expected cash flows. ROA does not take the time value of money or tax affects into consideration, and is greatly influenced by depreciation rates and capitalization policies.

Return on sales (ROS), on the other hand, does not include any allowance for the initial cost of creating the profit stream. Prior to making an investment, the entire expected costs of product development, capital investment, and advertising must be weighed against a product's expected return. ROS considers few of these outlays. Nor does ROS take into account the assets tied up in manufacturing, selling or delivering the product either, the timing of investments and their related returns, or the cost of capital.

Even reported net income is only an accounting convention. Note that accounting income is, in some way, included in ROE, ROA, and ROS calculations. Executives should manage for shareholder value, that is, discounted cash flow, not net income. Net income can understate cash flows by deducting depreciation expenses. However, net income usually overstates cash flows because capital investments are depreciated over many years and not expensed immediately.

While the distinction between cash flows and reported profits may seem trivial, it is hardly that. Concentrating on the net present value of cash flows versus reported profits dramatically changes individual decisions; it also changes a company's key value drivers. A profit orientation often leads managers to seek sales growth. They believe sales growth will further leverage economies of scale and meet ever-higher profit targets. A shareholder value orientation, on the other hand, carefully weighs the costs of all investment against discounted returns. The expected returns are discounted using the (risk-adjusted) cost of capital. Only if growth can be justified using a net present value analysis is an investment approved. For example, a profit-oriented manager is much more likely to invest in advertising for an enhanced product in a saturated market than a cash-oriented manager. A cash-oriented manager

---

Note: For the purpose of this discussion the definitions of ROE, ROA, and ROS are derived as follows:

Return on equity = Earnings per share/book value of equity per share

Return on assets = Earnings before interest and taxes – taxes/average total assets

Return on sales = Net income/total revenue

would only make the investment if the investment's return provided a premium over the company's cost of capital.

Suppose a company president discontinues a product line that was manufactured on a dedicated automated line. The president who is evaluated on shareholder value would immediately sell off the assets. The company would receive the salvage-value cash flow, as well as take a write-off against taxes. These steps would maximize the net present value of cash flows. However, if the same president was evaluated against book profits, he would hold on to the obsolete line until its book value was completely written off. Otherwise, the company would be forced to write off the remaining depreciation, reducing book profits.

During the 1960s, the "go-go" years, profit and shareholder value worked in concert. During these fast-growth years, most companies increased share value through sales growth and acquisition of other growing companies. However, as many markets began to mature, the disparity between strategies for profits and value creation began to grow. As markets matured, profit-oriented managers continued to invest in capital, new products, advertising, and marketing for sales growth. Because these investments were no longer made in rapidly growing markets, sales growth had to come at competitor expense. Since contested sales growth is difficult and expensive, many investments failed to achieve historical payoffs. In fact, too many projects failed to provide returns exceeding the cost of capital. This goal divergence led stockholders to undertake a wave of takeovers, leveraged buyouts, and restructures in the mid-1980s.

To create shareholder value, management concentrates on throwing off cash by reducing fixed and working capital, and by controlling capital and development spending. Management works to increase throughput and inventory turns. In addition, with SVA, management explicitly knows that with the vast majority of companies, more than two-thirds of a company's value is based on its cash flows more than five years into the future. Executives work toward increasing long-term market value. Yet, this also creates one of the greatest challenges to shareholder value analysis: estimating a company's value after five years, beyond the company's planning horizon.

To maximize reported profits, on the other hand, a company would seek to spend capital and build inventory to boost sales and drive down costs. A profit orientation causes managers to invest in vertical integration to reduce costs, regardless of the investment's return. Likewise, a profit-oriented manager is much more likely to introduce variations on current products. This product proliferation, hopefully, provides greater sales. The inventory implications of this decision are ignored. (In fact, one can show a paper profit by allowing product costs to escalate, which permits one to write up inventory. As a company's inventory increases in cost, its reported value also increases, registering a profit!)

The true measure of a company's value, as judged by its owners, is shareholder return. Companies like Dexter, Signode, PepsiCo, Marriott, and Westinghouse have embraced and committed to the idea of managing for shareholder value. All value-creation approaches seek to increase the values that investors place on all of the businesses of a corporation. To increase the values, management must invest above the cost of capital. Investments that simply return the cost of capital just break even; those returning less, actually destroy shareholder value.

However, because an individual business may consist of a number of businesses which do not have separately traded securities, you must, as closely as possible, estimate how investors would value a given business decision. The shareholder's return boils down to the present value of the company's cash flows, after being discounted by the company's risk-dependent cost of capital. These cash flows form the basis for dividends and share price appreciation, which benefit the investor. Cash flow and risk are the key measures of performance, not current earnings.

From the owner's perspective, a business is like a corporate bond or a T-bill—investments which yield a cash flow streams. These cash flows are judged on their magnitudes versus their riskiness and initial investment. As most shrewd investors know, a dollar today is worth more than a promised dollar tomorrow; therefore, the cash flows are discounted for their timing. The farther in the future the cash flows are, the less valuable they are. In addition, only higher expected return compensates for higher risk. A more risky investment is only attractive to an investor if the investment provides a higher potential return than a no-risk investment. Therefore, the cash-flow stream is discounted according to its risk. The present-value analysis compensates by discounting the cash flows by a market risk-dependent cost of capital. The more risky the investment, the higher the cost of capital will be.

The net present value of cash flows is the criterion by which managers should judge all decisions and investments. From the shareholder's point of view, net present value, as reflected in the share price of stock, is determined by two components:

$$\text{Share price} = \text{PVCF} + \text{PVRV}$$

Where

PVCF =   Present value of future cash flows over the forecast
         period (These cash flows, whether paid out in dividends
         or stock buybacks, or reinvested for capital appreciation,
         are realized by the shareholder.)

PVRV =   Perceived present value of residual value of investment at the end
         of the investment period

While this formula is a simplification of the well-known present-value equation, it demonstrates the critical leverage points for management to build shareholder value. Management can seek to raise shareholder value by

- Lowering the cost of equity by lowering the variability and risk of the company's cash flows.

- Increasing dividends to provide the investor with a predictable cash yield.

- Accelerating or strengthening cash flows by shedding underutilized assets, by reducing or deferring tax obligations, or by improving expense and investment discipline.

- Increasing the company's growth by improving its position in faster growing markets, employing superior technology, taking on appropriate debt leverage, or executing a superior strategy.

- Increasing the residual value of the business by improving its long-term competitiveness, raising market share, or investing in R&D with high potential payoffs.

However, the formula is not valid if the company's liquidation or breakup value exceeds this calculated price. In the first case, the company is worth more dead than alive. In the second case, the sum of the parts exceeds the value of the whole. Each of these options must be considered.

ABC links resource consumption via activities to products and customers. Since resource consumption can be translated into fixed and variable costs, while products and customers can be converted into revenues, ABC can calculate the difference between them. This difference between variable costs and revenue is incremental cash flow. Shareholder value analysis depends upon calculating discounted cash flows, more specifically, incremental cash flows. ABC identifies which costs are truly variable, versus fixed, over a given time horizon—a crucial ability in calculating incremental cash flows. For example, occupancy costs may be fixed over a fairly long time, supervisor salaries may be variable in the long term, and premium overtime pay is variable in the short term. In addition, incremental cash flows cannot be accurately determined without an understanding of product-specific overhead. This understanding is the strength of an ABC system. Therefore, ABC is critical in calculating shareholder value accurately.

The shareholder value approach fits well with an activity focus. A focus on activity ensures that, when shareholder value is projected financially, the underlying assumptions of the projections are linked to specific activities and to the performance of those activities. With an activity focus, you become accustomed to looking at all resource expenditures as creating or changing activities, and then looking at the activities' output. Future capital spending, advertising, and promotional programs, as well as new products and services, can all be tied to specific activity performance measures; for example, the contribution to shareholder value from a retailer's promotional program. Prior to initiating such a program, the marketing department estimates the number of new customers and changes in revenue and costs. These numbers are converted into an estimate of value that the program expects to add. Once the promotional program begins, the company tracks and verifies the number of new accounts that the promotional program has added. The company now has a baseline cost for adding new customers—a benchmark for other promotional programs.

The value creation sand activity-based philosophy changes the way managers view their businesses. Executives learn to manage for cash flows and not for conventional book profit. Under ABC, executives begin to see their customers in a broader perspective, as a set of activities that consume resources. The company can then work to satisfy activities directly, with the most efficient products and services possible. Products are seen as a bundle of activities that are managed by controlling the triggering of activities and efficiency of the activities through Process Value Analysis (PVA). Therefore, ABC and shareholder value, operating together, drastically change the philosophy of business management, as well as the methods.

Yesterday's Business Focus	*Tomorrow's Business Focus*
Profits and losses	Cash flows
Markets	Sets of customer needs
Products	Processes (e.g., activities)
Budgets	Activity triggers
Efficiency	Process value analysis

While this type of analysis is possible without ABC, it is usually not done. With ABC, this analysis is typical because ABC changes the way managers fundamentally view their business. With ABC, managers view business as a series of activities, on the one hand, consuming resources and, on the other, satisfying customer needs. This perspective instills the view of causation between decisions, investments, policies, systems, and customer needs and costs. This philosophy forever changes a manager's approach to business.

Both the shareholder value concept and ABC focus on the strategic business unit. Shareholder value analysis converts a strategic business unit's cash flows into a contribution to the company's value. Shareholder value analysis links each strategic business unit with the company's objective of shareholder value creation. This allows each strategic business unit to be evaluated against a single business objective.

Because the use of ABC allows one to properly calculate the cash flows of operational, tactical, and strategic alternatives, management can use shareholder value analysis to evaluate every decision against a single companywide objective—shareholder value creation. In the past, executives using the shareholder value approach have concentrated their efforts on creating value above the strategic business unit (SBU) or division level with debt restructurings, leveraged buyouts, divestitures, etc. However, these benefits are short lived. A company can only buy and sell divisions for so long. The majority of leverage points for value creation are at, or below, the SBU level. Building and selling products create wealth. Therefore, the level at which products are bought and sold is the level where the greatest leverage exist, determining which products to make, how to sell them, and to whom. Executives do not apply shareholder value analysis below the SBU level because they are unable to calculate incremental cash flows. Financial analysts are unable to calculate incremental cash flows because they lack product-specific overhead, which only ABC provides. Therefore, value analysis without ABC is limited to changes at the SBU level.

From these leverage points, you can see how shareholder value analysis links to a company's value, that is, its shareholders' objective with the performance of each of its business units. ABC, on the other hand, portrays the buildup of a company's activities and costs into strategic business units. Therefore, using shareholder value and ABC together links all of a company's activities with the company's strategic objective. With ABC, every management decision can be evaluated against one consistent objective—shareholder value creation. ABC provides the basis for analyzing strategic and tactical moves, while shareholder value provides the criteria, against which each move is evaluated.

However, you must be very careful in applying shareholder value analysis. SVA depends on a business unit manager's predictions of returns and growth. While ABC substantially improves cost forecasting, projections of future revenue must always be suspect. Executives may exaggerate their prospects to make themselves look better or receive a larger portion of the company's resources. Corporate management must be diligent in questioning all the major assumptions underlying the business unit's financial projections. Corporate managers must not allow the "hockey stick" forecast to go unchallenged.

SHAREHOLDER VALUE AND SUPERIOR FAUCET

Superior Faucet, as described in Chapter 6, provides an excellent example of why ABC is so important to shareholder value analysis. By using Superior's financial returns, expected sales growth, projected investment levels, and depreciation rates, you can estimate the company's future cash flows. By discounting these cash flows by each division's cost of capital (based on the parent company's cost of capital adjusted for each division's risk), a present value or shareholder value is calculated. This approach is applied using both the standard and ABC cost information. As Exhibit 8-1 shows, using ABC drastically changes the reported shareholder contribution of each of the divisions. As costs shift from one division to another, each division's projected cash flows change as well. The commodity division's value more than doubles, while the custom division's drops $16 million. By using ABC, the differences in share contribution become much more pronounced. This analysis makes strategic changes even more imperative—something had to be done about the Custom Division.

The Electronics Division, in spite of its low volume and high current losses, is expected to grow dramatically. This growth would require infusions of both working and fixed capital. In addition, the division's greater risk merits a higher discount rate. The division's market potential is outstanding; yet, with the higher-than-expected overhead, the division still has a negative net present value.

Exhibit 8-1   **SUPERIOR FAUCET'S SHAREHOLDER VALUE BY DIVISION**

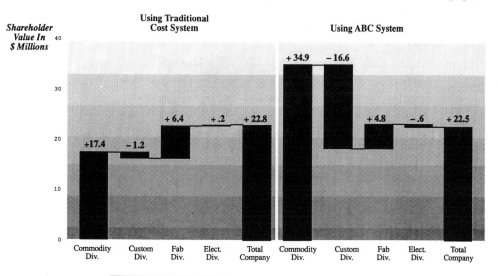

The traditional cost system and ABC show very different pictures of shareholder wealth creation

It is interesting to note that the total company's equity value declines slightly using ABC. This is caused by the more accurate cash flow projections that ABC allows. Under ABC analysis, overhead shifts to the faster growing businesses of the Custom and Electronic Divisions. Since these businesses were growing faster than the rest of the company and consuming more cash than previously thought, the total company shareholder value dropped.

After implementing the new strategy, as described in Chapter 6, the picture changes dramatically. Exhibit 8-2 shows the strategy's tremendous shareholder value creation—the company's value almost quadrupled. The Commodity Division reaps substantial overhead savings from the outsourcing, product line pruning, factory focusing, and streamlining. The Custom Division is sold off for $10 million.

The Fabrication Division decreases in value, despite operating improvements. More than half of Fabrication Division's sales were Custom Division parts that have been discontinued.

Other than forcing some streamlining, the strategy does not affect the Electronic Division. As such, this division still has a negative shareholder value contribution. Unless steps can be taken to increase its present value, the division should be liquidated.

Superior, being wholly owned by a parent company, has no publicly traded stock. Therefore, there is no established market value against which to compare the calculated shareholder value. However, you can compare the company's liquidation

Exhibit 8-2 **CHANGES IN SUPERIOR'S SHAREHOLDER VALUE BY DIVISION FROM PROPOSED STRATEGY**

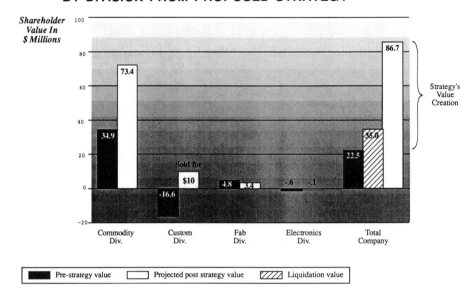

value against the current calculated shareholder value. Under current and projected operating conditions, Superior, with its large real estate holdings, has a liquidation value exceeding the company's operating value. Therefore, management would better serve the shareholders by liquidating the company than by continuing to operate it as it is.

Exhibit 8-3 details the value creation of each of the strategy's elements. The exhibit shows how much each of the strategy elements contribute to the $64 million in value appreciation. The methodology for assessing shareholder value creation will be shown later in this chapter.

It is important to note that all investments must have a positive present value—the investment's return must exceed the cost of capital. For many businesses, no investments with positive present values exist. In those cases, maximizing shareholder value may mean downsizing or even liquidating an otherwise healthy firm. A firm may possess valuable real estate holdings or other underutilized assets, which should be sold to the highest bidder. In other cases, maximizing shareholder value means building a company the old fashioned way—growing revenues and growing income. The vast majority of a company's value is, typically, the value of its cash flows more than five years hence. Contrary to popular opinion, a company managing for the long term is praised under a shareholder value approach.

In Superior's case, the Electronic Division has a negative present value. However, the division was not liquidated. Outside the scope of the strategy described here was a reorganization of the Electronic Division. The division's engineering,

Exhibit 8-3   **THE VALUE CREATION BY STRATEGY ELEMENT**

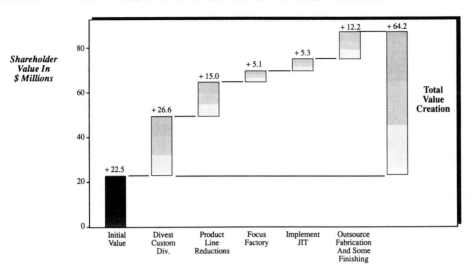

sales, and marketing efforts have been reoriented. The division's factory has been streamlined and almost all assemblies outsourced. These actions, combined with a new president, would, it is hoped, turn the division into a net cash generator.

Just as shareholder value is crucial to ABC, ABC is crucial to shareholder value. ABC provides the decision maker with more realistic cash flow projections by accurately assigning overhead to products and business units. ABC tells management which products are really creating wealth, and which ones are dissipating it. The ABC system, which segregates fixed and variable costs, allows one to accurately assess incremental costs of decision alternatives.

For a thorough discussion on shareholder value, calculating SBU value creation, and identifying the cost of capital, please consult Alfred Rappaport's *Creating Shareholder Value* (Free Press, New York, 1986). The book will not discuss how to value divisions or business segments, because the methods are not dependent on ABC. In any event, Rappaport does a better job than space allows in this book.

The following sections will describe how to evaluate a product line from the shareholder value perspective. Most past ABC applications have failed to evaluate product lines with a shareholder value approach. In fact, almost every conceivable measure to evaluate products has been used, except cash flow—ROS, ROA, ROI, residual income, net profit, etc. In some cases, the measures were used for simplicity, although it does reflect implementors' lack of exposure to a shareholder value approach to business. Most companies have not yet learned to manage for shareholder value. The following sections of this chapter will concentrate on evaluating product lines using shareholder value analysis. This methodology can easily be extended to other business decisions.

Assessing the Shareholder Value of Product Lines

Whether to Introduce a New Product

Product line decisions, like all shareholder value decisions, should not be "stand-alone", but should be a choice among various alternatives. A company chooses to introduce a product, or not to introduce it.

A company's decision to introduce a new product is both critical and complex. A grocery industry task group found that it costs manufacturers an average of $5.1 million to introduce a new supermarket product. Almost half of this cost comes from advertising and promotion. Sixteen percent went to trade deals to obtain shelf space in the stores, while 18 percent went into research and development and market analysis. Making the product is the least expensive step. A new product's cash flows must justify all these investments.

Likewise, the product line analysis must consider the possibility of competing product lines cannibalizing each others' sales, or of creating drag-along sales of other products. In addition, you must evaluate the present value of introducing the product versus the present value of selling off the excess assets. No decision should be made without considering it to forgone opportunities.

To properly analyze whether to invest in new product lines, one calculates a net present value (NPV). NPV incorporates three important elements: the product's cash flow stream, any net changes in investment, and the timing of the cash flows. To evaluate a product offering, one considers only incremental cash flow. The product's incremental cash flow in a given period is the difference between incremental revenue and incremental product cost plus incremental customer costs.

Incremental Cash Flow

A product's incremental cost includes all of its labor and material, as well as all variable overhead that the product triggers. These costs include production planning, tool repair, setups, sustaining engineering, and warehousing. The incremental customer-driven costs can include order entry, shipping, sales commissions, and freight.

The best way to identify incremental product costs is to simulate the company's activity levels both with and without the product. The difference between these activity levels is the product's incremental activity. Multiplying this incremental activity by the variable component of each cost driver's rate yields a product's incremental cost, as well as its incremental customer-driven costs.

The incremental costs do not include fixed costs (i.e., sunk costs) or costs that would occur without offering the product. The analysis excludes fixed costs such as occupancy, MIS, equipment maintenance, and supervision (naturally, if a proposed product line is large enough, many of these costs are not fixed). These cost elements are not included in the variable cost-driver rates applied. The incremental cost does not include any enterprise and market level costs, either. However, all costs are included in the calculation of income taxes. Exhibit 8-4 shows the difference between a delivered product's reported cost and its incremental cash flow.

Exhibit 8-4   **COMPARISON BETWEEN A PRODUCT'S FULL COST**
               AND INCREMENTAL CASH FLOW

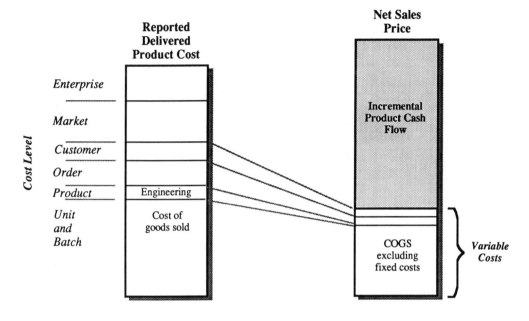

A product's incremental cash flow is very
different from its reported costs

The timing of cash flows is critical. A dollar today is worth more than a dollar tomorrow. One must factor all cash flows by the cost of capital and their timing. This process is known as *discounting.*

Discounting is especially important since much of a new product's investment is up front. The best time to evaluate a product is before its development. Exhibit 8-5 depicts the cash flows over the life of a typical product. A company must first invest in product development, and then tool up production, before receiving off-setting cash flows. Marketing and promotion campaigns must begin, dealers must be trained, and the product inventoried. These initial costs are significant and can vary greatly by product line—developing a power wheelchair is ten times more costly than developing a manual wheelchair.

New Product Costs

Most companies' budgeting processes greatly understate the costs of introducing a new product. A company's new product budget usually includes only engineering, tooling, and some minor prototyping charges. This is because most companies organize and budget product development around the engineering department. Non-

Exhibit 8-5 **NET CASH FLOW OVER THE PRODUCT LIFE CYCLE**

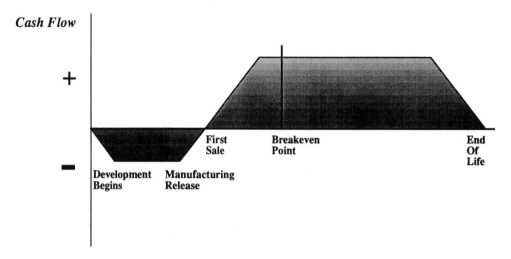

engineering costs, many of them variable, are buried within each operating department's budget and, subsequently, are not traced back to the new products. Marketing develops product requirements and promotional campaigns. Industrial engineers develop routings, time standards, and process plans. Usually, the industrial engineers must make new factory layouts to accommodate new product lines, in addition to specifying and buying new capital equipment. Purchasing frequently needs to find and qualify new sources for new product lines. Accounting must develop cost estimates, and quality assurance must write inspection procedures and audit vendors, to name a few additional costs. In addition, product introduction just disrupts production throughput and quality performance. With new products, a company must "ramp up" and debug production. As such, new products consume more production capacity and overhead than meets the eye. Since these costs are not engineering costs, the new product's budget usually does not include them. All these costs if variable must be captured by a new product line to make fair decisions.

To assess a new product, a company must estimate the changes the product will create in working capital. How much raw material, work-in-progress (WIP) inventory, finished goods, and accounts receivable will the new product add? The required inventory for custom products with long lead times will be proportionally greater than that required by fast-throughput standard products. Therefore, custom products require more working capital. Servicing certain market segments requires more investment than others. Retailers expect manufacturers to hold finished goods inventory to support JIT deliveries. Retailers are known as aggressive cash managers who withhold payments to the last minute, causing the supplier to carry many dollars in accounts receivables. Additionally, a customer may demand his own private label products, increasing manufacturer's inventory requirements and operating expenses.

To identify working capital needs, you must first estimate current working capital uses. You must assign all working capital to products or customers using ABC logic. After identifying the current levels of working capital required by each product, management must predict how working capital will change in the future. Various factors will influence the amount of required working capital. For instance, rising sales may increase the rate at which finished goods inventory turns. Therefore, while finished goods inventories must increase with sales, they may not increase at the historic rate.

Next, the company estimates how much capital each new product requires. This analysis highlights any products requiring new capital-intense assembly machines or test equipment. One aerospace company bought a $3 million piece of test equipment for just one product. Yet, the company did not include this up-front expenditure in its product decision. Chasing customers that require high capital or R&D outlays can drive down the company's shareholder value, unless management takes into account, not only the magnitude of the cash flows, but their timing as well.

Calculate a Present Value

Exhibit 8-6 shows a new product financial justification. The justification is a present-value calculation for the product line. This is the same methodology that was used to calculate each of Superior's division's shareholder value. The product costs are full product costs, including both variable and fixed components and depreciation. These costs are, of course, based on the forecast activity levels.

After calculating income taxes and depreciation costs, noncash-flow expenses are deducted. The project's analysis considers the total investment required to introduce the product, including engineering, capital, and working capital (finished goods and WIP inventory plus new accounts receivable and payables). However, these investments have no income tax impacts so they are added in after taxes are calculated. In the example, the company recovers all of the working capital as the product is phased out in five years. In this case the company assumes that there will be no cannibalized sales (sales stolen from other product offerings) or drag-along sales (sales of complementary products generated by this product). After cash flows are estimated, they are discounted to calculate their present value, at a cost of capital of 12 percent.

After calculating the new product's present value, you must subtract the present value of the alternative. In this case, the alternative to introducing the product line is allowing fixed costs to go unabsorbed. In Exhibit 8-7, all the fixed manufacturing and other costs that would have been absorbed by the proposed project remain. You must not only discount these costs, but adjust for income taxes as well. As you can see, not investing consumes cash, that is, destroys shareholder wealth. The present value of the D Series is $80,000 and the present value of not investing is –$28,000. Therefore, the project's net present value equals:

Net present value = Present value of project – Present value of alternative

$$\$108,000 = \$80,000 + \$28,000$$

Exhibit 8-6

CALCULATING THE PRESENT VALUE OF D SERIES PRODUCT LINE
A PROPOSED NEW PRODUCT LINE
(IN $000)

	YEAR				
	1	2	3	4	5
SALES	$120	$130	$140	$110	$50
COST OF SALES	($74)	($81)	($87)	($68)	($31)
GROSS MARGIN	$46	$49	$53	$42	$19
NEW PRODUCT DEVELOPMENT	($30)				
CUSTOMER COSTS	($16)	($17)	($18)	($15)	($10)
TAXABLE OPERATING PROFIT	($0)	$32	$35	$27	$9
INCOME TAXES	$0	($11)	($12)	($9)	($3)
OPERATING PROFIT AFTER TAXES	($0)	$22	$24	$18	$6
DEPRECIATION EXPENSE	$13	$15	$16	$12	$6
CASH FROM OPERATIONS AFTER TAXES	$13	$36	$39	$30	$12
INCREMENTAL WORKING CAPITAL	($11)	($1)	$0	$3	$9
FIXED CAPITAL INVESTMENT	($4)				
CASH FLOW FROM OPERATIONS	($2)	$35	$39	$33	$21
DISCOUNT FACTOR (AT 15% COST OF CAPITAL)	0.8696	0.7561	0.6575	0.5718	0.4972
PRESENT VALUE OF CASH FLOWS	($2)	$27	$26	$19	$10
TOTAL PRESENT VALUE	$80				

This net present value approach to product line evaluation supercedes all past attempts at *life-cycle costing*. The purpose of life-cycle costing is to recognize the changing cost behavior of a product as it ages in its life cycle. The concept was supposed to account for a product's initial investment, as well as for all service and warranty costs, as the product ages. However, the net present value approach includes all these factors without the complexity of arbitrary cost-accounting conventions.

One final word about product line profitability. One company expressed concern about accurately costing its product lines. Many of its products were low-volume prototype work which the company took in, despite knowing that the products lost money. The company ran the prototype jobs in its high-volume production plant, in spite of the disruption the prototypes caused. The company believed that you could not make a prototype in one plant and "hand it off" to the production facility. The

Exhibit 8–7

CALCULATING THE PRESENT VALUE OF NOT INTRODUCING
THE D SERIES PRODUCT LINE
(IN $000)

	1	2	3	4	5
			YEAR		
SALES	$0	$0	$0	$0	$0
FIXED COST OF SALES	($19)	($20)	($22)	($17)	($8)
GROSS MARGIN	($19)	($20)	($22)	($17)	($8)
NEW PRODUCT DEVELOPMENT	$0				
FIXED CUSTOMER COSTS	($13)	($14)	($14)	($12)	($8)
TAXABLE OPERATING PROFIT	($31)	($34)	($36)	($29)	($16)
INCOME TAXES	$10	$11	$12	$10	$5
OPERATING PROFIT AFTER TAXES	($21)	($23)	($24)	($19)	($11)
DEPRECIATION EXPENSE	$12	$14	$15	$11	$6
CASH FROM OPERATIONS AFTER TAXES	($9)	($9)	($10)	($8)	($5)
INCREMENTAL WORKING CAPITAL	$0	$0	$0	$0	$0
FIXED CAPITAL INVESTMENT	$0				
CASH FLOW FROM OPERATIONS	($9)	($9)	($10)	($8)	($5)
DISCOUNT FACTOR (AT 15% COST OF CAPITAL)	0.8696	0.7561	0.6575	0.5718	0.4972
PRESENT VALUE OF CASH FLOWS	($8)	($7)	($6)	($5)	($2)
TOTAL PRESENT VALUE	($28)				

company felt that the "hand off" compromised quality. This company believed that this philosophy differentiated it in its marketplace. By building the prototype, it knew it would obtain a high-volume contract if the product went into production. Management believed that if it accurately costed this work, the company would price itself out of the market or refuse the business entirely. While this is a very real concern, as long as management sets incentives that consider investing in, or "buying," new business, you can avoid this problem. Pricing contracts should not necessarily be based on costs. In this case, the company seemed to believe that it had to price prototype products on cost—when it did not. Obscuring your costs to avoid pricing errors is not an effective way to manage. There is just no substitute or excuse for not having the best information possible. As Peter Drucker said, "Management must manage."

Exhibit 8-8   **PRODUCT LINE CASH FLOW ANALYSIS**

CALCULATING THE PRESENT VALUE OF X SERIES PRODUCT LINE -
A CURRENT PRODUCT LINE

(IN $000)	YEAR				
	1	2	3	4	5
SALES	$45	$46	$47	$47	$47
COST OF SALES	($68)	($69)	($71)	($71)	($71)
GROSS MARGIN	($23)	($23)	($24)	($24)	($24)
NEW PRODUCT DEVELOPMENT					
CUSTOMER COSTS	($8)	($8)	($8)	($8)	($8)
TAXABLE OPERATING PROFIT	($31)	($31)	($32)	($32)	($32)
INCOME TAXES	$10	$10	$10	$10	$10
OPERATING PROFIT AFTER TAXES	($20)	($21)	($21)	($21)	($21)
DEPRECIATION EXPENSE	$6	$3	$3	$2	$2
CASH FROM OPERATIONS AFTER TAXES	($14)	($18)	($18)	($19)	($19)
INCREMENTAL WORKING CAPITAL					$3
FIXED CAPITAL INVESTMENT					
CASH FLOW FROM OPERATIONS	($14)	($18)	($18)	($19)	($16)
DISCOUNT FACTOR (AT 15% COST OF CAPITAL)	0.8696	0.7561	0.6575	0.5718	0.4972
PRESENT VALUE OF CASH FLOWS	($12.487)	($13.436)	($11.904)	($10.924)	($8.007)
TOTAL PRESENT VALUE	($56.759)				

Analyzing Existing Product Lines

Existing product lines are analyzed using the same present value approach, except that existing product lines require no development and usually no capital investment. When you identify a capacity constraint, an alternative to capital investment is to discontinue the least effective product absorbing the constrained capacity. In addition, you must seek to identify any assets that can be sold as used equipment, or even scrapped for salvage if a product line is discontinued. If sufficient product reductions take place, it is possible to sell a plant or lease out floor space. It may even be worthwhile to sell and write off underutilized equipment. Writing off equipment immediately allows the company to shelter income against taxes, thereby increasing cash flow.

Often, ABC identifies products which have such high variable overhead that their incremental cost exceeds their net selling price. These products consume cash and reduce shareholder value, even though they do not require any incremental investment (see Exhibit 8-8). As with all shareholder analysis, you must compare the product's ongoing production with the net present value of discontinuing it. In this case due to the series' high cost, the company loses less by discontinuing the product (see Exhibit 8-9). You must always determine which alternative will maximize a company's shareholder value. Every decision should be viewed at as a choice between different alternatives.

Exhibit 8-9

CALCULATING THE PRESENT VALUE OF DISCONTINUING X SERIES PRODUCT LINE (IN $000)

	YEAR				
	1	2	3	4	5
SALES	$0	$0	$0	$0	$0
FIXED COST OF SALES	($14)	($14)	($14)	($14)	($14)
GROSS MARGIN	($14)	($14)	($14)	($14)	($14)
NEW PRODUCT DEVELOPMENT					
FIXED CUSTOMER COSTS	($8)	($8)	($8)	($8)	($8)
TAXABLE OPERATING					
PROFIT	($22)	($22)	($22)	($22)	($22)
INVENTORY OBSOLESCENT	($1)				
ASSET WRITE OFF	($6)	$0	$0	$0	$0
INCOME TAXES	$9	$7	$7	$7	$7
OPERATING PROFIT AFTER					
TAXES	($19)	($15)	($15)	($15)	($15)
INVENTORY OBSOLESCENT	$1				
ASSET WRITE OFF	$6				
REMAINING DEPRECIATION	$3	$2	$1	$1	$1
CASH FROM OPERATIONS					
AFTER TAXES	($9)	($13)	($14)	($14)	($14)
INCREMENTAL WORKING					
CAPITAL	$2				
FIXED CAPITAL					
INVESTMENT					
CASH FLOW FROM					
OPERATIONS	($7)	($13)	($14)	($14)	($14)
DISCOUNT FACTOR (AT 15%					
COST OF CAPITAL)	0.8696	0.7561	0.6575	0.5718	0.4972
PRESENT VALUE					
OF CASH FLOWS	($6.170)	($9.531)	($9.078)	($7.895)	($6.865)
TOTAL PRESENT VALUE	($39.539)				

The next case, California Sunroof, illustrates how one company used ABC to evaluate cash-flow improvements.

CASE STUDY
California Sunroof—Choosing a New Strategy

California Sunroof was about to embark on a journey. Outside investors had recently bought the company in a leveraged buy-out (LBO) and replaced the president. The interim president, familiar with ABC, wanted a fresh look at the operations prior to putting the company on a new course.

California Sunroof employed 150 people and sold after-market pop-up sunroofs. The business was very seasonal—the majority of sunroofs being sold in the spring and early summer. With the market being seasonal and weather dependent, the installers did not wish to carry inventory. A cloudy summer could ruin the whole season. Therefore, quick, reliable delivery was very important to installers. With quick delivery they did not need to keep as much inventory on hand.

Being pop-up and not automatic, the sunroofs were usually installed in the after market on low-end automobiles—under $14,000. As with most after-market auto supplies, the market was very price conscious.

With the LBO, the company was very cash conscious. Immediately after being bought, the company was forced to lay off a third of its work force. The ABC study had many objectives, but the main objective, and the one this case will emphasize, was identifying net cash consuming products for elimination.

The manufacturing process consists of fabrication, in which extruded aluminum is sawed, bent, and welded. The next step is painting, in which the aluminum frame and trim are painted black. The next process is gasket assembly, in which extruded rubber is sliced and bonded into the frames as gaskets. The next department is components, in which components such as handles are assembled. These parts are brought together in assembly, where the glass is installed in the frames. From there, the assembly is packaged.

The company manufactured more than 120 different types of sunroofs in various sizes, glass types, trims, and styles. The ABC installation was challenging. The company had no MRP system and, therefore, lacked automated records of transactions. Just three months earlier, the product line had undergone a complete changeover; therefore, only limited historic cost information applied to for the current product offering. The business was seasonal, so the company costs would have to be amortized across the year's projected sales. In addition, the costs would have to compensate for the large seasonal work force. The accounting department had no departmental budgets, only a general ledger. Yet, within six weeks, one man working alone had developed an ABC cost model for the company (see Exhibit 8-10).

To identify incremental cash flows by product line, the company's overhead was split into variable and fixed components. Each department's variable and fixed overhead were allocated based on labor hours to each product, as it passed through each manufacturing department (in addition to direct labor and material, of course). The variable component included fringe benefits, expendable tooling, some utilities costs, paint, and other supplies. The fixed allocation included depreciation, engineering, maintenance, supervision, and other costs.

The costs of purchasing and inventory planning were assigned separately. Since material was planned by trim height and size, the analyst divided the total purchasing and planning costs by the number of different heights and sizes. This cost was then amortized across the number of units of that height and size.

All of the setup costs from the different manufacturing departments were aggregated. To obtain the number of setups that each product triggered, the analyst sifted through the records of the fabrication supervisor and counted up all of the different runs by product. These numbers were then adjusted to compensate for the manual adjustments that take place if a

Exhibit 8-10 **SUNROOF ABC ARCHITECTURE**

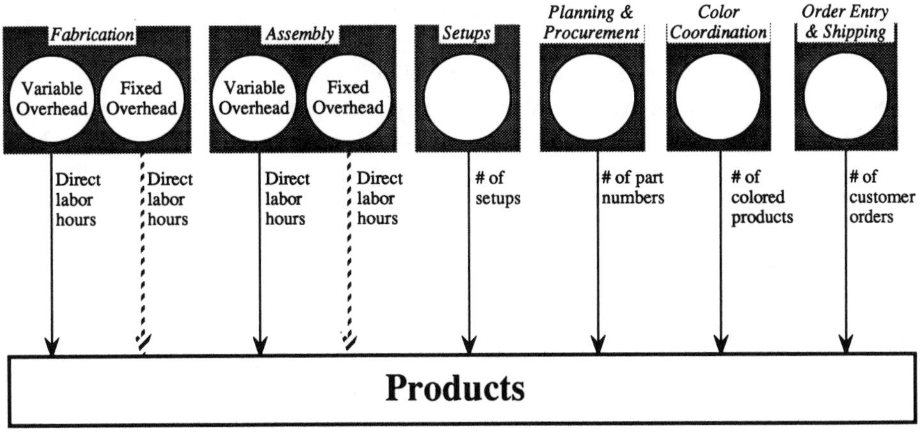

new lot of raw material is needed to complete a given batch. Setup costs, based on the number of setups required, were assigned to each product.

The lost labor efficiency—the difference between earned labor standards and actual labor performance—was significant. Since these costs were created by part shortages and poor scheduling, it was felt that these costs were generated largely by production changeovers. Therefore, these costs were assigned based on the number of production changeovers for each product. Both setups and lost labor were considered variable costs.

Using just a spreadsheet and the variable cost data, the analyst calculated incremental cash flow for each product. The analyst discovered that 40 percent of the products were net cash flow consumers. These products amounted to 15 percent of sales. The following year, the company eliminated these "cash hogs" and developed a new marketing strategy.

Lessons Learned

There are two lessons in this case. The first lesson is that one can develop an ABC system in a company lacking an MRP system—crude though the system may be. The data collection task was more time consuming and many shortcuts had to be taken. The analyst relied on surveys and manual records to a great extent. In addition, the analyst had to construct some very complex spreadsheets.

The second lesson is that you can use ABC to calculate incremental cash flows. In this system, by segmenting all process overhead into fixed and variable, the analyst calculated the variable costs of each product. This variable cost was used to calculate product-specific cash-flow contributions.

The Influence of Shareholder Value Analysis on Cost-Management Systems

The advent of shareholder value analysis is already influencing regulatory reporting. Money managers and shareholder rights groups have been pushing for greater reporting of cash flows and incurred liabilities, that is, pension commitments to better assess corporate worth. As regulatory agencies bow to this pressure, greater cash flow reporting will be required. In addition, as the awareness and understanding of shareholder value grows, managers will require more accurate information for calculating cash flows. These needs will drive changes in cost management.

Today, the greatest hurdle facing an executive who is attempting to perform shareholder value analysis below the strategic business unit is the difficulty of obtaining a true picture of product-specific overhead. ABC resolves this problem quite nicely. The next challenge is the identification of variable and fixed costs for product lines, given different scenarios and time frames. Analysts must be able to identify fixed and variable costs under a variety of different circumstances to calculate incremental cash flows. Therefore, the cost-management system of the future must support this need. The cost system of the future must allow analysts to peg accounts as fixed and variable, segregating costs in the final cost analysis. Therefore, the cost system of the future must be constructed as a database with simulation capability. The database would allow costs to be segregated and pegged as the costs flow through the analysis. The simulation capability would allow cost estimates under a variety of sales scenarios. These capabilities will allow the cost management system of the future to support value analysis.

Naturally, even with this futuristic cost management system, a substantial amount of other financial data is required. One must consider the opportunity cost of assets in any shareholder value analysis. The opportunity cost is the potential benefit that would be gained by pursuing an alternative course of action. This considers alternate uses of equipment and their outright disposal. The opportunity cost considers the rent or sale of buildings or floor space as a potential alternative. Closely tied to this idea is the consideration of any contingency costs. Contingency costs are the costs of pursuing an alternative course of action. These could include the closing costs of a facility such as toxic waste cleanup or severance programs. One must consider any net changes in investment, whether that is inventory, receivables, or installing new machines. Last, and frequently forgotten, you must consider the tax affects of any alternatives. All these factors, while they are essential to in the shareholder value analysis, are not part of the cost-management system. Therefore, while the cost system of the future will support value analysis, the usefulness of the data will always depend on the financial analyst's skills.

SUMMARY

Value-based planning methods provide a more rational framework for linking a corporation's business strategy with its contribution to shareholder value. This approach enables business unit executives to evaluate their corporate strategies, investments, and business decisions in terms of their contribution to corporate value creation. However, shareholder value creation depends on accurately estimating every decision's incremental cash flows. This is where ABC comes in. ABC identifies those costs which are truly variable and fixed and which overhead is product specific. This information allows shareholder value creation to be performed at the operating level of the business, by permitting the calculation of accurate net present value of cash flows. This application, as demonstrated, can tremendously affect a business unit's value.

CHAPTER 9

COST, CUSTOMER FOCUS
AND COMPETITIVE STRATEGY

The surest foundation of a business concern is quality.
And after quality—a long time after—comes cost.

Andrew Carnegie

This simple philosophy, together with the talent to find and hire master workers, allowed Andrew Carnegie to build one of the greatest business enterprises the world has ever seen. Carnegie, a penniless Scottish emigrant, worked his way up to division superintendent at the Pennsylvania Railroad Company. Always looking for opportunity, Carnegie helped invent and promote the Woodruff Palace Car—the world's first sleeping railroad car. Yet, in 1865, he left the railroad to pursue the more promising future he saw in iron.

With partners, he organized the Keystone Bridge Company, the first company to build iron bridges. From replacing wooden bridges, Carnegie moved into manufacturing iron rails and then locomotives. After meeting the "crazy Frenchman" Bessemer, Carnegie converted all his iron operations to steel. A former railroad worker himself, he foresaw the boon that steel would be to railroading, permitting larger tonnage movements over more resistant, yet flexible, tracks. Seizing the opportunity, he built new "million-dollar" steel mills modeled after the great English Bessemer plants. To gain further advantage, Carnegie shrewdly named these new mills the "J. Edgar Thomson Works," after his largest potential customer, the president of the Pennsylvania Railroad.

These mills were supplied with cheap ore shipments over the Great Lakes, and practically sat on top of the great coke fields of Pennsylvania. Carnegie captured the largest share of the insatiable American steel demand. Steel rails were being laid coast to coast, over steel bridges for steel locomotives. In 1883, Carnegie Brothers & Company was running day and night, shipping 10,000 tons of steel a month. The company made more than $1,625,000 a year.

Throughout these years, Carnegie never relented, always driving for greater economies and higher quality. Using the genius of Captain "Bill" Jones, Carnegie Steel built ever larger furnaces, with hotter blasts and more powerful blast engines. These innovations not only raised production yields, but improved the steel's consistency and strength. Carnegie built the first integrated iron and steel plant and eventually integrated backward into iron mining, as well as railroading and shipping. When the new, more efficient open-hearth furnace came along, he replaced the Bessemer converter that had served him so well. Carnegie Steel was consistently the low-cost producer of steel. Between 1878 and 1898, these developments pushed the cost per ton of steel down from $36.52 to $12.00.

By 1899, Carnegie Steel accounted for more than 70 percent of the country's exported steel and made more than $21,000,000 in profits. When J. P. Morgan bought Carnegie Steel Company for $492,000,000 in 1901, it was the largest financial transaction in history. While Carnegie devoted the rest of his life to philanthropy, the merger of Carnegie Steel and Federal Steel formed U.S. Steel. If there was ever a successful businessman, it was Andrew Carnegie.

If there is a danger lurking in ABC, it is that Andrew Carnegie's words will be forgotten, and a company will focus on cost rather than the customer. ABC and the cost of goods to the customer are important factors in the success of a business, but not the most important factor. Giving the customer what he/she wants is the key to success.

If a company puts today's profits before customer satisfaction, it erodes a company's value and competitiveness. Keeping the customers coming back generates future cash flows, without which a company is merely a collection of assets and liabilities. Putting cost before the customer is a very poor idea and a much worse strategy.

WHAT IS THE OBJECTIVE OF BUSINESS?

From Society's Viewpoint

From the capitalist society's viewpoint, the objective of business is to create and satisfy customer needs. The role of business in society is transforming resources such as raw materials, labor, knowledge, and capital into products or services that satisfy customer needs. In this system customers communicate their needs by voting with their pocketbooks. The more customers desire something, the more they are willing to pay. If society demands more of a product, prices rise; if society demands less, prices fall. To reward people for this transformation, an incentive called *profit* evolved. The greater the gap is between the price customers will pay for a product and the cost of resources, the greater the incentive to enter the business and satisfy the customer. With more customers satisfied, more efficient transformation of resources, or greater customer demand, wealth is created. Market pricing works to establish a balance between customer needs and resources applied. In the words of the marketing pioneer, Theodore Levitt, "The purpose of a business is to create and keep a customer."

Owners Have a Different Objective

However, a company's shareholders—its owners—perceive a different goal. They wish to increase their investment's return, the present value of their dividends and stock over their holding period. Looking at the average shareholder return of Dow Jones Industrial Average companies between 1984 and 1989, dividends amounted to only 16 percent of the shareholder's present value in 1984, while the stock price increase totaled 84 percent. Thus, the majority of almost every company's worth is the value of the company more than five years into the future. Hence, in most cases, to maximize shareholder return, growing companies should concentrate on increasing their long-term stock market appreciation. Management should not focus exclusively on short-term cash flows.

A company's future stock price derives, in large part, from its future growth and profitability, which in turn arise from a company's competitive advantage. To achieve a sustained competitive advantage, a company must either deliver products at the lowest price, like Whirlpool, or differentiate its products on customer value, like Maytag. Customer value is the product's desirability as perceived by the customer. However, over the long term, only differentiating its products on customer value is sustainable.

In the supercomputer market, when Cray first pioneered the market, the value of its stock jumped by 1,600 percent in four years. This high return attracted Fujitsu, NEC, Control Data, and Hitachi. While these entrants depressed Cray's profitability, Cray maintained unusually high returns by continually bringing computers of superior performance to the market. Thus, to maintain high profitability in a competitive market, a company must, like Cray, always work to stay ahead of the competition. A company must either fill new customer needs or increase customer demand.

Most Value Is Not Created in the Short Term

Many managers confuse shareholder value creation with short-term profit seeking. A short-term profit mind-set inherently undermines a business over the long term. Maximizing profits with no regard for the customers is shortsighted and destructive. Ignoring customer needs leads to customer dissatisfaction; simultaneously, unusually high profits attract competition. Thus, short-term profit maximization jeopardizes the company's future cash flows and business, which in the future is where the majority of a company's real value lies.

Misguided Cost Focus

As our owner-managers were replaced by "professionals," America's business philosophy increasingly became cost focused. This philosophy was reemphasized after the Boston Consulting Group expounded the experience curve's cost reductions. The experience curve became the centerpiece of many companies' strategies. Companies tried to drive their competitors out of the market by building an insurmountable cost advantage. Implicit in this strategy was the idea that competition is one dimensional—strictly based on price. A 1988 survey by Service 1st Corporation, of over 200 companies, found that three out of four respondents said that the only way to survive was to compete on price.

Yet, two different studies of competitive success found that price was almost irrelevant to business success. The PIMS (1) studies have analyzed the relationships between business performance and such factors as sales growth, capital investment, customer-perceived quality, relative price, and R&D spending in over 2,000 business units. PIMS found that the two most important factors in predicting a business's profitability were market share and customer-perceived quality. Researchers concluded, "we found unrelated to change in market share was businesses' price levels relative to competitors."(2)

Another study of competition concluded that a low-cost strategy, by itself, turned out to be ineffective in achieving or maintaining market share. For example, Intel dominated the eight-bit microprocessor market from 1975 until 1982. In spite of Intel having economies of scale and first entrant advantages, it lost its position as market-share leader to NEC in 1983. NEC, by focusing its products and distribution channels on particular groups of customers, was able to provide its customers with unique products and services. (3).

To observe a low-cost strategy's lack of sustainability, merely examine a list of companies that were successful low-cost competitors at one time: Texas Instruments in calculators, Osborne Computer in personal computers, Monarch in machine tools, Laker Airways in airlines, and Gemco in retailing. A customer-driven company is driven to react to the marketplace, while a cost-driven company is driven to entrenchment. A cost-driven company is much less able to respond to changes in technology or the environment. Cost-driven companies run lean, having less support staff and discretionary budgets to experiment with new ideas. Unfortunately, any significant market changes, such as opening a new channel of distribution or developing a new product, require investment. The low-cost strategy then works to stifle a company's ability to adapt. Competing on price makes a company least likely to adapt and, therefore, survive. This conclusion helps explain why Japanese companies, after entering on the low end of the market, always work to upscale their products.

Putting Cost Before Customers

As "by-the-numbers" executives rose through the ranks, most brought with them the idea that all competition was price based. These executives became enamored with the experience curve and relentlessly lowering manufacturing costs. They predicated their strategy on increasing sales volume and reducing prices. Unfortunately, attempting to drive the company down the experience curve to compete on price oriented the company toward its products and away from its customers. Even Texas Instruments, long the experience curve's leading proponent, has reoriented itself. As Jerry R. Junkins, chairman, president, and CEO of Texas Instruments said in *Industry Week*, May 16, 1988, "I don't think there is any substitute for looking at the world the way your customer looks at it. If you don't look out, in a product-driven company you will tend to optimize around your internal organization and force your customers to adapt to your organization—theoretically, it makes you more efficient. It is important, really, to do just the opposite."

One of the major problems with any cost leadership strategy is falling into the trap of becoming cost driven and not customer driven. As Schlitz Brewing Company and Texas Air discovered, becoming cost driven has disastrous results.

Until the 1970s, regional breweries dominated the slow-growing American beer market. However, interstate alcohol deregulation and the advent of larger, more efficient breweries began to drive out smaller competitors that could not afford to invest in the more efficient breweries. And with the greater interstate competition between 1970 and 1972, the number of breweries in the United States declined from 154 to 65. At the time, Schlitz, with its Schlitz, Old Milwaukee, Primo, and Malt Liquor brands was the number two beer producer. Watching the regional breweries being driven out of the market, Schlitz's management came to believe that the industry competed on price.

Therefore, Schlitz launched a strategy to become the industry's low-cost producer and undercut the competition on price. Schlitz constructed superbreweries with over 4 million barrels of capacity, twice that of the market share leader, Anheuser-Busch. These superbreweries required no more staffing than smaller facilities, cutting labor costs by $2 per barrel. Schlitz switched to lower-cost materials. All brewing starts with malted barley—barley grain steeped in water and allowed to germinate before fermentation. Breweries add either corn or rice to be fermented along with the malt barley. Schlitz once used corn grits, but switched to cheaper corn syrup. Hops are added to the fermentation to give the beer its aroma and bitter flavor. Most brewers, like Anheuser, use natural hops; Schlitz substituted hop pellets. Schlitz also shortened the brewing cycle by 50 percent with such innovations as an accelerated-batch fermentation process. By injecting air into the brew, the process caused yeast to grow faster, shortening the brewing cycle.

In the short term (1973), Schlitz's return on sales of 7.6 percent and return on equity of 21 percent exceeded Anheuser-Busch's of 5.9 percent and 13.8 percent, respectively. Unfortunately, problems began to surface. In 1976, Schlitz was forced to destroy 10 million bottles of "flaky" beer. Between 1976 and 1980, consumers began to taste the difference. Schlitz's volume dropped 40 percent, and its stock price collapsed from $67 a share in 1973, to $7 in 1980. By the time Schlitz decided to rethink its strategy and institute strict quality controls it was too late, Schlitz had lost consumer confidence. Schlitz Brewing Company ended up being acquired by Strohs Brewing Company in 1982.

Incidentally, to stop its market-share slide, Schlitz began a new advertising campaign. Schlitz aired a series of TV commercials featuring tough sports figures, renowned for their brawling ways. These boxers and like were supposedly responding to the suggestion that they abandon Schlitz for another beer. They demanded: "You want to take away my gusto?" While the ad was intended to be tongue in cheek, audiences were offended. This disastrous advertising series became known as the "Drink our beer or we will kill you" campaign. The commercials incited a blistering wave of complaints and were quickly pulled from the air. Once again, Schlitz demonstrated its insensitivity to the customer.

Texas Air—Failure at Any Price

Texas Air, which owns Continental and Eastern Airlines, has also pursued a low-cost strategy, principally by slashing wage rates. In 1983 after filing for bankruptcy, Continental replaced its union work force with nonunion workers, at much lower wages. Then, Continental began to force out experienced, that is, expensive, supervisors and middle managers. These were the very people who got the airline back in the air three days after filing Chapter 11. Not only did these policies lead to a disgruntled work force, but to intermittent service and reported maintenance violations (Eastern has also been indicted for maintenance violations). In 1987, passengers plagued by lost luggage, long ticket lines, and late and canceled flights gave Continental Airlines more complaints per passenger mile than any other airline. Eastern was a close second. Together, these two airlines received more complaints than all other airlines combined.

Continental's MaxSaver discount program demonstrates most of the disadvantages of competing on price. First, lowering prices makes it easy for competitors to retaliate. When Continental inaugurated MaxSaver, it incited a fare war. Second, competing on price attracts the least attractive customers—in this case—the vacation traveler. These infrequent travelers buy strictly on price, and willingly accept off-hour scheduling. Since the vacationer buys on price and travels infrequently, the company builds little repeat business. The MaxSaver program failed to attract the business traveler, the industry's most attractive passenger. The business traveler is more concerned with flight schedules, timeliness, and airline choice than with price. In many cases, a business traveler pays half again more for a ticket than a vacationer, even though the seat costs per mile are identical. Frequently, the business traveler even sits next to the vacationer.

Yet, despite their problems, Continental and Eastern were not ranked last among airlines. In one survey of frequent travelers, rating both domestic and international airlines on comfort, service, timeliness, food, and value, Aeroflot received the dubious distinction of being last; Continental and Eastern were only second and third from last.

Texas Air, relentlessly trying to lower costs without regard for customer needs, lost both competitiveness and money. In 1988, while the rest of domestic airlines had a record breaking year, earning more than $1.7 billion in profits, Texas Air managed to lose 3½ market-share points and $718.6 million. But not to be outdone, Texas Air racked up a loss of $885.6 million in 1989, the largest airline loss ever.

THE CONCEPT OF VALUE

What's missing from Schlitz's and Texas Air's philosophy? The concept of value. Experience shows that customers select a particular product from a group of competing products not because it has the lowest price, but because it has the highest ratio of customer-perceived quality to price. This relative customer-perceived quality is called *value*. Value includes all of the nonprice attributes that the customers believe the product or service possesses when compared to the competitor's. Value is not quality of conformance, the traditional manufacturing view, but a measure of relative customer desirability and satisfaction.

Value is a set of attributes on which the customer makes his/her buying decision. A washing machine's value can consist of its washing ability, load capacity, water usage, reliability, exterior styling, financing, and service options. These attributes are weighed with some attributes being more important than others. While no two people have the same desires or perceptions, value represents the collective sum of the market's needs and desires. For instance, consumers consistently rank washing ability as more important than exterior styling when choosing to buy. Each attribute's value is also relative to the competitor's products and current technology. How well Whirlpool's compares to Maytag's determines value. If a company improves value, it increases worth and, therefore, customer desirability.

The value concept looks beyond the product by itself, and examines the complete bundle of product and services that the customer buys. A customer does not strictly buy a product, but also buys delivery, a warranty, a brand image, courteous service, and a manufacturer's reputation. Whether you like it or not, a customer buys a product and an accompanying set of services. This customer perspective looks beyond the traditional product/market perspective. This customer-value view encompasses every customer interface from order entry to billing. Every step in the customer's purchasing cycle can be a source of customer dissatisfaction, from misordering to overbilling. An incorrect order can foul up a customer's delivery schedules and cost the customer sales. A billing error imposes work, that is, a cost on the customer to correct the mistake. As such, a company with a customer-value perspective examines each of these steps in detail. Many companies have learned that it is just as important to handle a customer order properly as it is to build a good product.

Take a recent survey taken by the University of South Florida. The survey asked customers to rate 110 factors ranging from price, quality, features, and service characteristics that were most important when choosing a supplier. While relative product quality was the most important characteristic overall, it was overshadowed by logistics factors such as

- Meeting promised delivery date
- Accuracy in order filling
- Advance notice of shipping delays
- Action on customer service complaints
- Length of promised lead times

As this example demonstrates, to raise customer desirability you must look beyond the product and toward delivery, service, and after-market support. No longer can manufacturers afford to concentrate solely on products; now they are forced to manage their sales, distribution, and marketing systems as well. Manufacturers are coming to realize that these systems are just as crucial to success as the product itself.

The Japanese Don't Compete on Price

The power of customer value has not been lost on the Japanese. Even though many Americans mistakenly believe that the Japanese success stems from relentless price competition—it does not. The Japanese compete on value. Japanese companies may enter a market in the low end or economy position. From this position, they learn the customers, access distribution channels, gain experience, and build volume. Then they scale up their product by pursuing precise quality conformance, duplicating their competitor's most successful attributes and devoting meticulous attention to customer desires. This closes the value gap; as economies of scale build, they maintain their initial price differential.

In Japan, during the early 1970s, for instance, Japanese CAT scanners performed at 60 percent of the Western model's level, but were 40 percent lower in price. Ten years later, Japanese CAT scanners were still 40 percent lower in price, but matched 90 percent of Western models' performance. Meanwhile, the Western market share plunged from 65 percent in 1976 to 16 percent in 1980. The Japanese held the line on cost and competed on customer value. The Japanese relentlessly and continually improved their products. They copied their competitor's best features and value engineered the design (designing out cost while maintaining performance).

Delivering Superior Value Creates Profit

Delivering superior value has been found to be a significant factor in determining a company's profitability, and vital in staying competitive. Data collected by John Grooncock (TRW's vice president of quality), presented in Exhibit 9-1, shows the strong correlation between a division's profitability and its quality. Notice that "Overall Product Quality," based on the traditional measures of quality (product tolerances,

Exhibit 9-1 **THE RELATIONSHIP BETWEEN QUALITY AND PROFITABILITY FOR 47 TRW DIVISIONS**

Group Average	Overall Product Quality			Customer's Opinion		
	Quality Index	ROS %	ROA %	Quality Index	ROS %	ROA %
Top 16	4.8	5.5	17.9	4.6	7.7	26.6
Middle 15	3.3	3.1	12.8	3.1	1.4	5.1
Bottom 16	2.0	3.9	12.0	1.9	2.9	8.9

Source: John Groocock, *Chain of Quality*, New York: John Wiley & Sons, 1986.

defects, and reliability) affect profitability less than the "Customer Opinion." The ranking called "Customer's Opinion" consisted of customer perceptions gained through interviews.

Besides high market-share companies, the only companies that consistently deliver high shareholder value are those companies that also deliver superior customer value. Such diverse companies as Alaska Air, Apple Computer, Rolm & Haas, Rubbermaid, Liz Claiborne, and Nucor all have consistently high profits. Each of these companies has, using very different methods, successfully differentiated itself in the eyes of its customers. In many cases, the high-value company even outperforms its market-share leader, as shown in Exhibit 9-2.

In addition, more than one high-value company can be successful in one market, as compared to only one low-cost competitor. In pianos, for instance, Steinway & Sons and Yamaha are both successful. Each company competes on different dimensions of customer value. Steinway pianos are renowned for their artistry and uniqueness, such as even voicing and fine cabinet work, while Yamaha delivers high reliability and consistency.

Value Allows Higher Prices

Value allows high profit margins, in part because products can command higher prices. According to a recent ASQC survey (see Exhibit 9-3), consumers are willing to pay anywhere from 21 to 72 percent more for high-quality products (e.g., superior customer value). Or, as Frank Perdue, the well-known chicken grower, put it:

Exhibit 9-2   **HIGH-VALUE COMPETITORS CAN OUTPERFORM MARKET-SHARE LEADERS**

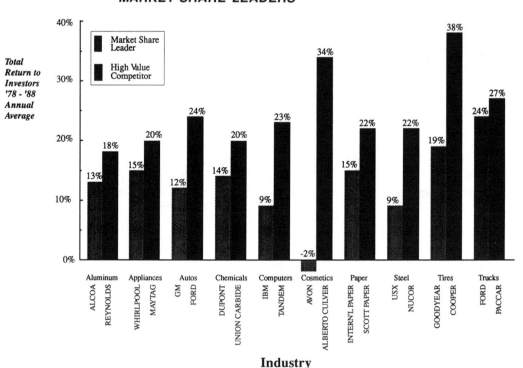

"Customers will go out of their way to buy a superior product, and you can charge them a toll for the trip."

Competing on Value Builds Loyalty

Competing on customer value attracts an industry's most desirable customers. When customers buy on value, they usually demonstrate loyalty to the seller, and are more likely to develop into a mutually beneficial partnership. A customer invests more time selecting a high-value product than a low-price one. It takes time for a company to evaluate a high-value product. A company must check references, evaluate and test products, and conduct quality and delivery audits. To evaluate a low price, all one needs is a quote. This qualification time and cost act as switching barriers. It takes time for the high-value customer to switch to a competitor. This cost, as well as the psychological investment, creates customer loyalty. When Komatsu entered the U.S. market with tractors 20 to 30 percent lower in price than Caterpillar's,

Exhibit 9-3   **SUPPLYING HIGHER VALUE ALLOWS HIGHER PRICES**

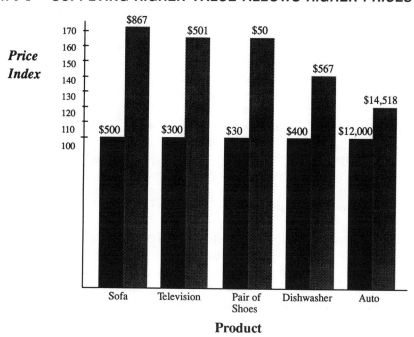

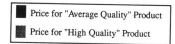

Source: 1988 American Society of Quality Control/Gallup Survey.

most Cat customers did not immediately switch. The customers gave Caterpillar time to make the investments needed to close the price gap.

Likewise, as Maytag, Inland Steel, and Cummins Engines found—each renowned for delivering superior customer value—loyalty pays. During the 1981–1982 recession, while the washing machine, steel, and diesel engine markets contracted, each of these companies picked up market share and financially outperformed its competitors.

Strong customer loyalty also makes the companies less vulnerable to price wars. A company like Allegheny Ludlum Steel, providing superior value with their extensive customer support and customized products, avoided much of the price competition in the early 1980s. Between 1980 and 1984, Allegheny averaged an annual return on investment of more than 15 percent. This return was in spite of a prolonged recession, heavy import penetration, a very strong dollar, and serious steel overcapacity. The steel industry was operated at 39 percent capacity at the end of 1982—83 percent is considered breakeven.

With high switching costs, customers are also more likely to work with companies to improve each other's operations. Manufacturers and their suppliers develop partnership arrangements. The manufacturers provide a valuable source of information, not only on the performance of their products, but on downstream applications and technological advances. Manufacturers can also provide management or technological expertise. For example, both Xerox and Ford have supplier consulting programs to raise their suppliers' quality levels and improve production methods. This provides Xerox and Ford with better components and avoids incurring switching costs. Suppliers, on the other hand, should be able to reduce their prices by sharing cost improvements.

When total customer satisfaction is the goal of the manufacturer, their suppliers are forced to reduce cycle times and deliver more quickly and dependably. These companies become more integrated and dependent on suppliers than before. By eliminating inventory and, more important, the need for it between the supplier and the manufacturer, both companies save money. Shortening cycle times improves operating efficiencies as well. This improves the manufacturer's competitiveness by reducing costs, raising quality, and increasing responsiveness.

High-value customers are attractive for another reason. High-value customers also tend to be high-value companies. The customer who buys value usually sells high-value products itself, and is, therefore, more successful providing ever-higher growth and sales. As such, it tends to be more profitable—and pay on time. High-value companies, as described here, also tend to grow more rapidly and be more successful. Therefore, they become an ever growing sales account.

Likewise, providing superior customer value also ensures repeat buyers, who require little marketing and sales effort, and provide free word-of-mouth advertising. A Forum Corporation survey found that the cost of keeping a customer is one-fifth as much as getting a new one—keeping the high-value company's marketing expenses down and future sales up.

In addition, delivering superior customer value increases market share. Market share, in turn, increases growth, economies of scale, and profitability. As an example, when General Electric culminated its eight-year effort to upgrade its dishwasher quality and image, they invested $28 million to automate its Louisville, Kentucky dishwasher facility. The automated facility, with its redesigned products, substantially improved customer value. When GE introduced the new dishwasher line in 1983, its service-call rate dropped 50 percent. According to *Consumer Reports*, which rated GSD 1200T as the best dishwasher buy, GE set a new washing standard. These value improvements allowed GE to penetrate the private label market and raised its U.S. market share from 31 to 41 percent between 1982 and 1986.

To others, like Corning Group President, Richard Dulude, providing superior customer value is "the ultimate issue of survival." He tells the story of how one day Ford Motor Company, one of Corning's biggest customers for a ceramic substrate used in emission-control systems, told Corning that its process controls trailed those of its Japanese competitors. More important, Corning could expect to lose more and more business. Corning was shocked; it had pioneered the substrate and opened the market. Corning took up the Japanese challenge and undertook an extensive statistical process control (SPC) program. Over the next three years, Corning created a whole new generation of processes, materials, and product enhancements. Corning not only saved its domestic market share, but significantly increased it. At one point, Corning converted a closed industrial flat glass plant to substrate production. Using its new processes, Corning built a European plant and secured a dominant share of Europe's dynamic and growing market. Finally, Corning doubled its market share in Japan.

Enjoying Employee Retention by Retaining Customers

An important by-product of customer satisfaction is employee retention. If customers are satisfied, employees with customer contact feel less stress and enjoy greater job satisfaction. These factors help keep experienced employees, reducing training costs and avoiding errors by new employees.

After a national automotive service chain began a customer retention program, customer retention increased by seven points and mechanic turnover dropped to a fraction of its previous level.

High Cost of Dissatisfying Customers

While the benefits of delivering superior customer value are substantial, the penalties of customer dissatisfaction are devastating. For example, research conducted for a telecommunications manufacturer found that over 90 percent of the customers who received inoperable equipment and did not complain would not buy from the same manufacturer again. Of those who did complain and were still not satisfied, over 80 percent would not buy again. The failure of a single piece of equipment, then, persuades most customers to switch to a competitor, and the manufacturer loses all those customers' future purchases. In this way, the failure of a $100 piece of equipment costs the company over $200,000 in future sales.

If that is not bad enough, dissatisfied customers told an average of nine people about their experience. It is interesting to note that consumers consider friends and relatives (in that order) to be the most trustworthy source of information on buying a new product. But it does not take a product failure to make a dissatisfied customer. The same research group (TARP) found that at least one-third of the time, dissatisfied customers stem from either an unfulfilled expectation or their lack of knowledge on how to use the product, while one-third stem from a manufacturer's policies and procedures, and only one-third stem from product defects.

I once asked Bob Arnold, a sales vice president at Norris Industries, if customers really hold a grudge when you disappoint them. He told me of a sales call during his first week at Norris Industries. When Bob showed up at the potential customer's office, the company president politely listened to Bob's sales presentation. At the meeting's conclusion the president told Bob he would never buy anything from Norris Industries as long as he was president. The company president told Bob, "You guys wouldn't sell me nails during the Second World War." Bob tried to explain that Norris Industries could not get material for any of its customers, but it was to no avail. This customer was lost for over 30 years.

Putting Profits Before Customers

Putting profits before customer satisfaction works against a company's long-term health as well. Kenmore, for example, sells what are probably very profitable installation contracts with its washing machines. For a fee, Kenmore servicemen will come out to install and balance its washing machine. I have installed washing machines many times so I did not buy the installation. I also resented the idea of having to pay for a washing machine that was difficult to install. Apparently, the washing machines are designed to be balanced at the consumer's home. From the day I installed the machine, it has never been balanced. Every time it runs through the spin cycle it squeaks. I swear I will never buy another Kenmore washer (in this case this dissatisfied customer tells thousands of people about his experience).

An ASQC survey found that 55 percent of consumers thought paying for service contracts was a bad idea. Moreover, the profitability of Kenmore's service contract creates a disincentive for Kenmore to eliminate the need for balancing. If Kenmore made the washer self-balancing, no one would buy the installation and a source of profit would be eliminated.

This also provides a competitor with an opportunity. Next time I buy a washer, I will specifically ask about balancing. A washer that needs no installation balancing will be more attractive to me.

Or take Fujitsu, in mainframe computers. Keeping computers on-line is very important to every mainframe user. IBM, with its worldwide service network, can have servicepeople and spare parts anywhere in the world, faster than its competitors. Fujitsu, like the rest of the computer manufacturers, is unable to match IBM's worldwide service network. Therefore, Fujitsu is striving to build computers that never break down. It is designing computers with extremely high reliability components and redundant systems. In this way Fujitsu foregoes the cost of building a comparable service network, at the same time providing the customer with something more desirable than quick service—service avoidance. Not only can this strategy nullify IBM's service advantage, but it will be much more cost effective.

For years, American machine tool builders, like Kearney & Trecker, Giddings & Lewis, and Cincinnati Milacron, built all numerically controlled machining centers to order. While each machining center can be customized, they had lead times of up to 18 months during boom times. Building to order allowed the machine tool builders to minimize their investment, hedge their inventory risk, and level their production. It also allowed Yamazaki, Mazak, Toyoda, and Okuma to capture a significant share of the market with their built-to-stock machines. These stock machines are configured with a limited number of options, and can be available in as little as a few days.

Therefore, concentrating on cost or profit, while ignoring value, typically results in both short-term profits and lost customers. On the other hand, building value increases long-term profitability, insulates the company from competition, and builds market share. Hence, building value, not increasing profit or reducing cost, best maximizes shareholder return.

Yet, American companies will continue to lose ground to Japanese, German, and even Korean competitors until they learn to manage for customer value, instead of short-term profits. At a seminar with 40 company presidents, noted management commentator and consultant, Tom Peters asked if long-term customer satisfaction was their company's number one priority. All 40 executives raised their hands. When asked how many measured customer satisfaction, no one raised their hand. Surprisingly, less than 10 percent of *Fortune* 500 businesses even measure customer satisfaction, much less manage their business by it.

CUSTOMER VALUE BUILDING THE COMPANY

To pursue a customer-based strategy takes a change in the traditional company's culture. To develop such a customer-focused organization, companies must do much more than expound the philosophy that the customer comes first. It takes leadership. Executives must talk to and listen to their customers. David Kearns, the president of Xerox, spends one day each month answering calls from customers. If he is in a meeting and a customer calls, he takes the call. Executives must prove commitment by example. For some companies, such as General Motors, this is quite a change. At GM, executives are insulated from the outside world in chauffeur-driven limousines, heated underground garages, executive dining rooms, and the cloistered fourteenth floor.

But more than just having executives listening to the "voice of the customer," every employee needs to. Salespeople, order entry clerks, credit analysts, shippers, billing clerks, repair personnel, and telephone operators are just some of the employees who regularly interact with customers. Each of them communicates an impression to the customers—favorable or not. Each point of contact can build personal relationships and pick up customer intelligence. Personal relationships increase buyer loyalty while they can learn of new customer needs. The point of contact can identify areas where the company has customer problems and find out what the competitors are doing. However, these actions only take place if employees are encouraged and a mechanism is established to take actions. By getting the employees to talk and listen to the customers, employees discover how their activities can better serve the customers.

Xerox's hourly workers visit customers. Shippers discover how squaring off boxes on the pallets saves on customers' shipping costs. Packers learn how poorly applied glue on cartons can foul the customer's material handling equipment. Companies from BASF, to Phillips Petroleum, to Metropolitan Life have established quality improvement teams to find and solve customer problems. Pillsbury established award programs for outstanding customer service. At Digital Equipment Corporation, every corporate officer is assigned an "Executive Partner" within a corporate account.

MEASURING CUSTOMER VALUE

Our management culture needs quantification. One must measure value. Measurement is needed to gauge the alignment between customers' expectations and the company's performance. One must give the organization improvement targets and feedback. Companies must track customer value and compare it to competitors. Companywide objectives must be established to ensure teamwork toward a common goal.

While many companies have internal measures that customers value, such as on-time delivery, fill rate, and call answering time, these internal measures rarely match the customers' perceptions. For example, one computer manufacturer proudly reported a 98 percent on-time shipping record. However, the customers claim that 24 percent of shipments were late. Why the discrepancy? The company's measure tracked the time up to shipment and assumed two days for delivery. However, subsequent investigation found that two of the manufacturer's carriers took, on average, four days to deliver products. Internally, the manufacturer was doing great, but not from the customers' perspective. To avoid this pitfall, companies must strive for true performance measurement from the customers' perceptions.

To center your business on customer needs and satisfaction, the company must measure and track value through customer surveys on an ongoing basis, like Florida Power & Light Company (the first American winner of the prestigious Japanese Deming Award), L. L. Bean, Metropolitan Life, DEC, Citytrust, Caterpillar Tractor, and IBM.

To measure value, the firm must identify what its customers perceive as desirable in its product or product lines. How does your product satisfy the customers' needs? What is it about your product that causes customers to buy it? How fast do the customers want delivery? What do they perceive they get now?

To start answering these questions, a company undertakes a customer value study. To communicate effectively, the study team establishes a common vocabulary that both the customers and the company will understand. This allows customers, engineers, and marketers to understand each other's language when describing the product and its uses. First, the team identifies all the sources of contact between the company and the customer and then documents how the product's nonprice attributes satisfy the customer's needs and expectations.

Questionnaires

The team develops structured questionnaires and tests them with a sample group. The team identifies the customers' market segments based on buying patterns, product mixes, and other customer characteristics. The company is even forced to define what its markets are, and who its customers are. One usually finds that each market segment has different weights for different attributes. The team then identifies a cross section of the company's market segments to interview. By interviewing and surveying the company's customers, potential customers, and distributors, the company identifies its needs, expectations, and perceptions by market segment. Typically, the survey results uncover new market segments with unique needs.

Identifying Customer-Value Attributes

After identifying the attributes, each is assigned a weight that reflects its relative importance to the customers. In the washing machine example, the customers rank washing ability as the most important characteristic; therefore, washing ability would get a higher weight than reliability.

Weighing the Attributes

After determining the attributes and their weights, the customers rate the company's and its competitors' products as vastly superior, superior, average, inferior, or vastly inferior relative to the competition for each product attribute. The responses are scaled so that vastly superior ratings are worth one point, superior one-half point, average zero, inferior negative one-half, and vastly inferior negative one. After summing the ratings for each attribute, the total is multiplied by its weight, creating the attribute's score. The sum of the attribute's scores equals the product's relative value rating, which can range from a high of +100 to a low of −100. This value rating represents the customer's perception of a product's relative desirability. The higher the value rating, the bigger the gap between your product and its competition. This value rating will vary by different segments. A producer may be strong in one segment and weak in another, reflecting design and service trade-offs.

To emphasize the need for undertaking a customer value study, typically the team first surveys management for the executives' perceptions of customer needs and relative importance. After developing the customers' rankings, one compares them to the managers' expectations. In all cases the gap between the managers' perceptions and customers' real needs is wide. For example, Allen-Bradley's Industrial Control group surveyed its distributors and found they rated "ease of use" most important. Management, on the other hand, rated distributor training as most important. Allen-Bradley was surprised to discover factory response to inquiries and repair service as needing the most improvement. Not surprisingly, executives had ranked these two items third and insignificant. These surveys opened the managers' eyes to their customers' needs, because they realized they didn't understand them.

Exhibit 9-4   **BULLDOG'S TRACTOR VALUE**

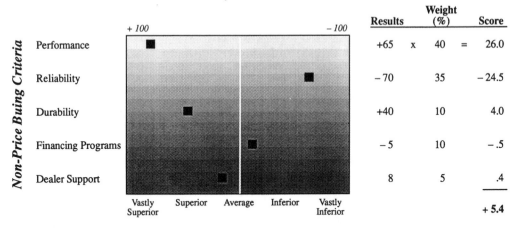

Linking Value to Performance Measures

Exhibit 9-4 shows a Bulldog tractor's value. Bulldog's customers, construction companies, identify performance, reliability, durability, financing programs, and dealer support as their nonprice buying criteria. As the chart shows, the customers perceive Bulldog's tractors as superior on performance and durability, but inferior on reliability. After applying the appropriate attribute weight, Bulldog's value rating is 5.4, or average.

The team tries to translate customer needs into product attributes and activities that the company can control. For example, measuring the time it takes a Bulldog to move 2 tons of dirt can be used as a benchmark for part of the performance attribute. For spare parts availability, Bulldog can measure the elapsed time between a customer order and delivery. This search for valid measurements, as with cost drivers, may be difficult, but necessary.

Linking Value to Performance Measures

By relating specific performance measures to each attribute, Bulldog can monitor its value rating, as well as its competitors', over time. It is important to remember that this performance measure grades actual performance, not customer perceptions that really count. When customer perceptions lag actual performance, management can reduce this lag with market education through advertising.

Measurement Drives Continuous Improvement

A company must push measurement into much greater detail to maintain continuous improvement and effectively manage the organization. A company finds that it must work hard to get continuous customer feedback. A company has to make it easy for the customer to contact it; installing toll-free telephone lines for customer service and ongoing customer surveys are two ways. Sales call reports and customer information cards enclosed with the purchased products are other ways. By using open-ended questions, management can identify emerging trends to anticipate customer needs, instead of just reacting to them. The feedback and its processing must also be timely so that the company can take corrective actions.

Management can use this value and activity data to set rigorous performance specifications for the critical customer interfaces. Companies such as Swissair and American Airlines record how long it takes to check in, deliver luggage, answer the phone, and open the doors on landing.

Rubbermaid makes extensive use of customer feedback, and more than 90 percent of its new products are a success. It generates reams of customer data from user panels, focus groups, brand awareness tests, and diaries that consumers complete with notations about product use. Most executives read customer letters to find out how people like their products and glean new product ideas.

American companies must learn to tie executive compensation to customer satisfaction like Domino Pizza, Perdue Farms, or Xerox. At Xerox, the in-field performance of products is measured by its own customer satisfaction management system. A chief engineer has 25 percent of his performance evaluation based on the results for his products. Executives must ensure that new product designs are driven by customer needs as they are at Ford, Texas Instruments, and Procter & Gamble. Customer value must drive everything from capital spending to manufacturing policies, and R&D to personnel recruiting.

The firm should use these measurements to drive a company to improve customer service. The goal should be to meet customers' expectations 100 percent of the time. Failing to meet expectations can cost a company a customer. If Federal Express loses one $18 parcel, it can cost the firm a customer forever. That one parcel then costs Federal Express all of that company's business over the next 20 years, or $300,000 in sales.

Both the identification and problem solving process depend heavily on measurement. It puts perspective on how important different problems are. This identification helps eliminate any customer dissatisfiers. This measurement can gauge the effectiveness of complaint management and its effect on customer loyalty. The measurement, by identifying gaps between the company's performance and the customer's perceptions, provides the ideas for actionable results by management.

This program is not a one-time occurrence, but must be ongoing. The company must constantly measure performance and solicit feedback. The company should also continue to validate the attribute and test the weightings—the weightings change over time.

By expanding the mapping of a customer's functions, you can gain great insight into their needs. A company maps out how the company's activities are consumed by its customers' activities. As with ABC, your customers consume the company's activities. By mapping out the linkages, the company can identify and leverage truly value-adding activities from the customer's viewpoint. For example, by studying the activities of a dealer when ordering a medical product, the company identified the opportunity to standardize the ordering process with the reimbursement process. Both require nearly the same information, but both forms were very different. By changing its order forms to parallel the reimbursement forms, the company reduced its dealer's ordering cost and effort.

A few years back, managers at FMC's juice machinery divisions found that their customers, orange and citrus juice producers, had little interest in juice processing equipment. The citrus producers cared only about production throughput and juice quality—percent oil and rind and pulp content. Since these factors were largely influenced by process control and maintenance, FMC decided to add the services of maintaining and repairing juice machinery. These services were an immediate market success. Today, FMC's machines produce 75 percent of the free world's citrus juice. By identifying unmet needs, FMC was able to open a new business and substantially improve the market penetration of their existing lines.

Besides, mapping helps identify unmet customer needs. Unmet customer needs are always revenue enhancement or differentiation opportunities. Since needs can never be fully satisfied, this provides opportunities and targets for constant improvement.

ACTIVITY-BASED CUSTOMER FOCUS

However, a customer-based focus is a logical extension of activity-based management. Activity management looks at a business as a set of activities. A customer focus looks at a customer as a set of needs, not as someone who buys their product. A customer's needs are satisfied by activities. Customers want to consume a supplier's activities in return for payments. In other words, activity management throws out the traditional product/market focus and looks at business as activities satisfying customer wants. It is the change from the internal to the external viewpoint.

This perspective is broader than the traditional product focus. In this environment, companies always look to satisfy customer needs, even as those needs change. A customer-focused company looks for unspecified wants and ways to satisfy them. It works to build closer relationships with current customers, as opposed to finding new ones. Building current customer sales works to keep transactions down, just as reducing suppliers does. By concentrating on selling more to current customers, a company creates fewer new customer orders, invoices, bills of ladings, and freight charges. In addition, marketing and selling expenses are avoided completely. A customer-focused company will even work to change the customer's perception of their own wants, so the company can satisfy them.

By examining how much customers are willing to pay for different products and services, you can estimate how much company activities are worth to the customers. In other words, you can associate revenue with activities. For example, UPS can tell you exactly how much its express delivery system is worth by how much customers are willing to pay. UPS can then compare this revenue to the delivery system activities that provide guaranteed two-day delivery versus the standard ten days.

ABC plays a critical role in improving a company's customer focus. ABC concentrates management's attention on activities. ABC defines how much each activity costs. It also bores in on what is triggering the activity. To be truly customer focused, management must look beyond the company into the customers' activities. While a company's products consume activities, so do a company's customers. The customers' activities consume the company's activities to fulfill their needs. The next generation of customer-focused companies will look past their products and directly at their customers' activities. They will realize that activities that satisfy customer wants are those creating profits. To manage their business effectively, they must concentrate on managing these activities, not output.

First, a company must make itself easy to do business with. A company must make it obvious to customers whom to call, what products are offered, and how to order products. A company must have knowledgeable people on the phones to talk to customers. These service reps must be empowered so that they can be responsive to the customers' needs. Product literature must be easy to use. One company I worked at had not updated their catalogues in seven years, in spite of changing over 30 percent of their product lines. Talk about confused customers.

With an activity focus, one can link all customer needs with a company's activities and how these activities satisfy customer needs. To become truly activity focused, a company must look at how well it performs in the customer buying chain (see Exhibit 9–5). From the customer's perspective: Are the customers aware of the company? How many are aware of the company's product offering? Does the company's product offering meet the customers' needs? etc. To develop an activity-based focus, you must answer these questions, as well as assess every step in the customers buying chain.

One relates the company's activities, policies, and systems driving the activities to steps in the customer's buying chain. Using the customer-value survey results, management can target the steps with the greatest leverage. If you can develop a detailed understanding of a customer's operations, you can even estimate the revenue generated by satisfying each customer need. By understanding how much a customer's warehousing, financing, and handling costs, a company can estimate how much quicker delivery would be worth to a customer. Using this information and value surveys the company evaluates how effectively the customers are being satisfied at every step, how much it is costing the company, and how effective the trade-offs are between different activities.

As current customers take on more importance with this outlook, customer retention becomes much more important. As one can imagine, a company can lose customers or commit defects at each step in this cycle. Some companies relate a percentage lost on each step and compare the loss to competitors as part of their customer retention program. An important question is how much fallout is being

Exhibit 9-5 **STEPS IN TYPICAL CUSTOMER BUYING CHAIN**

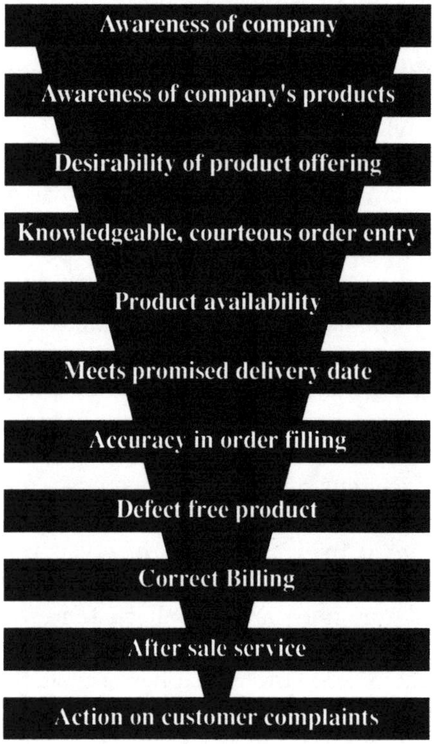

Awareness of company

Awareness of company's products

Desirability of product offering

Knowledgeable, courteous order entry

Product availability

Meets promised delivery date

Accuracy in order filling

Defect free product

Correct Billing

After sale service

Action on customer complaints

lost at each step? Listening to why customers defect, managers learn exactly how they are falling short and where to direct their resources. Defecting customers have corrosive affects on profitability. Losing customers forfeits the investment that a company has already sunk in developing the customer, as well as their future business. Retaining customers provide many benefits, sales expenses are avoided, loyal customers provide free advertising, and longtime customers buy more products.

Executives must manage the company's and customers' activities to complement each other, irrespective of the company's organization. Executives must set company-wide service goals that overcome the traditional functional performance measures. If the customer is dissatisfied, the customer does not care if the service department or the shipping department is at fault; the customer wants action. Customers do not want to talk to three different departments. They want the customer service representative, or whoever answers the phone, to resolve their problem—quickly. Internally, the company cares who made the mistake, but the customer doesn't. Therefore, firms must empower the customer points of contact. Management must give employees the authority and responsibility for customer satisfaction. The customer contacts must have the ability to respond to individual customer needs.

By increasing responsibility and streamlining the system, one can simultaneously improve customer satisfaction and reduce cost. At one company, they were handling over 500 credit adjustments a month, each of which the credit department took over a month to process. An investigation discovered that each credit adjustment cost $45 to process, and more than 40 percent were under $100. By developing new procedures, the company empowered the customer service reps to authorize all credits under $100. They improved customer satisfaction by immediately authorizing many nuisance claims and cutting the cycle time of all credit adjustments—saving close to $100,000 a year. The changes had one other significant benefit, they improved customer service rep morale. By empowering the reps to help the customer, the reps felt more fulfilled in their jobs.

Combining tasks and empowering employees to act slashes cycle times. One credit card company switched from having one person open mail, another write back to the customer, and a third track down receipts to having one person handle it all. It reduced the average processing time from 35 days to 6 days.

The successful company will manage its customers' needs. The company will satisfy its customers' needs, and identify and fill unspecified needs. They continually create and adapt to changes in the customers' needs. Once measured, value can become part of every executive's performance measures, as well as an integral part of all decision making. Assessing customer value can be part of new product planning, R&D, advertising, and, as the next section describes, capital justification.

Putting Customer Value into a Financial Justification

The PIMS database has statistically proven a relationship between value improvement (which PIMS calls customer-perceived quality) and market share increase for different types of businesses. Using this quantification of the relative value's attributes, Bulldog can estimate a capital project's resulting value improvement. Using the PIMS data, this value improvement can be converted into an estimated cash-flow stream.

Today's Capital Justifications Are Flawed

In most companies, the analysts use discounted cash flows to analyze investments, but they use the incorrect product costs for many of those estimates. Product costs include depreciation, but depreciation is not a cash-flow expense. Depreciation only affects income taxes; it does not affect cash. By including depreciation in the product costs, cash-flow changes are understated, making it more difficult to justify investment. Therefore, companies must learn to use the proper product costs when calculating savings.

Japan spends more on capital investment than does the United States with an economy little more than half as big. Why? Over 90 percent of American executives continue to use our current labor-based cost systems and conventional financial analysis to make investment decisions. Our current cost systems, by failing to identify overhead savings, greatly hinder any justification. Moreover, the whole conventional financial analysis is deeply flawed; it relies on erroneous assumptions and fallacious payback calculations. Conventional financial analysis only compares an investment's cost versus expected cost savings. This excludes any revenue enhancement or revenue protection from the analysis.

Cone Drive Operations, a manufacturer of heavy-duty gears, could never justify an investment of $2 million for a computer-integrated manufacturing system on cost savings in an operation bringing in only $26 million in sales. Yet, in 1985, the project paid for itself in just one year. The traditional justification procedures—so-called intangibles of better quality, faster time to market, and quicker order processing—all led to greater customer desirability. This greater desirability raised sales.

The Cost of Inaction Is High

The traditional capital justification makes no allowance for lost opportunities. The analysis assumes that sales will remain constant with or without the investment. This simply is not true. Failing to invest, or inaction in general, has disastrous consequences. Opportunity is fleeting.

After World War II, there were several efforts to develop a commercial jet. The British with their Comet was one of the first. The plane was based on the standard propeller wing design with jet engines attached. Unfortunately, the Comet was unstable at high speeds and the project was scrapped. For 25 years, Douglas Aircraft was the leading commercial aircraft manufacturer. When, in the 1950s, Donald Douglas failed to follow his aeronautical instincts and, instead, listened to his bankers, he decided to hold off on making the investment in the unproven jet market. His delay gave Boeing, the number three commercial aircraft manufacturer, a three-year head start in developing the 707. Its engineers gambled that a swept-wing jet would be more stable. After the successful introduction of the 707, Boeing had enough cash to immediately start the design and prototyping of its next aircraft, the 727. Even with its limited resources, Boeing was able to bring on the 727, just as McDonnell Douglas (the companies had now merged) brought out its first jet the DC-8. By failing to invest, Douglas, Lockheed, and Curtiss-Wright lost their dominant positions in the commercial aircraft business.

In 1975, Johnson & Johnson introduced a nonaspirin pain reliever called Tylenol into the U.S. market. A competitor, Sterling Drug Co., was marketing its own nonaspirin called Panadol, already introduced overseas. Sterling Drug Co. decided not to introduce Panadol domestically, to avoid competing with its own Bayer aspirin. In 1975, Bayer was the leading over-the-counter pain reliever. In 1983, when Sterling finally introduced Panadol in the United States, Bayer's market share had fallen to 8 percent. Sterling did not make its decision in 1975 knowing it would permanently lose almost 50 percent of the over-the-counter pain reliever market.

When Gillette decided not to match the introduction of stainless steel razor blades by Wilkinson Sword, a gardening and ornamental sword manufacturer, the decision was not based on permanently losing 15 percent of the razor blade market. Gillette made its decision to avoid cannibalizing its very profitable carbon steel razors. Gillette failed to invest in stainless steel, despite the knowledge that it provided a closer, more comfortable shave. In less than two years, with market share diving, Gillette relented and introduced stainless steel blades.

As Sterling, Douglas, Gillette, and countless others have learned, inaction can be just as destructive as poor execution. Opportunity is fleeting. Competition never stops. Competitive advantage, whether it be from superior knowledge, methods, or designs is always shortlived. Only through relentless drive and vigilance can a company expect to remain viable.

The Comprehensive Justification Approach

Fortunately, using the concept of value, one can incorporate customer value and the risk of inaction into the justification analysis. This puts customer needs into the management decision making process and brings it to the forefront.

Justifying an automation project can now include not only the project's cost savings, but also its increased market share. The increased market share's heightened sales and asset utilization are all included in the justification. As an example, Bulldog is considering installing a flexible manufacturing cell (FMC) to machine its engine housings. Engineering studies revealed housing failure as the principal cause of poor tractor reliability and a contributor to only adequate durability. This proposed investment would result in a direct impact on customer value, and, therefore, the project's justification includes the improved market share that the project would generate.

To incorporate this value improvement into the financial justification, the firm must estimate the project's effect on customer value. Exhibit 9-6 shows the FMC's expected value improvement. The project increases reliability by 70 points, and durability by 15 points. However, these improvements must be weighted by the attribute's importance. The firm expects the cell to improve Bulldog's value score by 26 points over two years.

To compensate for competitor actions, relative value is expected to drop by 3 points each year without investment or process improvement. Therefore, in year 1, the FMC improves value nine points, or six net points. The analysis converts Bulldog's six-point value improvement into a market-share change by multiplying it by the PIMS value/market share coefficient (see Exhibit 9-7) for the capital equipment businesses listed in Exhibit 9-8. In this case, Bulldog's will gain 0.9 percent of market share in year 1, and 2.1 percent in year 2. Exhibit 9-9 shows Bulldog's tractor sales

Exhibit 9-6   **THE EXPECTED VALUE CHANGE FROM FLEXIBLE MANUFACTURING CELL**

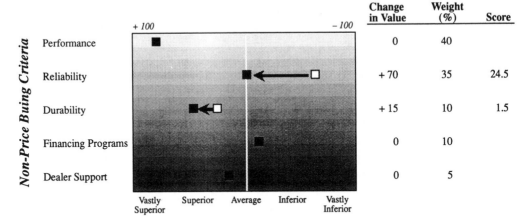

Survey Results

	Change in Value	Weight (%)	Score
Performance	0	40	
Reliability	+ 70	35	24.5
Durability	+ 15	10	1.5
Financing Programs	0	10	
Dealer Support	0	5	

Project's Value Improvement	**+ 26**

with and without the new FMC. Using market size, a $5.9 million sales increase is estimated with the new cell, over the sales without. This additional revenue is incorporated in the project's financial justification.

The analysis includes a declining market share over time. Competitors never halt innovation and new product introductions, and, therefore, if a company fails to invest, it should assume a deteriorating competitive position. To estimate competitive loss over time, a company first identifies its most aggressive competitor. The company compares this competitor's products over the last five years to estimate the average

Exhibit 9-7   **QUANTIFYING THE MARKET-SHARE INCREASE OF A QUALITY IMPROVEMENT**

Business	Expected Value Change	Value/Market Share Coefficient	Forecasted Market Share Change (%)
Capital Equipment	+ 6	.15	(+ 6 x .15) = .9

Exhibit 9-8   **COEFFICIENTS RELATING QUALITY IMPROVEMENTS TO MARKET-SHARE INCREASES**

Business

	Consumer Durables	Consumer Nondurables	Capital Goods	Raw & Semi-finsihed Materials	Components	Supplies
Quality/Market Share Coefficients *	.17	.38	.15	.30	.16	.38

* From Phillips, L.W.; Cheng, D.R.; Buzzell, R.D.; "Product Quality, Cost Position and Business Performance: A Test of Some Key Hypotheses." Journal of Marketing - Spring 1983

value improvement in its products. It must be assumed that at least one of Bulldog's competitors will improve their product at this rate, and the project's analysis must consider this improvement.

This approach overcomes one of the traditional financial procedure's greatest failings, the bias for inaction. The financial mind-set associated with the traditional justification is that the decision can always be made later. The decisions are not portrayed as time dependent. However, all decisions are time dependent. Douglas's decision to wait on investing in jets was catastrophic for his company. That decision could never be reversed. Opportunity is fleeting. The justification approach described penalizes inaction with lost market share.

A company should strive to meet and exceed customer expectations. As such, companies should be willing to invest capital to help meet those needs. It is not merely an issue of financial justification; it is an issue of competitiveness and keeping the customers satisfied. If a project dramatically improves customer value, it should not need a financial justification; companies should just do it.

This approach can be used to develop financial projections and has many advantages over the traditional method of extrapolating on past trends. This approach puts a premium on customer desires. It assumes that only a growing market or increased desirability leads to higher sales. A failure to invest in product or service improvement does not maintain the status, it leads to a deteriorating competitive position. This quantified approach avoids overly optimistic financial projections characteristic of sales and marketing organizations. Only by proving rising customer desirability does higher market share follow. This in turn leads to more realistic sales and financial forecasts.

Exhibit 9-9

BULLDOG SALES WITH AND WITHOUT
FLEXIBLE MANUFACTURING CELL

BULLDOG WITH FLEXIBLE MANUFACTURING CELL

YEAR	MARKET SIZE ($MIL)	MARKET COEFFICIENT	RELATIVE VALUE RATING CHANGE	MARKET SHARE CHANGE	MARKET SHARE	TRACTOR SALES ($MIL)
CURRENT	$21				32.0%	$6.7
1	$23	0.15	6	0.90%	32.9%	$7.6
2	$25	0.15	14	2.10%	35.0%	$8.8
3	$28	0.15	-3	-0.45%	34.6%	$9.7
4	$31	0.15	-3	-0.45%	34.1%	$10.6
5	$34	0.15	-3	-0.45%	33.7%	$11.4

BULLDOG WITHOUT FLEXIBLE MANUFACTURING CELL

YEAR	MARKET SIZE ($MIL)	MARKET COEFFICIENT	RELATIVE VALUE RATING CHANGE	MARKET SHARE CHANGE	MARKET SHARE	TRACTOR SALES ($MIL)
CURRENT	$21				32.0%	$6.7
1	$23	0.15	-3	-0.45%	31.6%	$7.3
2	$25	0.15	-3	-0.45%	31.1%	$7.8
3	$28	0.15	-3	-0.45%	30.7%	$8.6
4	$31	0.15	-3	-0.45%	30.2%	$9.4
5	$34	0.15	-3	-0.45%	29.8%	$10.1

Companies must commit to and expound a philosophy of customer satisfaction first. Every business decision should be judged by how much customer value is created. Executives must ask themselves will a particular investment increase customer value, and how much? What service policies will best fit customer needs? Customer satisfaction is and should be, a key objective of every business.

CHAPTER 10

BUSINESS STRATEGY
AND ABC

*Knowledge is the only instrument of production
that is not subject to diminishing returns.*

John M. Clark, University of Chicago

Art's long, life short, judgement difficult, opportunity transient.

Johann Wolfgang von Goethe

Greece was being invaded. Over 100,000 Persian troops landed on the beach in front of the plain of Marathon. The opposing Greek force numbered a mere 11,000 Athenians. Spartan reinforcements were detained, observing religious rites. After landing, the Persians established a camp and deployed, in a deep formation, near the shore.

Miltiades, the Greek general, knew their numerical disadvantage. While his troops were better trained and equipped than the Persians, these facts hardly made up for an almost ten to one disadvantage in men. For nine days he and his troops waited for the Persian attack on the hills above the plain, barely a mile away. Then Miltiades saw the Persian army reembarking. Obviously they intended to land their troops elsewhere. Miltiades decided to attack while many of the Persian troops, including their formidable cavalry, were trapped on their ships.

Miltiades did not follow the usual order of battle. He could not spread his small force the length of the Persian lines in the standard Greek phalanx formation—the phalanx required soldiers eight deep to complete the formation of overlapping spears and shields. Yet Miltiades decided that he would deploy his troops opposite the entire Persian line—by making his center thin while keeping his wings eight men deep. Brooks, on both sides of the Greek advance, provided natural obstacles to attacks on his flanks.

Instead of advancing at the usual slow pace of the phalanx, the Greeks charged down the hill at the enemy. This surprise maneuver caught the Persians off guard in the midst of forming their lines. The front rank of Persians went down. The Persian wings collapsed. However, their comrades drove back the weak Greek center, and they followed the retreating Greek middle.

As the retreating Greeks reached their initial position, Miltiades sounded the trumpets. With this signal, the two victorious Greek wings wheeled inward, striking both sides of the advancing Persians. Meanwhile, the Greek center rallied and struck the Persians in front. The Persians fought hard, but being attacked on three sides was a tremendous disadvantage. At last, the Persians broke and fled. The Greeks chased the invaders to the water's edge, managing to burn many of the Persian vessels before they fled. Great skill won the Battle of Marathon and saved Greece from invasion.

Even though this battle took place over 2,400 years ago and was fought on the field of combat, not commerce, its lesson holds true for today's executive. A force using a superior strategy and tactics can defeat a larger and stronger foe. However, a strategy is only as good as the information on which it is based. Just as the Greeks employed a superior strategy based on their unobstructed view of the enemy's movements, management can create and sustain competitive advantage based on the superior intelligence provided by ABC. ABC provides a company with a new perspective for viewing the business. ABC uncovers a wealth of information that can give the company competitive insights and opportunities. This chapter describes how to strategically use this information to create shareholder value.

THE ACTIVITY-BASED FOCUS

Activity management creates a fundamental change in the way a business is viewed. Under activity management a business is viewed as a set of activities. The philosophy of ABC is: Activities consume resources and products consume activities. However, products are merely surrogates for activities. Optimally, a customer's activities consume the company's activities as the company's activities consume employee's activities. In the ABC environment, managers strive to control the creation and operation of activities. This philosophy changes the focus of competitive strategy from the traditional product market to activities. This holistic activity perspective looks beyond the delivered product and examines how effectively the product is delivered and serviced. The activity focus even looks at how the product satisfies customer's activities. The entire approach is one that looks at how effectively activities are being consumed and why.

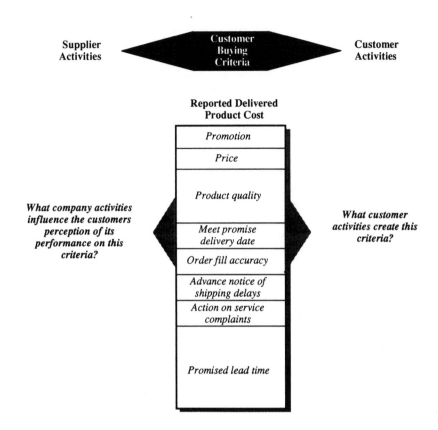

Under activity management, firms learn to manage their activities to satisfy a customer's activities. Management makes cost and service trade-offs to best satisfy the customers' activities. Management can evaluate the cost of each activity performed versus the benefit and importance to the customer. This evaluation can be quantitative or intuitive.

The company has the option of changing the frequency of activities, investing in capital or training to improve activity performance, outsourcing activities to specialists, not providing the activity, and many other choices. Since a business is a bundle of activities, a company can choose which activities it cares to perform. All other customer-required activities can be outsourced. No firm can perform all activities as well as some outside specialists. This philosophy allows the firm to build a competitive advantage by selecting the "best of the best" performers for each activity. The company, therefore, improves the leverage of its activities with the greatest value added.

Executives should use this information to develop the most effective strategy for the business—to increase shareholder value. No matter what strategy a firm is pursuing, understanding the trade-offs of fulfilling customer needs is critical to a business's success. How the firm configures its activities defines its strategy. A firm may configure its activities to be the low-cost supplier or to provide superior customer value. A company must understand the costs of satisfying different customers' needs.

USING ABC FOR COST MANAGEMENT

The first strategy for achieving competitive advantage is cost leadership. A successful low-cost strategy hinges on the ability to sustain a cost differential, while meeting minimum customer needs. A firm such as Emerson Electric will maintain this advantage as long as competitors cannot replicate it. The low-cost strategy leads to successful performance only if the firm provides enough customer value to satisfy the buyer's needs at the lowest cost. Unless the low-cost supplier continually improves its cost performance, a competitor will eventually supplant the cost leader. Obviously, ABC is critical to this strategy in that ABC provides new insight on a firm's basis of competition. ABC identifies key activities and helps diagnose systems and policies that drive cost.

Using ABC, Excel Medical discovered that its low-cost strategy was not feasible. In this case, the company knew enough about its competitor, GAC, to identify key cost advantages that Excel could not overcome. Management decided not to compete on price. Cost leadership was the competitor's strategy as well. Their head-to-head battle had a destructive effect on both companies' profits, although their price war did successfully drive most of the small players out of the market. Unfortunately, this strategy slashed share price by 30 percent over three years. Based on the ABC findings the president elected to reorient the company toward a differentiation strategy.

Providing superior customer value is the second means of attaining competitive advantage. Cost is critical to differentiating one's company successfully, because the firm must maintain cost proximity to the competition. This differentiation is successful if the superior customer value allows the company to charge a price premium. This premium price must more than compensate for the added costs of being unique. Unless a price premium exceeds the cost of differentiating, a company will fail to achieve a successful advantage in differentiation. This superior value may appeal to only a few customers or to the whole market. Either way, it is critically important that a company manage its activities to provide superior value while controlling costs.

ABC can also help identify value improvement opportunities. ABC can identify links between a company's activities and those of its customers. Such links can simultaneously reduce both companies' costs and raise quality. For example, by understanding what activities a customer performs to order and pay for products allows a company to develop a mutually beneficial interface with the customer. By installing electronic data interchange (EDI), the customers can check the company's on-hand inventory, query the status of their orders, and enter new orders. With automated billing, the company's credit position improves and billing costs fall, while cutting the customer's accounts payables costs and allowing them better financing terms.

One chocolate manufacturer discovered that one of their major customers melted down the bars of chocolate after delivery to make its candy. Since it cost the manufacturer money to pour, form, and package the bars, the manufacturer suggested the customer receive rail tanks of chocolate instead. This saved the customer the natural gas to melt the bars down, as well as the company's handling and packaging costs. All of these cost-cutting actions worked to reduce costs for both parties by integrating company and customer activities. Moreover, this integration increases customer dependency and creates switching costs.

From an ABC study's results, one may find that the company is not organized to service customers' needs. The company may need to focus the factory or outsource processes. One can find its distribution channels unsuited to current or future needs. Some of the channels may be too expensive or unresponsive.

ABC provides valuable insight to the company focusing on a particular market segment. By focusing, a company targets only a limited market segment. One way a company can satisfy a niche is to underprice the competition by avoiding some costly options that broader line competitors must offer. Another way is by offering special options and services that broader firms would find too expensive to match. The principal danger a focused firm faces is usually not competition, but a loss of focus. The company loses sight of its original target customers and begins to pursue others. This pursuit diverts management attention and upsets the company's economics. The company loses its competitive edge in its original market. The market becomes confused about the company's direction and the business becomes vulnerable to competition.

ABC helps avoid this situation. By reporting customer profitability, the ABC system immediately informs management when the firm starts losing focus. New markets usually have some entrance costs. They may be advertising, specialized salespeople, or promotions. These costs immediately show up in the customer profitability analysis. If a company begins to take on different types of customers, its cost drivers reflect it. The number of units per order, the number of invoices, and the number of bills of lading to each market begin to change. While these changes will initially be very subtle, as their affects become greater, trends are unmistakable. These trends alert management to conscious or unconscious changes in strategy.

Developing a successful strategy is impossible without considering the customers. The strategy transforms the customer's needs into operational goals for the organization. The strategy defines the criteria by which the company strives to differentiate itself. These points of differentiation guide the development of the marketing, manufacturing, and distribution strategies. The company configures each of these functional strategies to support its overall strategic plan. The strategy guides trade-offs on issues such as product line breadth, pricing, and level of service offered.

Manufacturing can support a technological leadership strategy by allowing rapid new product introductions, providing an innovative working environment, or developing proprietary processes. The distribution system can support a differentiation strategy by providing rapid deliveries with full service installations. Marketing enhances a focus strategy by recruiting salespeople from the targeted industries and specially training them in customer applications. Whatever strategy the company pursues, all the company's functions must cooperate.

If, on the other hand, the company does not articulate its strategy, the manufacturing or distribution systems may undermine it. If, for example, a company's differentiation strategy is based on market responsiveness, the strategy may be undermined by allowing the purchasing department to contract with Far East suppliers for critical components. Long procurement lead times would hamper design changes or preclude prompt delivering of custom orders.

RETHINKING STRATEGY

Because ABC drastically changes a company's perception of their business, after undertaking an ABC study, the company frequently rethinks its strategy. A company undergoing strategic change must ensure that the organization moves toward a common objective. To this end, it is recommended that the company conduct a customer-value survey in concert with any ABC study. The survey defines which product and service attributes each market segment finds most important. It also ranks the company versus its competitors on these attributes, and identifies what products a company must offer (product line reductions are a frequent ABC recommendation).

This customer survey information is invaluable. Many companies base their marketing strategies on fallacious assumptions about their customers and why they buy its products. These assumptions go untested for years, and in many cases are wrong. In company after company, survey after survey, the executives find wide divergence between their perception and their customers' perceptions of which attributes are most important when buying the product or judging different competitors. A marketing survey can lead a company to rethink their marketing, manufacturing, or distribution strategies.

Typically, the customers determine many of the minimum performance standards, such as delivery time, quality levels, product capability, and price. This still leaves the company plenty of room for differentiation in the services, product features, product quality, and product breadth offered. The successful company is sensitive to these minimum expectation levels. In addition, the company identifies the level of performance that customers perceive as superior.

An ABC study coupled with a marketing survey, inevitably, leads a company to rethink its strategy. Which customers merit the highest priority in resources and effort? On which factors will the company try to compete? The resulting business strategy guides the trade-offs between the dimensions of customer value and cost.

Most companies' overhead and SG&A costs dwarf their pretax profit by a 4-to-1 margin. When one recasts these costs, one suddenly find that many products are unprofitable. The results of an ABC study at Torquematic, a motor manufacturer, are typical. The study found that some products had a return on sales of worse than −3,500 percent. Exhibit 10-2 shows how profits accumulated across their numerous motor products. The first 20% of their products created profits, while the rest of the product line dissipated them. If Torquematic had sold only the top 74 products, while aggressively eliminating the overhead associated with the other products, their profits would have been $480,000 instead of $1,100,000.

Likewise, pursuing unprofitable customers is not bad—it is disastrous. It takes years to effectively reorient a company's marketing strategy. Usually, a company must reeducate the customer and reconfigure the manufacturing and distribution process, while introducing different types of products. Additionally, by pursuing the wrong customers, a company passes up opportunities and squanders resources.

Take the case of a door lock manufacturer deciding to reorient its business. The lock manufacturer shifts away from the mature builder market to the faster growing do-it-yourself (DIY) market. Exhibit 10-3 lists some of the differences between the builder and retail markets. The retail market demands different sales skills than does the builder market. The company needs to invest in consumer packaging point-of-sale displays, promotion, and advertising programs. Furthermore, the company would have to reconfigure its factory and distribution system. It takes the door lock manufacturer years to move its orientation from the builder market to the retail market.

Now, imagine the company repositioning itself as a manufacturer of retail products, only to discover the retail market is substantially less profitable. Despite fewer transactions and higher volumes, the retail chains' bargaining power enables them to aggressively negotiate away all of the manufacturer's cost savings, and more. As the company focuses on the retail market's needs, it alienates the builder customers. With unhappy builders, it would take the company years to reclaim its lost position. The company would have squandered years and countless millions of dollars chasing an imaginary pot of gold.

You see the most common manifestation of these doomed strategies when watching companies battle foreign competitors. Often, Far East competitors successfully compete against domestic companies using traditional cost accounting systems. The domestics consistently overcost high-volume products and price them accordingly, allowing the foreign companies to undercut these prices and gain share. Faced with declining sales, the domestics, using their standard labor-based cost systems, expand their product offerings to recover lost sales. This product line expansion creates more low-volume products that, in turn, needlessly drive up overhead and dissipate profits. The Japanese, in particular, concentrate on manufacturing only a limited product line. Rather than "dumping" their products on the American market, the Japanese can price their products substantially less, because they are not burdened with the losses stemming from low-volume products.

In the late 1960s, the distortions of the traditional cost system misdirected at least one company's business strategy in the antifriction-bearing market. In

Exhibit 10-2 **SHRADER BELLOWS PROFIT VOLUME PROFILE
FOR FLOW-CONTROL VALVES**

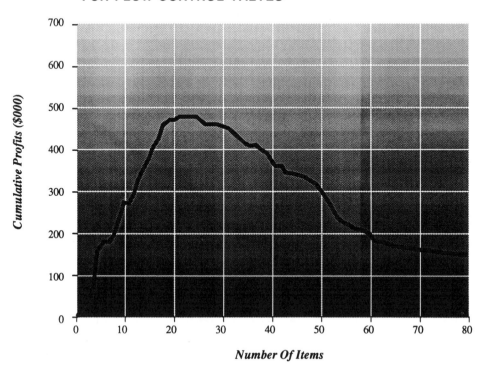

Source: Schrader Bellow (D-2): A Strategic Cost Analysis, Harvard Business School
Case Service Order Number 9-186-278.

Exhibit 10–3

CHARACTERISTICS	BUILDER MARKET	RETAIL MARKET
PRODUCT OFFERING	WIDE - MANY OPTIONS	LIMITED - ONLY FAST TURNING ITEMS
SALES & MARKETING	TECHNICAL SALESMAN	SOPHISTICATED MARKETERS PROMOTIONAL PROGRAMS CONSUMER ADVERTISING
MANUFACTURING	ASSEMBLY-TO-ORDER	BUILD-TO-STOCK
PACKAGING	BULK PACKING	CONSUMER PACKAGING
DISTRIBUTION	LARGE SHIPMENTS	SMALL FREQUENT SHIPMENTS

this market, Japanese companies fielded product lines having one-half to one-quarter the variety of their western competitors. One company that was nearly driven out of the market by the Japanese was Svenska Kullargen Fabrickn (SKF).

In 1971, SKF had factories in all of the major European countries, each geared to produce a broad product line for the local consumption. When the Japanese invaded its market, SKF avoided direct competition by introducing specialized bearings. The Japanese ignored this segment of the market. The Japanese not only had a limited product offering, but a limited marketing focus as well. Initially, the Japanese companies only focused on the largest ball bearing users, such as automobile manufacturers. These products commanded higher prices and were more profitable.

Unfortunately, SKF saw its total costs mysteriously rise as its factories became increasingly complex. Passing these cost increases along to its customers further increased its loss of sales. SKF's cost system, by failing to accurately portray its products' overhead costs, misled management. The greater SKF's reaction, the more ground they lost.

Finally, SKF changed to a bolder strategy. It focused each of its factories on a limited product offering. Factories manufactured the products they made most efficiently. If a product did not fit into one of the "new" factories, SKF dropped the product. This factory focusing cut overhead dramatically, and closed the price gap between SKF and the Japanese, halting the Japanese advance. (1)

SKF successfully blunted the Japanese onslaught without ABC; however, if SKF had had ABC, could it have preempted the Japanese invasion? Probably. ABC would have driven SKF to streamline and focus its factories before the Japanese invasion. Likewise, SKF would not have presented such an attractive target to the Japanese.

As this example illustrates, good information is imperative to a successful strategy, and the business strategy is the essence of a company. No matter how good a company's people, not matter how much capital or other resources a company has, lacking an effective strategy dooms a company to failure.

The next case describes how ABC changed one motor manufacturer's picture of product profitability. This new picture, in turn, led the company to reassess its business strategy.

CASE STUDY
Torquematic—Where the Price Is Not Right

In 1989, Torquematic was a division of Multinational Machinery Manufacturing Company. The division produced and sold 250 different types of dc servomotors for an annual revenue of $55 million. Under corporate's growth-oriented management, Torquematic was expected to increase sales 10 percent a year. Torquematic had one plant in the United States that machined many of the motor parts, as well as wound the armatures, and assembled and tested the motors.

A dc servomotor is a direct current motor with closed-loop feedback that provides torque and precise speed control over a wide operating range. DC motors were required in applications where stop-start and variable-speed are necessary, such as OEM, specialty equipment manufacturers, aerospace applications, and electrical equipment distributors.

OEMs accounted for half of Torquematic's sales dollars and two-thirds of its unit shipments. The OEMs were automation and equipment manufacturers of machine tools, electronic insertion equipment, and large engineering plotters. The OEMs bought large quantities of relatively simple motors on long-term contracts to be used as components in their systems. Being volume buyers, competition for their orders was tough and had recently gotten tougher as Korean firms had entered the market.

The specialty equipment manufacturers made custom material handling and automated machines usually requiring custom or semicustom motors. However, within the last few years, these manufacturers had begun to specify particular families of components from which their engineers should design. This standardization would not only increase buying economies and cut manufacturing overhead, but also reduce systems' maintenance and repair costs. However, in practice, specifying custom motors was still very common. The specialty manufacturers tended to buy motors in small orders throughout the year. Due to the customized nature of the products and the lack of competition, these motors provided Torquematic's highest profit margins.

Motors for aerospace applications were Torquematic's smallest market. These motors went into space vehicles and military hardware. As such, the motors had to withstand extreme environmental operating conditions and satisfy a number of unique applications, which required substantial engineering investment.

The last major buying group was distributors. Distributors would buy Torquematic's products and resell them to users for applications ranging from door openers to wire-winding machines. While distributors would buy large quantities of motors throughout the year, they rarely bought many of any one kind. In fact, over the course of a year a distributor would buy just about every kind of motor Torquematic made. In general, a manufacturer's margins through distributors were fairly good.

In 1989, seeing the increased competition in the price conscious OEM business, Torquematic would then use cash to build market share in the specialty equipment market by increasing its investments in marketing, sales, capital, and R&D resources. This would allow the company to reach more customers and upgrade their present motor line, as well as introduce larger frame size motors. Torquematic's management believed that they could take advantage of their superior motor technology and successfully move into manufacturing larger customized motors.

However, before embarking on this new strategy, Torquematic's vice president of Finance wanted to verify their planning assumptions with an ABC study. He convinced the president to have a consulting firm develop a PC-based ABC model. Over the next two months, consultants working with Torquematic's management developed a model that attached manufacturing, engineering, sales, marketing, and distribution costs to a sample of products.

The study results flabbergasted management. Specialty orders, with their small volumes and short production runs, were found to create a huge number of setups, inspections, work orders, expedites, customer orders, and so on. The military products not only suffered from these ills, but required substantial engineering, documentation and testing, plus special packaging. All of these costs were spread on labor hours by the traditional system. Not only were specialty and military motors costing more than management thought, these products were losing money (see Exhibit 10-4).

Distributor products had their margins eroded by the large number of small orders that created large order entry, packaging, shipping, and freight costs. In addition, the study pointed out that there were much greater differences between models than met the eye, as reflected in the number

Exhibit 10–4. **CHANGES IN MOTOR COST AND MARGIN USING TORQUEMATIC'S ABC SYSTEM**

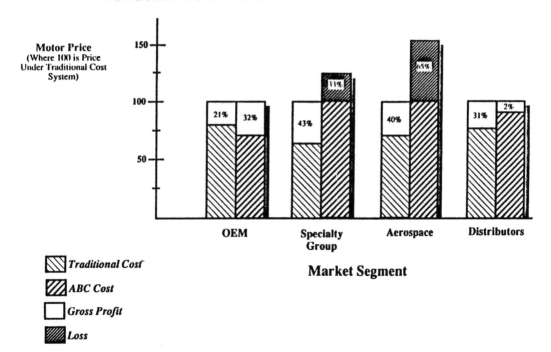

of manufacturing transactions caused by these products. The OEM market, with its high production volumes, steady sales demand, and large customer orders, cost much less than previously reported. In fact, the OEM products created 160 percent of the company's profits.

Initially, many members of management refused to believe the numbers. In fact, a skeptical engineering staff was tasked to validate the ABC methodology and conclusions. Over the next two months, further cost analysis and marketing studies verified the ABC data.

Torquematic was faced with a bleak situation. Competition was intensifying, driving down prices in its most profitable market while corporate headquarters was pressing the division for higher sales and profits. Torquematic saw price reductions and margin erosion as eventual unless the company could enhance the differentiation of their OEM products (see Exhibit 10-5).

The company's executive committee conducted a series of off-site strategic planning sessions to reassess the company's strategy. Fortunately, the vice president of engineering and R&D had a proposal. He recommended that the division expand the motor lines into drive systems. Torquematic's motors in almost all cases were sold as part of a drive system, where the drive system consisted of a power supply, a control, and a motor. By moving into drive systems, Torquematic would increase product differentiation and simultaneously increase sales and profits. The vice president proposed that leveraging the company's technology might, along with the advances in microprocessor technology, help to develop complete single-unit drive systems. These systems would be entirely self-contained, saving production costs, system weight, and volume. Since the majority

Exhibit 10–5. **COMPARABLE OEM DC MOTOR PRICES 1986–1989**

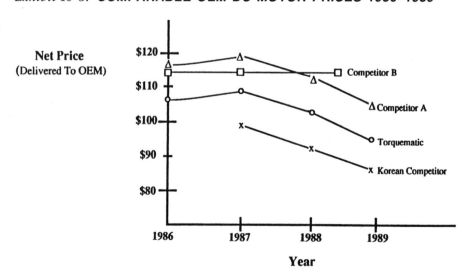

of Torquematic's customers integrated their own drive systems, a single-unit system would save them considerable expense. However, this option was not without serious risk—about 30 percent of the company's sales were to drive system assemblers, who would take a dim view of Torquematic integrating into their market. However, after further analysis and debate, management accepted Engineering's proposal and decided to enter the drive systems business.

The OEM product line would be the first to be expanded into drive systems because this was the company's largest and most profitable market. In addition, the OEMs designed and integrated their own drive systems. Not being particularly good at drive integration, the OEMs would welcome Torquematic taking over that function. The division's long-term strategy was to differentiate its products by providing enhanced services like design engineering and complete systems to the OEMs.

In the specialty market, subsequent ABC studies found some products were actually making a profit (see Exhibit 10-6). Therefore, management

Exhibit 10–6. **TORQUEMATIC SPECIALITY EQUIPMENT PRODUCTS**

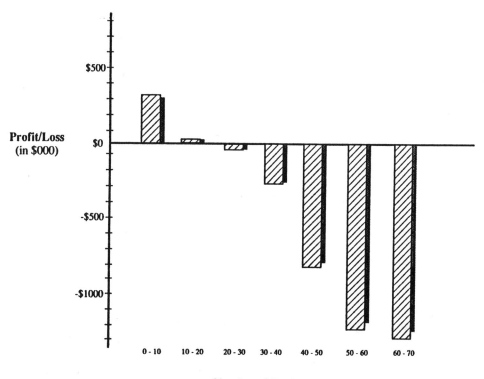

**Number of Products Arranged
In Descending Profitability**

undertook a number of actions to stem the market's losses. The company slashed the product offering and the market's sales, marketing, and engineering budgets. The minimum order quantity was raised and an ordering charge was added to all pricing. The division's long-term strategy in both this market and the distributors' was to standardize components, modularize the design and upscale the motors into drive systems. The first action would reduce manufacturing costs and the second would increase differentiation.

In the aerospace market, the company decided to develop a new pricing model. If they could convince the government to accept the new bidding method and its higher prices, Torquematic would stay in the aerospace business. Otherwise, Torquematic would withdraw from the market.

Lessons Learned

The traditional cost system can lull management into making disastrous decisions, as was almost the cast at Torquematic. If Torquematic would have pursued its original strategy of milking the OEM market, the company would have unwittingly forfeited its position in its most profitable market. As this case shows, ABC provided information of strategic value and as in many cases created a trigger point for developing a new business strategy.

ESTABLISHING A PRICING STRATEGY

Many executives and economists argue that the market sets prices, not cost. While true in theory, this is rarely the case in practice. Almost all companies set prices on a cost-plus basis. One well-known exception is Cray Research, Inc. For Years, Cray's supercomputers' performance so far exceeded that of the competition, Cray set its prices strictly according to the value realized by the customer. Unfortunately, most companies are in this position.

Yet, market dynamics play a key role in setting prices. In a free market, pricing transmits information. Pricing reflects each competitor's costs, barriers to entry and capacity, as well as customer desirability, available income, and other factors. In today's manufacturing environment, most companies rely on the traditional labor-based cost accounting system to establish a cost-based price. Therefore, each company has its costs systematically skewed in the same direction—underpricing low-volume, custom products and overcosting high-volume, standard products. This distortion, no doubt, influences pricing.

In addition, many companies blunder when setting prices. Many companies base prices on a fully burdened product cost that includes sunk as well as fixed costs. This error stems from the misconception of managing for the income statement and not cash flows. Sunk costs, such as depreciation and product development, have no place in pricing decisions after the investment has been committed. Likewise, fixed costs are just that—fixed with or without sales—and should not influence pricing. Pricing decisions should be made only with respect to incremental cash flows since that objective directly supports the company's goal of shareholder value creation.

An ABC system is a cost planning system. As such, one can set prices according to future production levels and resulting costs. In this way, a company can price products more competitively at less risk. With ABC and its cost stimulation, management is given a much more accurate picture of its future costs under a variety of outcomes.

Price Hikes

Underpricing products is quite common. In addition to distorted cost information, underpricing may be the result of neglect or a poor market assessment by the sales force. Whatever the reason, it is an opportunity. Take the case of a controller at one electronics manufacturer. He discovered that one product was not covering its variable cost. The controller called up all of the company's competitors and found that the few who did carry a comparable product all charged twice as much for the product. After seeing this evidence, the vice president of sales was not persuaded to raise the product's price or drop the product. The company president, on the other hand, agreed with the controller and ordered the product's price raised 175 percent. This price hike had no discernible effect on the number of units that were sold the next year.

Superior Faucet thought it was making a return of 20 percent on the sales of its spare parts and installation and repair kits. The ABC study found these products to be losing more than 30 cents on every dollar of sales. The following year, Superior raised prices on these items an average of 40 percent. This price increase had no discernible effect on the sales of these items, and increased revenue by $300,000. This phenomenon is described as *price inelasticity of demand* in the microeconomics literature. Inelasticity implies that customers are insensitive to price. This occurs when items purchased constitute an insignificant portion of the customer's costs, or when no acceptable substitute is available.

One industrial supply manufacturer believes that price changes are ABC's most important benefit. In this company's markets, most products are built to individual customer specifications. Therefore, the company prices each order as it comes in. In this custom environment, the company has immediately reaped the benefits of ABC with new pricing formulas for these products. The company claims first-year benefits in the tens of millions.

Another manufacturing company also believed that the new pricing policy, resulting from ABC, was one of its greatest benefits; however, for different reasons. This manufacturer had a large number of captive fabrication operations, such as casting and machining. In recent years, these operations were forced to compete for external, as well as internal work. From the insight ABC provided, the manufacturer learned to price its work on forecasted variable-cost basis, instead of bidding on all work at a full product-cost basis. ABC, by causing management to rethink its cost systems, drove them to question, and then develop new pricing policies. The company's new policies excluded sunk and irrelevant costs from pricing decisions. In addition, the company forecasted costs and took the cost advantages that greater volume would provide when setting its pricing. This company found that these chances drastically increased the number of successful bids.

Customers have one of three ways to respond to a price hike:

1. The customer accepts the price hike and continues to buy the product.
2. The customer switches to a comparable product from the same supplier.
3. The customer buys the product from a competitor. This usually results in the competitor losing money on the unprofitable product rather than the price-increasing firm.

Rarely will a customer drop a supplier over a price hike on a few, unimportant items. After an ABC study, a company typically raises prices only on a limited number of low-volume products. As such, these products cannot represent a significant portion of revenues. The risk of lost sales through selected price hikes is typically very small. If a significant portion of any customer's purchases is affected by the price hikes, the customer must be small. A study by the National Retail Hardware Association found that fewer than 100 items, in the average hardware store, were purchased on the basis of price. All these items were available at mass merchandisers with lower pricing. This study confirms the considerable price flexibility in the majority of a company's product offering.

Frequently, managers believe that they can avoid the tough choice of whether to drop a product by simply doubling the price. They believe the market should be left to choose whether it is willing to pay the higher price for those products. In some cases, raising prices can be a very effective means of returning a product to profitability. Products with low-price elasticity, such as custom products and spare parts, are especially amenable.

In Exhibit 10-7, the current selling price of an LA5 motor is shown as $200 per unit. This sales price was based on the standard cost system's reported product cost of $120 per unit. However, the LA5 motor is a complex, low-volume motor, and an ABC study shows that the incremental cost of an LA5 motor is $180. If the company wanted to raise the LA5's price to make the standard margin, it would have to charge $305.

However, if the LA5 motor's price is raised to $305 the demand for the motor will drop to 3,100 units (see Exhibit 10-8). This lower production volume increases per unit costs. In fact, at an estimated production volume of 3,100 units, the average incremental cost would be $310, at which point the company loses $5 a unit. Therefore, the price increase trims cash flow from $128,000 to a $15,000 outflow.

Exhibit 10-7 **PRICE VERSUS COST OF LA5 MOTOR**

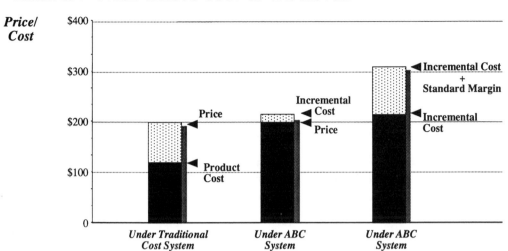

Exhibit 10-8 **COST DEMAND CURVE**

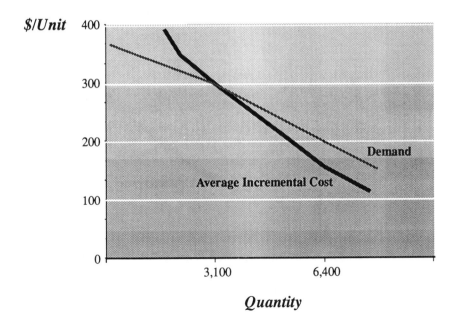

Optimal Pricing

Optimally, to maximize profit, a company chooses a price at the intersection point of the marginal cost and marginal revenue curves. While it can easily simulate the cost impact of a volume change on a product's manufacturing cost, few companies know what a product's price elasticity is; that is, what the demand curve looks like. The company does not know precisely how much sales volume it will lose by increasing the product's price. Therefore, it is only possible to estimate the optimal price for the highest cash flow.

However, this insight puts a new perspective on raising prices. In the vast majority of cases, production cost curves rise so sharply as volume drops, that no price hike is profitable. Exhibit 10-9 shows the demand curves of a product with high price elasticity (such as a custom product), a product with average price elasticity (studies have found this curve to have a −1.7 slope; for every 10 percent price increase 17 percent of sales are lost), and a commodity product with little leeway for switching costs from one supplier to another.

Exhibit 10-10 shows how the average incremental cost of a product from discrete manufacturing (a screw machine department and a punch press department) and one from assembly operations (assuming the assemblies contain no unique parts) change with volume. As one can see, per unit cost rises dramatically as volume production drops, especially in discrete manufacturing.

Price hikes only increase cash flow if, as volume drops, revenues are increasing faster than costs are rising. So, in spite of increased revenue per unit a company may never make a profit on some products. Therefore, in low-volume regions of discrete manufacturing, it is impossible to raise prices to turn a product profitable. However, there is little cost penalty for assembling low-volume products from high-volume components. With other products, whether a price hike can be successful is less obvious. Thus, you must simulate how a product's costs would change under various production volumes to assess how viable a price hike can be.

Another pitfall of raising prices befell Sulzer-Bingham, a manufacturer of pumps for power plants, oil fields, refineries, and chemical plants. In 1987, Sulzer, a Swiss pump manufacturer, bought Bingham, an American pump maker. The merger created significant overlap in its product lines. However, Sulzer-Bingham never consolidated these product lines. In addition, a far greater problem for Bingham was its schism between engineering and manufacturing. This division resulted in many pump designs being difficult to manufacture.

In 1989, the company president decided to end the product-line overlap and manufacturability problems in one fell swoop. To avoid upsetting customers, the president decided to continue offering these products, but to double their prices. This move had unforeseen consequences.

Doubling the prices inadvertently doubled each pump's sales commission. The president sent the wrong message to the sales force. By doubling its reward, salespeople began to concentrate on trying to sell these higher priced products. Orders for the difficult-to-manufacture pumps jumped, bogging down the factory, creating

Exhibit 10-9 *DEMAND CURVES FOR DIFFERENT PRODUCTS*

Custom Product

***Typical Product
With Average
Demand Curve***

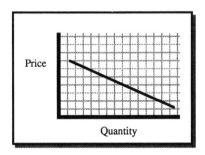

***Commodity
Product With
Low Switching
Costs***

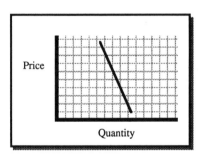

delivery problems, and escalating costs. Despite instructions to the contrary, the president found the sales force pushing these difficult-to-manufacture products with surprising vigor. The price doubling had created the wrong incentive for the sales force, with disastrous results.

Therefore, prior to raising prices a company must

1. Examine pricing on comparable competitor products
2. Assess potential customer reaction to a price change

Exhibit 10-10 **PRODUCTION ECONOMIES AS REPORTED**
                BY AN ABC SYSTEM

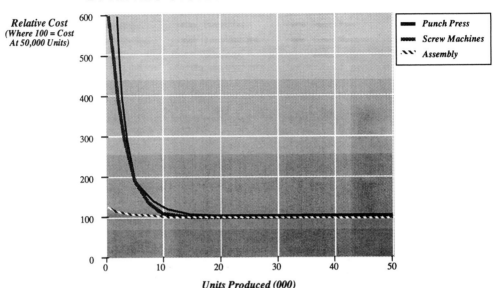

Fabrication processes have large economies of scale
while assembly operations do not

3. Simulate manufacturing costs with the expected change in unit sales

4. Coordinate the pricing plan and the commission structure

In addition, management must consider what margins are wanted on different
products. Typically, products with a lower price elasticity will contribute a greater
relative profit than those with low price elasticity. Keep in mind that higher price
elasticities result from a product's having a variety of substitutes and/or being
relatively expensive. An executive must consider each product's margins in this
light—availability of substitutes as well as the absolute cost to the customer.

DEVELOPING A PRODUCT LINE STRATEGY

The next section discusses what actions can be taken if a company is losing
money on some of its products.

Buying It Elsewhere

One option for dealing with unprofitable products is to buy the part and resell
it. One company discovered that one of its competitors was offering the company's

product in the competitor's catalogue. The product was difficult to manufacture and the competitor found it cheaper to buy than build. Not surprisingly, when the company conducted its ABC study, they found that this product was grossly undercosted. So, unfortunately, the company was on the receiving end of this effective tactic.

Killing Product Offerings—The Final Option

Pruning product lines is not a new idea. Many companies have reaped substantial savings from narrowing their product offering. For example, Hunt, in 1947, was a medium-sized cannery. Over the next 11 years, it cut the 30-plus product lines to just three: tomato products, peaches, and fruit cocktail. Likewise, within each of these lines, Hunt reduced the variety offered. For example, Hunt offered peaches in only one syrup grade (thick). This simplification paid off handsomely for Hunt. Sales increased from $15 million in 1947, to $120 million in 1958. By 1958, Hunt had the top-selling tomato sauce and tomato paste brands, and the second-best-selling brands in peaches and catsup. Despite the benefits of streamlining product lines, most companies find it much easier to add products than to subtract them. Food companies introduce an estimated 30 new products into the retail channel every week! Long ago, the famous industrial economist, John Clark, observed, "Discrimination is the secret of efficiency."

However, before deciding to prune product lines, management must answer two questions.

1. How much money will cutting the product line save? In the ABC system, every product's cost is volume dependent. Eliminating sales volume impacts products with common components, as well as fixed costs. To estimate true savings, one must simulate the cost effects of eliminating the products. Many overhead costs simply migrate to other products, unless one eliminates all requirements for the product's subcomponents. Assume, for example, that a product to be discontinued contains part number XYZ, as does a product to be retained. By discontinuing the first product, you lower the production volume of part XYZ, which increases XYZ's per unit cost. The company ends no-batch activity on part XYZ. The batch costs from the discontinued product must now be absorbed by the retained product, raising its cost.

True savings only come from eliminating unique subcomponents. If one reduces volume on common parts, pruning product lines increases costs. To calculate the company's costs without the proposed product lines one must calculate changes in activity levels. Multiplying this change in activity times the variable component of each cost-driver's rate calculates the incremental cost savings from a product-line reduction. In many cases, the volume drop is not significant enough to eliminate any "fixed" costs, or any noncash-flow expenses, such as depreciation. The product of the variable cost and the change in activity is the product line reduction's true cost savings.

If one's time horizon is more than one year, that is, the "long run" when evaluating product line decisions, all costs are variable except equipment depreciation and maintenance, management, supervision, and occupancy.

Sunk costs should not be confused with variable costs. If a company has already invested significant dollars in product development and inventory, that is, sunk costs, there are no savings if the product is eliminated. As a matter of fact, one may only avoiding any possible recovery of these costs. For example, a publisher significantly overspent its budget developing a new book series. Before introducing the series, a market survey revealed that the books would fall far short of the sales forecast, and would lose money. The publisher decided to minimize costs and forego any marketing investment on the series. The publisher did not realize it had already sunk the bulk of the series' cost. Without marketing spending, the series would surely fail. The publisher neglected to look at the development expenses as sunk and the decision to invest in marketing as incremental.

2. Before deciding to prune a product line, management must ask: What products and product options do the customers really require? To answer this question you must survey the customers. A company must conduct a study identifying what product offerings the market requires. The study identifies and weighs the attributes that are most important to the customers. Only an impartial customer survey can defuse the internal concern about possible customer reaction to a product-line reduction. There is always sales organization resistance to pruning a product line. One company, considering a product line reduction, had such a survey conducted by outside consultants to avoid prematurely signaling its intentions to its customers.

The marketing survey usually finds quick, reliable delivery to be much more important to customers than product line breadth. By reducing the product offering slightly, one eliminates many low-volume products. These products are the very ones that inevitably ruin a customer service reputation. Many companies offer products that can be neither stocked nor supported by a sufficient component inventory to meet random demand. Upon receiving an order for a low-volume product that requires a unique part, the factory must fabricate the unique part from raw material. Hence, this product takes at least the entire manufacturing lead time, rather than the shorter quoted lead time, to be produced (low-volume parts are usually bumped off schedule time and again). Since the factory must produce the unique part from scratch, delivery is delayed—infuriating the customer. So, one can usually improve its customer value by reducing the product offering.

Before making the product reduction decision, one should conduct some further analysis.

- Which customers buy the items to be dropped?
- How much sales volume do they represent?
- If all of last year's customer orders that contained these products were never received, how much revenue would have been lost?

- Are the products to be discontinued easily replaced by substitutes within the firm's product offering?

Answering these questions helps management assess the risk of dropping the products. This next case concerns a company that did not follow this recommended approach.

CASE STUDY
C.A. Logan—Killing Products: Opportunity Lost

The C.A. Logan (CAL) company was founded during the Second World War to manufacture brake systems and hydraulic components for military aircraft. After the war, the company continued to supply parts to the depressed aircraft industry and diversified into furniture, industrial equipment and other markets. In the early 1960s, the company sold the brake systems portion of the business. In 1966, the founder C.A. Logan retired and sold the business to a large conglomerate.

By the mid-1980s, CAL's major products were spring-loaded pistons. These pistons were mainly used in seating systems such as recliners, airline seats, and wheelchairs. In addition, CAL's products included items ranging from door openers, to hospital beds, to lift trucks. While the parent company spent the 1980s restructuring—spinning off and selling acquisitions—CAL concentrated on its core business and expanding its product offering into new applications. In 1988, the company had record sales of $97.4 million.

CAL competed with a number of small competitors, as well as divisions of larger companies, each specializing in their own niche. Accordingly, each company produced a set of nonstandard products that could not be easily replaced by a competitor's product without a redesign. Management perceived CAL's strategic advantages as being its broad line of quality products and having the largest and best trained sales force in the industry.

Between 1985 and 1988, sales declined and profits plummeted. Although divisional management attributed the declining profitability to reduced sales associated with a dramatic drop in orders, the facts suggest otherwise. Between 1985 and 1987, sales actually grew from $92.2 to $97.4, while profits dropped more than 57 percent.

In fact, CAL was allowing their competitors to capture the majority of the market's high-volume product sales. The competitors were leaving CAL with a few high-volume products, but mostly with low-volume, nonstandard products.

To turn the situation around, the parent company's management decided to undertake a product profitability study of CAL's business. Two men from corporate staff, along with two outside consultants, were assigned the task of conducting the profitability study. The consultants convinced the team to use activity-based costing to conduct the product-line analysis. They began the process with a plant tour and interviews of the heads of support departments. As the team toured the plant, you could not help but notice the great disparity in production batch sizes. The staffers frequently saw batches with thousands of pieces, as well as batches with fewer than 50.

After completing the interviews, the team assigned support costs to process overhead pools. The interviews determined how the system would assign overhead costs to products. For each overhead function, the team attempted to identify an output measure that tracked to a product and was correlated to resources that a product consumed.

For CAL's plant, the team established four activity centers: fabrication, numerical control machining, extrusion, and assembly. Each activity center had two cost pools to assign its overhead costs: numbers of setups, and direct labor hours. The other overhead costs, such as material movement, purchasing, inventory control, order entry, and packaging, were assigned directly to products using the following measures:

Number of purchase orders

Number of work orders

Number of material moves

Number of shipments

Number of receiving receipts

Number of customer orders

Sales dollars

Using a computer listing of the prior year's sales, the team created a list of all components manufactured last year. Against this part database, the team applied costs using the cost drivers. Programmers then had the computer sum up the component costs into end-item product costs. The study took months of analysis and debugging because CAL maintained more than 28,000 unique parts.

The results were startling. The study found that some products were causing overhead activities that cost 30 times more than the company was being paid for the product. Of the company's 2,612 products that were sold the previous year, only 369 products created profits, while the remainder dissipated them. If CAL had only sold these top 369 products, its profits would have been $3 million instead of $1.8 million.

The ABC study identified 2,243 products as being unprofitable. CAL seemed to be an ideal candidate for product-line pruning. The study team, after distributing the ABC study results, surveyed the marketing staff for their recommendations. For each product, the survey gave a menu of choices:

1. Raise the price.
2. Drop the product.
3. Lower the product's cost.
4. Challenge the data.
5. Buy the product from an outside vendor.
6. Take no action.

The marketing staff decided to respond as a group to the survey. However, prior to completing their survey, the marketing staff demanded more information. They developed a set of questions to identify products that were "safe" to drop. They wanted to know:

1. Did any major customer buy the product?
2. Could the product be substituted for with a similar product?
3. How much sales are exposed, if, by eliminating the product, CAL would have lost all orders containing that product?

The marketing staff wanted to avoid alienating any major customers and dropping any products that would result in large losses in sales. The marketing staff recommended raising prices on more than 230 products. They recommended dropping 510 products, which would decrease sales by 3 percent. With these recommendations in hand, the study team presented their finding to the executive committee.

The president and the VP of sales & marketing believed that dropping over 500 products was too drastic, and they were not sufficiently confident in the study's accuracy. The president ordered the VP of Finance to investigate the findings and make his own cost savings estimates.

Three weeks later, the VP of Finance presented his conclusion. While the study team estimated that the annual savings from eliminating these products, and their associated overhead, was $1.2 million, the VP was more conservative at $950,000 in additional profit. The president agreed to approve the product-line reduction.

Yet, by September of 1990, CAL had only dropped 25 products—the natural attrition rate. This seems incredible, given the savings estimates and the approval of the pruning project. Even before the ABC study, everyone admitted knowing that many products were unprofitable. The president and his staff all agreed that CAL needed to rationalize its product line. The product line redundancy not only raised manufacturing costs, but also confused CAL's customers.

The product pruning project got derailed in early 1989, when one of CAL's major competitors announced their exit from the market. CAL's president put the pruning project on hold. He thought that the product line reduction would send the wrong message to its customers, at a time when CAL was struggling to pick up these now free accounts. Yet, after temporarily halting the project, the president never reactivated it—the time never seemed right.

Management gave two reasons for failing to follow through with the product-line reductions. While management believed the ABC study up to a point, they felt that cutting the product line would immediately lose revenues, but the cost savings would never materialize. Second, the president and marketing vice president believed that product line breadth was a very important buying criterion to the customers and distributors. By cutting the product line, these executives believed that CAL would put other product sales and the company's perceived strategic advantage at risk. Since CAL did not conduct a customer survey, this assumption was never validated.

Lessons Learned

CAL invested a great deal of time and money in an ABC system. The team worked hard to develop consensus and middle-management support. Yet, despite this investment and ample evidence of great potential savings, the company undertook no action. This would seem to indicate that the majority of the challenge of successfully implementing an ABC system is not technical, but managerial. The team failed to win sufficient top management commitment, and this failure doomed the system.

Unless a company is in a crisis, product line reductions are extremely difficult to implement. Ironically, a sister division of CAL conducted a smiliar study concurrently with CAL. This division successfully reduced its product line and enjoyed significant profit improvement. However, the sister business was operating at a loss when the study was done. The division's management, therefore, had considerable incentive to make changes.

DROPPING PRODUCTS IS HARD TO DO

If the company is losing money, management is more willing to make tough choices. One survey of turnaround companies found that 92 percent eliminated money-losing products from their product line! On average, the troubled companies discontinued 17 percent of their products. Additionally, 72 percent of the companies dropped customers. In one case, a company slimmed down from 250 products to 33, yet increased sales!

In good times, management typically avoids cutting products, an action that is perceived as very risky. Management fears that pruning products will alienate customers and devastate sales. Many executives believe that their companies must sell a broad product line. They think that customers want one-stop shopping with lots of choices. In some cases this is true; in many it is not. Low-volume products have proportionally much greater demand variability than comparable high-volume products. Therefore, to satisfy demand when it comes, distributors and retailers must either carry safety stock or rely on quick delivery. Unfortunately low-volume products usually have poor delivery from manufacturers because these products have high demand variability. Distributors and retailers make their money turning inventory. Slow-moving items cost them money by tying up inventory and stretching out delivery times.

Sales and marketing groups vehemently resist pruning the product offering. The sales department believes that pruning products cuts sales and, therefore, its commissions, while making its sales quotas harder to fulfill. Likewise, salespeople and marketers prefer the ease with which they can sell customized products. They find it much easier to sell a product that has no competition.

Executives worry about how the market will react to a product-line reduction. If we cut back our product offering, will the customers think of it as a precursor to leaving the business? Sometimes, executives intuitively do not believe the overhead reductions will actually follow. They have heard savings estimates before and the estimates never seem to materialize. They realize that this is one decision they cannot reverse or hide. Once the products are gone, they are gone. Alternatively, a price increase can be used as a prelude to eliminating the products. Unfortunately, a price hike does little to discourage future product proliferation, allowing the old products or new variations to creep back into the product offering.

The company must manage the product reduction transition. The sales department must inform key customers of the changes and explain the rationale. The marketplace must understand the reduction. Customers must not believe the reduction is a prelude to exiting the business. The company must distribute new catalogues and price lists. The company must work down inventory of these products and its components to avoid write-offs. Surprisingly, when the company announces a product reduction, the volumes of the products to be dropped rise dramatically as customers stock up.

Another surprise of a reduction is that total sales do not decline. Most customers switch to comparable products within the company's line and the low-volume products that were customer dissatisfiers are eliminated.

DEVELOPING A CUSTOMER STRATEGY

As ABC suddenly uncovers many unprofitable products, it reveals many undesirable customers. The next case will show how one company analyzed customer profitability (the profits the company makes on the customer, not how much money the customer is making selling his products) and used this information to raise profits.

CASE STUDY
Colter Industries—Choosing the Right Customer

Colter, a manufacturer of vibration isolation tables, mounts, and systems, served over 8,000 customers with 20,000 different end items. Colter sold their products to universities, research centers, laboratories, and optical manufacturers. Given the unique nature of its products, Colter sold a substantial portion of their products overseas. Sales increased from $81 million in 1987 to $86 million in 1988, fueled in part by "Star Wars" research. In 1988, when a new president took office, Colter was a successful, profitable company, with a return on equity exceeding 18 percent.

Unsatisfied, the new president laid out an aggressive plan for stronger performance. He devised a new strategic plan. As part of the plan, he wanted additional growth without additional distribution, sales, and administrative resources. A strategy for achieving higher growth and profitability was to promote high-margin products to desirable customers. The president intuitively knew that Colter's SG&A costs, which amounted to 46 percent of total expenses, varied widely by customer. To meet his stated goals, the president felt that he needed a new system to determine the real cost of each customer order. Colter implemented an ABC system as part of the new strategy. To meet their goals, Colter had to understand which customers were the most profitable to serve, and which were not.

The finance manager, with the help of a consulting company, worked to design the new cost system. The new system needed to not only track manufacturing costs, but SG&A costs as well. The production overhead of each department was split into two pools. The first pool assigned all of the batch costs directly to piece parts based on the number of batches run. This batch cost was then spread across all of the parts in that batch. These costs included setups, first article inspections, material handling, and production planning. The second pool included all of the remaining production overhead: tooling, maintenance, utilities, etc. The second overhead pool was assigned on volume through the work center, as measured by machine hours in the fabrication work center and the labor hours in the assembly department. The team analyzed each type of cost to determine if it was related to the volume of sales and production, or to the processing of individual production and sales orders—volume-driven versus batch-driven costs. The team interviewed members of every department to identify how their people's work split between these two categories (see Exhibit 10-11). The system split SG&A costs into volume costs and order costs. The team assigned all order costs to customers based on the number of customer orders bought. They assigned volume costs to products based on sales dollars.

Exhibit 10–11 **SPLITTING COLTER OVERHEAD COSTS INTO ABC POOLS**

MANUFACTURING

OVERHEAD ACCOUNT	VOLUME POOL	BATCH POOL
MATERIAL HANDLING	NONE	ALL
PRODUCTION PLANNING	NONE	ALL
OPERATORS	DIRECT LABOR	INDIRECT LABOR
SUPERVISORS	SUPERVISING	EXPEDITING
WAREHOUSING	NONE	ALL
QUALITY CONTROL	FINAL INSPECTION	FIRST ARTICLE

GENERAL, SELLING AND ADMINISTRATION

OVERHEAD ACCOUNT	VOLUME POOL	ORDER POOL
ACCOUNTING	GENERAL ACCOUNTING	ACCOUNTS RECEIVABLES
	PAYROLL	CREDIT PRICING
SALES	COMISSIONS FREIGHT	SALES FORCE ORDER ENTRY
MARKETING	ALL	NONE
GENERAL MANAGEMENT	ALL	NONE

After completing the study, the results surprised everyone, even the president. While most executives were not surprised by the direction of change in reported profitability, they were shocked by its magnitude. Many people did not believe the reported costs. Exhibit 10-12 shows the ABC study results of Colter's profitability serving different customers. Only 32 percent of their customers were found to be profitable to serve. The study identified order size as one of the key factors in determining the customer's profit contribution. The other was ordering nonstock items, which was roughly 80 percent of the product offering.

The sales force was very resistant to the new cost system. Most of the sales force just did not grasp how much work was entailed in processing a small order or short production run. However, by educating and working with the salespeople, the team convinced the sales force of these true costs. Frequently, senior executives led these discussions with the managers.

Exhibit 10–12 **COLTER PROFITS BY PERCENTAGE OF CUSTOMERS**

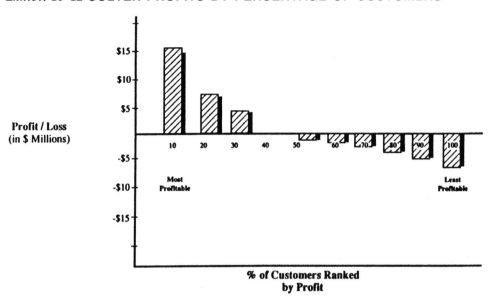

% of Customers Ranked
by Profit

After developing the ABC system with firm management backing, Colter devised a plan for increasing customer profit contributions. Salespeople raised prices on small, custom orders with surcharges and handling fees. Product managers reduced the number of product offerings in various product lines. Colter turned over small accounts to manufacturers' representatives to cut sales expenses. The company taught the salespeople to emphasize standard products, and not to accept small build-to-order requests. The minimum buying quantities were doubled. Colter worked with a number of customers to reduce their service and ordering costs. A number of customers cut the number of different end items purchased and the frequency of small orders. Furthermore, customer service worked to establish a purchasing schedule for the customers to improve customer service and Colter's production planning.

Colter gave a number of its largest customers direct on-line order entry terminals to reduce both firms' order entry costs. Colter converted one large state university into a distributor! This university began to consolidate all of the purchases from the other universities in its university system for a larger discount. This move slashed per unit freight, shipping, order entry, and packaging costs. On the production side, management encouraged engineers to reduce setup times and improve the factory layout to reduce nonvalue-added batch costs.

The results were impressive: the average customer order size increased by 87 percent. While the number of different end items sold was slashed by 40 percent, sales increased in 1988 and 1989 by 11 percent and 6 percent, respectively. In addition, actual SG&A costs declined as sales rose. Colter increased the number of profit-contributing customers by 15 percent. Simultaneously, the number of customers with a negative net profit contribution was reduced by half.

Colter considered itself fortunate in applying these changes in a growing market. In a tight market, competitors might have touched off a price war or mirrored Colter's actions. However, Colter gained total market share, as well as a greater share of the more desirable customers. By 1990, sales were up 18 percent, while profits doubled from 1988.

Lessons Learned

This case shows the powerful effects of ABC on customer selection and management. It shows the cost diversity of serving large numbers of customers. Of course, within this cost diversity is opportunity. Customers with many small orders and a high percentage of nonstock items are not profitable to serve. Wisely, Colter used its study results to maneuver its customers to greater margin contributions. Because Colter was the first company in its industry to use ABC, Colter was able to "cherry pick" the market's most profitable customers. The company also dropped many of the transaction-intense customers that were unprofitable to serve, allowing their unwitting competitors to pick them up.

This case also demonstrates the success of having ABC driven by the company's president. In this case, the president used the ABC information to challenge the status quo and take decisive and strategic action.

LEARNING TO IMPROVE CUSTOMER MARGIN CONTRIBUTIONS

Undesirable customers, once identified, should be transformed into profit contributors, if possible. The first step in this conversion is to discover why the customers are unprofitable to serve. Do they buy low-margin products? Do they require an abnormal amount of sales, customer service, or engineering support? Or, are they given discounts that are simply too high? Fortunately, ABC identifies the factors driving the customer's high service costs.

If sales expenses are too high, can one refocus the sales force? If more drastic action is required, a company can sell using telemarketing or through manufacturer's representatives. It costs a company roughly $100 to $150 for a salesperson to make a sales call, versus a telemarketing call of $25–$35. Naturally, a telephone call is less effective than a person-to-person meeting, but telemarketing can efficiently supplement the sales force. Sales management can also change the commission structure to encourage salespeople to sell higher-margin products to the more desirable customers.

If a customer frequently orders large volumes of products, one may consider installing electronic data interchange (EDI) at the customer's facility. With EDI, the customer checks the supplier's inventory availability and outstanding order status and enters new orders, thereby saving both companies time and money. This allows both companies to handle smaller order quantities economically.

If a customer's contributions to profits are negative, that customer's discounts should be examined. Typically, sales contracts are based solely on sales volume, and not on service costs, because suppliers lack service cost information. With ABC, a company now has service cost information on which to make more profitable/less costly sales contracts. A company with ABC knows exactly how much shipping a full truck order saves versus ten smaller shipments. A company knows how much a faxed order costs versus a phone order. With ABC, a company knows the cost of stocking a private label product, and much more.

In many cases, a company can even force a customer to renegotiate a sales contract prior to expiration. Sales contracts typically require minimum sales volumes to qualify for certain discounts, whose provisions are rarely enforced. One can start enforcing the contract, or one can renegotiate contract terms, thereby increasing sales volume or reducing discounts.

One can change distribution policies to reduce costs. By raising the minimum order quantity, one save money on shipping, billing, and freight. Suppose a company had a minimum order quantity of three. Using the ABC rates, one can calculate how many billing, order entry, shipping, and freight transactions will be reduced if the minimum order quantity is raised to five units. The transaction rate changes, times the variable cost driver rate, estimates the savings. Against these savings, management can weigh the market impact. Alternatively, one can also charge handling fees and require customers to pay freight on small orders. Using ABC data, a company can even determine the cost difference between offering three-day delivery versus ten-day delivery costs.

Sometimes the high cost of service is created not by the customer, but is self-induced. At Excel Medical, the high customer-service costs made many customers appear unprofitable to serve. However, this problem actually stemmed from confusing and obsolete product literature. When talking to customer-service representatives, the customers always asked many questions, which consumed both parties' time. It took a customer an average of 20 minutes to figure out which product to order. The company was imposing this cost and frustration on its customers! After replacing the catalogue, customer-service overtime disappeared, and the customer-service phone bill dropped by 20 percent.

Another option when dealing directly with small, high-cost customers is to require them to make their purchases indirectly through distributors. Distributors consolidate many small orders into large ones and usually have a limited number of ship-to locations—keeping order and freight costs down. Since distributors create few customer orders, bills of lading, invoices, etc., they are relatively inexpensive to serve. The distributors make their money selling groups of products from many manufacturers to the small accounts that a manufacturer cannot afford to sell to directly.

On the other hand, in 1965, the Norton Company pursued the opposite strategy. The Norton Company, an abrasives manufacturer, decided to sell grinding wheels directly to large accounts. Norton's sales plan established an annual volume usage for each grinding wheel. If a customer exceeded a specified sales level, it received a lower price than was previously available. The plan also included a consigned inventory at the customer's facility. Norton shipped the wheels directly from the factory, thereby, bypassing the distributors and eliminating their margins. The distributors continued to serve the low-volume accounts.

The move reversed Norton's slide in market share. Sales rose from $250 million to $340 million within four years. However, before developing its new discount schedules, Norton decided not to conduct a detailed cost analysis—an analysis to identify the trade-off between the new discounts and higher distribution costs versus the previous distributor margins. Norton management felt it could not justify the time or expense of the cost study. Consequently, after implementing the plan, sales advanced $74 million in three years. Yet, income before taxes declined by more than $4 million.

ABC—A Cornerstone of Performance Measurement

ABC provides the data for a much more robust performance measurement system. A performance measurement system assesses how effectively the company is implementing its business strategy. This system helps guide decision making by providing information to manage the business. Since people do what is rewarded, and what is measured is typically what is rewarded, the measurement system also drives behavior. If the performance measurement system is effective, it will drive the company's employees toward its strategy, making the company more competitive. If the system is not effective, it will steer the company toward the wrong objectives, squandering resources and degrading performance.

Over the years, working with some of the country's largest companies, I have been struck by the poor performance measurement systems being used. Companies consistently use obsolete financial measures in lieu of true measures of shareholder value creation. General Motors, for example, while expounding a commitment to the shareholders, measures performance against earnings per share and return on equity, not shareholder value creation.

Financial and cost measures dominate the systems creating a very short-term orientation. Lacking nonfinancial measures that are characteristic of process improvements, managers have no quantitative benefits to point to when undertaking any long-term investments. Therefore, long-term investments, whether it be R&D, preventive maintenance programs, quality improvement teams, or training programs, are all discouraged.

In addition, the performance measurement systems are not structured to support the company's strategy. The systems lack linkages from one organizational level's objectives to the actions of the next. If all the divisions meet their objectives, there is no guarantee of fulfilling the corporation's objectives or successfully implementing the corporate strategy. This lack of linkages undermines the business unit's support of the company's business strategy, because the business unit's performance measurement system is not driven by the strategy. The missing linkages also result in an unbalanced set of measures. While some departments, such as manufacturing, are buried in metrics, other critical business processes go completely unmeasured. In most companies, few measures exist to determine if engineering, marketing, research and development, and human resource management are successfully supporting the company's strategy or not.

A company should develop a family of measures by rigorously translating corporate objectives into actions that each business unit must satisfy. ABC translates corporate objectives into activities that measure output and productivity. In addition, ABC traces the triggering of activity to its responsible sources. Therefore, ABC provides an extensive data source for an integrated performance measurement system. For example, instead of evaluating the engineering department solely on schedule and budget attainment, one can hold engineering accountable for the number of engineering changes, new part numbers, tools fabricated, and uncertified suppliers used on each new product. Therefore, engineering is held accountable for the activity it triggers in other departments, as well as its own. As one can imagine, these measures must be carefully balanced between functional measures that are hierarchical up through the organization, and measures that encourage cross-functional cooperation.

The selection and weight of performance measures must reinforce the company's strategy and its competitive environment. For example, the telecommunications manufacturer must concentrate engineering on creating products quickly and error free, while a pump manufacturer with long product life cycles must encourage engineering to respond to and resolve customer complaints. The company's strategy must drive the selection of performance measures.

Yet, analyzing data and implementing new performance measures do not make money. Action is the result of a successful strategy. Companies must seize the opportunities that ABC provides. In 1917, American Locomotive and Baldwin Locomotive dominated the steam locomotive market. By 1970, both were out of the locomotive business and today neither exists. These companies failed to adapt. When General Motors introduced the first mainline diesel-electric locomotive in 1934, American and Baldwin redoubled their efforts in steam engines. It was a losing battle; diesels cut fuel costs by as much as 80 percent. Yet, American and Baldwin's loss was General Electric's and General Motors' gain.

Just as GE and GM capitalized on new technology, American companies can employ ABC to defeat the competition. Change offers opportunity. However, nothing disseminates faster than information, and ABC is information. ABC is a tremendous opportunity, but can be a tremendous disadvantage if your competitors implement ABC first.

## CHAPTER 11

REDESIGNING THE FACTORY WITH ABC

Results are gained by exploiting opportunities, not by solving problems.

Peter Drucker, Claremont College

A successful manufacturing strategy provides a company with a competitive advantage. The manufacturing strategy is oriented to the customers and is integrated with the company's overall business strategy. The manufacturing strategy configures the manufacturing operation to support and enhance the factors on which the company intends to compete. Consider the contract printed circuit-board assembly business. One company, Solectron, differentiates itself by providing customers with high production flexibility at low cost. Solectron can ramp up production to meet customer demand on short notice. To support this strategy, Solectron cross-trains its work force, maintains some excess production capacity, and has equipment configured for quick changeovers. These features allow Solectron to respond quickly to rapidly changing customer needs. These characteristics are in high demand from companies with high-demand variability or frequent design changes.

Another company, Array Technology, also a printed circuit-board assembler, differentiates itself with its "design-for-manufacturability" services to customers. Array uses its design skills to help lower a company's cost and raise customer products' reliability through improved design. The company has integrated its computer-aided design (CAD) systems with its manufacturing operation. Process controls feed data back to the design system, ensuring that all design parameters are within process capability. This not only ensures that designs are compatible with Array's equipment, but it allows a quick, efficient transfer of designs to production.

In both these cases, the company's manufacturing capability helps support the company's strategy. Operations proactively meet and satisfy the customers' needs. While the company's marketing strategy can help define customer needs, it is the manufacturing and logistics strategy that deliver it. A manufacturing strategy, in most cases, is not a means for producing products at the least possible cost; rather it molds the factory's capabilities to support and enhance the company's competitive position. The factory provides products and services to help differentiate the company from its competitors.

It sends a clear message to the company about what's important, why, and how—and this is what ensures successful implementation of the strategy. It is critically important that the manufacturing organization, as well as the rest of the company, reach consensus about these critical capabilities. Only through consensus will the whole company work toward the common objective. As one work toward developing this consensus, one will find widely diverging perceptions about the company's and its competitor's strengths, as well as customer needs. These are the reasons why conducting a market survey is crucial. A market study gives all the players a common perception of the customer's needs as well as expectations

FOCUSING THE FACTORY

Just because ABC uncovers a product as unprofitable does not imply it must be discontinued. The company may decide that the product is a "loss leader," without which the company could not sell other products (the sales department frequently expounds this view, although I have never run across either a leprechaun or such a mythical product).

Instead of accepting elimination or continuation of a loss leader, management can radically change a product's cost. A factory, by trying to produce a very broad product line that has different and conflicting requirements, becomes very complex. Complexity, in turn, causes high overhead costs. By separating the factory into smaller and simpler operations, one can dramatically change a product's manufacturing costs, as well as quality and delivery performance. This separation is called focusing the factory.

Focusing the factory entails reconfiguring it to manufacture a limited group of products organized along product lines. Focusing a factory usually converts a job shop to repetitive manufacturing and brings scale economies to the production process.

In a focused factory, machines are moved closer together, thus cutting inventory levels, lead time, and distance traveled. This saves warehousing, material movement, and shop floor-control costs. Shorter lead times and well-defined material flows improve operator accountability and feedback. Operators quickly discover any errors on their part. As the factory is organized around products, machines run similar components all the time. This reduces setup times, allows the use of modular jigs and fixtures, and makes easier the implementation of statistical process control.

By organizing around products, the factory is more customer responsive. Everyone, from the general manager to the machine operator, identifies with the customers, on whom success depends. This pride heightens the operator's morale and flexibility, which, in turn, increases customer responsiveness and raises quality levels.

A factory may be focused by separating nonhomogeneous products such as high-volume from low-volume products. Typically, high-volume products are built to stock, while low-volume products are built to order. These two different production approaches require very different systems and procedures. For example, build-to-stock products are planned at the finished-goods level, while build-to-order products are planned at a major-component level. Build-to-stock components are scheduled in large batches with fixed schedules. Build-to-order products are scheduled in small batches with short lead times.

The customer requirements or critical success factors of each business are also different. Build-to-stock products are usually "commodity-like," with low cost an important competitive factor. Build-to-order products are less price sensitive. These products usually compete on high quality, reliability, and fast delivery.

Typically, factory managers are measured on operating efficiency; consequently, they prefer large production batches. Factory production managers invariably concentrate on shipping the high-volume products, forsaking the build-to-order products. Large batches tie up production capacity and, as a result, create long lead times. To reduce production costs, production managers buy high-volume machines that, unfortunately, have long setup times. Because most cost systems do not tie setup costs to specific jobs, the low-volume products burden the high-volume products with high overhead rates. If these two types of products are produced in the same factory, not only does the build-to-order products customer service suffer, but so does the build-to-stock's. Additionally, the two types of products, with their different quality requirements, lead to many conflicts over just what is "acceptable."

If a factory attempts to build these different products, with their diverse requirements, on the same production lines, the business will have cost, quality, and customer service problems. ABC reflects these problems by reporting many of these products as unprofitable.

By splitting the factory into high-volume and low-volume operations, these problems can be overcome. By improving operating efficiency, the build-to-stock production lines can concentrate on lowering production costs. The company could streamline warehousing and planning costs by installing Kan Ban, for example.

Meanwhile, the build-to-order lines can make themselves more flexible and more responsive to the marketplace. As the build-to-order operation increases its flexibility by reducing setup times and by streamlining, the low-volume products are made more economically. This process transforms the products into profit generators. By splitting the factory, both operations are greatly simplified and overhead is reduced. The build-to-stock operation only worries about a very small number of high-volume end items. Concurrently, the build-to-order operation will forecast at a major component level.

CASE STUDY
Acme Machining—Bidding to Win

Acme Machining was a captive machine shop for a major commercial aerospace manufacturer. Thus, it had to produce a wide variety of machined parts used in the aircraft interiors and landing gears. Due to the slump in private aircraft sales, Acme was operating at well below 50 percent capacity in 1988. Acme's machine shop was organized into five departments based on machine type. The largest department consisted of N/C machining centers. The other departments were grinding, turning, manual milling machines, and, located in another building, secondary operations. Many of the parts went to secondary operations after machining for broaching and deburring.

In 1987, corporate headquarters decided to allow the aircraft division to begin sourcing parts from outside vendors. Headquarters wanted to decentralize decision making and force the captive operations to become more responsive and less costly. For the first time, Acme was going to compete for work. In early 1988, the aircraft division put one such package out for quote, which Acme bid on. The results shocked Acme's management. While there was wide variation in all of the vendor quotes, Acme consistently overbid all of the high-volume jobs. In fact, Acme won only 34 out of the 118 parts that were bid. In addition, the parts won were the low-volume ones, the very ones Acme thought they were least competitive in making, given the nature of their equipment. On the high-volume jobs, Acme's bids were as much as 40 percent higher than the vendor quotes.

From this shock, management conducted a series of high-level meetings to examine the bidding process and its results. Acme's management came to the conclusion that their cost accounting system was providing inaccurate information. Therefore, management decided to have a new cost system developed. Acme established a two-person team consisting of the plant controller and the industrial engineering manager. The team conducted a detailed study of the shop process flow. They interviewed key employees and undertook specific studies of several overhead drivers. They spent six months developing the new system.

The new system assigned costs to products using five different drivers for each of the production departments. Their cost drivers were direct labor hours, machine hours, setup hours, number of moves, and number of inspection points. The new system assigned 43 percent of the overhead on a measure of activity such as setup hours, and number of moves or inspections. This study generated results that were much more believable to management. Acme's ABC study found that the low-volume machined parts were greatly undercosted. From Exhibit 11-1, you can see that the percentage of overhead per labor dollar for low-volume parts was more than twice that of high-volume parts. The low-volume parts had proportionally more production order, material handling, machine setup, and inspection overhead than high-volume parts.

Acting on this information, Acme set out to reduce the high cost of their parts. Acme rearranged the factory, setting up manufacturing cells centered around the N/C machining centers to machine families of parts. For example, sleeves, latches, and brackets each had their own cells. Acme invested in new and more flexible tooling to slash setup times in the cells. Manufacturing engineers also reevaluated methods to move as much machining as possible onto as few machines as possible.

Exhibit 11–1 **ACME MACHINING ABC OVERHEAD SORTED BY BATCH SIZE**

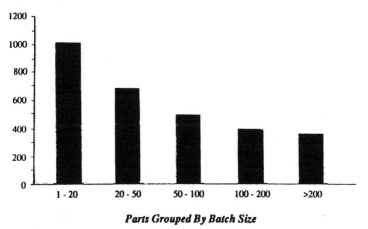

Parts Grouped By Batch Size

Low volume parts had substantially more overhead per direct labor dollar than high volume parts

The remaining machines that were not arranged in cells, which were mostly manual, continued to be arranged in a job shop fashion. While the job shop produced low-volume items very economically, it was expensive to run large batches. The job shop had lower machine-hour cost-driver rates, but much higher batch rates than the manufacturing cells.

Acme knew that they needed to raise the volume going through the shop to become more cost competitive and profitable. With the private aircraft business in a terrible slump, Acme solicited work from the outside. Unfortunately, as the quotes had shown, currently Acme's pricing was not cost competitive. Acme decided to find high-volume work that suited their high-volume manufacturing cells. Acme specifically targeted machined parts that could fit into their manufacturing cells with little or no modifications. Determining whether parts could be run in the cells became the key marketing and bidding criteria.

The cell bid rates were substantially below the job shop department. In addition, Acme decided to price the work based on each job's incremental cash flow. Since Acme's ABC system provided job specific overhead, Acme had an excellent idea of how much variable cost each job created. Acme intended to maximize cash flow and ignore sunk costs. Excess capacity costs would not burden Acme's quotes. Acme believed that this approach would substantially improve their chances of getting the additional work and maximizing economic performance. Therefore, Acme bid work strictly on incremental costs with a variable markup. Acme varied the markup based on their forecasted work load and competition for the job. Acme bid one job with only a 16 percent markup, however, while operating near capacity, bid a job with a markup of 58 percent. They believed that this approach, coupled with ABC, gave Acme a significant advantage in finding new work in the marketplace.

While, initially, only 32 percent of the company's units went through cells, by late 1990 more than 82 percent did. By focusing on specific types of part configurations, Acme was able to target and successfully solicit business from a local material handling equipment manufacturer. In addition, higher prices on low-volume work caused Acme's sister division to design out many of the low-volume parts, and in some cases, buy the parts from other vendors. Likewise, engineers worked with the customers to standardize part features, such as holes and threads, to reduce the number of different cutting tools each cell required.

Over the next two years, Acme managed to run the shop at almost 80 percent of capacity. Meanwhile, throughput time dropped by 75 percent, while quality soared. In addition, Acme's return on sales went from a negative 6 percent to a positive 3 percent.

CASE STUDY
AJ Wheelchair—A Tale of Factory Focus

AJ Wheelchair was suffering from stagnant sales and virtually no profits. The company manufactured both high-volume, simple products (called Chevys) and low-volume, complex products (called Cadillacs in this case). The factory was vertically integrated. It bent tubes, fabricated parts, finished components (plating and polishing), and assembled finished components into end items.

Customer surveys found that the most important buying attribute to the Chevy customers was rapid delivery. The customers wanted their Chevys in three days and were very price conscious. The Cadillac customers, on the other hand, wanted reliable delivery in ten days and picked their products based on quality—its features, appearance, and sturdiness. Even though both products used many of the same components, customers could only buy the Chevys in a very limited range of configurations, while the Cadillacs were fit to every driver's size and disability, extending the number of permutations possible into the millions.

The competitors were gaining ground as AJ continued to fight delivery and quality problems. One of their competitors in the Cadillac business was providing deliveries of custom chairs in less than a week. This was causing AJ great concern; AJ could not even meet their three-week promises. While the factory had a huge slow-moving inventory, the Cadillac products were frequently late. The more numerous Chevys always seemed to get top priority when scheduling the factory, but frequently missed their promised dates as well. The factory did a poor job of satisfying both market's needs.

On the other hand, the Quality Department always tried to impose the Cadillac's strict quality standards on the Chevys, despite the Chevy product managers' contentions that the Chevy market didn't require them. The factory was confused, but it had a lot of improvement opportunity. Manufacturing overhead could be trimmed, inventory levels could be lowered, etc.

Desperate for change, the president had an ABC study conducted of AJ's manufacturing operations. One consultant, the cost accounting manager, and information systems analyst conducted the ABC study over a six-week period.

The study revealed that the Cadillacs, with their extensive planning, scheduling, quality, engineering, and testing requirements, were much more expensive than anyone thought. The Cadillacs, on average, had four times as much overhead activity per unit as the Chevys (see Exhibit 11-2). This higher activity level caused almost three-quarters of the Cadillacs to lose

Exhibit 11-2 **AJ WHEELCHAIR'S AVERAGE OVERHEAD PER UNIT BY MARKET**

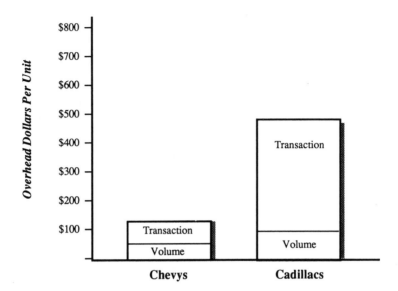

money. Management was in a quandary. It knew that it had to slash its manufacturing costs and, concurrently, improve its customer service.

What the company needed was to focus its factory. The company had not realized its products had conflicting requirements. AJ built the Chevys to stock and assembled the Cadillacs to order. The Chevys and Cadillacs each required a different manufacturing system. There was only one way the Chevys could be organized to meet a three-day delivery. The factory would enter and pull the order from stock in one day and have it delivered by truck in two days. This meant that the company had to inventory the Chevys at six distribution points around the country. From six distribution points, UPS can deliver a wheelchair-size parcel, anywhere in the country, in two days.

On the other hand, it would cost billions of dollars to stock all the possible combinations of Cadillacs. To meet the Cadillac customer's ten-day delivery requirement was tough. The factory would have one day for order entry, three days for assembly and shipment, and six days for delivery. To assemble Cadillacs to order required AJ to inventory the finished (that is, plated) components. From this inventory, the factory would pull the necessary components to assemble the order.

To focus its factory, the company split the factory into two smaller factories (see Exhibit 11-3). Each factory had its own workers, organizational struc-

Exhibit 11-3 **CHEVY/CADILLAC FACTORY BEFORE AND AFTER FOCUSING**

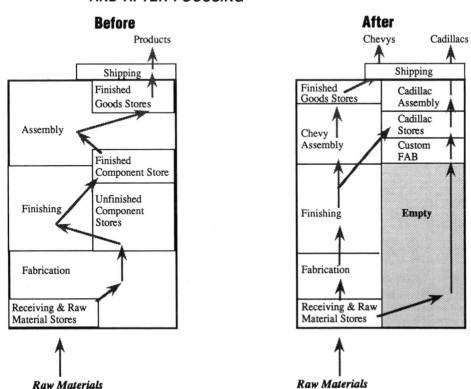

ture, support departments, and performance measurements. Furthermore, each factory had to have its own inventory and inventory planning and control system.

The Cadillac factory kitted each customer order in its finished-components stores area. Workers then assembled these components under strict quality standards and shipped within three days. Its planning group only planned the requirements for the 1,000 or so finished components in their inventory. From these 1,000 components, workers could assemble millions of products. If the finished components were in stock, the Cadillac factory would be able to ship the products in four days. Only with its own inventory could management hold the Cadillac group responsible for their delivery performance. This segregation also avoided schedule conflicts with the Chevy group. Management measured the Cadillac factory on delivery performance, inventory levels, and cost.

By stocking all the required Cadillac components, AJ practically ended the expediting of parts. No longer were long production runs broken up by expedited runs of only a few pieces. This change saved setup, material handling, and scheduling costs, to name a few. The new system significantly simplified and improved planning. With fewer components, planners could more accurately plan their parts.

The Chevy factory manufactured all its products or components to a forecast. This allowed most of the parts to flow through the plant on a Kan Ban system. The Kan Ban system pulled parts through the factory by using cards. These cards practically eliminated planning, shop floor control, and warehousing costs. This system simplified manufacturing so much that it eliminated most of the intermediate stores locations, although some batches remained queued up waiting for plating.

Management measured the Chevy factory's performance on delivery performance (against three-day delivery), cost, and inventory levels. By focusing this factory, both groups improved delivery performance, raised quality levels, reduced inventory, and cut costs.

Over the next year, delivery performance finally met market needs, and activity levels dropped throughout the factory on higher sales volume. Exhibit 11-4 shows each factory's costs before and after focusing. The Cadillac factory lowered its cost by over 20 percent. Almost all the reduction came from transaction overhead. Flexible assembly fixtures, new

Exhibit 11-4 **AJ WHEELCHAIR COSTS BEFORE AND AFTER FOCUSING**

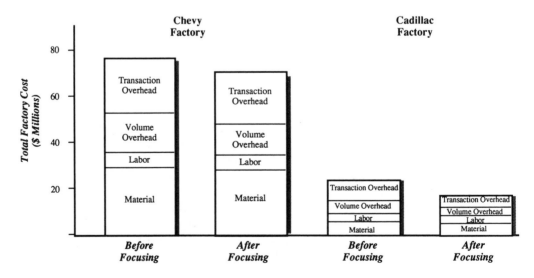

methods, and a new layout reduced the cost per transaction, while part standardization and new planning procedures greatly lowered activity levels. The focusing was a success.

Separating the Chevy factory also uncovered opportunities. A robot welder was justified on scrap savings. Previously, the factory had brazed the tubes together. Brazing leads to heat deformation, which, in turn, causes a high scrap rate. The robot welds a piece so fast, the heat does not have time to distort the metal. The Chevy factory also established standard assembly lines that cut changeover and handling times. This lowered the Chevy factory's cost by almost 10 percent.

Lessons Learned

As this case demonstrates, dramatic cost reductions are possible, which eliminate the need for product pruning. While AJ did trim its product line, AJ's focusing saved a variety of products from elimination.

ABC, by identifying transaction costs and how transaction costs differed across the product line, pushed AJ to make changes. The transaction costs between the different products were so great it forced management to look at the products separately—a view reinforced by AJ's marketing study. This view of separation was instrumental in convincing AJ to focus its factory. If AJ reconfigured the factory to support only one of the two product lines, ABC forecasted disaster.

The outcome showed the dramatic changes that one can make on transaction costs with new systems. Just by reorganizing the Cadillac assembly area and instituting kitting, indirect time plummeted. In addition, after splitting the factory, the improvement in delivery performance came as quite a shock, especially to the sales force. Simply by taking the problem apart and putting it into smaller pieces, dramatic improvements were made possible.

Splitting the factory allows the company to set consistent goals for each new factory, which best satisfy the customer's needs. The focused factory, with a narrower range of customer demands, is better able to adapt to these demands. The factory is then able to establish measures, facilities, equipment, a labor force, and systems that best support this environment. If the factory is supporting repetitive production, then fast throughput and hard tooled machines equip the shop. If the factory supports low-volume customized jobs, then the shop needs quick changeover, flexible machines.

With a narrower range of products, the factory's economies improve. The industrial engineers can make standardized setups and fixtures to reduce changeover times. Fewer jobs require fewer process adjustments that improve quality. The company can make the process flow linear (straight-line flow), trimming inventory buffers. Trimming inventory buffers frees up floor space while reducing handling and material movement. This continuous product flow simplifies production scheduling and enhances quality feedback, in addition to reducing cycle times and improving delivery reliability.

The narrower product line simplifies forecasting and production planning, which, in turn, reduces the number of part shortages. Engineers can groom paperwork to fit each product group's data requirements. In one factory, engineers cut cycle times and expenses by customizing the paperwork for assemblies and spare parts. The customized assemblies had work orders with detailed work instructions and test parameters. Spare parts, on the other hand, merely had routings and test codes. These changes slashed the time and cost to process spare parts. By focusing the factory into different product lines, the company could match the systems to the products more effectively.

An important point to remember when designing a focused factory is to physically separate the two product groups. Each factory must also have its own organizational structures, including planning, quality, and data processing. Since each factory requires a different manufacturing system, the two factories should not use the same MRP system. Planners should master schedule the Chevy and Cadillac products at their inventory level. The factory planned and inventoried Chevys as the end item, and Cadillacs as finished components. Most MRP systems cannot support both of these requirements concurrently. Using only one planning system is disastrous for one of the factories.

CASE STUDY
Westgate Electronic's SMT—Driving Toward World-Class Manufacturing

Westgate was one of the first firms with a companywide ABC program (although they call it by another name). One element of that program is a standard ABC configuration for surface-mount technology (SMT) printed circuit-board assembly.

In the mid-1980s, Westgate found that almost every Westgate installation in the world had through-hole printed circuit-board assembly equipment. Through-hole technology is the precursor to SMT (described on next page). There was no standard equipment, and most sites operated this equipment well below capacity. When SMT began to replace through-hole, Westgate decided to avoid the expense of duplicating facilities and overhead across the company as had happened in through-hole. Therefore, Westgate established an SMT committee of representatives from across the firm. One of their objectives was to limit the number of SMT facilities. In addition, the committee standardized the SMT equipment so that production could be easily shifted from one site to another.

To support this manufacturing strategy, Westgate developed a corporate SMT ABC model. This model would ensure consistent and fair interdivisional pricing of SMT work. The model would also allow productivity and cost comparisons across all the SMT sites. It would aid in identifying superior methods and systems at one site that could be transplanted to others. Last, Westgate wanted to be a "world-class" manufacturer. To meet this objective, Westgate believed they must compare (i.e., benchmark) themselves with external competitors and peers. To make this benchmarking practical, Westgate wanted to manage and set goals for only a few high-level metrics such as cost per placement. This desire drove the need for only a limited ABC system at the corporate level.

Exhibit 11-5 shows Westgate's corporate ABC SMT model. The corporate model was relatively simple. In spite of being simple, the model was flexible. A site can create as complex an ABC system as desired within this framework. For instance, at one site, the test and repair cost pool was broken down into three different pools with one pool for each type of test equipment. The corporate model then consolidates this data into one pool for corporate reporting.

The model did not have activity centers per se. The system aggregated costs into cost-driver pools, independent of process. The materials engineering, purchasing, material handling, manufacturing specifications, and scheduling costs were all procurement costs. Westgate assigned these

Exhibit 11-5 **WESTGATE'S SMT ABC MODEL**

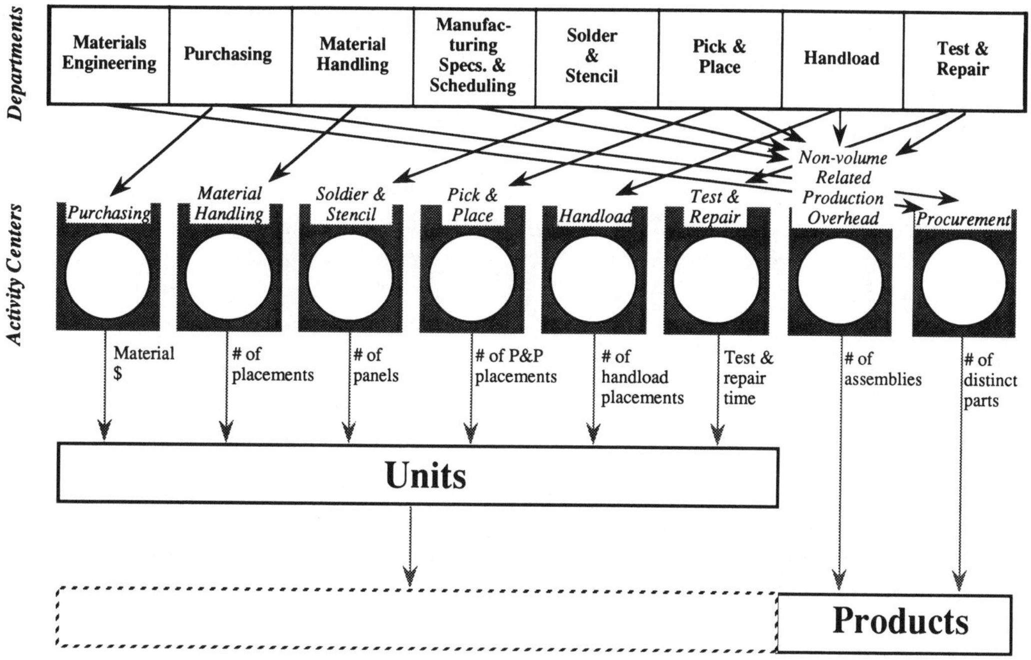

costs on number of distinct parts, material price, and number of placements. Westgate used material price to reflect the greater purchasing effort required for complex parts such as DRAMs versus simple parts such as capacitors. This method contrasts with Wang, which developed cost pools and rates for major groups of components. The number of different parts was chosen as a driver to represent the tasks to evaluate and qualify new part numbers. Material handling costs were split into two pools—the number of placements and the number of distinct parts cost pools.

All the batch production costs, such as test setup and pick and place setup, the system collected in the assemblies cost pool. The system does not report a total cost of pick and place. However, an analyst can calculate a total cost from the cost detail.

Process Description

Through-hole: Through-hole components are electrical components, such as resistors, capacitors, and integrated circuits. These components have metal legs that are inserted into drilled holes in circuit cards. After insertion, the legs are bent to attach the components to the board. Then a wave solder machine feeds the circuit cards through a solder bath that welds the legs to the boards.

Surface-mount technology: Surface-mount differs from through-hole, in that the components do not have any legs, which makes the components considerably smaller. A pick and place machine sets the SMT components on the circuit board's metal pads that have had a mix of solder and paste stenciled on. After that, the circuit card is heated or run through a solder bath to weld the components to the board as the solder and paste temporarily liquefy.

Westgate believes that their ABC system is an integral part of their manufacturing strategy, and that it is helping them make their SMT sites more efficient. However, over the long term, they claim that the biggest benefits have been achieved in product design. Using ABC, Westgate attributes many product successes to better designs resulting from ABC analysis.

CASE STUDY
McKormick Chemical—Blending the Right Mix

One speciality chemical manufacturer undertook a similar approach of establishing a companywide ABC program. Management felt that the current cost system focused attention on past variances that reflected historical, rather than future, or even current conditions. Overhead was growing at an alarming rate. The company wanted to seek out and drive operating improvements proactively, instead of just responding to variances. Management also believed that they spent too much time analyzing incomplete data, most of which they did not believe.

All SG&A costs were being allocated to plants as a percentage of sales. Management found some plants' management complaining that they received little, if any, sales support. In addition, the company wanted to refocus its sales force and marketing groups on the more profitable business. Unfortunately, the company wasn't sure what business that was.

Management felt that they needed better product-line profitability information. They intended to make capital investments in the near future and wanted to make sure they invested in the most profitable products. In addition, management was concerned about pricing. The sales force had complained about a number of once "profitable" products that McKormick was being priced out of. The sales force believed that their processes were superior to the competitors, and did not understand why McKormick was increasing its prices.

To solve these problems, McKormick developed a companywide ABC system. A design team was assembled with representatives from each plant. This system was implemented concurrently across all the company's four plants. The system, using a common design, compared all the factories. The ABC incorporated all the company's complex cost variables into its simulation. Each plant had different costs for making the same product, resulting from different

Vessel and reactor sizes

Distances to customers

Raw material costs (including inbound freight)

Process equipment

Operating efficiencies

Yield

Overhead

Storage capacity

These factors created different cost driver rates for each different plant. However, not all these factors were incorporated in cost drivers. A simulation model was also built that encompassed capacity constraints and different vessel sizes and shipping distances. By simulating different product mixes and run lengths at different sites using ABC, the company calculated the optimum product mix for each site. The company excluded all fixed (i.e., sunk) costs from these calculations.

This information was used to benchmark each site's capability and rationalize the facilities. By comparing different plants that were making the same products, management identified critical leverage points that made one plant more efficient than another. While McKormick was not contemplating any plant closings, this information would have been invaluable for such a purpose. However, the company did eliminate some production lines as a result of the system. These production lines were so old and inefficient, the study proved it was more profitable to write them off than to continue production. The ABC study, as always, provided excellent information for overhead reduction and improved pricing. One surprising finding was the discovery of just how much a mechanical breakdown actually cost in lost production, scheduling interruptions, overtime, etc. This cost justified the implementation of an expanded preventive maintenance program.

OUTSOURCING ACTIVITIES

For a hundred years, companies operated on the philosophy of building for oneself as much as possible. Companies believed that they saved suppliers' profit margins and avoided being at the mercy of suppliers. Twenty-five years ago, the domestic steel industry was dominated by large, vertically integrated companies. U.S. Steel, Inland, and Bethlehem each owned its own coal, ore, and limestone mines, as well as railroad and shipping lines. U.S. Steel sold steel products ranging from barrels to oil field equipment. This is no longer the case—big integrated steel producers are a dying breed. These dinosaurs have been put on the endangered species list by minimills, composites, aluminum, and efficient foreign producers. One sign of the times is the announcement in 1988 by USX—alias U.S. Steel—of its intention to sell all its rail and shipping facilities.

One key strategy that more companies are undertaking is outsourcing the purchase of parts, components, or end units from outside suppliers. This supplants vertical integration, where parts are manufactured in-house. GE Medical farmed out the manufacturing of printed circuit boards, harnesses, and certain mechanical parts as part of a cost-reduction program in CAT scanners. Vendors with greater production economies and expertise saved GE 25 percent on these components.

One consumer appliance manufacturer saved over $2 million a year by outsourcing screws. The screws used to travel a quarter of a mile in the company's plant from cold headed to plating, to packing, to shipping. By buying them from a Far East vendor, they received the screws plated and in bags, ready for shipment to the customer. The vendor, using highly automated equipment, was able to produce, plate, and pack the screws untouched by human hands. For the company, outsourcing eliminated a huge number of work orders, moves, setups, and other transactions throughout the plant. The move also allowed the company to concentrate more resources on what they did best—manufacturing appliances.

Allows Strategic Make/Buy Decisions

ABC identifies the true costs of buying. Often, management makes the decision to buy based on a vendor's quoted price versus the in-house cost. As an example, take the case of a pump manufacturer analyzing a quote to buy Korean castings. The in-house manufacturing cost is $125. Since the Korean casting's quote is for $100, management decides to buy the casting from Korea. This ignores the very significant transaction costs of acquiring the material. In Exhibit 11-6, ABC shows the hidden costs of buying Korean castings. Not only are there procurement charges like duty, brokerage, and freight, but there are also purchasing, planning, and scrap costs to consider. Together, these costs added $54 to a $100 casting's price. With ABC, the company decides to make the casting in-house and saves $29.

Using ABC, reported overhead shifts from labor-intense processes to capital-intense ones. With this new overhead, one may discover processes that the company is no longer competitive in. If so, the company may decide to investigate "outsourc-

Exhibit 11-6 **PURCHASING COSTS IN A TRADITIONAL VERSUS ABC SYSTEM**

PURCHASING COSTS IN A TRADITIONAL VS ABC SYSTEM

CASTING - BEARING HOUSING	TRADITIONAL SYSTEM	ABC SYSTEM
VENDOR QUOTE	$100	$100
PURCHASING		12
PLANNING		4
RECEIVING		2
FREIGHT		10
DUTY		5
BROKERAGE		3
SCRAP & REWORK		22
TOTAL	$100	$154

ing," that is, buying all the process's output from a vendor. However, outsourcing is a difficult undertaking infested with pitfalls.

The first pitfall is the flawed methodology typically used to evaluate make/buy decisions. Companies do not make the decision based on discounted cash flows, they base it on comparing in-house product costs versus vendor quotes. Evaluating outsourcing on product costs makes no allowance for fixed and working capital investment. This favors in-house production.

Most outsourcing decisions are based on whether the in-house manufacturer or the vendor has the lowest operating cost. Yet, this is not the criterion against which decisions should be judged. All decisions should be weighed against shareholder value creation. In many cases, the more expensive course of action provides the greatest value improvement. Many companies underemploy assets providing lower-cost components. However, the capital tied up into this process may not be reducing cost sufficiently enough to provide an adequate return on this investment. For example, one manufacturer maintained a million-dollar investment in gear cutting, despite the fact that a recent study had found that it saved only $30,000 a year. From the perspective of the shareholders, the company would have been better off selling the equipment, working down the inventory, and buying the gears complete from outside vendors. The cost savings were not worth the investment.

Don't Ignore Working-Capital Investments

When outsourcing, the company receives large immediate cash infusions by reducing inventory and selling off assets. When a process goes outside, the company works down in-process inventory and avoids future capital investments.

When analyzing outsourcing, one must identify the net present value of outsourcing. Purchasing must compare the difference between the total in-house cost and the vendor cost (vendor prices plus procurement costs) discounted into the future. The outsourcing alternative must also include the immediate infusion of cash from selling the in-house equipment (and stepping down the processes work-in-process inventory) and from the excess space the department presently occupies. Likewise the in-house alternative must include the discounting of all future capital investments in the process. A process may actually be less expensive in-house, but the analysis must consider selling the assets, leasing the space, lowering inventory levels, and foregoing future capital investments. Hence, outsourcing throws off a lot of cash and, thereby, in many cases, creates more present value.

An outsourcing candidate does not have to be a fabrication department like machining, it can be one's truck delivery fleet. No activity should be off limits. In most cases vertical integration has a negative affect on the company's value creation. Yet manufacturing executives frequently claim that a process is of strategic value and cannot be outsourced. While sometimes a valid argument, it is frequently overused. The operations vice president of one large aerospace company makes this claim about his blanket shop. The blanket shop sews together insulation blankets that surround the passenger compartment of commercial airlines. Many were somewhat skeptical of this claim. The technology used to sew the blankets is a Singer sewing machine. It is difficult for one to imagine why the company pays union labor rates— $14 an hour not including fringes, for sewing. The same company also has one of the world's largest wood shops—their principal product—crates to ship landing gears overseas.

In addition, the process for evaluating outsourcing is flawed. Typically, companies only send out for quote a limited quantity of parts, which forfeits buying leverage. Companies usually use only in-house variable costs to compare to vendor costs. When considering outsourcing the whole manufacturing process, one needs to consider the entire cost of maintaining and supporting the process. In the case of outsourcing, all these costs become variable. When looking at strategic make versus buy decisions, one needs to assume that all your process's costs are variable. Over the long term, all costs are. The company can use freed-up floor space for another department or lease it out. The company can sell equipment and so on.

On the other hand, one also needs to calculate the true costs of buying from a vendor. When buying from the vendor, one still plans and schedules each part's arrival. One must pay freight, place purchase orders, and receive the parts. Therefore, before approaching a vendor, one must decide how one wants to manage the supplier relationship. Does the company want long-term contracts, receiving by-passed, blanket POs, integrated planning systems, etc.?

With a JIT partnership, the company and the vendor both benefit from many, if not all, of the advantages that come from vertical integration. With a long-term arrangement, buying and selling costs are very low and supplies are guaranteed. One can integrate forecasting and planning to keep lead times short and inventory low. Close supplier relationships can give each other access to technologies and changes in each other's business. Suppliers can justify greater capital investments with firm orders in hand, and gain higher credit lines. Vendors can design your subcomponents, saving development time and money. Ford, for example, under a broad agreement with Bendix Automotive Systems Group, is responsible for the entire brake system—from design to manufacture. Ford merely specifies the brake system's function and lets Bendix do the rest. Each party maintains its specialization and efficiency.

Physio Control, a manufacturer of defibrillators, avoids costly transactions on their resistors, capacitors, and diodes. Physio does not order, receive, inspect, or invoice any of these parts. It has a bank of parts in its printed circuit-board assembly area that a vendor keeps filled. The vendor then bills Physio, once a month, for the parts consumed. This eliminates nearly all transactions on these components whose average cost is less than 5 cents.

If one wants such a JIT arrangement, a very cautious approach is suggested. First the company sends out a quote package of all its work to interested vendors. After analyzing the first set of quotes (the quotes may be higher than your in-house costs at this point), one narrows the field of vendors. One will find it is too time consuming to work out all the questions and issues with many vendors. By explaining one's methods, equipment, and tooling, one reduces the vendor's risk. One can even sell him one's equipment and allow him to hire one's operators. After working with the vendor, he becomes convinced that the company is serious about a JIT/sole source relationship, and is not going to "cherry pick" his quotes. This all works to bring down his quote (25 percent from the original starting point is typical).

At this point one has the numbers to determine if outsourcing will save money. Comparing quotes with a vendor is very interesting. Since vendors do not have an ABC system, they tend to overcost high-volume parts and undercost low-volume parts (see Exhibit 11-7; the vendor price is the landed price with procurement costs included). Vendors tend to charge jobs many transaction costs; their costs are much more realistic than the typical company's. This makes comparing the quotes and ironing out misunderstandings a long and involved process.

Some suggest taking advantage of the vendor by just outsourcing the low-volume products. This is a bad idea for two reasons. The first reason is that most fabrication processes usually have large fixed costs and minimum operating rates; reducing the volume usually hikes per unit costs. So, by outsourcing only the low-volume work, both companies end up losing money. Unfortunately, a common problem with out-

Exhibit 11-7 **COMPARING OUTSOURCING QUOTES WITH ABC'S COSTS**

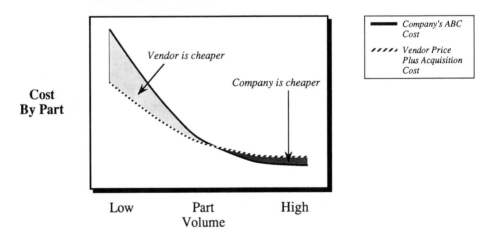

Vendors lacking an ABC system make cost comparisons difficult

sourcing low-volume parts is unreliable delivery. In every factory, managers and supervisors concentrate on the higher-volume production. This phenomenon is compounded by the production people's intuitive knowledge that the company doesn't make any money on these products. This tendency almost always results in erratic scheduling of low-volume parts. Since the late end-item delivery of a single part causes late deliveries, these parts, even if outsourced, are expensive. The second is that driving your vendors out of business is not a very effective long-term strategy.

However, before entering into a contract with this new vendor, it is the company's responsibility to determine whether or not the vendor really can support your needs. Vendors frequently oversell their capability and underestimate the difficulty of transferring production and supporting a JIT relationship. One must conduct quality, production planning, and technical capability audits. This includes trial runs and test parts. In addition, one must perform a credit check and talk to the vendor's references. One should share cost data, and make certain both companies will make money. This is essential for a successful relationship. One must take all these steps, even if one knows the vendor very well already. Once the company commits to outsourcing, there is no turning back.

Outsourcing a department can reap substantial savings and it also makes a company more focused and flexible. However, a hasty transition can put a company out of business.

Typically, one finds it very difficult to convince management to investigate outsourcing. Many executives do not want to lessen their control. They have come to believe that no vendor can compete with their in-house operations. The flawed methodology used to decide make or buy has reinforced this view. In 1987, while conducting a capital planning study of an aerospace company, one consulting firm could not help but notice the company's enormous outsourcing opportunities. The consultants conservatively estimated that the company could save over $400 million annually, and free up over $700 million in assets through more extensive outsourcing. The aerospace concern could outsource capital intense processes such as machining, sheet metal fabrication, wire harness assembly, tube bending, and gear manufacturing. Out of the 12 senior executives who presented these findings, only the controller seemed interested.

However, one somewhat disheartening benefit from outsourcing is that it forces a company to fix unaddressed quality problems. It is not uncommon to find companies operating for years with error-ridden engineering drawings, worn-out machines, and defective tooling. Consequently, the company must correct these problems before outsourcing. A company cannot expect a vendor to make a part that is not to print. Likewise, the company must fix its tooling. To outsource the department, the company must first correct all these problems. It is sad that it takes outsourcing to get management action. Many employees even feel betrayed. The employees believe they could have beaten the vendors if the company would have fixed these problems earlier.

USING ABC FOR DECISION MAKING

When performing any analysis using ABC information, the costs one uses depend on the decisions that need to be made. Depending on the decision's time horizon and the magnitude change in activity, costs change from fixed to variable. Suppose, for example, that a company is analyzing a make-versus-buy decision for one part. It is unlikely that occupancy costs and depreciation are going to change based on the outcome; these costs are fixed. If, on the other hand, the same company is looking at outsourcing the whole department over the next year, these costs are variable.

If the analysis evaluates investments or strategic alternatives such as which market to chase, the product costs should exclude noncash-flow items such as depreciation. However, an analysis must consider items such as capital costs and changes in working capital.

In addition, in an ABC system, there are costs at different levels. There are costs assigned to units, batches, products, orders, customers, and markets. One should include only costs at or below the decision making level. If, for example, a company is evaluating whether to drop a product line, the decision affects unit, batch, and product-level costs. The channel and market segment costs, like advertising, will be unaffected. Yet the costs to plan raw material will change. The analyst needs to use judgment when evaluating costs, as well as different rates.

To support this type of analysis, the ABC system must have the flexibility for an analyst to choose which cost elements are fixed and which are variable for all cost analysis. The system must have the capability to "flag" general ledger accounts as fixed or variable based on the decision being evaluated. The system will then report fixed and variable costs for every cost object queried.

CHAPTER 12

ACTIVITY MANAGEMENT

The only truly effective way to cut costs is to cut out activities altogether. To try to cut back costs is rarely effective. There is little point in trying to do cheaply what should not be done at all.

Peter F. Drucker, Claremont College

With these few simple words, Peter Drucker sums up activity management. Costs are not just incurred, they are caused. Activity management controls the occurrence of activities and the efficiency of their operation. Since activities create cost, regulating activities controls the source of costs. When action is taken to reduce the causes of activities that consume the resources, then a lasting reduction in costs takes place.

Companies of all kinds—McDonnell Douglas, Citicorp, General Electric, Chrysler, and Sears—have sharply cut staff in recent years, yet few have realized the expected cost savings. In some cases, costs have actually increased. Most companies have found that with less staff, performance suffers. This is in addition to frequent employee complaints about increased work load and stress.

Companies find that while staff is reduced, work remains and employees scramble to maintain throughput, yet throughput invariably suffers. The company can reluctantly let customer service slip or increase production by hiring temporary workers or worse yet, consultants. While the idea behind these staff reductions is always the same—make the company more efficient (and most companies are far from efficient)—they fail. Why? The companies are only eliminating the symptom of the problem. By reducing staff, a company is only reducing the resources to performing activities. With fewer resources, fewer activities can be performed. Since activities are consumed by products or customers, performing fewer activities means building fewer products or satisfying fewer customers. Building fewer products or serving fewer customers means the company generates less revenue. Since management does not understand the relationship between resource consumption, activities, and the products or customers triggering them, management leaves fate to decide which products or customers remain unsatisfied.

This process puts the cart before the horse. One must learn to manage the activities to control costs. Without an understanding of which costs are driven by which activities, or which costs are driven by which customers, only blind luck allows management to cut costs effectively. Costs are cut effectively only if the tasks eliminated are not desired by the customer anyway. Ending such nonvalue-added activities have no effect on the customers. Therefore, costs are lowered while revenue remains unchanged.

What activity management seeks to do is manage costs and customer value at their source—activities. Activity management looks at customer needs, and how the company's activities should be configured to fulfill those needs. Activity management focuses on controlling activities.

In 1975, McKesson Drug Company rolled out, nationally, its Economost electronic order-entry system. This system is a marvel of activity management. McKesson, a nationwide wholesale drug distributor, initially developed the system to lower their order-entry costs. Later, McKesson expanded the system's capability to provide its customers with more and more benefits.

The Economost system allows independent pharmacies to order products by making a single pass through the store with a hand-held electronic order-entry device. A stock clerk then sends the device's information, via a modem over phone lines, to McKesson's national data center, automatically entering the customer's orders. The same or following day McKesson delivers the ordered items.

This system cuts the retailer's costs and lowers his required inventory. The system allows the retailer to carry less inventory with next-day delivery and the McKesson-supplied inventory management reports. This cuts the drugstore's working capital and space requirements. The system even delivers the items with pricing labels, and comes in cartons matching the drugstore's aisle assignments. The retailer needs fewer clerks to inventory and order products.

McKesson has also reaped benefits. McKesson slashed its order-entry staff from 700 to just 15, and dropped half its sales force. McKesson then transformed the remaining sales force from order takers into business consultants. The sales force now aids the druggist in laying out the shelves, setting up inventory controls, and developing ordering procedures. McKesson built into the automated pricing higher discounts for larger orders. These higher discounts have successfully encouraged retailers to buy in larger quantities. Most drugstores no longer ordered items once or twice a day, but once or twice a week. These changes slashed the number of transactions in McKesson's billing, warehousing, shipping, and trucking departments.

McKesson has passed on some of these savings to the retailers. This creates switching costs for the retailer not to leave McKesson. The system has been so successful that it has raised the average profitability of independent pharmacies. Most of these pharmacies were at break-even levels in the early 1970s. These independent pharmacies were very important to McKesson, because McKesson has a high market share with them.

Before expanding the pilot system, McKesson's controller decided that the Economost system was a very bad idea. This is not surprising—McKesson's traditional cost accounting system hid the transaction savings that the Economost system would provide. The controller asked the strategic planning department to prepare a formal operations research model to demonstrate the system's economics. Only after developing a formal model were the system's savings quantified. The controller opposition relented.

ABC transforms this intuitive activity management into a structured system. With an ABC system, McKesson would have known how much electronic ordering would have saved. McKesson could have calculated the optimum discounts for the increased order sizes. An ABC system portrays how all activities interrelate and create cost. This allows a business to manage and control all its activities.

Every business can be thought of as a set of activities. Earlier, we defined the principle of ABC that activities consume resources and products consume activities. In the broader sense, products are merely surrogates for activities. Optimally, a customer's activities consume the company's activities, as the company's activities consume employee's activities.

Yet every company has activities that its customers do not consume and that are not required to do business. These surplus activities are called nonvalue added. While the traditional cost-focused organization concentrates on efficiency, the activity-focused company concentrates on simplicity—eliminating nonvalue-added tasks. It is one of management's prerogatives to seek out and end these activities. The more effective the management, the fewer nonvalue activities the company has.

This chapter describes how to use ABC to manage activities and identify true savings opportunities. It describes how to use the results of ABC and avoid the pitfalls, and what type of options are typically available, and how to carry them out effectively.

THE NEW BUSINESS PHILOSOPHY

Strategy ABC is a new management philosophy. It is a philosophy of managing activities and not symptoms, that is, costs. It looks at every business as a series of activities. Furthermore, a customer's activities consume the company's activities. The efficiency with which the company consumes resources is critical to its competitiveness. However, it is not as important as the effectiveness of one's competitiveness—

doing the right things. Business is no longer defined in terms of products and markets, but in terms of activities performed. With this system, management learns to manage the company's activities to satisfy a customer's activities. Management makes cost and service trade-offs to best satisfy the customer's needs. The company can add or subtract activities, change the frequency of activities, and improve activity performance.

Activity management provides a holistic and integrated system of management. ABC links resource consumption—that is—cost to activities, and then to products and services. Customer value, on the other hand, relates revenue to customer needs. By capturing cost and customer need information in terms of activities, executives can incorporate cost and customer value trade-offs in decision making. Activity management then uses a single criterion to evaluate every decision alternative—the highest net present value (see Exhibit 12-1). This single objective function ensures that every decision is in agreement with the company's objective—shareholder value creation. Therefore, activity management integrates the entire business process. The business process has only a single objective. The management system incorporates all the company's activities, as well as customer needs.

Exhibit 12-1

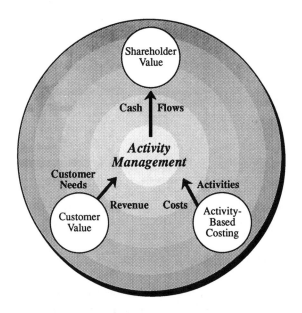

Activity management integrates Activity-Based Costing and Customer Value to maximize shareholder value

Choosing Activities

In the ABC environment, managers strive to control the creation and operation of activities. Since a business is a bundle of activities, a company can choose which activities it cares to perform. All other customer-required activities can be outsourced. No firm can perform all activities as well as some outside specialists. This philosophy then allows the firm to build a competitive advantage by selecting the "best of the best" performers for each activity. The company, therefore, improves the leverage of its activities with the greatest value added. More significantly, this philosophy changes the focus of competitive strategy from the traditional product and market orientation to one of activities.

Controlling Activity Frequency

To control the creation of activities, management seeks to improve the company's effectiveness. Effectiveness measures how well the company aligns its activities with customer needs. Are the activities and their occurrence on target? How much are different activities worth to the customers? The perfectly effective company is one in which all the company's activities add value to the customers.

ABC helps identify which policies create activities, so that management can judge the effectiveness of these policies. Management can compare how much a policy costs versus how much customers are willing to pay.

For example, at one company, management found freight costs per unit dropped dramatically if customers ordered five units or more. Using an ABC system, management calculated the number of transactions cut by raising the company's minimum order quantity to five. Then the company quantified the change's cost savings. Since raising the order quantity would cause some customers to carry more inventory, the analyst discounted the savings against lost sales. The analyst examined each different customer group's buying frequency. The analyst estimated the cost impact that raising the order quantity would have on each customer group's costs. If the cost impact was significant, the analyst considered the sales lost. From this analysis, the company raised its minimum order quantity, but lowered discounts by 1 percent. This cut the company's billing, shipping, and freight costs, as well as saved 85 percent of the customers' money as well.

Efficiency Is Important as Well

By managing activities, one configures them to be consumed by their customers. One strives to satisfy customer's needs at the lowest price possible, while providing the company with a profit. A company must configure its activities so that customers are willing to spend resources to consume the company's activities. This is the effectiveness of our activity management. ABC plays a role in improving a company's effectiveness. By managing its own activities, a company gains insights into its customers' activities. This insight helps the company understand its customers and configure its activities better.

Efficiency is the last component of activity management. Efficiency is how well the company converts resources into activity. The efficiency of each activity depends on the systems, people, scheduling, and equipment performing the activity. The better a firm manages these factors, the higher the ratio of activities to resource consumption.

Even today, most companies focus exclusively on efficiency. When facing a cost reduction, management seeks out and lays off workers who don't seem busy. However, even with the employee gone his or her work remains. This work may or may not be important to the customer. Management lacks tools to help them understand the trade-offs between customer value and cost. Management does not know what policies to change to end activities and remove costs.

Learning to Manage Activities

One should try not to manage costs, one should manage activities. Costs are but a symptom, activities are the cause. Unless a nonvalue activity is consuming costs, trying to control costs only blindly lowers throughput. This insight and ABC provide management with one of the best opportunities for cost reduction a company has ever had. It provides the company with activity information that invites cost reduction, in that only traceable costs are controllable and ABC makes overhead traceable. ABC

- Describes which activities drive costs
- Allows overhead productivity to be measured
- Provides information for trade-off decisions
- Identifies what creates activity

Describes which activities drive costs. Surprising as it sounds, most managers fail to concentrate their attention on the company's most expensive and critical activities. This is caused, in part, by the cost systems' overemphasis on direct labor, as well as departmental structures. Departmental structures concentrate attention on functions and not the performance of activities.

ABC focuses management on the activities that result in costs. In addition, ABC provides a clear picture of which activities are the most expensive. It shows management that costs are only symptoms and that systems and policies create costs. Management learns that the only way to control costs is to change the way business is conducted.

One also knows, from ABC, the interrelationships between all the departments—which indirect departments are supporting which production departments, and which ones are not. These insights are invaluable as one tries to slash overhead spending.

Allows overhead productivity to be measured. ABC, by measuring the costs of activities against the number of activities, creates productivity measures. With ABC one knows how much an activity costs to perform, allowing one to compare internal costs to external costs. A company can use this information to benchmark themselves against comparable companies and competitors, or decide make versus buy questions. In addition, one knows whether overhead is becoming more or less expensive over time. These measures should be easy to understand because they mirror how the company actually operates and incurs costs. This allows executives to question the way the overhead departments operate and to identify improvement opportunities.

One can use this information to set cost reduction targets and track progress toward those goals. An executive can track the cost of processing a shop order or creating an engineering drawing to scrutinize the department's productivity. By quantifying the cost of processing a PO as $45, management can track whether the purchasing department is becoming more or less efficient. This encourages managers to streamline their operations and make them more flexible. As Lord Kelvin once said, "The first step in understanding something is to measure it."

Without measurement and an understanding of what causes overhead, setting performance improvement targets is difficult at best. ABC gives management this information. The company can set realistic targets and track progress toward them. Management is no longer forced to put blind faith in panaceas like CIM, JIT, and MRP for, as yet, unidentified benefits.

Provides information for trade-off decisions. ABC, by identifying how much different activities cost, provides the basis for all forms of trade-offs. For example, how much is a discount worth versus buying in full truckload quantities? This information allows management to negotiate more effective sales contracts or establish more profitable policies. Moreover, how much does qualifying a vendor, whose products skip receiving, inspection, and warehousing, save? These data give purchasing the justification to upgrade vendors.

From ABC, the company knows how much the total cost of processing material receipts is. The firm knows how much each receipt costs and how much time it takes. They now have productivity measures for every department. These data, in turn, allow the company to estimate how much purchasing department capacity is absorbed by processing purchase orders versus how much is taken up in qualifying new vendors.

Identifies what creates activity. ABC tells the company which products, customers, processes, and product attributes trigger activity, in turn, creating costs. ABC clearly links a product to the moves, setups, purchase orders, and planning tickets it creates. Management can then analyze what causes these cost objects to trigger these activities. What business processes, policies, and systems do products encounter that trigger this activity. For example, how production is scheduled determines how many transactions a customer order triggers. If a customer order has 1,000 units and the shop is scheduled in batches of 500, the order creates two batches. These batches, in turn, trigger two shop orders, two setups, two inspections, and so on. A company's systems determine how much cost a particular product or customer triggers.

ABC gives management insight into what induces cost. By examining high cost-driver rates, management identifies the policies or procedures driving many costs. At one company, the cost per purchase order was abnormally high. Upon investigation, the company discovered that it required the completion of more than 15 separate forms for each purchase, regardless of purchase price. The original intention of many of these forms was to control cost by requiring justification and management approval. Unfortunately, the result was a slow, cumbersome, and inefficient procurement system. When management became aware of the exorbitant cost of processing each purchase order, it eliminated many of the forms and initiated changes in the approval cycle. Manager signatures are now only required for items of more than $1,000, applying to only 5 percent of the purchase orders. These improvements cut purchasing costs and avoided bogging down management. In addition, purchase order processing time was slashed by more than 90 percent.

In another case, during an ABC study, it was found that a company's customers were averaging two units per order of a particular product that had high freight costs. This was very surprising because the customer was entitled to free freight for purchases of only three or more units and the customer was receiving free freight. Further investigation revealed that the customers were always ordering custom units and two standard units. The customers ordered the two standards to receive free freight. Because the custom product took three weeks to build, the company always shipped the two standard units immediately and placed the custom on backorder. Therefore, the company paid for freight on two shipments. The company's policy of encouraging larger customer orders had backfired, doubling freight costs.

ABC quantifies changes in activity levels alerting management to changes in the environment or the effect of policies. This allows management to see and understand what triggers changes in the organization and creates costs.

PROCESS VALUE ANALYSIS

Every time an operator stores, moves, inspects, sorts, counts, or expedites a part, he creates costs. Despite the fact that none of these tasks add value to the product. Value-added tasks are those that increase the value of the product from the customer's perspective. Nonvalue-added tasks are all other tasks—those tasks that are not part of the process of providing a product and meeting customer expectations.

Some ABC systems identify all costs as either value added or nonvalue added. By highlighting the total cost of nonvalue added activities, some people believe companies will be driven to eliminate them. Therefore, many consultants try to separate costs into value added and nonvalue added as part of the ABC system. This segregation forces needless and confusing detail in the ABC system.

As one undertakes an ABC analysis, the steering committee examines each overhead department's costs with its managers. The committee develops an understanding of what each functional group is doing, what is consuming its resources, and how the work flows. Just by going through the ABC analysis, management puts each process step under a microscope. Management questions why it costs $12.50 to store and move material from the warehouse. Is the paperwork excessive? Do the forklifts have to drive too far? Can we have parts skip the warehouse and be delivered directly to the next department? Can we move the equipment closer together, eliminating the movement all together?

The process one goes through to ferret out improvement opportunities is called process value analysis (PVA). PVA is a dynamic process of examining the business to make it more efficient and effective. PVA seeks improvements to meet the needs of the customers with less cost and higher quality. PVA takes a systems approach to a business process. It looks at the conversion of input to output and how well that output matches customer needs. When conducting a PVA, one typically breaks down activities into many tasks, which is a much greater level of detail than an ABC system provides.

The PVA has four steps:

1. Define existing process

2. Determine customer needs

3. Design improvements

4. Monitor results

1. *Define existing process.* This is the step where one develops an understanding of the current process and how it is performed. One identifies the events triggering the process, as well as all inputs, that is, information, documents, labor power, equipment, etc. One flowcharts the process to document and understand the tasks involved. One identifies all the process outputs and interfaces to other functions and processes. One also estimates the cost and cycle time of the process. It is frequently useful to break down cycle time into waiting time versus work time, and value-added work versus nonvalue-added work. One must also identify how the process is being measured, and to what objectives.

It is important to identify process variations, that is, if certain products take longer to process than others. Typically, these variations provide a great deal of insight into the process. For example, at one engine repair and overhaul facility, the average engine was not meeting customer turnaround times. While the study group was busy streamlining the operations, it was not until it looked at the turn times of individual engine classes that the root cause of the delays was identified. Turn times varied significantly by engine type. When investigating why, the team discovered that delivery problems with one supplier were causing delays for that engine class. Only by investigating process variation was the true cause of the delay uncovered—supplier deliveries.

2. *Determine customer needs.* Once the process has been defined, customer requirements must be validated. First one needs to identify who the process's customers really are. After figuring out who the customers are, one next needs to discover the

customer's perceptions of the process output. Typically, one will use either interviews or surveys, or both, to identify customer perceptions. One seeks to discover whether the process output satisfies customer needs and why. One must then attempt to understand the customer well enough to understand how and why the process output satisfies the customer's needs. Once one understands the customer's needs, one identifies how well the company is meeting those needs. From this analysis, one identifies gaps between the customer needs, their perceptions, and the company's performance.

3. *Design improvements.* After developing an understanding of the process and the gaps with customer needs, one can seek to identify process improvements. If the process has nonvalue-adding steps, one can simplify the process by consolidating steps. If the process has wide variation based on output type, one should consider splitting up processing by output type. If customer needs are not being met, one should consider changing the process's outputs. If costs are excessive, one may consider changing the process's frequency or its inputs. One may find that performance is being measured against the wrong objectives, and simply by changing incentives, problems disappear.

To identify these opportunities, one should get the involvement of operating people, sharing the information discovered about the process with them. Brainstorming sessions with small groups are one of the best environments for soliciting new ideas. The operating people are the ones who must develop ownership of any changes to the process. In addition, they are also the ones who know the system the best. Once the improvement opportunities are identified, one must estimate the resources needed to implement them, as well as the expected benefits. Then the case for the improvements can be taken to management for their approval.

4. *Monitor results.* After obtaining approval and implementing the project, management must measure performance of the process against the project's benefits. One must implement key performance measures to ensure that the project achieves the desired results, as well as provides feedback for continuous improvement.

Process Improvements

Using PVA, management should question how it is doing business. It is usually difficult to break ingrained mind-sets regarding the way one has always done business. Nevertheless, PVA provides management with the perspective to look beyond the cost and look at what is creating it. This uncovers duplication between functions and identifies nonvalue-adding activities, inviting their elimination.

For example, Exhibit 12-2 shows the elements of a company's die-casting and punch-press department's batch costs. Each time the die-cast department runs a batch of parts, the batch consumes $610. This transaction cost includes $118 for tool cleaning and $397 for indirect labor. After completing this analysis, management undertook a program to reduce these transaction rates.

Exhibit 12-2 **ELEMENTS OF TWO DEPARTMENTS' BATCH COST-DRIVER RATES**

```
ELEMENTS OF TWO DEPARTMENTS BATCH
COST DRIVER RATES
```

	DIE CASTING	PUNCH PRESS
SHOP FLOOR CONTROL	$3.90	$27.40
MATERIAL HANDLING	$2.00	$13.30
INSPECTION	$16.40	$10.20
INDIRECT LABOR	$397.00	$67.50
TOOL CLEANING	$118.12	–
LOST LABOR EFFIC.	$73.10	$13.50
COST PER BATCH	$610.52	$131.90

The industrial engineers working with the die-cast operators developed new methods for quicker changeovers. The engineers modified the machines so that dies could quickly slide out on to a waiting dolly. The engineers replaced nuts and bolts that secured the tooling to the machine with spring lock pins. Instead of preparing the die while they were on the machine, the operators completed most of the tasks off-line. Responsibility for cleaning the dies transferred from the tooling department to the die-cast operators. This change eliminated time spent moving dies back and forth between the department and tooling. Moreover, it freed up valuable tool and die-maker time. These and other changes allowed the company to cut their cost per batch by over $100 in just two months.

However, the punch-press department had a relatively high shop floor control and material-handling cost. When management investigated, they found that shop floor control was creating a large number of expedites for the punch-press department. Every expedite, in turn, created a shop floor control work order, a material movement, and a setup. But what caused the expedites?

The expedites were caused by a fastener house with a new sales contract. This large customer had recently negotiated a special two-week delivery program (four weeks was the normal delivery period). This customer was ordering many special delivery items. Because their delivery cycle was half of the MRP system's four-week planning cycle, the system never scheduled most of these fastener orders. Moreover, these orders had a severe penalty clause for late delivery. This forced shop floor control to expedite these items. The expedited items, in turn, disrupted production, upsetting other schedules and creating even more expedites.

To resolve this problem, in the interim, management created a finished goods inventory for the fastener house's orders. In the long run, the company changed its MRP system for a shorter planning cycle. The company also began working toward shortening its manufacturing cycle times.

While management rightly sacked the shop floor control supervisor for failing to either solve the problem or bring it to management's attention, the other responsible parties deserve mention. The information systems group helped create this problem through its rigid MRP design. However, management bears responsibility for this situation as well. When this special program was negotiated, management worked with the fastener house to develop a more efficient way of handling its sales orders. Yet management gave no consideration to the factory's ability to meet this new demand. Many believed that this was due to management's sales orientation and the low status the company gave manufacturing.

One question you might ask is: Shouldn't management have seen this problem without an ABC system? From a theoretical standpoint—yes—from a practical standpoint—no. In most organizations, management lacks quantification of problems; as a result, they end up misallocating resources and pursuing the wrong problems. A lack of measurement forces management to rely on opinion and judgment as to what the problems are and how they can be solved. Suggestions and opinions percolate up the chain of command, where multistep communication and political motivations distort this information. Thus, without ABC attaching dollars to measures of activity and an understanding of what's causing activity, management is handicapped in its understanding of the problem.

True Cost Centers

Supported by a meaningful cost system, activity-center managers understand and are able to control their costs. If they want support from an indirect department, they know it will cost them. At Hewlett-Packard's Loveland Division, the test manager discovered how much equipment calibration truly cost his test department. Seeking to control his department's budget, he began to investigate ways to reduce calibration costs. He found that his own people could perform 25 percent of the calibrations. He also found that outside contractors were being scheduled too frequently and cut them back. This manager was able to cut his calibration costs by more than 35 percent.

However, you must be very cognizant of nonvalue-added tasks as you study the organization, its flows and processes. As you trace the product's flow through the factory, you identify many nonvalue-adding tasks (see Exhibit 12-3). Eliminating nonvalue-added tasks is one of the most effective ways of reducing cost and decreasing cycle time. Each of these discoveries is another cost reduction opportunity. Eliminating redundant activities removes steps from a process and also cuts errors and slashes cycle time. Cutting cycle time exposes waste and error faster, once again cutting costs.

Cellular Manufacturing

One effective way to reduce nonvalue-added tasks in manufacturing is to rearrange your factory into a cellular plant layout. Most companies arrange their factories in a job-shop fashion (see Exhibit 12-4). The machines are grouped by process type (Taylor's notion of specialization?). In this layout, the factory produces

Exhibit 12-3 **ELIMINATING NONVALUE ADDED**

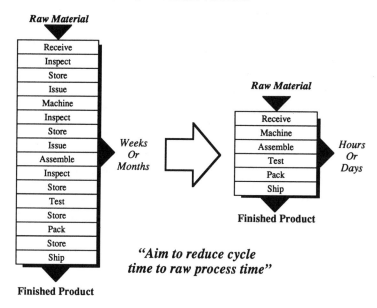

*"Aim to reduce cycle
time to raw process time"*

Exhibit 12-4 **JOB SHOP LAYOUT**

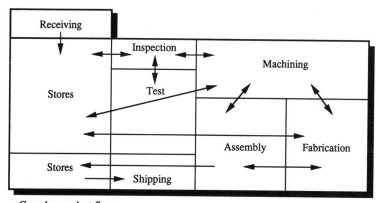

• Complex product flows
• Conflicting objectives
• "Protectionist"
• Poor feedback

This layout results in long leadtimes, poor
quality and unresponsiveness

products in batches that must move from one process area to another. While this layout increases production flexibility to respond to changing product mixes, it creates inventory buffers throughout the plant.

These inventory buffers cause long manufacturing lead times and reduce quality feedback. Studies have found that parts are experiencing value-added processing only 2 percent of the time with this type of layout. The rest of the time the parts are waiting for processing. Operators typically receive little timely feedback on their quality. Downstream operators do not know who worked on the job and their workstations are too far apart. This layout encourages supervisors to manage for departmental efficiencies, creating large batch sizes with long setup times.

The cellular plant arrangement (see Exhibit 12-5) reduces travel distances, smooths production flow, and allows setups to be standardized. With machines colocated and in a U-shape, one operator can even work more than one machine. By arranging the machines in a flow with no inventory buffers, quality feedback is immediate and scheduling is easy. This works to reduce manufacturing lead times, as well as eliminating nonvalue-added activities. One can trace most nonvalue-added activities to either inventory management or quality problems. Personnel must move, count, and store inventory. Likewise, quality deficiencies create waste and the need for inspection and rework.

Exhibit 12-5 **CELLULAR LAYOUT**

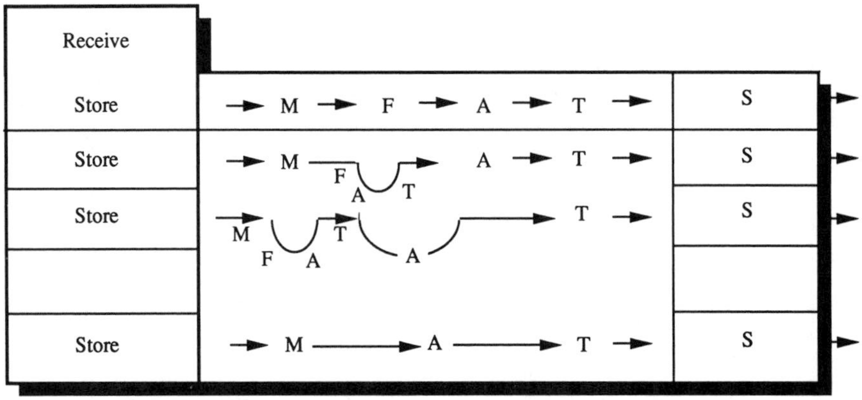

• Grouped by product family
• Economies of scope
• Common objectives
• Immediate feedback/good communications

This layout improves leadtimes, flexibility and quality

At John Deere, the ABC system identified the high cost of material handling and transporting parts. While the plant facilities constrained any major rearrangement, Deere made some layout changes. They established a dedicated cell of 12 machines strictly to manufacture two parts for General Motors. Deere also moved secondary operations back into the main floor to reduce traveling distances. Another outcome was moving the process engineering group from a half mile away to the center of the shop. This change tripled the engineers' output and improved communications with the operators.

ACTIVITY MANAGEMENT AND COST REDUCTION

When one identifies a high-cost activity, the first step is to determine whether the cost is an efficiency or an effectiveness problem, or no problem at all. To reduce cost, one should always emphasize effectiveness over efficiency. A job not worth doing is not worth doing well. If an activity does not add value to the customer, one should not try to perform the activity efficiently; the company should not perform the job at all. One should always question why the company is performing the activity—is it necessary? One should always investigate what is triggering the activity (see Exhibit 12-6). If the activity must be done and has a high cost per activity, one should assess the activity's efficiency.

Exhibit 12-6 **ACTIVITY-BASED COST REDUCTION**

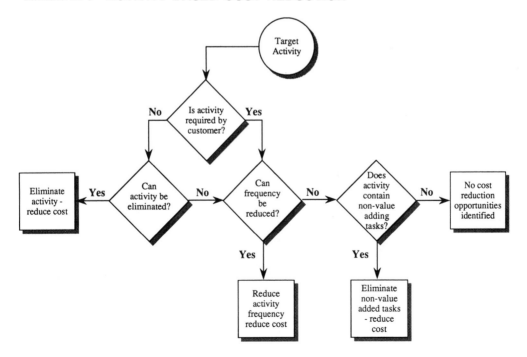

One should investigate what is triggering activities. Determine whether a company or customer requirement is causing the activity's frequency. If the high-cost activity is triggered by the company itself, a more efficient policy might be in order. If the high frequency of the activity is triggered by the customer, one should understand the reasons. For example, does the customer really require frequent customer orders? One should also attempt to determine how much this frequent activity is worth to the customer. One may be able to come to an agreement with the customer limiting the activity and splitting the savings.

In the case of a high cost per activity, one will investigate the process for non-value-added tasks. The best way to do this is to flowchart the process. One should identify every step in the activity, who is responsible, how long it takes, how the activity is processed, and what function each step performs. After flowcharting the process one can quantify any critical performance variables, such as cycle time or cost per task. Next, a team can evaluate each step in the process, looking for a more efficient process. One looks to eliminate as many steps in the process as possible. Each time a part or document is moved, it incurs more cost and a great deal of queue time.

First, one would like to eliminate any time the part or document is stored, inspected, moved, or counted. Next, any redundant tasks, or ones that can damage the part, should be eliminated. Last, any steps that can be eliminated through cross training should be.

In the die-cast department described in Exhibit 12-1, inspection cost each batch $16.40. Once the study identified this cost, quality control had "go/no-go" gauges fabricated for some of the high-volume parts. All an operator had to do was successfully insert the part into the gauge; if it fit it passed inspection. These gauges cut inspection costs by two-thirds. In the other case, a machining department's inspection cost of $9.20 per batch, together with the department's scrap, amounted to over $150,000 a year. These dollars provided management with the justification for implementing statistical process control.

By having the operator measure his own parts, quality control shifts from catching defects to preventing them. Management can hold operators responsible for part quality. SPC allows operators to catch tool wear and spindle run-out immediately. Operators track and correct process variation before it leads to defects.

ABC identifies the processes with the highest scrap and inspection costs—the best opportunities for SPC implementation. The costs of SPC training and the additional operator time for recording data are more than offset by scrap and inspection savings.

Looking at the order entry area, one printing company found that new orders and repeat orders both had the same order-entry costs because both types of orders were processed the same way. However, all the information for the repeat orders was already available. By changing the processing of repeat orders, the company saved order-entry time and the customer's time, plus reduced data-entry errors. In addition, the old order called out the production specs, which saved production planning time.

Looking at the organization as a whole raises issues beyond parochial interests. Management discovers that one department's shortcomings create costs further downstream. For instance, at one aerospace company the N/C programmers were recreating the engineering drawings for machined parts on the computer-aided manufacturing (CAM) system before generating the tool paths. The N/C programmers explained to us that they could not use design engineering's computer-aided drafting (CAD) drawings. Engineering did not draw the drawings to "geometric dimensioning and tolerancing" standards. Without proper tolerancing, the parts could be machined—even inspected—to the original drawing but still not fit together. Management discovered that it could save over $300 per part number by training the designers in "geometric dimensioning and tolerancing."

When management makes a policy decision, rarely does it ever know its true costs. By tracking ABC costs, one can finally close this loop. One can identify the cost of certain activities, and frequently you can trace these activities to a particular management decision. Management can learn what its decisions cost.

For example, at a medical equipment manufacturer, credit adjustments were sharply curtailing the company's sales and profits at the end of each month. These adjustments upset the controller and stymied the company's continuing effort to make "their numbers." The high cost of these credits ($80,000 a month) was another source of irritation for the controller. He instructed the credit manager to approve each credit adjustment personally.

When the ABC system pegged the cost of processing a credit adjustment at almost $42 a piece, the cost startled management. To explain this high cost, the team investigated the credit adjustment process. It discovered that more than 40 percent of credits were under $100. By requiring the credit manager to approve all the adjustments, the adjustments were burying her. She was unable to investigate the high-value credits over $5,000. The credit adjustments were backlogged three months, and more than 13 percent of the customer service calls were credit adjustment inquiries.

Why did the company have so many credit adjustments in the first place? The credit adjustments were the result of billing errors that, in turn, were caused by over 2,000 different sales contracts. With so many sales contracts, each with its own individual terms, the data-processing department could not keep up with the updates and corrections, while errors were rampant. Obviously, customers would only notify the company if the error was in their favor, so it was likely the company was losing money by underbilling. A management decision that was made years ago allowed all sales representative to negotiate their own contracts, with management merely approving them. With no guidelines or standards, each sales contract was unique. That decision was a costly one—$171,080 a month, or over $2 million a year. Exhibit 12-7 shows all the activities, and their costs, that the team attributed to the credit adjustment problem.

To end this problem, the company standardized the sales contracts. This, in turn, reduced billing errors and requests for credit adjustments. The company also

Exhibit 12-7 **ESTIMATING MONTHLY COST OF NONSTANDARD SALES CONTRACTS**

```
ESTIMATING MONTHLY COST OF NONSTANDARD
SALES CONTRACTS

    Credit Processing:     668 Credits  X $42/credit  = $27,972
    Rebills:               210 invoices X $18/invoice =  $3,780
    Customer Service:     1440 calls    X $31/call    = $44,640
    Data Processing:       184 updates  X $77/update  = $14,168
    Average Value of Credit Adjustments:                $80,520
                                                       ---------
                                       Monthly Cost    $171,080
```

changed the policies. Ten standardized sales contracts were created for all but the top 20 customers. Therefore, the company reduced the number of sales contracts from more than 2,000 to 30. In addition, the credit adjustment policy was changed also. The customer service reps were allowed to approve credit adjustments under $100 (to implement required training and control mechanisms). After a trial period, the company hoped to have reps approve all credit adjustments. They believed that this policy would slash credit processing and billing costs. Simultaneously, the changes would lower the number of customer service calls, while raising customer satisfaction with more accurate billing and quicker customer response.

Identifying the abnormally high cost of a credit adjustment led the ABC team to investigate the problem. ABC allows one to quantify a problem's cost, and by following the philosophy of ABC, track it to its source. In this case, the company found that the real culprit—a low-priority issue—was standardized sales contracts. By identifying its real costs, standardized cost sales contracts were no longer a low-priority issue.

One may wonder why this, apparently obvious, problem went unsolved. First, the problem and its cause were not obvious. Only looking at the problem from the perspective of activity management did the credit adjustment activity begin to make sense. The team initially investigated the situation because the team heard complaints about slow credit approvals. Only after looking at the cost of credit adjustments, and then the number of credit adjustments, did someone begin to question what was triggering this activity. Looking for what triggered the activity led them to find the real source of the activity.

Prior to the ABC system, the credit department, aggravated by the large number of credit adjustments, blamed the billing department for sloppy work. In fact, the credit problem caused rancor between the departments, and their members barely spoke. The billing department felt victimized by the MIS department for not maintaining the automated billing system. The MIS department thought of the billing system as a rather large, never-ending nuisance, caused by the sales department's lack of discipline in filling out the billing system forms. The sales force looked at the sales contracts as a good way to get the customer some of the little things they wanted so desperately, such as 90 days credit or price breaks on certain products. The entire credit adjustment issue was clouded in parochial perspectives. No one saw, or had jurisdiction over, the whole problem, and nobody saw its true cost either.

A different situation plagued an air filter manufacturer's purchasing cycle. The company found that the cost of processing its 5,400 purchase orders (POs) averaged $52 per PO. The company had a complicated procurement system to meet the regulatory requirements of its Swedish customers. The cost of this process nearly doubled the average PO purchase total of $54. The least expensive PO totaled $4.18. Realizing this procurement process was burdening the purchase of small items with needless cost and cycle time, the company changed its purchasing policies. All noncontrolled items, worth less than $100, could be bought directly by each department head, by passing the entire purchasing, receiving, and receiving inspection departments, saving more than $10,000 annually. The company ensured control over these items by tracking expenditures against each department and monitoring the buying with audits.

In other cases, the constraints imposed by a particular software system may create cost. At one company, data-processing reports showed a very high number of customer returns. Upon investigating the problem, the IS manager found that the reports inflated the number of returns. The computer system did not allow customer bills to be edited, so every bill with an error had to be "returned" and reentered. The system did not allow anyone to change invoices or even make corrections. This computer policy created a needless workload in order entry and billing, plus fallacious reporting.

On the same system, operators had to repeat data entry over and over again on different inventory status screens. The selection committee needs to identify this type of inefficiency when buying a software package.

ABC even helps to control the seemingly uncontrollable cost of corporate headquarters. At Weyerhaeuser, corporate headquarters "charges back" its costs to the operating divisions on measures of activity. The corporate accounts receivable department charges divisions like the Paper and Forest Products Company based on the number of invoices processed and customer files maintained. Information Services charges divisions based on the number of report pages run and hours to develop reports. The salaried payroll department is charged back to the divisions, based on the number of payroll checks created. The chargeback is based on the budgets of each department. For example, Payroll's budget, including salaries, utilities, floor space, and fringe benefits, is divided by the number of payroll checks processed. This cost per check is then charged to each division's budget based on the number of checks the division generated.

By charging these services back to the user's budgets, Weyerhaeuser claims that the corporate services are more responsive to the divisions. The services develop a sense of ownership of the output. Charging back invites detailed scrutiny of services and costs. The chargeback also creates a teamwork atmosphere between the divisions and these service groups. The divisions see how their needs create work for the corporate services. The divisions no longer feel like they are paying taxes to corporate. The corporate groups see themselves as selling their services, and the divisions see themselves as customers. Corporate services are no longer a monopoly, but must compete for business. The system also allows the divisions to buy the same services from outside organizations, or do without the services entirely. This puts price restraints on the corporate groups. In fact, the information services (IS), faced with competition from minicomputers, was forced to cut costs. The IS laid off workers and began to try to sell its services outside the company to get the department's utilization up.

DESIGN IS THE ROOT OF ALL PRODUCT ACTIVITIES

Viewing a company as an integrated series of activities linked to customer needs complements a fast-cycle-time company. This activity-based philosophy leads to organizing a company around customer needs and the activities to support them. In such an organization people understand how they relate to the rest of the company and the customer. They know how work flows and that time is critical to the customer. The faster their job is completed, the sooner the customer will be satisfied.

In an era where quickly reaching the market with new products is becoming more and more important, streamlining design would seem to be a very good application of ABC. When Xerox sent a group of engineers to Japan in 1981, they came back with a startling conclusion. Their competitors were able to design a new product in half the time, at half the cost. The Japanese burn rate—the dollars per day—was the same; however, their development cycle was only half as long as Xerox's. This realization led Xerox to redesign and revitalize its development cycle, saving $30 million on a single copier.

Like all the other organizations in a company, ABC works to streamline. Since the product's design determines 60 to 70 percent of its manufacturing cost, by simplifying design, great savings result. Typically, a company's new product development budget only includes engineering and some minor prototyping charges. This is because most companies only organize and budget product development in the engineering department. This underestimates the real cost of introducing a product. This approach buries many new product costs in each operating department's budget, and results in the true costs not being tracked back to the products. Marketing develops product requirements, manufacturing engineering develops routing and process specifications, cost accountants provide cost estimates, and quality assurance writes inspection procedures, to name a few additional costs. Since these costs are not engineering costs, the new product's budget does not include them. This understatement distorts decision making by understating the true cost of new product development. It also hinders the inclusion of nonengineering departments early in the development cycle, because they lack budget for it.

ABC corrects these shortcomings. ABC identifies this true cost and every activity involved in the new product. ABC identifies the total development budget, ensuring that all groups are privy to early design involvement. This avoids duplication of effort and rework.

Close examination of the product development cycle reveals an incredibly high rework cost. Typically, 30 percent of product development costs stem from part redesign. Herein lies one of the largest potential savings from reducing product development cycle times. By speeding up the design cycle, one does not have a chance to redesign the product. The designers are forced to get it right the first time, or incorporate new features in the next product.

Unfortunately, the product development process is so poorly understood, it is very difficult to design an ABC system for the engineering of a product. It is very challenging to develop reasonable activity measures in this unstructured development environment, since the process is so complex and so poorly measured. By its very nature, engineers design each product only once. An engineer never repeats the same product. I know of only one company, an auto parts supplier, that has tried it. However, if perfected, I believe an ABC system for the engineering process would be very beneficial.

Such a system would assign costs to products in the design phase on measures of activity such as the number of drawings created, bills of material, specifications, and tools built to estimate engineering hours. By identifying and tracking the parameters that cause new product development costs, management could improve the design process. The number of activities per product could be lower, the process streamlined, and rework avoided. The numbers of drawings, routings, and bills of material would be cost drivers in the "new product development" activity center.

For example, drawing a new part from scratch takes 25 hours, including analysis, while modifying an existing part only takes 3 hours. Add to this the cost of developing new tooling, inspection criteria, routings, documentation, and test procedures, and the new part costs $4,000 compared to $145 for the modified part.

Engineers, product managers, and manufacturing managers would all see the savings in developing generic parts. Generics are standardized parts that engineers can easily customize. These generics would slash development time and manufacturing costs.

The ABC system would provide information to help streamline the new product introduction cycle and to accelerate design cycle times. For example, if a new product principally contained off-the-shelf components, it would require fewer drawings and less test time and documentation. The savings from having vendors design components would be apparent. Additionally, this new product would avoid the fabrication of new tooling. This would slash the development cost and cycle time. While these benefits are intuitive, without accurate data, managers are forced to rely on intuition—almost always suboptimum.

The ABC system would capture development costs by process type. For example, constructing a mold for an investment casting is much more expensive than a sand casting. The ABC system would supply this information.

CONTROLLING WITH ABC

ABC provides managers with productivity measures for the whole organization. Managers know how much it costs to process a purchase order or issue materials from stores. While management can use this information to encourage continuous cost reduction and improvement, management should not rely on these measures entirely. It can lead them into a terrible trap—the trap many face in industry today. Our management philosophy has forced financial measures down deep into the organization. This is to manage the business "scientifically." Unfortunately, the premise that optimizing each component of a system optimizes the system as a whole is wrong. *To maximize a system's output, some parts must be suboptimized.* Pushing down costs in one area may simply drive up costs elsewhere.

Also, management should not reduce cost at the expense of customer satisfaction, but work toward more enterprisewide measures such as

Customer delivery performance
- Number of returns
- Product lead times
- Unplanned downtimes
- Customer retention
- Market share

Companies realize profits through activities by satisfying customer needs and consuming resources effectively. Therefore, companies should work to manage activities, not output. Management should use cost information not to manage costs, but to know the financial consequences of efforts to manage activities.

Management should work to

- Motivate positive behavior
- Measure progress to attaining goals and objectives

BUDGETING USING ABC

ABC improves the budgeting process in ways very similar to flexible budgeting. Before forecasting activity levels for next year, management will review their cost drivers. Management identifies any policy changes, new products, streamlining, and capital investments that will affect next year's costs. These changes can influence the number of activities or the cost per activity.

After running the production forecast, finance should provide each department with an estimate of the number of cost-driver units forecast for next year. The purchasing department receives an estimate of the number of POs they will process next year and the number of vendors to be qualified. The reports tell the warehousing department how many issues to expect. This information allows the departmental manager to estimate, more accurately, his work force and other requirements for the upcoming year.

For example, by changing policies and allowing customer service reps to approve credit adjustments under $50, the credit department could expect its activity level to drop. The three clerks in the credit department had each processed an average of 3,700 credit adjustments last year, for a total of 11,100 adjustments (see Exhibit 12-8). Since the supervisor's records showed that adjustments under $50 were 40 percent of the total, the work load should drop even with the expected increase in sales volume. The forecast estimated that the department would process 6,993 credit adjustments next year. If the company cut the number of people processing credits to two, they should be able to handle 3,497 apiece.

To develop next year's budget, we divide the cost-driver pool into variable and fixed elements. The variable elements include the costs that will vary as the quantity of cost drivers increases and decreases. In this case, we assumed the indirect head count was reduced from three to two. However, the clerks received an average pay increase of 5 percent. Fringe benefits went up accordingly. The other variable expenses went down the same percentage as the drop in work load. The fixed costs had some minor changes. While it may seem counterintuitive, the cost-driver rate went up, but only on credit adjustments over $50. Credit adjustments under $50 are virtually free. The $50 adjustments, and below, are assigned no transaction cost; the total budget went down. The higher rate indicates that the credit department can investigate the remaining credit adjustments more thoroughly.

PROFITING FROM ABC

ABC by itself provides no benefits; ABC is only a tool. However, the information ABC provides is a great catalyst for change. The benefits of ABC are in the actions taken from the information ABC supplies. While these benefits are tremendous, most companies will never achieve more than 10 percent of them. Until the ABC system becomes the integrated cost system, executives, managers, engineers, and purchasing agents will continue to use their standard cost system for decision making. People will always perform to their measurements, and, in the end, they are measured against the standard cost system.

People do not like working in ambiguous environments, such as having two cost systems. People just do not have confidence in a cost system that the controller has no confidence in. The perception will be: if the controller had confidence in ABC, it would be the standard cost accounting system.

Another hindrance to ABC is the counterintuitive nature of some of its conclusions. Most managers in the real world make their decisions based on past experience and not intellectual arguments. The argument that cutting product lines will increase profits is not obvious. Only if the managers can understand activity-based

Exhibit 12-8 **CREDIT DEPARTMENT BUDGETING**

CREDIT DEPARTMENT BUDGETING

	LAST YEAR ACTUALS	FORECAST
QUANTITY OF COST DRIVER		
- CREDIT ADJUSTMENTS	11,100	6,993
VARIABLE COST POOL ELEMENTS		
- INDIRECT LABOR	$61,000	$42,700
- FRINGE BENEFITS		
& PAYROLL EXPENSE	17,080	11,956
- SUPPLIES	3,500	2,205
- UTILITIES (1)	850	536
- MIS CHARGES (2)	1,200	736
TOTAL VARIABLE BUDGET	$83,630	$58,133
FIXED COST POOL ELEMENTS		
- SUPERVISION (3)	$16,000	$16,800
- SUPPLIES	300	350
- DEPRECIATION	1,450	1,310
- OCCUPANCY	2,160	2,350
TOTAL FIXED BUDGET	$19,910	$20,810
TOTAL BUDGET	$103,540	$78,943
COST PER CREDIT ADJUSTMENT	$9.33	$11.29

(1) UTILITIES ARE PRINCIPALLY PHONE EXPENSES.
(2) MIS CHARGES ARE ASSIGNED ON USAGE.
(3) SUPERVISION IS ONLY 1/3 OF A MANAGER AND INCLUDES HER   FRINGE BENEFITS AND PAYROLL EXPENSES.

management, from the standpoint that some products create much more work than others, will the managers truly understand the results of ABC. This understanding can be reached only through education.

Furthermore, unless a company is in crisis, many executives lack the desire to change the company's direction radically. Cutting product lines, reorienting the business toward different customers, outsourcing departments, and implementing JIT are uncomfortable. Each of these actions is risky and challenging. Many managers also have their egos on the line. In the past, they have argued exactly the opposite, which is why the company is in its current condition. Most managers have insufficient incentive to take on these actions, despite the benefits each of these actions promise. Only if the board of directors rewards executives to take such risks will they take risks. Or, only if the company is in crisis and the board tells them to turn the company around or the shareholders will fire them, do they take bold action.

To improve a company's competitiveness dramatically with ABC, a company must implement ABC as their integrated cost system. The president and staff must commit to an ABC philosophy and follow its conclusions. Last, the shareholders must reward management for outstanding performance. Outstanding performance is the benefit of following ABC.

CHAPTER 13

THE 1990s—CROSSROADS OF AMERICAN MANUFACTURING

We should all be concerned with the future because we will
all have to spend the rest of our lives there.

Charles F. Kettering

The only thing certain about the future is that it won't be like the past. Neither size nor past success guarantees success in the future. Only the ability to adapt and change to meet new threats and challenges allows an enterprise to survive and prosper. This was just as true for the Roman Empire and the Ming Dynasty in the past as it is for General Motors and IBM today. To prosper, an enterprise must adapt itself to new threats and challenges.

To survive the 1990s, companies face a new set of challenges. They must become fast, focused, and flexible. Today, these factors are transforming competition and will forever change its basis. This chapter explains why customer focus, speed, and flexibility will drive competition in the 1990s; where Japan stands on these initiatives; and how ABC plays a critical role in pushing American business to win on these points.

BEING CUSTOMER FOCUSED

The Rise of Global Quality

From the late 1940s through the 1960s, American manufacturing could not expand capacity fast enough to meet demand. Television sets, garbage disposals, dishwashers, copiers, and computers went from being novelties to necessities. People scrimped and saved to buy their first TV set. In an economy characterized by scarcity, price was the most important criterion for any purchase. Consumers were easy to satisfy. They had nothing but radios to compare with an RCA or Zenith television set.

However, times change. Prosperity arrives. Markets become saturated, prices fall. Consumers are no longer naive first-time buyers. Consumers need a reason to replace their TVs—a bigger screen, new features, better resolution, or higher reliability. Quality increasingly becomes the buying criteria, not cost.

In addition, television, satellite communications, and jet travel have seemingly brought the world closer together. Names like Sony, Michelin, Panasonic, Mercedes-Benz, and Nestle become more familiar as trade barriers fall. Consequently, consumers develop global quality standards. Today, customers can locate the best of whatever they want, anywhere in the world—Italian shoes, Swiss chocolates, Japanese robots, and American workstations. This has led not only to heightened trade, but to competition and greater expectations.

Japanese manufacturers set new listening standards for stereos in the 1970s, and new reliability standards for autos in the 1980s. On the other hand, Japanese consumers want to know why they cannot own spacious homes like Americans do, while South Koreans and Russians want to own appliances and automobiles.

American machinists always expected machine tools to seep hydraulic fluid. The machinists were used to working in filthy machine shops—machine tools dripping oil, with sawdust covering the floor to absorb it. This was so until Japanese machine tools arrived in the early 1980s—the Japanese mills and lathes never leaked. Suddenly, American machinists became dissatisfied with their leaky American machine tools.

The world's consumers developed a new set of standards by which to judge products. Fortunately, during the 1980s, American companies responded to these new global standards. After the invasion of foreign goods in the late 1970s and early 1980s, America responded with a quality renaissance. While companies made great improvements in products ranging from automobiles to resistors, in most industries the Japanese have maintained a lead in product quality. A 1990 Planning Forum Conference found that the quality of goods and services continues to be the chief competitive issue.

What Is Quality?

Initially, the results of their quality improvement efforts disappointed American executives. While companies devoted thousands of hours and millions of dollars to improving quality, many found that their customers did not appreciate their effort. Executives discovered that customers have their own perception of quality.

Traditionally, American companies viewed quality as "conformance to requirements" or defect identification and prevention. One can trace this philosophy to the origins of the quality organization—quality control began strictly as an inspection function. The War Department's World War II procurement practices reinforced this view. During World War II, the armed forces bought and inspected half the country's output to acceptable quality levels (AQL). These criteria covered everything from bullets to aircraft, from ships to soap. Later during the 1960s, this idea was taken to its extreme with the Martin Company's zero defects program for the Pershing missile program. At Martin, all defects had to be avoided or eliminated—no defect was too small. More recently, Phil Crosby also expounded this philosophy in his influential 1979 book, *Quality Is Free.*

Under this internally focused view, the quality organization does not distinguish between what is important to the customer and what is not. The quality department collects mountains of inspection data trying to eradicate all defects, irrespective of which defects cost the most or are most important to the customer.

Customer Value Replaces Conformance as the Basis of Quality

As the companies invested time and money into lowering scrap rates and achieving zero defects, they discovered that their customers did not appreciate many of their efforts. Initially, the companies complained "the customer does not understand what quality is." Later it dawned on them that as the customer is always right, he always defines quality.

This is a lesson even American Express was forced to be reminded of. Despite a strong tradition of excellent service, when American Express expanded card operations with too little investment, complaints surged. To remedy this embarrassment, James Robinson, the chairman, wanted performance standards and quality controls instituted. He ordered the department heads responsible for card operations to implement such a system. After installing the new system, Robinson found the departments doing superbly by their own standards, but no better from the customer's vantage point. American Express then developed an entirely new tracking system, a service tracking report that measured the impact of each department's actions on the customer. Complaints plummeted.

As some American firms moved toward JIT (just-in-time), they discovered how unimportant price really was. The companies found that they could not continue to buy strictly on price. Only if the vendors delivered defect-free parts on time could companies expect to eliminate receiving inspection and inventory buffers. Executives have also seen and used the services of companies like Federal Express and Nordstroms. They see how successfully these quality leaders compete on customer value and not price. In many industries, their own company has seen their export prices fluctuating wildly as the dollar soars up and crashes down. These observations helped convince executives that service and product quality were more important to their company's health than was price.

The experiences of Ford, Allen-Bradley, and Coors Brewing Company are typical. These companies learned to shift their quality focus from internal conformance to customer value. In 1980, some influential people at Ford Motor Company saw the NBC documentary, "If Japan Can, Why Can't We?" which paid great tribute to Dr. Edward Deming. Someone suggested that Ford invite him to teach the company what he taught the Japanese in 1950. He came to Ford in January 1981. Dr. Deming helped convince Ford that quality was a matter of life and death for every enterprise. However, quality had to have a common purpose, and had to be driven from the top. In 1981, Ford initiated its "Job One" quality improvement campaign.

Yet, in July 1985, Chairman Donald Petersen overhauled Ford's approach to quality. In a corporate policy letter, he redefined quality, "Quality is defined by the customer; the customer wants products and services that, throughout their life, meet his or her expectations, at a cost that represents value." One result, was that Ford required all dealers to participate in its customer satisfaction surveys in 1986.

Allen-Bradley and Coors both had begun companywide quality improvement programs in the early 1980s. By 1987 and 1988, respectively, they had expanded these efforts into customer satisfaction programs. These programs centered on collecting customer feedback and translating the results into operational measures. The satisfaction ratings, in turn, provided the basis for continuous improvement programs.

Just as the Hopi Indians have no word for time, America has no universal term for customer-perceived quality. Some companies call it customer satisfaction, this book calls it customer value. However, both value and quality have many interpretations, which make things somewhat confusing.

Recognizing its importance, America's Malcolm Baldrige National Quality Award weights customer satisfaction as 30 percent of the total scoring. This is double the next closest category of "Quality Results." The 1980s have forced American companies to learn that there is more to competitiveness than price.

Customer value provides a company with more buying loyalty and the ability to charge higher prices. As Ford's chairman Donald E. Petersen says, "If we aren't customer-driven, our cars won't be either." We are seeing a clear trend toward customer value as a key factor of success in the 1990s.

The successful company will ride this wave and learn to work toward continuous improvement of its customer value, while its competitors will watch their market share and profits erode. To support this move toward customer value, companies will have to accelerate their quality improvement efforts. Simultaneously, companies will have to increase their "speed" and "flexibility."

BEING FAST

As Benjamin Franklin said, "Time is money!" One of the critical dimensions of competition in the 1990s will be speed—both dimensions of speed, the speed of

Exhibit 13-1 **THE BASIS OF COMPETITIVE ADVANTAGE IN THE 1990s**

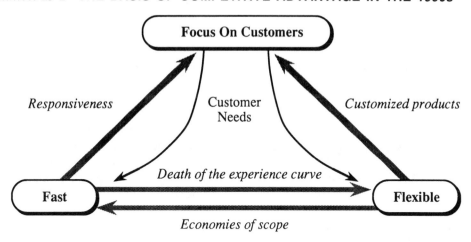

customer responsiveness and the speed to market. The time it takes to satisfy customer needs is critical to raising customer value. Shortening the time from product design to manufacture will forever change the basis of production economics.

With Federal Express, microwave ovens, and the facsimile machine, consumers are becoming more and more time conscious. As consumers become more obsessed with time, the speed of service becomes a more and more important buying criterion. As customers become used to immediate gratification, they come to expect it.

Achieving fast cycle times is a reflection of organizational ability. It is not easily copied, and is very difficult to compete with. It locks up channels of distribution and positions a company as an innovator. The first mover can also charge a price premium, set industry standards, and grow market share.

Many companies are already successfully differentiating themselves on speed. Citicorp's mortgage business is growing at a rate of 100 percent per year, powered by its 15-day mortgage approval program. Domino's Pizza, with its guaranteed 30-minute delivery, is the second fastest-growing franchise in the United States. Everex Systems, a maker of personal computers, has a system called "Zero Response Time." This system adjusts the factory production to phone orders every two hours. Rapid delivery has propelled the company to grow 41 percent last year.

In 1985 Northern Telecom concluded that it had to increase customer satisfaction by 20 percent over the next five years to stay competitive. To meet this goal, it had to do business faster than ever before. It reoriented the company to a whole new strategy based on time. It developed a time-reducing strategy in three parts: manufacturing process improvement, new product introduction, and procurement. The company requires each division to carry out one of these programs and share its findings. Preliminary results show that:

- One product's manufacturing cycle dropped from nine to two and half weeks.

- Some divisions reduced their product introduction cycle by as much as 50 percent.

- Research Triangle Park Division now receives 84 percent of their materials from certified suppliers.

The same phenomenon exists in industrial markets. JIT is forcing manufacturers to be more responsive to retailers, in turn, forcing manufacturers to accept nothing less from their suppliers. Quickly processing orders and delivering products holds down inventories. This saves money for the supplier, manufacturer, and distributor. It reduces financial risk by having fewer goods on hand. Cycle time reductions soften demand fluctuations and make companies more responsive to their customers—everyone wins.

While in 1989 the appliance industry was fighting a price war, General Electric was dazzling its appliance dealers with its superfast distribution system. In many cases, major dealers receive deliveries overnight from GE warehouses. This system, according to one Frigidaire distributor, "had more to do with Frigidaire losing market share than pricing had."

As speed becomes more and more important and companies become more and more customer focused, the drive for speed will accelerate. Time from order to delivery will shorten, forcing delivery systems and manufacturing organizations to organize for rapid response. The only way operations can respond faster is through efficiency and flexibility, which, in turn, lower cost. Fast cycle times reduce feedback loops. The time to detect, correct, and verify mistakes collapses. Fewer mistakes mean less scrap and rework, enabling more learning to take place. In fact, learning is the heart of strategic leadership.

More significantly, the electronics revolution, and the integrated circuit in particular, are accelerating the introduction of new products into the market place. While electronics have brought about computer-aided design (CAD), computer-aided engineering (CAE), and other design tools that raise the productivity of designers, the effect of electronics on products themselves is much more significant. Electronics are becoming are a larger and larger part of many product's cost. Electronics improve product performance and reduce cost, while cutting weight and volume. A good example is a submarine navigation system, an electromechanical system made up of a computer, gyroscopes, and accelerometers. In 1978, less than 40 percent of such a system's manufacturing cost was electronics; within ten years electronics and software had grown to over 80 percent. The new units are one-fourth the size and much more accurate.

Advances in electronics are leading to many of the performance improvements in today's products. In automobiles, they have already found their way into engine controls and fuel injection systems, raising the miles per gallon. Electronic systems in the antilock and air suspensions have improved handling and riding comfort, while diagnostic systems have reduced repair costs. In the future, electronics will allow smart suspensions, multipoint electronic fuel injection, and traction control.

In commercial jets like the 767, the electronic cockpit systems have allowed Boeing to reduce the cockpit crews from three persons to two. This innovation not only saves personnel costs, but reduces weight as well. As digital avionics replace analog systems, aircraft performance improves with more accurate flight paths and lower maintenance costs. These and other advances reduce the air carrier's operating costs and help sell new airplanes.

Microprocessors, sensors, and other electronics are now a significant part of even air conditioners. Electronics now control the air-conditioning cycle and the electric motor of many models. Consequently, these innovations improve energy efficiency, increase reliability, and make the system easier to service.

Yet even the 50 percent annual increase in computing power per chip understates the magnitude of the electronics revolution. Advances in electronic packaging technology such as application-specific integrated circuits (ASICs), flexible circuit boards, surface-mount technology (SMT), software tools, and the advent of fuzzy logic, leverage every improvement in chip performance. Surface-mount technology reduces the space needed on a circuit board by 40 percent. This space reduction allows more circuits per board and, thereby, reduces the number of boards, interconnections, cables, and components. These part number reductions, in turn, slash manufacturing costs and improve reliability. ASICs, customized circuits in the form of chips, improve performance even more dramatically, cutting electronic costs by more than 50 percent in some cases.

There are great advances in technology in just a few years. Since much product performance and cost depend on electronics, technological improvements provide significant cost reductions and performance improvements in just a single year. And, unlike an F-15 jet fighter, for most products, swapping out and replacing electronics modules with the next generation is not feasible. Therefore, companies must rapidly introduce products to keep up with the latest product features and technologies. This means that the product design cycle must be fast to get products to market with the latest technology. In addition, with shorter life cycles, companies have less time to amortize the new product introduction (NPI) costs, so the company must slash development costs.

The Death of the Experience Curve Strategy

These shorter product life cycles put to death the experience curve strategy, a strategy made famous by the Boston Consulting Group in the early 1970s. Using this strategy, companies try to drive their competitors out of the market by building an insurmountable cost advantage. This lower manufacturing cost comes from large economies of scale and cost reductions, which follow from more cumulative production. To gain this edge, companies quickly build production capacity and pre-emptively price their products down the experience curve. By pricing the products lower than the competition's, the company builds more sales volume than the competitors and, therefore, gains greater cost reductions.

However, speed forever changes these economies. Economies of scale first evolved from mechanization, the replacement of human labor with mechanical labor. Mechanics greatly leveraged workers' labor, and the more specialized the mechanics the greater the leverage. Once the factory established the mechanics, more and more repetitive production would amortize its costs. As more production went across the machines, supervisors and engineers would permanently resolve more problems. This problem elimination decreased the need for engineering, inspection, tooling, and supervision. The factory would also identify and make operating improvements to further reduce cost. The more production volume forecasted, the more investments the accountants could justify. Economies of scale also relied on large batch sizes. The large batch sizes keep transaction costs proportionally very low.

However, as Henry Ford discovered with the Model T, relentlessly driving down the experience curve destroys a company's ability to innovate, not to mention change over to new products. (It took a year for Ford Motor Company to retool for the Model A, during which time, Mr. Ford lost $200 million and idled over 60,000 workers.) Henry Ford drove the cost of a Model T down from $3,000 to $900 between 1908 and 1923. Meanwhile, he shunned major automobile innovations like the automatic starter, demountable rims, and closed body structure, to avoid upsetting his Model T's experience curve. The reason—over 51 percent of experience curve savings come from the very departments who bring about innovation—design engineering, tooling, and industrial engineering.

As Casio found, speed beats the experience curve. In the late 1960s, competing in electronic calculators with the likes of Sharp, Cannon, Seiko, Hitachi, and Sony, Casio was at a disadvantage. Casio's competitors were all vertically integrated with dedicated integrated circuit (IC) production facilities. The competitors had substantial economies of scale in production and established sales channels. Casio was basically an engineering, marketing, and assembly company. Casio had limited production facilities and only a small sales force. Recognizing its competitors' strengths and its own weaknesses, Casio decided to compete by accelerating the product life cycle. Casio reorganized its company, combining engineering and marketing. The company installed computer-aided design and manufacturing (CAD/CAM) systems and developed extensive subcontracting arrangements to support rapid product introductions. The entire company was geared toward rapid new product introductions.

No sooner had Casio introduced its card-size calculator than Casio started driving prices down to discourage new entrants. Only a few months later, Casio introduced a new product with new features. Casio introduced products as soon as their competitors matched theirs. Casio competitors were always competing on price, while Casio was always competing on new product features. This strategy not only nullified their competitors strengths, but resulted in Casio's Japanese calculator market share rising from 12 percent to over 36 percent in six years—while Sharp, as the market share leader, based its strategy on the experience curve. Against Casio, Sharp saw its market share fall from 34 percent to 17 percent. As this example shows, the advantages of speed nullify the advantages of the experience curve.

Competitors' products are obsolete before achieving a cost advantage and vertical integration slows reaction times. The first to market gains market share. In the electronics industry, the rule of thumb is that the first two companies to market lock in up to 80 percent of the business.

Many Companies Are Already Speeding Up

Many companies have already recognized this trend. Last year Ingersoll-Rand announced "Operation Lightning" to produce a new hand-held pneumatic grinder in one year, instead of the usual three. Tektronix's new graphics terminal took only nine months from design to production, versus three years for its predecessor. Motorola's Paging Division designed and built its very successful Bravo pager in just 18 months, including an automated factory. A 1988 benchmarking survey of printed circuit board (PCB) manufacturers, by A. T. Kearney, found that PCB manufacturers expected to drop the design cycle turnaround time from 17 months to 10.5 by 1990, a 38 percent drop in just two years.

Motorola has even gone a step farther to ensure it is first to market. Motorola tries to anticipate customer desires. Then Motorola invests in a solution, hoping that by the time the product is ready, the customer has woken up to the need.

Speeding Up the Organization

To decrease the design cycle demands improvements throughout the organization. The factory must be flexible, able to change over to new products quickly and with minimum disruption. The delivery system must be quick to market and not absorb large inventories. Short life cycles also lead to rapid product obsolescence.

Companies must remove overhead of all kinds, because it retards new product introduction. The more steps a piece of paper has to travel, the longer it takes to process and the more it costs. A company can no longer afford to spend the time and money to identify and qualify new vendors, test new components, write new test procedures, and build special tooling for each product. These areas are where ABC is critical. ABC encourages companies to streamline and eliminate nonvalue-adding activities, saving resources—time and money. As Xerox found by reducing its new product development time from six years to three, costs are cut in half.

Designs with as few part numbers as possible save development time and money, as well as reduce manufacturing and service costs over the long term. Designs with fewer parts require fewer drawings, specifications, tooling, routings, and other documents. This also reduces risk, as fewer part numbers increase reliability. There are fewer batches to schedule, fewer setups, and less warehousing, which cuts overhead. Fewer parts also translates into higher-reliability products, fewer chances for defects and wear.

Using off-the-shelf components saves time and money. Hewlett-Packard has a companywide database of preferred vendors and parts. It certifies vendors, determines part reliability, and ensures availability. With the reliability of the vendors and parts already known, the components are less risky and less costly to use. This restrains qualification and test costs. It also avoids part shortages, a common occurrence in the electronics industry. Recently introduced components of a new technology frequently encounter yield problems or capacity constraints limiting availability. The qualified parts have proven supplies. The ABC system penalizes the unproven parts by adding the qualification costs into the product. Using off-the-shelf components also increases their volume, which reduces per unit cost.

Using a modular design (one of the rules of design-for-manufacturability) saves time and cost and improves flexibility. In Romeo, Michigan, Ford is building a flexible factory to build engines. The factory will produce V-8 and V-6 engines built around a common combustion chamber and using 350 common parts. The multi-disciplined design team using design-for-manufacturing rules was able to cut the overall number of components in the engines by 25 percent. Ford expects new V-8 variations to cost just $60 million, compared with as much as $500 million for a typical new engine. While the factory's 500,000 engine capacity is comparable to that of the typical engine plant, its ability to produce a dozen engine sizes and configurations represents a sharp drop in the minimum practical engine volume.

Working with suppliers can provide a competitive edge as well. Compaq leaped ahead of IBM with its DeskPro 386. Compaq built the DeskPro around Intel's powerful 386 microprocessor. Compaq worked closely with Intel to ensure compatibility with existing PC software. Once Intel finished redesigning the chip, it took Compaq only a month and half to introduce the DeskPro 386.

By using suppliers to design the components they will manufacture, companies ensure that their parts will fit the supplier's processes—reducing risk, cost, and time simultaneously. In Japan, some suppliers start work on projects even before the customer awards the contract. These suppliers are willing to take this risk, due to their long-term relationship with their customer. For example, Yamashita Rubber Co. began independent work on an advanced engine mount three years before Honda began the Accord redesign. When Honda designed the car, it was able to plug the mount into its engine system.

One key factor in getting the design finished and ready to build is autonomous multidisciplinary teams. The team must be small, colocated, and able to make its own decisions. These teams work toward a common goal, avoiding functional conflicts which mar the traditional design structure. Motorola's Bravo project, which designed and built its new pager and factory, had only 24 people. The team included representatives from marketing, quality, and most important of all, manufacturing. Management gave the team autonomy to make their own decisions. The team did not have to wait for approvals or second-guessing from corporate headquarters.

Pacific Scientific, as part of its strategy to become totally customer focused, worked to quicken its customer responsiveness. The motor company nixed the traditional organization structure of engineering and manufacturing. Pacific Scientific is now organized in cells, comprised of representatives from marketing, engineering, and manufacturing. Each cell is dedicated to either a particular product or a customer, whichever makes more sense. The company has strived to eliminate all time that isn't devoted to enhancing the product. By living for one particular customer or product, the cells can design and build a motor, from scratch, in two weeks. This time is down from 18 weeks in 1985.

To reach the customers quickly, engineers must design their products for manufacturability. Components must fit the limitations of their equipment or suppliers. Engineers, by using Taguichi methods, a system of designed experiments, can identify tolerance requirements for products. Together with statistical process control that identifies process tolerance capability, the engineer knows whether present equipment can produce the design.

Since the mid-1980s many companies have returned to concurrent engineering, the process of designing the product concurrent with the design of the process. Before the mid-1950s, this is how all American companies designed products. Concurrent engineering is the development of both the product and production process simultaneously. This brings both the design and manufacturing engineers together from the project's conception, ensuring that the products are manufacturable. The results have been dramatic. At NCR's checkout counter terminal division, concurrent engineering cut in half, to 22 months, the time to introduce a product. The product also has 85 percent fewer parts than its predecessor. Moreover, the product takes only one-fourth of the time to assemble. While the results have been impressive, it still leaves a large potential untapped.

Companies need to extend concurrent engineering beyond manufacturing and into a program for the whole company. Companies must incorporate all the aspects of the business that determine time to market and life-cycle cost. A company accomplishes nothing if the factory can build a new product in a few hours, but the order entry system cannot accept these orders. This is the situation of one company with a successful concurrent engineering program. Support functions are holding up the products. A company besmirches its image reputation if they introduce a product before their dealers can support it. Dealers must be trained and inventoried before dealers can sell products. Very few failings discourage a customer more than being convinced at a trade show to buy a product, and not being allowed to.

Caterpillar, for instance, never introduces a product before it has a two-month supply of spare parts. In this way, Cat can ensure that it always meets its guarantee to deliver spare parts, anywhere in the world, in 48 hours, or the customer gets them free. To accelerate the new product, introduction cycle companies must adapt everything from their order entry systems to their field service groups.

To get products to market faster, Hewlett-Packard has initiated its "Product Generation Team." This group is spearheading an effort to cut the product introduction cycle in half across the whole company. The team is going beyond concurrent engineering, where the product is designed simultaneously with manufacturing planning. H-P is working toward integrating CAD/CAM systems, improving the design process, and developing new information systems to speed and improve the introduction process. The team is developing cash-flow models to justify or cancel new products. The justification rests on when the product will hit the market, and how fast it will generate profits. Implicit in this approach is that successful competition is time dependent.

Not surprisingly, shorter development cycles cause the biggest changes to take place in the engineering organization. The company cannot afford for engineering to make mistakes and design defective products, correcting errors with engineering changes later. A company must understand its process limitations and design within them. One study estimated that 80 percent of process deviations are designed in.

Engineers must design quality in, fit the production process, and meet the customer's needs. In a study of new consumer products, 80 percent of the products that failed in the marketplace had the same or worse product performance than the previous model. New product success depends on improving customer value. Poor definition of product requirements is also the number one cause of product development delays. The lack of understanding of customer needs causes frequent changes in the product development and marketing plans. Thus, only the customer-driven organization can successfully get a product to market fast.

Accordingly, companies with the shortest design cycle are those that are best able to respond to rapidly changing market needs. A short design cycle eliminates the absurd rework cycle in most companies' design process. Collapsing the design cycle greatly reduces the chances that customers' needs, or management's perceptions of their needs, will change before the company brings the product to market. With a short design cycle, companies just do not have the spare time to redesign.

Another benefit of faster design times is that designers become more proficient. Engineers gain more new product experience faster. They interact more frequently with all aspects of the product's team—manufacturing, marketing, quality, test, and service.

Innovation Becomes Process, Not Product Focused

With short life cycles, a company can no longer rely on continual cost reductions during the product's production. The cycle is too short. A company must design and build the product to the ultimate cost on the first unit, benefiting from all of the experience curve's savings of higher yields, less supervision, and less rework on job one. This requires a company to design, plan, and manufacture a product better than they ever have before. This will change product development from emphasizing the product, to one of emphasizing the process. In the future, engineers will design end products around process parameters, instead of product parameters. This will ensure that products are manufacturable as well as functional.

The success of concentrating on process and not design development, was seen in the 64K DRAM (dynamic random access memories) market. While American firms dominated the 16K DRAM market, with over 50 percent of the world's market share, the Japanese came to dominate the next generation 64K products. The Japanese' success resulted from their successful introduction of the 64K, while American merchant producers were snarled with production problems. By early 1981, six Japanese firms had introduced the 64K DRAM, versus only two U.S. firms. By the end of 1981, the Japanese controlled 70 percent of the world DRAM market.

Arguably, the principal reason for this loss was the different development strategy followed by Japanese versus American firms. While the Japanese concentrated on developing the 64K DRAM by adapting and improving Mostek's successful 16K DRAM with process technology, American firms followed the more complex approach of designing in the greater circuit density. The complex American designs were plagued by yield and design problems. Indeed, design problems caused Intel to halt its 64K development in 1981. National Semiconductor and AMD could not introduce a 64K product until 1983. By concentrating on process innovation and not design innovation, Hitachi, NEC, and Fujitsu stole the DRAM market from the likes of Mostek and National Semiconductor.

When the next generation 256K DRAM was introduced by Hitachi in 1982, the Japanese companies had a substantial lead. By the beginning of 1985, not one American company was yet in volume production, while NEC, Fujitsu, and Hitachi each were shipping a million 256Ks a month. By 1987, only two American manufacturers continued to commercially sell 256K DRAMS, and the prospects for the future are bleak. Speed to market drove American companies from the DRAM battlefield. However, American manufacturers, unwilling to concede the war, changed venue by moving the battle to the courts, where they filed dumping charges against the Japanese. In addition, the industry went to Washington and solicited money for a government-sponsored consortium, called SEMATECH, to manufacture DRAMs.

Likewise, companies that are experienced in concurrent engineering programs have discovered that they cannot engineer products and processes simultaneously. The process development cycle takes much longer than product development; therefore, engineers are forced to begin developing processes for products that are not yet specified. However, this approach has large benefits—proprietary process technology is easier to protect from competitors, and provides greater leverage than product technology. Products can be reverse engineered and copied; processes cannot.

Fast Cycle Times Force a Global Perspective

As design cycle time shortens, so does a competitor's reaction time. Aggressive companies are becoming more sophisticated and resourceful than ever before. These companies try to stay abreast of all technological developments, no matter where they take place in the world. With a fax machine and a telephone line, someone can transmit knowledge to just about anywhere in the world in minutes. This reduces the life of a technological advantage and makes speed crucial to competitive success. And since knowledge has no diminishing returns and is easily copied, companies must provide products to the whole world as soon as possible.

In 1953 after IBM introduced the 701, it took four years for a comparable computer to reach Japan. In 1979 the time lag between introducing a computer in the United States and a comparable model in Japan was five months. In 1980, the introduction of comparable computers was simultaneous.

Today, technology spreads surprisingly fast to developing countries as well. In mid-1986, as Intel came out with its 386 microprocessor, personal computer makers around the world rushed to design a PC using the new chip. Taiwan's computer maker, Acer, was no exception. Acer's five-man team worked around the clock to complete a 386-based computer. Acer shocked the PC world when it introduced its computer in November, only weeks after Compaq, the U.S. leader. As the time from product introduction in one country to others shortens, companies cannot afford to give their competitors a time advantage.

Hewlett-Packard, like many companies, used to delay introducing products overseas. This is no longer so. In 1987, it successfully introduced the Vectra personal computer in Europe and the United States. But in Asia, production of software and manuals in local languages was delayed. This delay permitted competitors to thwart Hewelett-Packard's market penetration. So, when it came time to introduce a line of graphics terminals, the mistake was not repeated. The equipment and documentation came out in 15 different languages simultaneously, including Japanese and Chinese.

For years, EMI (originally Electric and Musical Industries, Ltd.) was a modest English recording company. In the early 1960s, EMI's U.S. subsidiary struck it big with a rock and roll group from Liverpool. The profits created by the Beatles fueled a diversification effort that moved EMI into electronics. In 1972, with this new cash flow, EMI developed the computer-assisted tomographic, or CAT, scanner. This computerized x-ray machine, which allowed doctors to view the human body in three dimensions, was a remarkable advance. For years, the company enjoyed remarkable growth, by 1977 EMI had sold 704 of the world's 1,130 scanners at prices between $300,000 and $1 million each.

Yet EMI did not expand globally, restricting its manufacturing and financial resources. CAT scanners continued to be manufactured only in England. As demand outstripped capacity, EMI's delivery times stretched to 12 months. Its geographic isolation also caused nearsightedness. EMI relied only on feedback from its local market—concentrating enhancements on improving image resolution. EMI ignored the American markets' demand for shorter scan time. Meanwhile, 16 other competitors entered the market. In 1979, EMI's Godfrey Hounsfield shared the Nobel Prize for his CAT scanner invention. In that same year, EMI, which had started to lose money in the business, was taken over by Thorn Electric. By 1980, after three years of losses, the company withdrew from the market it had pioneered. EMI failed to develop a global market and financial presence. EMI's decision making was slowed, and it needlessly distanced itself from its customers' needs.

Companies forfeit, or at least seriously constrain their foreign market penetration if they lack local manufacturing presence. Exhibit 13-2 shows a very high correlation

Exhibit 13-2 **CORRELATION BETWEEN SALES AND MANUFACTURING**

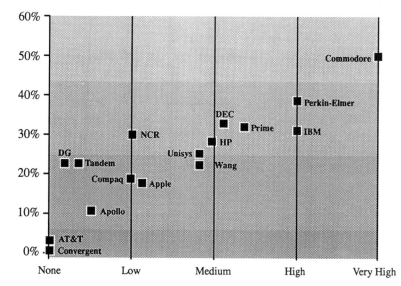

Degree Of European Manufacturing

* Based on 1986 sales
Sourse: Pittigilio, Rabin, Todd & McGrath, Electronic Business, May 1, 1988

between successful market penetration of American electronic firms in the European market and integrated manufacturing capability.

Companies manufacturing on distant shores suffer from a time lag and transportation costs. It takes a commercial cargo six weeks to sail across the Pacific Ocean. JIT purchasing and supplier integration force companies to develop the local manufacturing capability. Witness the invasion of Japanese automobile suppliers following the construction of U.S.-based assembly plants.

In addition, offshore manufacturing suffers many of the pitfalls of competing on the experience curve—it stifles innovation and flexibility. By divorcing the domestic design engineers from production, feedback and process innovation suffer. Communication and cultural barriers breed distrust. Typically, low-wage countries lack technical support personnel, making it difficult to maintain and calibrate capital equipment, subsequently leading to intermittent quality problems. The work force also lacks skills and, frequently, literacy. A lack of skills, combined with a high turnover rate (in the Mexican border cities of Tijuana, Nogales, and Juarez a turnover rate of 10 percent per month is not uncommon), makes the work force very inflexible for quickly changing to meet new production requirements or new products with a high level of competence. These problems force companies to invest time and resources such as production engineering and tooling to make the worker tasks very simple and repetitive. These companies must have long production runs to recover this investment—making their plants inflexible.

Firms perceived as invaders fall prey to protectionism and import restrictions that close the doors to these markets. Foreign firms with local manufacturing can become true insiders and exempt from trade sanctions. For example, Sony's large San Diego television assembly plant has been excluded from dumping lawsuits brought against other Japanese television manufacturers.

Since technology diffuses much faster than distribution and service channels, companies with new technologies frequently find themselves constrained by limited distribution channels and resources. Lacking a local manufacturing and distribution channel frequently forces companies to resort to joint venturing. Joint venturing provides a company with access to distant markets immediately by licensing additional production capacity. Unfortunately, joint venturing, by giving away part of the business, as well as technology, limits future growth opportunities.

To become fast, a company must concentrate on the business process. ABC supports becoming fast by focusing management on the process. ABC shows management what activities are consuming resources, and what is triggering the activities. Management learns to manage activities, not outcome. Managing activities is the key to increasing speed, as well as flexibility.

BEING FLEXIBLE

Initially, American companies will narrow their product lines as they implement ABC. They will uncover product lines that they have no hope of making profitable, and that merely drag down earnings. They will focus their factory to improve service to different market segments. After this initial period, the company will come to realize that it must reduce costs through streamlining. It will also see marketing opportunities in new product lines. It will find that it must make the factory more flexible to build these new product lines.

As firms give more and more attention to the customers, it drives focusing the factory and distribution systems. The factory becomes configured to support customer needs. For example, the Excel (as described in Chapter 7) needed to support the rehab and home-care markets with different channels of distribution. It also needed two focused factories. The rehab was a build-to-order business, while the home-care business was build-to-stock. The customer segmentation followed all through the company, even to order entry, where the rehab products required experienced service reps to take customer orders.

ABC encourages companies to reduce costs through streamlining. ABC identifies the cost of taking orders, processing purchase orders, receiving parts, making setups, loading trucks, etc. ABC drives management to reduce these costs. This increases the economies of scope. Companies can produce a much wider product offering at lower cost. Management will push for a system that has no additional costs for a lot size of one. As management simplifies the organization by eliminating duplication and nonvalue-adding activities, its cycle times collapse.

However, the move toward JIT does not go far enough. Companies must make their factories flexible, able to produce a far wider range of products, at no additional time or cost. Engineers must make processes more flexible, while design rules constrain engineering to design for the processes available. At Hewlett-Packard, they have begun a process called manufacturing-for-design. This project is working to integrate all the systems between the computer-aided engineering (CAE) system and the automated machines on the factory floor. This integration will speed up and reduce cost in the new product development process. The team is also working toward improving process capability to support more design parameters. The intent is to drive the manufacturing organization to become more flexible and robust, to allow more design flexibility.

Companies will install flexible automation and robotics to raise productivity and quality while increasing throughput. With companies now able to justify flexibility, sales of flexible manufacturing systems will increase, as will capital equipment, with quick changeover times. Integrated CAE systems with automated process planning will help accelerate the design cycle and reduce transaction costs. This increase in flexibility will also reduce the cost and disruption of product introductions.

With the economies of development and production greatly reduced, new products will be profitable with much less volume. This will allow greater product customization. As companies become more customer focused, they will be able to identify subtler differences among customers. By identifying these differences, and with lower economies, companies will drive to exploit these opportunities. They will develop specialized products and services for smaller and smaller market niches.

Knowledge-Based Competition

While many manufacturing experts have foreseen the need for flexibility and flexible manufacturing systems to support it, business requires a much more significant change. A company's overhead must become flexible. A company's overhead (including SG&A) is the largest piece of a company's total cost.

Economies of scale disappear with greater product variety, which is created by greater customer focus. The more specialized the mechanics, the longer it takes to change over the mechanics to produce another product. The more time it takes, the greater the costs of changing over. As attention to the customer grows, management identifies more and more differences between different market segments. To satisfy the different customers better, the company's products become more differentiated for each segment. This increased product variety diffuses production volume, nullifying economies of scale.

In the overhead areas, economies of scale derived from specialization. As companies specialized and people performed repetitive transaction processing, the costs of these transactions fell. Offsetting these overhead economies is the cost of complexity. As manufacturers introduce more and more products and find new customers, new requirements are created. Simple rules no longer work. The complexity of more products and customers creates more exceptions to rules, requiring deviations in procedures. A deviation from established procedures creates a new task. New tasks increase the cost of activities or create more activities. This causes complexity, confusion, and errors in the overhead areas and, thereby, cost.

To allow more product and customer variety, and avoid an escalation in overhead cost, requires a more flexible system—a new information system. Our management information systems must change from their present hierarchical design to a rule-based system to support flexibility.

Today's hierarchical information systems require every option and choice to be defined, as well as every dependent option. In the hierarchical database, a crane assembled from a motor, winding, and gearbox with options of four different motors, three windings, and three gear boxes, has 36 different bills of material, routings, and product costs—one set for each end item—each created separately.

A rule-based system does not structure data in every conceivable option, like a hierarchical design. It structures data into decision rules. In a rule-based system, the rules configure the end item from only 10 bills of materials (4 motors + 3 windings + 3 gear boxes), routings, and product costs. The system only configures the end unit as it is ordered.

Since the rule-based system does not look at every product as a particular end item, but as a set of rules, it simplifies all overhead activities. In order entry, for example, a rule-based system allows an easy-to-use customer interface to be designed. The system asks for the product configuration in terms of customer options. The customer service rep no longer needs to input the exact end item configuration—part numbers. This substantially lowers the training and order-entry knowledge required by the service reps. Since rules are simple for a computer to process, the order-entry system creates the bills of material, routings, and costs on-line.

This innovation is extremely important in companies selling products with many features and options. Many simple products can be built in an incredible number of combinations. For example, a door lock can come in 3.1 million different combinations with all of the styles, functions, finishes, and backsets (excluding keying combinations).

Rule-based processing substantially cuts ordering time and identifies order problems while the customer is still on the phone. Configuration problems do not pop up later, delaying the order and forcing a customer to be called back. In the rule-based system, if the customer orders an unbuildable product, the system flags the problem for the service rep immediately. For example, the system informs the rep that a number two gear box does not fit with a 3-horsepower motor and gives the reason why. On the other hand, a hierarchical system identifies only unbuildable options for the rep if the programmer hardcoded each unbuildable option into the system, an approach not feasible in broad product lines. Unfortunately, this product validation, with a broad product line in a hierarchical database, takes a very long time. Worse yet, if the system does not have the unbuildable options programmed in, the system releases unbuildable configurations to the factory. This creates havoc. After releasing the material from stores and planning the schedules, the factory must correct all these activities. Worse yet, customer service must call back the customer. The rep must tell the customer not only that we cannot build his order, but it is going to be late. These sources of customer dissatisfaction are ended. The service rep can even price a complex product on the phone with the customer. This system dramatically improves all aspects of customer service. This is critically important as customers place more emphasis on time and service when choosing their products.

The rule-based system records the configuration as a set of decisions. It configures the set of decisions as a percentage bill of material, simplifying production and capacity planning. All planning is based on generic (the most common product) configurations— production hours and number of changes required for each product line. Rule-based systems simplify capacity planning and increase their accuracy by loading in the generic work load and the net changes from the different decision rules.

The rule-based systems do not require artificial intelligence (AI) or relational databases, although AI and relational databases support rule-based systems. I have worked with a rule-based order entry system that has been in operation for over five years. The company designed the system in-house using off-the-shelf hardware. In addition, rule-based process planning and engineering systems are already on the market.

A rule-based system is actually much simpler to use than the traditional MIS design. All the rules are self-explanatory and follow the designer's decision making process. The system will vastly increase productivity of the overhead functions. The computer performs most of the mundane tasks within the company. No longer do engineers waste time writing up individual bills of materials and routings for products with new combinations of options. No longer will accountants have to create costs for each new product. Merely by inputting their logic into the computer, the computer applies it to every product. The system automatically configures the products with the rules that the engineers have established. The system transforms engineers from clerks into knowledgeable workers. They spend most of their time analyzing process and product parameters to establish rules.

Process plans describe how to build a product and should have rule-based routings. With process planning, a computer reroutes a part if a machine is at capacity and an alternative is available. Unfortunately, with today's hierarchical systems it is too complex to input every conceivable option. Therefore, alternative routings are done manually, requiring human interaction and updating in the MRP system. The MRP system always assumes that parts follow their primary routing. Frequently, neither production planning nor shop operators update shop records when parts use alternate routings. This results in bad historical data. The rule-based information systems follow the same rules, but automatically reroute the parts. Rule-based systems will dramatically improve planning by allowing alternative routings and schedules. The system also avoids creating errors and it reflects how people think and act.

The rule-based system takes the product design and, using its parameters and rules, determines the optimum processing. The optimum routings, given sufficient capacity, are always chosen. Process planning embeds the process capability in the rules. This ensures that similar parts are given similar routings.

Rule-based systems will be a crucial test of American competitiveness, because American companies use computers much more extensively and have more advanced software than do the Japanese. This rule-based system will usher in all the benefits claimed by computer-integrated manufacturing (CIM)—improving productivity, increasing flexibility, and reducing cycle times. Using rule-based information systems is one of America's best advantages over the Japanese threat.

Small Is Beautiful—In Factories Too

As ABC shifts reported costs from labor-intense processing to capital-intense ones, companies will discover that the capital-intense fabrication of parts is much more expensive than previously thought. Companies will also discover that they have neither the capital nor the expertise to be truly competitive or flexible in many diverse manufacturing processes. In many cases, the small, focused vendor can provide better delivery and prices than in-house operations. As an example, the Big Three auto companies produced 55 percent of their parts in-house in 1985; industry analysts expect this to fall to 48 percent by 1992.

Vendors, not being captive suppliers, offer much more flexibility by having greater production capacity than in-house operations. This provides the company with greater flexibility, without any accompanying fixed costs. One of the important criteria in a successful product introduction is the ability to ramp up production. This requires sufficient capacity to meet demand, which vendors allow.

Increased outsourcing by cutting the number of in-house processes reduces plant size. At one plant, outsourcing reduced the facility's employess from 1,100 to just over 400. Outsourcing also reduced the plant's square footage by 60 percent.

A customer focus also leads to small factories. As companies become more customer focused, they cannot help create new market niches. Every customer is different with different needs. As a company works to satisfy more individual needs, it customizes its products and its delivery system for that customer. For example, one small used-furniture dealer made an interesting discovery simply by talking to his customers. When he asked them why they bought used furniture rather than new furniture, many replied, "I need the furniture now, if I ordered new furniture it would take three months to be delivered." The dealer discovered an unfulfilled customer need for quick delivery of new furniture. The dealer began to carry a limited line of new furniture and advertised, in the local papers, new furniture with a 48-hour guaranteed delivery. Customers loved it. The dealer's sales grew to over $50 million in just ten years.

The most successful retailers, The Gap, The Limited, 7-Eleven, and Nordstroms, are all niche creators. Niche creators, by limiting themselves to a particular market segment, can customize their products and services to provide superior customer value. With a limited market size, the niche creator has an effective barrier to entry. Large companies find niches with entrenched competitors unattractive. Niching drives a company to smaller enterprises.

Size invariables lead to complexity, which leads to overhead and management layers. This bureaucracy retards responsiveness. As speed negates economies of scale, one will find economies in reducing overhead through simplicity, which, in turn, comes from smaller focused plants. Likewise, a company focusing on customers reconfigures and focuses its factory for particular market segments. While companies can configure factories with "plants within a plant," usually the focused factories are physically separated. This physical separation allows the company to have more areas with local manufacturing presence, and takes advantage of a focused vendor base. The local presence gives the company more diverse marketing and political clout.

Just-In-Time (JIT) is lowering inventories around the world. As JIT forces inventory out of a company's entire value chain, an incentive is created for the company's suppliers and customers to be close. Market responsiveness (i.e., delivery time) becomes a much more important buying criteria. This encourages smaller plants. If, for example, a company finds that its customers require one-week delivery for assemble-to-order products, the company needs only one assembly point (for most parcel sizes) to meet this delivery requirement. If, on the other hand, the customers require four-day delivery (assuming the company can take the order and assemble the product in a day), the company needs two assembly points. If the customers require three-day delivery, the company needs six assembly points. The faster the response required, the more shipping points are required, and, consequently, the greater is the incentive for smaller plants.

Greater electronics content in products is also affecting the size of plants. As electronics become ever more powerful, the size, weight, and cost of electronics drops. This trend accelerates the replacement of mechanical systems with their stampings, castings, and machined parts, with circuit boards. This eliminates the need for capital-intense fabrication equipment.

The economies of operating smaller facilities are also improving. Last year a mainframe MRP system would cost around $3 million for software, installation, and hardware. The same system on a minicomputer costs only $500,000. This decline reduces the plant's break-even point. In addition, the growth of professional services allows the plant to convert otherwise fixed costs into variable costs. A company can contract out so-called "fixed costs" such as printing, personnel, payroll, sales, distribution, and even secretarial support.

These trends will push manufacturing enterprises to decrease in size. In fact, the number of large manufacturing enterprises (over 1,000 employees) has been falling since 1958 (see Exhibit 13-3). The initiatives of customer focus, speed, and flexibility will accelerate this trend.

As speed and flexibility reduce the size of the manufacturing enterprise, and customer responsiveness becomes crucial for success, the successful global company

Exhibit 13-3 **TRENDS IN FACTORY SIZE 1958–1985**

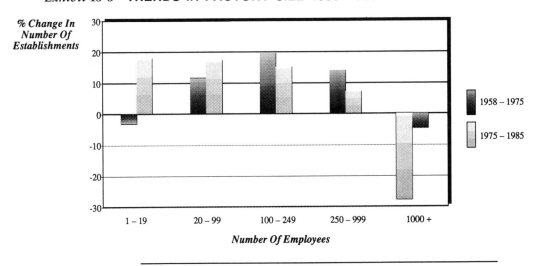

The trend is toward smaller manufacturing facilities

Source: Managing Automation, Sept. 1988

will be one with local operations. With economies of scale replaced by the focused factories' economies of scope and market proximity and quick customer responsiveness becoming more important, international trade will slow. Companies will propagate small regional plants around the world to provide quick customer responsiveness. Each plant will produce a narrow range of products for the surrounding region. In this way, the plants will have volume and economies of scope, as well as the advantages of local presence.

While currency, skills, technology, and knowledge are telecommunicated across borders, the local manufacturing enterprise will replace international manufacturing trade. This trade will make merchandise trade irrelevant. Globalization will increasingly show up only as capital and information flows, and not imports and exports.

As the size of the manufacturing enterprise shrinks, our ABC systems will become simpler. With short life cycles, the idea of life-costing will die. The life-cycle costing concept originated in the defense industry, the only industry whose product life cycle is getting longer. Fortunately, few other American industries are burdened with the excessive regulation and poor management practices that plague the aerospace contractors. ABC encourages companies to become fast, focused, and flexible. Our business culture has transformed American executives into extremely analytical managers. Up until this time, analytical managers have put America at a competitive disadvantage, because the numbers they have used have all been wrong. Yet, if

American executives aggressively follow the path that ABC lays out, U.S. manufacturing will return to predominance as the world's foremost manufacturing and service power. One must ruthlessly drive transaction rates down, increasing flexibility. One must streamline and accelerate design cycles to get products to market faster. One must quantify and measure customer value to manage businesses by it. If American executives fail to embrace ABC and the route it lays, they will watch Japan eclipse us.

THE JAPANESE CHALLENGE

In the fourth century B.C., philosopher Sun Tzu said, "Know thine enemy, know thyself and win a hundred battles." These words are just as true today as they were then. To meet the Japanese challenge, one must understand them, their many strengths, and their few weaknesses.

Today, Japan's leading companies have advantages in all the dimensions of competitive advantage of the 1990s—in customer value, speed, and flexibility. This advantage was born in their defeat.

After World War II, Douglas MacArthur's occupation headquarters staff were appalled by Japan's miserable product quality. The quality of the Japanese phone system inhibited the staff's control and communications. To help rebuild the phone system and the economy, the staff brought American quality experts to Japan, such as Edward Deming and Joseph Juran, to educate Japanese companies on quality control. These quality experts believed that the American companies slighted quality. Deming and Juran thought this stemmed from a lack of top management involvement. Therefore, after arriving in Japan, they demanded that the leading Japanese executives attend their quality seminars. The new leaders of Japanese industry willingly agreed. These business leaders had only recently ascended to their posts. The American military had purged top executives from the Zaibatsu (family-owned holding companies like Mitsui, Mitsubishi, and Sumitomo, which controlled most industrial production) for their wartime ties. The American military then replaced these top executives with Japanese operating managers who best fit the "classical American" manager mold.

In 1950, Deming predicted, to an astonished audience, that if they followed his advice, "Japanese products would within five years invade the markets of the world, and that the standard of living in Japan would in time rise to equality with the world's most prosperous countries." Convinced, these executives would lead their companies with total quality control for the next 40 years.

In the 1950s, Japan, boosted by the Korean conflict, grew rapidly. The wartime devastation had left little industry. As such, thousands and thousands of start-ups fought bitterly for every sale. This intense competition fueled tremendous growth. Japan's GNP grew four and a half times between 1950 and 1970. In the 1950s, Japan had over 100 automobile and 200 motorcycle manufacturers. (It is an interesting comparison that in the United States, in the early 1900s, there were more than 250 automobile manufacturers; the survivors of this intense competition came to dominate the world auto production. However, by 1950 there were only 6 left and today 3.) Only the best survived. The survivors developed a strong bias for growth and a preoccupation with the actions of competitors.

During the 1950s, Honda increased its production 50 percent faster than demand called for. In less than five years, Honda challenged Tohatsu as Japan's leading motorcycle manufacturer. Eventually Tohatsu went bankrupt, while 45 other manufacturers left the business. To survive in this environment, the Japanese companies had to learn to expand aggressively and pay special attention to the needs of their customers.

In Japan, it is still a rarity for a Japanese business executive to have a business degree. This may be one reason they have not learned to rely on western-style marketing research. Often, they do not depend on marketing departments either. They view marketing as too important to be left to midlevel specialists.

For example, when Sony researched the market for a lightweight portable cassette player, results showed that consumers wouldn't buy a tape recorder that didn't record. Akio Morita decided to introduce the Walkman anyway. Japanese executives continue to rely on personal visits to dealers who carry their products. This is the same approach that Alfred Sloan used when he ran General Motors and built it into the dominant automobile manufacturer. Sloan used to work as salesman or assistant service manager for a few weeks a year to stay in touch with the customers.

To hear the voice of the customer, Japanese auto companies have installed hidden microphones at auto shows. They listen in as the customers sit in, try out, and comment on the new cars. The Japanese supplement this "soft" data with "hard data." The Japanese closely follow shipments, inventory levels, sales figures, and most important, market-share data. They even identify their share of each major customer's total purchases. Aggressive Japanese companies calculate the percentage shares of each customer's business that are repeat versus new business—Are the customers buying new product lines from the company? They also record how many customers are giving referrals and how many customers are going to competitors. They also follow up and find out why they do not have all the customer's business.

The Japanese also conduct surveys aggressively. Ford surveys 2.5 million customers a year and regularly invites owners to meet with engineers and dealers to discuss quality problems. However, Ford is still far behind the Japanese auto companies. Every customer who buys or services a vehicle at a Nissan Motor Corp. dealership gets a call from an outside research firm. Nissan wants to know how every customer was treated.

Of course even with their relentless striving for quality, Japanese companies can stumble. In 1989, Toyota had to recall the LS400 to fix three different defects. However, Toyota did seem to try to appease its customers. Each owner got a personal phone call and two choices: Bring the car in yourself and have it fixed on the spot or have a Lexus representative pick it up at night and return it ready to go the next morning. Either way, Lexus not only fixed the defect but washed the car, cleaned the inside, and filled the gas tank. Some customers even received a small gift like an ice scraper on the front seat. This unheard of level of service impressed many owners.

One of the tenets of total quality control is kaizen, or continuous improvement. The Japanese have been applying this idea to their products for years. Merely to survive the intense competition of the 1950s and 1960s, the Japanese firms had to adopt every superior feature from competitors' products. This created an intense preoccupation with their competitors' actions. It is also one of the ways Japan closed the technology gap with western competitors. For years, the Japanese have gone to American trade shows with notebooks, copying down the best features of every company's products. These features could then be found in next year's models. From this approach, the Japanese developed the habit of frequently introducing products.

The development of generalist engineers, along with their consensus oriented management, has led to very effective new product development teams. For example, Honda can typically have cars rolling off its assembly lines just 24 months after making its first hand-built prototype. This is at least a year faster than Detroit.

The Japanese can attribute part of this speed to their practice of rotating engineers through production and design. The Japanese engineers have not only learned the design trade-offs and manufacturing problems that can be encountered, but have a number of personal relationships in both departments. America, on the other hand, after World War II, followed the idea of specialists to an extreme and split production engineering from design. The system, as intended, made specialists in both departments, but no generalists.

A 1984 study of American and Japanese flexible manufacturing systems (discussed in more detail later) found that the American systems took far longer in system development. The Americans took 25,000 worker hours, while the Japanese took only 6,000. The American companies used larger groups of specialists than the Japanese. While the Americans designed the systems for greater flexibility, the implementation is problematic and results are far below expectations. The American design teams are usually broken up after the design and turned over to new line personnel. The Japanese depend on generalists who know they will inherit the system. These engineers limit the new technology in the system and work to avoid every possible production problem.

On the other hand, many Japanese companies still manage their worldwide operations out of their headquarters. Even low-level decisions must come out of face-to-face meetings in Tokyo. This can have nothing but a detrimental effect on responsiveness and speed. According to Shoichiro Irimajiri, Senior Managing Director at Honda Motor Co., Japanese companies are 10 to 20 years behind in internationalization. The trend toward smaller regional manufacturing will, no doubt, aggravate this problem as more Japanese production and engineering are forced overseas.

Japanese Source of Advantage

Ever since World War II, Japanese manufacturers have concentrated on high-volume repetitive production—first in shipbuilding, textiles, and steel—to take advantage of their low labor rates. As labor costs escalated during the early and mid-1960s, Japanese companies began to invest capital to build economies of scale. As more companies vertically integrated into assembly operations, they continued to concentrate on high-volume repetitive products. By concentrating only on high-volume products, the Japanese companies retained the low-overhead structure that came from simple, repetitive manufacturing. These focused factories also continued to improve the quality of their products (Japan registered the first Quality Circle in 1962).

Over the same years, another significant development was taking place. In 1948, with inflation running rampant, Toyota wanted to control in-process and finished-goods inventories. Taiichi Ohno, an engineer by profession, began experimenting with the idea of a pull system of production to lower inventory levels. Ohno had read about such a system in American supermarkets. Ohno was impressed by the efficiency with which stores managed their inventory. The produce closely followed customer demand and never spoiled. Ohno came to understand that as customers removed lettuce from the shelves it triggered replenishment. The system pulled inventory from its sources. This pull system, by only building components when needed, cut inventory. To that end, Taiichi Ohno instituted the first "pull" system in Toyota's engine machining shop.

Over the years, a new production system began to evolve. Operators began to operate more than one machine, inspect their own work, and were given line-stop buttons. In 1953, Toyota introduced a system of exchanging paper tags to signal replenishment orders. This system came to be called "Kan Ban." Concurrently, Toyota instituted a standardization program for car and truck components. Other Toyota shops became synchronized to reduce inventory further.

By 1962, this system spread throughout the factory and to some outside suppliers. Toyota had their stamping press changeover times down to less than 15 minutes. In the late 1960s, Toyota began to teach this system to its subsidiaries and affiliates, like Hino and Daihatsu. This new system of production became known as just-in-time.

By the early 1970s, JIT began to spread throughout Japanese manufacturing. This development worked in concert with the Japanese focus on quality and provided industry with a large economic advantage. As JIT spread, it still was a system for repetitive manufacturing, but by driving down setup times and streamlining operations it also increased flexibility. Nevertheless, Japanese companies still pushed to provide all the options of the job lot–oriented western competitors. This drove the Japanese to increase flexibility while maintaining the economics of repetitive manufacturing.

At Mazda's giant U-1 plant in Hiroshima, the Miata, 323, 929, and the RX7 are all produced on the same assembly line. After the sudden success of their Miata, they were able to reshift their 1990 production to triple Miata's original capacity of

20,000 cars per year. Not only is Mazda building six different cars on the same assembly line, they can have two or three assembly lines in the same factory.

Thirty-five robot arms hold the main parts of a Nissan Sentra body in virtually perfect alignment. Then 16 other robots weld the parts together in 62 spots. This system installed at the Zama plant was the first in the world to use computer-programmed robots instead of fixed jigs. No longer are jigs required to align main body parts, including the floor, body, and side panels. This system allows one production line to handle up to four models and eight body types at once. It only requires 45 seconds to change from assembling a four-door sedan to a hatchback or station wagon. Down the line, robots paint each body a different color and receive different parts. All these steps are determined by computer control. With this system, Nissan can take the computer program to another plant, instead of bulky new jigs and equipment. Nissan can change over production at a new plant in just three months. Before it took 10 to 11 months to transfer production. Use of this technology allows Nissan to shift production rapidly to new and popular models, as well as introduce products.

This kind of flexibility allowed Nissan to create its Infiniti line of luxury cars for only $500 million. It saved this money by building the car at an existing assembly plant in Tochigi. The Infiniti shares an assembly line with the Cedric and Cima, luxury cars sold only in Japan.

American car companies have nowhere near this sort of flexibility. Ford's Wixom, Michigan installation is arguably the most flexible Big Three assembly plant. Wixom is the only American plant that builds both front-wheel- and rear-wheel-drive cars on the same line. Yet Ford produces only three models—the Lincoln Continental, the Lincoln Town Car, and the Continental Mark VII, even though these cars are nearly identical with different name plates.

At Mita Industrial Co., it is not uncommon to find one shift producing over 1,000 different copiers on its assembly line. This variety of models will find their way to different markets around the world. While some of the differences are minor, such as language notices and brand names, others are sizing and electrical specifications.

A 1984 study of 60 Japanese and 35 American flexible manufacturing systems (FMSs) by Ramchandran Jaikumar is even more discouraging. The study, which included half the FMSs in both countries, found the Japanese systems substantially more flexible than the American systems. The average number of parts on the American system was 10, while on the Japanese system it was 93, nine times higher. The American batch sizes were larger and their utilization was two-thirds less (see Exhibit 13-4).

Marching Toward Different Goals

It is also important to note that Japanese executives drive their corporations toward different objectives than do American firms. While American firms drive to

Exhibit 13-4 **COMPARISON OF FMSs STUDIED IN THE UNITED STATES AND JAPAN**

	UNITED STATES	JAPAN
SYSTEM DEVELOPMENT TIME (YEARS)	2.5 TO 3	1.25 TO 1.75
NUMBER OF MACHINES PER SYSTEM	7	6
TYPES OF PARTS PRODUCED PER SYSTEM	10	93
ANNUAL VOLUME PER PART	1,727	258
NUMBER OF PARTS PRODUCED PER DAY	88	120
NUMBER OF NEW PARTS INTRODUCED PER YEAR	1	22
NUMBER OF SYSTEMS WITH UNTENDED OPERATIONS	0	18
UTILIZATION RATE (TWO SHIFTS)	52%	84%
AVERAGE METAL-CUTTING TIME PER DAY	8.3	20.2

SOURCE: Jaikumar, Ramchandran, "Postindustrial Manufacturing" Harvard Business Review, November-December 1986.

increase return on investment (an obsolete measure that reflects the distance between corporate management and the desires of shareholders) and stock price, Japanese firms drive toward increased market share and then return on investment. There is an extreme bias for growth in Japan. This attitude is fostered by the banking industry's pervasive influence, which wants high growth to spur greater lending and reduce the chances of default. The Japanese have a cultural responsibility to their workers that encourages growth so that employment levels are never forced down. Japanese tax rates are lower on stock appreciation versus dividends, which encourages companies to reinvest money rather than pay out dividends. With the limited powers of their shareholders, stockholders are unable to force the companies to pay out dividends, even if the companies have only poor investment opportunities. In addition, the prestige of your company is important to one's status. A company's size, growth, and technical accomplishments are more important to prestige than profitability. This environment creates a very aggressive competitor, who may make seemly irrational investments by American standards.

Contrary to many pundits, it was the quality movement and Japan's fierce competition that was the source of Japan's industrial resurgence and not state planning or just-in-time. The Ministry of International Trade and Industry (MITI) has historically done a poor job of picking winners and losers in industry. Its efforts to shape the computer and auto industry have failed totally. Subsidies to industry have been trivial when compared to in-house R&D and capital spending. Likewise, long before JIT spread from Toyota, Japanese industry was making major inroads into foreign markets.

THE CONCLUSION

The traditional American manufacturer is going to have to undergo gut-wrenching changes to meet the Japanese challenge of the 1990s. Many Japanese competitors have already demonstrated surprising ability in competing on fast, focused, and flexible initiatives. However, the first step to regaining American competitiveness is implementing ABC. ABC changes a company's focus from products and markets to activities. An activity focus ties your whole company to all the customer's needs. This philosophy removes a company's self-imposed tunnel vision. Activity management weds revenue creation with resource consumption based on activities. Activity management integrates all aspects of a business to support a single objective—shareholder value creation. Activity-based costing is the crux of the first truly integrated business philosophy.

ABC guides companies to realign their operations for customer focus and to streamline overhead. Unlike the traditional cost systems, it does not push a company toward automating direct labor out of the process or moving operations overseas. Companies attack overhead. Companies slim down, dropping uncompetitive products and processes, eliminating nonvalue-added activities and needless layers of management.

Today's challenges demand that companies become more responsive to their customers in time and fulfilling needs. To provide this speed and flexibility, you must reconfigure your engineering, manufacturing, and distribution organizations and systems.

As one looks toward the future, one must remember that the battle has yet to begin. This country can do anything, as long as America takes up the challenge—manufacturing resurgence. America must drive to victory with better products, better services, faster responsiveness, and lower costs. ABC is only one small, yet critical part of the solution. Victory depends on the desire and drive to defeat the Japanese threat. As Alfred P. Sloan, the man who built General Motors said, "There is no resting place for an enterprise in a competitive economy."

NOTES

CHAPTER 1

(1) Zeleny, Milan, "Descriptive Decision Making and Its Applications" Applications of Management Science, 1, 1981.

CHAPTER 2

(1) Carman, James M. and Eric Langeard, "Growth Strategies for Service Firms," *Strategic Management Journal*, First Quarter (1980).

(2) Kaplan, Robert and S. Kallapur, "American Bank," Harvard Business School Case Services, Order Numbers 9-187-194.

CHAPTER 3

(1) Kaplan, Robert, "Kanthal (A) and (B)," Harvard Business School Case Services Order Numbers 9-190-002 and 9-190-003.

(2) Berlant, Debbie; Reese Browning and George Foster; "How Hewlett-Packard Gets Numbers It Can Trust," *Harvard Business Review*, January-February 1990.

CHAPTER 4

(1) Turning, Peter B.B. and James Reeve; "Impact of Continous Improvement on the Design of an Activity-Based Costing System," *Journal of Cost Management*, Summer 1990.

CHAPTER 9

(1) The PIMS (Profit Impact on Market Strategy) data bank contains the strategy experience of over 2000 business units for as many as 18 years. The database includes measures and performance of all kinds, such as market share, R&D expenditures, customer-perceived quality, and profits. In all the database records over 200 separate characteristics of each business experience.

(2) Buzzell, Robert D. and Frederik D. Wiersema, "Successful Share Building Strategies, *Harvard Business Review*, January-February 1981.

(3) Birnbaum, Phillip and Andrew Weiss, "Competitive Advantage and the Basis of Competition," Seventh Annual International Conference of the Strategic Management Society, Oct. 14-17, 1987.

(4) Abegglen, James C. and George Stalk Jr., Kaisha, *The Japanese Corporation* (Basic Books, Inc., New York, NY 1985).

CHAPTER 10

(1) Stalk, George Jr. and Thomas M. Hout, *Competing Against Time* (Free Press, New York, NY 1990).

CHAPTER 13

(1) Jaikumar, Ramchandran "Postindustrial Manufacturing," *Harvard Business Review*, November-December 1986.

FURTHER READING

The books discuss general strategy and not activity-based costing. While the number of articles on ABC is enormous I have limited the following list to the very best articles.

I find case studies to be one of the best teachers of ABC. Copies of the case studies listed below can be obtained through either Harvard or Darden Business Schools. In addition, books and articles which include ABC case studies are marked with an asterisk (*).

BOOKS

Abegglen, James C. and George Stalk, Kaisha, *The Japanese Corporation* (New York, NY: Basic Books, 1985).

Bibeault, Donald, *Corporate Turnaround* (New York, N.Y.: McGraw-Hill, 1982).

Garvin, David, *Managing Quality* (New York, NY: The Free Press, 1986).

Groocock, John, *The Chain of Quality* (New York, NY: John Wiley & Sons, 1986).

Halberstam, David, *The Reckoning* (New York, NY: William Morrow & Co., 1986)

Hayes, Robert H., Steven C. Wheelwright and Kim B. Clark, *Dynamic Manufacturing* (New York, NY: The Free Press, 1988).

Johnson, Thomas and Robert S. Kaplan, *Relevance Lost* (Boston, MA: Havard Business School Press, 1987).

Kaplan, Robert S., *Measures of Manufacturing Excellence* (Boston, MA: Havard Business School Press, 1990). (*)

McNair, Carol and William Mosconi and Thomas Norris, *Beyond the Bottom Line* (New York, N.Y.: Dow Jones-Irwin, 1989)

O'Guin, Michael C., "Strategic and Financial Planning for the Automated Factory," in *The Automated Factory Handbook* (New York, NY: TAB Professional and Reference Books, 1990)

Ohmae, Kenichi, *The Mind of the Strategist* (New York, NY: McGraw-Hill, 1982).

Rappaport, Alfred, *Creating Shareholder Value* (New York, NY: The Free Press, 1986).

Schonberger, John, *Japanese Manufacturing Techniques* (New York, NY: The Free Press, 1982).

Stalk, George, Jr. and Thomas M. Hout, *Competing Against Time* (New York, NY: The Free Press, 1990).

ARTICLES

Beaujon, George J. and Vinod R. Singhal, "Understanding the Activity Costs in an Activity-Based Cost System," *Journal of Cost Management*, Spring 1990.

Berlant, Debbie, Reese Browning and George Foster, "How Hewlett-Packard Gets Numbers It can Trust," *Harvard Business Review*, January-February 1990. (*)

Cooper, Robin and Robert S. Kaplan, "How Cost Accounting Distorts Product Cost," *Management Accounting*, April 1988.

Cooper, Robin and Robert S. Kaplan, "Measure Costs Right: Make the Right Decisions," *Harvard Business Review*, September-October 1988.

Cooper, Robin, "Implementing an Activity-Based Costing System," *Journal of Cost Management*, Spring 1990. (*)

Cooper, Robin, "The Rise of Activity-Based Costing—Part One: What is an Activity-Based Costing System," *Journal of Cost Management*, Summer 1988.

Cooper, Robin, "The Rise of Activity-Based Costing—Part Three: How Many Cost Drivers Do You Need, and How Do You Select Them?" *Journal of Cost Management*, Winter 1989.

Cooper, Robin, "Cost Classification in Unit-based and Activity-Based Manufacturing Cost Systems," *Journal of Cost Management*, Fall 1990.

Cooper, Robin, "When Should You Use Machine-Hour Costing?" *Journal of Cost Management*, Spring 1988.

Eiler, Robert G., Walter K. Goletz and Daniel P. Keegan, "Is Your Cost Accounting Up to Date?" *Harvard Business Review*, July-August 1982.

Govindarajan, Vijay and Shank, John K., "Strategic Cost Analysis: The Crown Cork and Seal Case," *Journal of Cost Management*, Summer 1988.

Johnson, H. Thomas and Dennis A. Loewe, "How Weyerhaeuser Manages Corporate Overhead Costs," *Management Accounting*, August 1987. (*)

Johnson, H. Thomas, "Beyond Product Costing: A Challenge to Cost Management's Conventional Wisdom," *Journal of Cost Management*, Fall 1990.

Johnson, H. Thomas, "Activity Management: Reviewing the Past and Future of Cost Management," *Journal of Cost Management*, Winter 1990.

Jonez, John W. and Micheal Wright, "Material Burdening," *Management Accounting*, August 1987. (*)

Kaplan, Robert, "The Four-Stage Model of Cost Systems Design," *Management Accounting*, February 1990.

Kaplan, Robert, "Accounting Lag: The Obsolescence of Cost Accounting Systems," *California Management Review*, Winter 1986.

Kaplan, Robert, "The Evolution of Management Accounting," *The Accounting Review*, July 1984.

Keegan, Daniel; Robert Eiler and Joseph V. Anania, "The Factory of the Future," *Management Accounting*, December 1988.

Kim, Il-woon, and Ja Song, "U.S., Korea & Japan Accounting Practices in Three Countries, *Management Accounting*, August 1990.

Miller, J.G. and T.E. Vollmann, "The Hidden Factory," *Harvard Business Review*, September-October 1985.

O'Guin, Michael C. "Focus the Factory with Activity-Based Costing," *Management Accounting*, February 1990. (*)

Ostrenga, Michael R. "Activities: The Focal Point of Total Cost Management, " *Management Accounting*, February 1990.

Ostrenga, Michael R. "A Methodology for Identifying Your Excess Capacity Costs," *Journal of Cost Management*, Summer 1988.

Romano, Patrick "Where is Cost Management Going?" *Management Accounting*, August 1990.

Rotch, William, "Activity-Based Cost in Service Industries," *Journal of Cost Management*, Summer 1990.

Sapp, Richard W., David Crawford and Steven A. Rebischke, "Activity-Based Information for Financial Institutions," *The Journal of Bank Cost & Management Accounting*, V. 2, No. 2 1990.

Sapp, Richard W., David Crawford and Steven A. Rebischke, "Activity Framework for ABC in Financial Institutions," *The Journal of Bank Cost & Management Accounting*, V. 2, No. 3 1990.

Shank, John K., and Vijay Govindarajan, "Transaction-Based Costing for the Complex Product Line: A Field Study," *Journal of Cost Management*, Summer 1988. (*)

Turney, Peter B. B., "Activity-Based Costing: A Tool for Manufacturing Excellence," *Target*, Summer 1989.

Turney, Peter B. B., "Ten Myths About Implementing an Activity-Based Cost System, *Journal of Cost Management*, Spring 1990.

Turney, Peter B. B. and James Reeve, "The Impact of Continuous Improvement on the Design of Activity-Based Cost System," *Journal of Cost Management*, Summer 1990.

Turney, Peter B. B., "What is the Scope of Activity-Based Costing?" *Journal of Cost Management*, Winter 1990.

Worthy, Ford S., "Accounting Bores You? Wake Up," *Fortune*, October 12, 1987.

MANUFACTURING CASE STUDIES

Bottenbruch, Dagmar and Robert Kaplan, "Metabo Gmbh & Co.," Harvard Business School Case Services Order Number 9-189-146.

Bottenbruch, Dagmar and Robert Kaplan, "Mueller-Lehmkuhl GmbH.," Harvard Business School Case Services Order Number 9-187-048.

Cooper, Robin, "Schrader Bellows: A Strategic Cost Analysis, Software Module," and supporting cases (A)-(H), Harvard Business School Case Services Order Numbers 9-186-272, 1-186-052, 1-186- 278, 1-186-054, 1-186-055, 1-186-056, 1-186-139.

Cooper, Robin and Peter B. B. Turning, "Hewlett-Packard: Roseville Networks Division," Harvard Business School Case Services Order Numbers N9-189-117.

Cooper, Robin and Peter B. B. Turning, "Powell Electronics: The Printed Circuit Board Division," Harvard Business School Case Services Order Numbers N9-189-054.

Cooper, Robin and Peter B. B. Turning, "Tektronix: Portable Insturments Division (A), (B) and (C)," Harvard Business School Case Services Order Numbers 9-188-142, 9-188-143 and 9-188-144.

Cooper, Robin and K. H. Wruck, "Siemens Electric Motor Works (A) and (B)," Harvard Business School Case Services Order Numbers 9-189-089 and 9-189-090.

Cooper, Robin, "Ingersoll Milling Machine Company," Harvard Business School Case Services Order Numbers 9-186-189.

Kaplan, Robert, "Kanthal (A) and (B)," Harvard Business School Case Services Order Numbers 9-190-002 and 9-190-003.

March, Artemis, "John Deere Component Works (A) and (B),"Harvard Business School Case Services Order Numbers 9-187-107 and 9-187-108.

SERVICE INDUSTRY CASE STUDIES

Colley L., John, "Data Services, Inc." Colgate Darden Graduate Business School Sponsors Order Number UVA-OM-581 and UVA-OM-582.

Kaplan, Robert, "Union Pacific (A) and (B)," Harvard Business School Case Services Order Numbers 9-186-117 and 9-186-178.

Kaplan, Robert and S. Kallapur, "American Bank," Harvard Business School Case Services Order Numbers 9-187-194.

Rotch, William, "Alexandria Hospital, 1987." Colgate Darden Graduate Business School Sponsors Order Number UVA-C-2007.

Rotch, William, "Amtrak Auto-Ferry Service" Colgate Darden Graduate Business School Sponsors Order Number UVA-C-988.

APPENDIXES

APPENDIX A

EXAMPLES OF FIRST STAGE DRIVERS

COST CATEGORY	COST DRIVER
OCCUPANCY (RENT, LEASES, TAXES, FIRE INSURANCE)	SQUARE FOOTAGE
DEPRECIATION	DEPRECIATION BY LOCATION
PAYROLL	# OF CHECKS
PERSONNEL	# OF EMPLOYEES
WORKERS COMPENSATION INSURANCE	# OF EMPLOYEES
FRINGE BENEFITS	% OF LABOR COSTS
MRO PURCHASING (NONPRODUCTION ITEMS)	# OF MRO PURCHASE ORDERS
JANITORIAL	SQUARE FOOTAGE
PREVENTIVE MAINTENANCE	# OF MACHINES IN PROGRAM TIME CARD CHARGES # OF BREAKDOWNS
MACHINE REPAIR	TIME CARD CHARGES WORKER ASSIGNMENTS TIME CARD CHARGES
TOOLING	# OF TOOLS (or DIES)
UTILITIES	METERS
INSPECTION	# OF INSPECTIONS DEPARTMENT ASSIGNMENTS
MANAGEMENT	SURVEYS
WAREHOUSING	# OF RECEIPTS AND ISSUES
SHOP FLOOR CONTROL	# OF MOVES
INDUSTRIAL ENGINEERING	I.E., WORK ORDER ROUTING CHANGES SURVEYS
QUALITY ENGINEERING	DEFECTS PROCESS SPECIFICATIONS TEST PLANS

John Deere Component Works ABC System

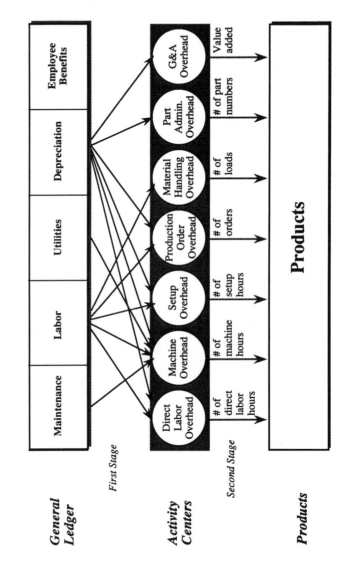

Source: John Deere (A)

Schrader Bellows Second Stage ABC Architecture

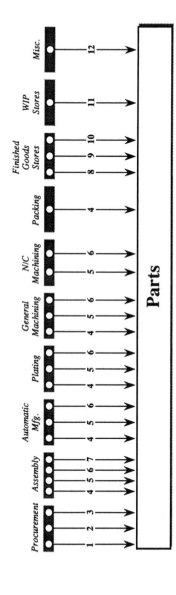

Drivers

1. # of purchased parts
2. # of raw material shipments received
3. # of purchase orders received
4. Direct labor hours
5. Setup hours

6. # of setups
7. # of times direct labor reported
8. # of customer orders
9. Sales dollars
10. # of shipments

11. Average Value in WIP inventory
12. Cost of goods sold by total, automotive manufactured and component item, flow control and couplers

APPENDIX B

EXAMPLES OF SECOND STAGE DRIVERS

PROCUREMENT

FUNCTION	COST DRIVER
SCHEDULING, WRITING & TRACKING PURCHASE ORDERS	# OF P.O.S/# OF LINE ITEMS
ACCOUNTS PAYABLE	# OF CHECKS/# OF LINE ITEMS
QUALIFYING VENDORS (AUDITS TO ELIMINATE RECEIVING & REC.INSP.)	# OF QUALIFIED VENDORS
RECEIVING	# OF DOCK RECEIPTS
RECEIVING INSPECTION	# OF INSPECTIONS
WAREHOUSING (FROM DOCK)	# OF STORES RECEIPTS

Buyers spent most of their time placing or coordinating purchase orders. The cost of the purchase orders is divided by the number of line items in the P.O. One item on a 200 line item P.O. is much less expensive to process than one item on a P.O. with only one item (this also encourages vendor and P.O. consolidation).

In some cases, like at Wang, procurement costs are very important and effective material acquistion is paramount to competitiveness. Wang developed activity procurement centers for major classifications of parts; boards, ICs, OEM products, mechanical and electro-mechanical. Since the cost of buying, inspecting, and storing each of these components varied widely, each had their own procurement rates. A company can assign buyer costs by the commidity codes the buyers work on. Inspectors are usually dedicated to particular types of components and different procedures exist for receiving purchased parts than raw materials.

At Hewlett-Packard they have gained substantial benefits from developing a preferred parts list. Any parts not on the list are given a qualification and risk charge. With preferred parts H-P avoids qualifying parts and is able to negociate large discounts with vendors. But more importantly planning, inspection and other transaction costs are dramatically lowered. At H-P, 5000 part numbers make up over 80% of the company's total part insertions. This even makes factories easier to design, in that the designers know how many parts the products will require which determines how many insertion machines they will need.

Qualifying vendors is a step another toward JiT, where the vendors can skip receiving and receiving inspection. In most cases the P.O. costs and accounts payables and receiving, receiving inspection and warehousing to dock costs can be consolidated into two pools.

PLANNING

FUNCTION	COST DRIVER
REQUIREMENTS PLANNING & SCHEDULING	# OF BATCHES PLANNED
SHOP FLOOR CONTROL	# OF MOVES
EXPEDITERS	# OF EXPEDITERS

Requirements planning costs are proportional to the number of batches planned. These costs are irrespective of the number of departments routed through. Costs are very different between build-to-stock and build-to-orderproducts. Stock units tend to have much larger batches and therefore greater economies. Parts of Kan Ban are not planned and therefore receive no planning costs.

Shop floor control chases down parts. The more times a part moves the more chance of it getting lost.

QUALITY ASSURANCE

FUNCTION	COST DRIVER
QUALITY PLANNING	# OF NEW PART NUMBERS
INSPECTION	# OF FIRST PIECE INSPECTIONS (SETUPS)
CHEMICAL LAB	# OF TANK CHANGES
TEST	# OF TEST HOURS # OF TESTS (1)

(1) Test hours vary widely from product to product, some parameter which relates the test time to the product is usually required.

TOOLING

FUNCTION	COST DRIVER
TOOL DESIGN & FABRICATION	# OF NEW DIES CONSTRUCTED (1)
TOOL REPAIR	MACHINE HOURS PUNCHES
TOOL CLEANING	CHANGEOVERS

(1) Since fabrication costs differ widely by process, some estimating parameters are usually required to conpensate for the differences.

WAREHOUSING

FUNCTION	COST DRIVER
FORK-LIFTS AND OPERATORS	# OF MOVES # OF RECEIPTS AND ISSUES
STORAGE COSTS (OCCUPANCY)	# OF LOCATIONS ASSIGNED (BY PART NUMBER)

MAINTENANCE

FUNCTION	COST DRIVER
MACHINE REPAIR & PREVENTIVE MAINTENANCE	MACHINE HOURS
CALIBRATION	MACHINE HOURS
TOOL ROOM	# OF TOOLS PER JOB MACHINE HOURS

FABRICATION DEPARTMENTS

FUNCTION	COST DRIVER
DIRECT LABOR (Includes percent of fringe benefits)	MACHINE HOURS
INDIRECT LABOR (Includes percent of fringe benefits)	# OF SETUPS
LOST EFFICIENCY	# OF SETUPS (2)
DEPRECIATION	SPLIT BETWEEN TIME SPENT ON PRODUCTION AND SETUPS

(2) Most the difference between standard and actual is caused by changing over from one job to another.

PLATING

FUNCTION	COST DRIVER
DEPRECIATION	PROCESSING TIME
DIRECT LABOR	PROCESSING TIME
UTILITIES	PROCESSING TIME
CHEMICALS	SURFACE AREA

ASSEMBLY DEPARTMENTS

FUNCTION	COST DRIVER
DIRECT LABOR (Includes percent of fringe benefits)	LABOR HOURS
INDIRECT LABOR (Includes percent of fringe benefits)	# OF SETUPS
LOST EFFICIENCY	# OF SETUPS (3)
DEPRECIATION	SPLIT BETWEEN TIME SPENT ON PRODUCTION AND SETUPS

(3) Most the difference between standard and actual is caused by changing over from one job to another.

SALES

FUNCTION	COST DRIVER
SALES FORCE	# OF SALES CALLS
ORDER ENTRY	# OF CUSTOMER ORDERS
CUSTOMER INQUIRIES	# OF PHONE CALLS

SOFTWARE DEVELOPMENT

FUNCTION	COST DRIVER
PROGRAMMING	# OF LINES OF CODE

NEW PRODUCT DEVELOPMENT

FUNCTION	COST DRIVER
PROJECT MANAGEMENT	# OF NEW PRODUCTS
COST ESTIMATING	# OF NEW PRODUCTS
PRODUCT DESIGN	# OF NEW PART NUMBERS
RELIABILITY ANALYSIS	# OF PART NUMBERS
DOCUMENTATION	# OF NEW PART NUMBERS
TOOL FABRICATION	# OF NEW PART NUMBERS
MODEL SHOP	# OF PROTOTYPES
VENDOR QUALIFICATION	# OF NEW VENDORS

Index